GUERRILLA DIPLOMACY

GUERRILLA DIPLOMACY

Rethinking International Relations

Daryl Copeland

Viva Books

New Delhi | Mumbai | Chennai | Kolkata | Bengaluru | Hyderabad | Kochi | Guwahati

First Indian Edition 2011

VIVA BOOKS PRIVATE LIMITED

- 4737/23 Ansari Road, Daryaganj, New Delhi 110 002
  E-mail: vivadelhi@vivagroupindia.net, Tel. 42242200
- 76, Service Industries, Shirvane, Sector 1, Nerul, Navi Mumbai 400 706
  E-mail: vivamumbai@vivagroupindia.net, Tel. 27721273, 27721274
- Jamals Fazal Chambers, 26 Greams Road, Chennai 600 006
  E-mail: vivachennai@vivagroupindia.net, Tel. 28290304, 28294241
- B-103, Jindal Towers, 21/1A/3 Darga Road, Kolkata 700 017
  E-mail: vivakolkata@vivagroupindia.net, Tel. 22836381, 22816713
- 7, Sovereign Park Apartments, 56-58, K. R. Road, Basavanagudi, Bengaluru 560 004
  E-mail: vivabangalore@vivagroupindia.net, Tel. 26607409, 26607410
- 101-102 Mughal Marc Apartments, 3-4-637 to 641, Narayanguda, Hyderabad 500 029
  E-mail: vivahyderabad@vivagroupindia.net, Tel. 27564481, 27564482
- Beevi Towers, First Floor, SRM Road, Kaloor, Kochi 682 018, Kerala
  E-mail: vivakochi@vivagroupindia.net, Tel: 0484-2403055, 2403056
- 232, GNB Road, Beside UCO Bank, Silpukhuri, Guwahati 781 003
  E-mail: vivaguwahati@vivagroupindia.net, Tel: 0361-2666386

www.vivagroupindia.com

Published by arrangement with

Lynne Rienner Publishers, Inc.
1800 30th Street, Suite 314
Boulder, Colorado 80301
USA

ISBN : 978-81-309-1527-2

Published by Vinod Vasishtha for Viva Books Private Limited, 4737/23, Ansari Road, Daryaganj, New Delhi - 110 002. Printed and bound by Raj Press, R-3, Inderpuri, New Delhi - 110 012.

S0000 / S0810

For Glyn Berry,
a colleague and Foreign Service officer,
who was killed on January 15, 2006, by an improvised explosive device while on duty as political director with Canada's Provincial Reconstruction Team in Kandahar, Afghanistan

* * *

and for all my colleagues, of any nationality,
who have given their lives practicing diplomacy.

* * *

In honor of Glyn, all royalties from the sale of this book will go to the Glyn Berry Memorial Scholarship in International Policy Studies, which has been established by Dalhousie University, Glyn's alma mater. Details may be found at www.alumniandfriends.dal.ca/giving/glynberry.

Contents

Preface

The evil that is in the world almost always comes of ignorance, and good intentions may do as much harm as malevolence if they lack understanding.
—Albert Camus

It was the early 1980s and the world was a very different place. The cataclysms in Southeast Asia had subsided, and the Cold War was on: the Soviets were in Afghanistan, the Cubans in Africa, and the Vietnamese in Cambodia—and the United States was most everywhere else. But in Bangkok—where I was working as a junior political and consular officer at the Canadian Embassy—life seemed mainly, well, exotic. Except for the faint echoes of recent violence in the border refugee camps; a low-level, vaguely Islamic insurgency along the Malaysian frontier to the south; and occasional accusations regarding the use of chemical and bacteriological weapons against minority tribes in neighboring countries, Thailand seemed tranquil, very much the "land of smiles." I had actively sought my assignment, and if there was to be the occasional ripple in the sea of calm, I was confident in my capacity to smooth it out. I had enough worldly experience on the one hand and formal education on the other to help me think my way through whatever challenges might ensue. Or so I thought.

My first full day in country was a hazy, super-hot Sunday. The night before, colleagues had taken me out to the Foreign Correspondents Club, which at the time was habituated mainly by diplomats, expatriates, and journalists—including a slightly forlorn if not dissolute group of correspondents who just couldn't leave Indochina behind. Upon walking into the club for the first time,

I was reminded of the intergalactic bar in *Star Wars,* where creatures from across the cosmos gather to mix and mingle.

When it closed for the night, we flagged a three-wheeled tuk tuk with veteran Australian cameraman Neil Davis. (He became a friend, but a year after I left he was caught in a crossfire and killed while covering an abortive palace coup.) Through the flashing lights and heavy night air we traveled past the throngs still streaming out of the legendarily sin-soaked Patpong Road and crossed town to arrive at an after-hours bar called The Thermae. Because the front doors of the putative barbershop and beauty salon were locked, we entered through a dank and dingy back alley to find ourselves in a cavernous space filled with dense smoke and pulsating music. By three in the morning it was crammed with everyone in Bangkok who either hadn't yet found what he or she was looking for—from pleasant conversation to every conceivable vice—or just couldn't sleep.

The scene made the earlier part of that evening appear tepid by comparison. Murray Head's huge hit "One Night in Bangkok" wasn't released until a year or two later, but the setting in The Thermae inspired the lyrics to the song. This was underground Bangkok, a superstore for footloose and lonely insomniacs, a kind of wonderland for aficionados of the bizarre—a place where, when the going got weird, the weird turned professional. Not unlike Lewis Carroll's Alice, I found myself unsure which side of the looking glass I was on. We finally left just before dawn.

The next morning, while I remained discombobulated, my predecessor Marius, who would be leaving in a few days, called to invite me on a trip to the former Thai capital of Ayutthaya, which lies about fifty kilometers up the Chao Praya River from Bangkok. An hour later we were en route to the site, accompanied by the locally engaged consular and administrative assistants, Nipha and Saranya.

This was prior to the real estate bubble of the 1990s, and Bangkok, home to about 7 million, was still predominantly low-rise. With the exception of soot-belching buses, beat-up taxis, and the long-tailed boats that plied the river and the few remaining canals, or *klongs,* modern public transit was then nonexistent. The density of the crowds, the extent of the gridlock, and the severity of the air pollution, which my colleagues seemed not to notice, dumbfounded me. I was especially surprised whenever we stopped at an intersection, which for the people of Bangkok meant commercial opportunity. Children would clean the grime from your windshield for a few baht or hawk snacks, garlands, and newspapers. In some neighborhoods, the kids themselves were for sale.

As we cleared the sprawling suburbs, I remember thinking about the hazards of trying to eke out a living in the grinding traffic and noxious fumes. I recall reflecting on my good fortune to have been born in a place where the standards of public health and social service were such that I would never see our children working the streets. I never imagined that "squeegee kids" would soon enough become a prominent feature in Western cities, too.

In about an hour we arrived. Sacked by the Burmese in the eighteenth century, the ruined emerald city with its palm-fringed vistas remains a visual feast, the immense Buddhas and giant, bell-like *chedis* providing strikingly serene contrast to the vitality and chaos of Bangkok. We parked near our first stop, a magnificent temple featuring a giant reclining Buddha. As we walked along a shaded path by the riverside, I noticed a small crowd of Thais clustered around a vendor's stall that featured a large cage full of small birds. Somewhat to my surprise, Nipha walked over to the hut and came back with one of the little birds in a portable bamboo cage. She then walked down to the riverbank, turned a simple clasp that opened the gate on the front of the cage, and freed the bird, which flew off across the water.

What was this amazingly graceful gesture all about? I thought that something so poetic must surely have symbolic or religious meaning. When I inquired, Nipha looked at me with a gentle blend of understanding and pity and offered a brief explanation of the Buddhist practice of making merit through token good works.

We were about to move on when a tall, blonde, slightly disheveled young male visitor—perhaps German or Dutch or North American—approached the vendor and also bought a caged bird. He, too, had apparently been struck by the proceedings. He made his way down to the bank of the river and waited in line for his turn to join in the ritual, seemingly wanting to fit in and to do the right thing.

But the clasp on his cage appeared to be jammed. Fumbling with the gate, he was beginning to draw an amused crowd. The attention only made him try harder, and the episode was beginning to take on the quality of a minor spectacle. In embarrassed desperation, the young fellow grabbed the corners of the cage and torqued it mightily in a final attempt to force the latch. Instead the entire edifice exploded into a cloud of bamboo shards.

A murmur of disbelief passed through those gathered on the bank. All eyes then moved to the bird, which had escaped the wreckage unscathed. It circled in a wide arc over the water, crossed the tree line on the far shore, and then, incredibly, flew back to the vendor and landed on his outstretched arm. A knowing smile passed fleetingly over the face of the savvy small businessman as he casually returned the fortunate flutterer to the larger cage for resale.

* * *

What to make of it all? This was shock and awe of a cross-cultural kind. On that saffron-tinged, frangipani-scented morning, I began to realize that my own perceptions would have to change fundamentally. I was indeed in a very distant place in all respects—where missteps could be made, where not everything was as it seemed, and where much of what was important occurred at levels other than the obvious.

Clearly, for all the fragments of insight I may have picked up in my years of backpack travel and studies in international affairs, I was still far from where I wanted—or needed—to be. Living on the other side of the world would be quite different from passing through it. To come to terms with my new surroundings—and certainly to operate effectively as a diplomat—I'd have to do more than just look. I would have to learn to see.

* * *

Twenty-five years have passed between my arrival in Bangkok and the start of this project. Some things are the same, but much more is different. This book is mainly concerned with what has changed and what those changes might mean for diplomacy, security, and international relations in the era of globalization. More than anything else, though, it is about seeing, above all seeing the world in new ways. In publishing it, I hope to advance our understanding of what is going on, why, and what might be done about it.

I began this enterprise in the late spring of 2006, motivated by the conviction that the moment was ripe for a holistic, synoptic treatment of the topic. After so many years of diplomatic practice, I thought it time to stand back, to reflect, to research, and to analyze. I was certain that, by fusing grand strategy and multidisciplinary analysis, I could find a better way forward and break new ground. This book is the result.

I advance the case that diplomats must be empowered to manage globalization—which can occur only with the reinvention of diplomacy itself. In that respect, diplomacy's inherent dedication to dialogue, whether through open communication or more discreet channels, has great appeal, especially as an alternative to the threat or use of force. I argue that diplomacy, reimagined and linked integrally to development, can and should displace defense at the center of international policy and global relations.

In the course of my research, and somewhat to my surprise, I found the near-complete absence of a user-friendly guide to the conceptual geography and the operations of the international system as we know it. Without such a framework, I would have difficulty articulating my analysis. I have tried to close that lacuna and to map the insecure present by building a model of the new world order, interpreting the recent Cold War past, assessing the meaning of development and the role of science and technology therein, and, finally, offering some thoughts on the future of diplomacy, the foreign ministry, and the foreign service.

The task, as it happened, was somewhat larger and more complicated than I had anticipated.

While I have a couple of degrees and over the years have kept in close touch with colleagues in the scholarly community, I am at heart a practitioner, not an academic. In order to cover all of the ground necessary to make my case, I have had in places to draw on personal experience, to rely on instinct, and to traverse great chunks of entire disciplines, often at high altitude and sometimes cursorily. Meanwhile, I have barely touched upon international organizations, multilateral financial institutions, or many other aspects of international policy and relations, including trade and immigration, that might usefully have been considered. I have doubtless missed important authors and sources. The nature of academic publishing, moreover, means that some circumstances may have changed since the book was written. Perhaps I can correct these shortcomings, and countless more, another day.

Whether or not I have done it well, I have done something unusual in the study of international relations—namely, explore relationships between subjects rarely considered in tandem, let alone all together: the Cold War and globalization; development and security; science, technology, and international policy; and the constituent elements of the *diplomatic ecosystem* (which I define as the mutual habitat of foreign ministries, diplomacy, and foreign service). In my efforts to reveal the relationships between and among these components to produce a synthesis at the level of grand strategy, I have also drawn on the full spectrum of sources, from academic to popular and conservative to radical, from literature and film to conversations and interviews. While this is essentially a book about diplomacy, it is intended for a broad audience, both specialists and those with more general interests. As a result, the argumentation is, of necessity, heavily research-based in some cases and more intuitive in others. This differentiation reflects the sprawl and uneven surface of the intellectual terrain traversed.

I recognize that the synoptic approach may have created occasional moments of analytical tension or chasms between pieces of the argument. I have tried to ease the transitions and lay at least token bridges across the greater divides, but the scaffolding may still appear a bit shaky in places. While I have done my best, I don't doubt that it could be improved.

For this; for any errors of omission, fact, or interpretation; and for any other failings, I apologize in advance and ask but a small measure of forbearance. I am certainly open to all suggestions for reconsideration.

* * *

This book would not have been possible without the generous support of the following organizations: Foreign Affairs and International Trade Canada, École Nationale d'Administration Publique at the Université du Québec, the Canadian Centre for International Governance Innovation, the Canadian Institute of

International Affairs/Canadian International Council, the Norman Paterson School of International Affairs at Carleton University, the Munk Centre for International Studies at the University of Toronto, and the Diplomatic Academy of London at the University of Westminster (UK).

Research assistance was provided by James Gaede, Anurag Singh, and Aaron Shull; editorial assistance was provided by Scott Bury, Ruth Tobias, and Shena Redmond. Bruce Gregory's detailed and thoughtful review provided countless insights and sources. Early drafts, in whole or in part, benefited greatly from detailed comments provided by Sarah Pothecary, Mike Taylor, Evan Potter, Kristen Rundle, Chris Lowry, David Edwards, Sean Moore, Barry Nesbitt, Nabil Ayad, Rhonda Zaharna, Nick Cull, and Chris Brown.

The helpfulness, kindness, and encouragement of each of the following individuals also contributed greatly to the completion of the project: Davey Copeland, Deborah Dunton, Maureen O'Neil, Nelson Michaud, John English, Andy Cooper, Martin Rose, Kevin Fitzgibbons, Thierry Weissenburger, Anne Carlisle, Gordon Morrison, Marie O'Shea, Denis Stairs, James Eayrs, David Dewitt, Nelson Michaud, Gerard Hervouet, Maureen Molot, Fen Hampson, Rachelle Lamb, John Kirton, Bob Bothwell, Margaret Macmillan, Marie-Lucie Morin, Peter Harder, Michael Small, Drew Fagan, John Curtis, Mackenzie Clugston, Michael Calcott, Adriaan de Hoog, Brian Hocking, Nadia Hall, Corey Copeland, George Copeland, Lillian Copeland, Gaston Barban, Colin Jennings, Jennifer Barbarie, Bijana Scott, Simon Anholt, Ian Burchett, Ian Barnes, Colin Roberson, Donna Lee, Debra Hulley, Ron Cochrane, Randolph Mank, Doug Gould, Louise Dupere, John DiGangi, Michele Pichette, Fredericka Gregory, Jan Melissen, Paul Sharp, Sean Riordan, James Eayrs, Josh Fouts, Richard Isnor, Tim Dottridge, François Taschereau, Mark McLaughlin, Robert Johnstone, Janice Stein, Rima Berns-McGown, Sarah Whitaker, Doug Thompson, Tim Shaw, Stewart Beck, Peter Singer, Peter Nicholson, Mary Anne Dehler, Neil Reeder, Mark Lahey, Philip Fiske de Gouveia, Barbara Darling, Louise Terrillon Mackay, Craig Hunter, Gerald Wright, Ken Merklinger, Randolph Gherson, Sam Hanson, Steve Wollcombe, and, last but by no means least, Tim Shaw and Jane Parpart.

While responsibility for the contents of this book is mine alone, its making has been very much an exercise in collaborative intelligence. I can overstate neither the value of nor my gratitude for the contributions so generously offered by my many partners.

Finally, none of this would have been possible without the interest, guidance, and encouragement provided from the very beginning by my publisher, Lynne Rienner, to whom I am particularly indebted.

—Daryl Copeland

1 Diplomacy, Development, and Security in the Age of Globalization

It is impossible for words to describe what is necessary.
—Colonel Walter E. Kurtz in
Francis Ford Coppola's *Apocalypse Now*

It's a jungle out there. Even Joseph Conrad, whose novel *Heart of Darkness* provided the basis for Coppola's film, would have been awestruck to discover just how far up the river, as it were, the world now finds itself. Pick up a newspaper, turn on the television, or log on to your favorite political website or e-zine. The big stories, from political violence to religious extremism, transnational market meltdowns to weapons of mass destruction, pandemic disease to climate change, all point to the conclusion that the human project is facing major challenges.

Headlines, of course, don't tell the whole story. Now as always, a good deal of what matters takes place *behind* the headlines, sometimes in the little-known habitat of diplomats. But increasingly, the things that count are happening in the open, in the public domain. Breaking events are reported and broadcast, often by citizen journalists using the new digital media. Nowhere are these changes more clearly evident or important than in the case of international relations.

Today, world affairs are less a matter of conducting official business between states than of managing the effects of the colossal force widely known as globalization, a powerful engine of integration. Paradoxically, it can also generate insecurity, splinter polities, and enlarge cultural divides.

With the economic crisis that begin in mid-2008, globalization may be down, but it is far from out. Indeed, its persistence continues to render the planet and its problems, and hence the challenges facing diplomacy, immensely more complex. A new range of issues rooted in science and driven by technology must increasingly become the focus of the diplomatic enterprise. Multiple threats to global order, which are at least as likely to stem from the activities of supranational or intranational collectivities as they are from the machinations of traditional nation-states, have rendered the peaceful administration of the international system increasingly difficult.

In our wired world, security has become indivisible and diplomacy, dedicated by definition to solving problems and resolving differences without the use of force, matters. Each year many more die from poverty-related causes than are killed as a result of any kind of political or religious violence. By addressing issues of underdevelopment, which only fifty years ago were all but ignored, agents of diplomacy can play a critical role in the achievement of international security. But diplomacy is a neglected, almost obscure subject within contemporary academic research, and its practice has not been adapted to the transformed environment in which it must operate. Not only has it lost its monopoly on intergovernmental communications across borders, but a panoply of thorny challenges, most related to globalization, have either gone unaddressed or have been dealt with by other means, mainly military. The results have been dismal.

Understanding the volatile alchemy of underdevelopment and insecurity, assessing the crisis of diplomacy, bridging the diplomatic performance gap, and identifying ways to transform diplomats into globalization managers are the goals of this book. Yet no one size fits all. I offer no single-factor explanations or sole-source solutions, instead contributing to the debate by synthesizing and encapsulating sets of complex interrelationships under the rubrics of public and, especially, *guerrilla diplomacy*.

* * *

The Book of One Thousand and One Nights tells the instructive tale of a one-time king of Persia. Betrayed by his first wife, the king neither trusted nor respected any possible successor; each day he would choose a virgin, marry her, and have her beheaded the following morning.

One day the king encountered the vizier's cunning and beautiful daughter, Scheherazade, who, against her father's wishes volunteered to spend a night with the king. Sizing up her predicament, Scheherazade used her knowledge, intellect, and imagination to tell stories of Ali Baba, Sinbad, and Aladdin, among others, until the king was won over by satisfaction and gratitude. He sent the executioner home. Scheherazade was granted full pardon; they were wed and had three sons.

Moral of the story? *Keep talking*. That is the message that diplomacy brings to the world of international relations.

Twenty-First-Century Alchemy

Development and security are worthy ends; diplomacy and defense, like trade, immigration, and international law, are available means. History illustrates that diplomacy can be crucial to the prevention and, more commonly, to the resolution of conflict. Much less widely appreciated is the fact that diplomacy can also make a durable contribution to international security at much lower cost than can armed force, namely by addressing not only the immediate causes of organized violence—anger, resentment, humiliation—but also the underlying, structurally embedded ones. Even with absolute poverty diminishing in places, relative disparity and the popular discontent it creates are becoming more acute.

Diplomacy can be used to address and ultimately manage these discontinuities, tensions, and imbalances. Diplomats, however, are languishing in the bleachers as the legions march by.

When the Soviet Union imploded, the distinction between the first, second, and third worlds ceased being either accurate or relevant. Since then, analysts have been without a world order model that effectively captures globalization. To better identify and understand the emerging contours of the twenty-first century, a better framework is required—one that will distinguish among those whose prospects are improving, those whose dispositions will be contingent upon future developments, those whose well-being is at risk, and those who are excluded.

Almost twenty years have passed since the end of the Cold War, yet the Manichean, radically simplistic worldview of the Cold Warriors remains. Among major powers, foreign policy remains to a great extent militarized and may become even more so. The Cold War habit of binary perception—whereby everything is seen in terms of good or bad, friend or foe, black or white—as well as that of threatening and brandishing hard power haunts us still. The domestic politics of fear and the ubiquitously advertised danger of terrorism have obscured a larger truth, namely that it is people, not countries or politics or ideas, that constitute the foundation upon which all else rests.

I propose a solution: the acceptance of human-centered development, whereby the well-being of people is paramount as the basis for a new international policy upon which the world can construct a new kind of security. Achieving this goal will require moving well beyond discredited notions of "modernization." Much greater focus is needed on scientific research and the development of new technologies, as well as on the balance between human and environmental needs. If scientific discovery is the fuel of globalization, then technological innovation is its motor. Special attention will have to be devoted to finding ways to better connect diplomacy to the research and development (R&D) agenda in support, for example, of the health of the ecosphere—without compromising the present or future requirements of economic development, social progress, or justice. Growth must proceed, yes, but it must be of an intelligent and informed variety, rather than the reckless, speculative greed and fear fest that has recently wrought such havoc. I propose a holistic, sustainable ethic of development as the defining characteristic not just of aid programs but of diplomacy and international security as a whole.

An important implication of this argument, with consequences for spending priorities and the distribution of resources, is that we must rethink the nature of diplomacy, which has been driven in all kinds of new directions by globalization. Traditional diplomacy, predicated on the conduct of formal relations between states, is in disarray. It is equipped neither to address the complex challenges of the twenty-first century nor to deliver the kinds of remedial policies that the era of globalization requires. The growing number of unresolved transnational issues and the increasing incidence of violence and conflict in the world attest to diplomacy's failure. In the face of the new constellation of unconventional, irregular threats—from explosive devices to pandemic diseases—international policy planners and diplomatic practitioners need to innovate rigorously and to adopt irregular responses. Technology, for example, can create economic opportunities and solve problems, but it can also intensify alienation and spread disaffection. Bridging the R&D gaps that divide the beneficiaries of globalization from those consigned to its underside or lost on the periphery requires specialized knowledge. Many diplomats, however, especially those in senior positions, are saddled with outdated skills and rigid sensibilities acquired during the Cold War. They are without the flexibility to combine a nuanced understanding of the political economy of knowledge with its strategic application.

Diplomats, as they have traditionally been trained and developed, are particularly ill prepared to diagnose or treat the growing range of political, economic, and, especially, science-based global problems that have become a prominent feature of the evolving international landscape. Like the bases for the new security, the diplomat, too, must be reimagined. Class, pedigree, and social status, once among the defining elements of the trade, have been eclipsed by personal and professional skills not easily acquired at Ivy League schools. These new skills are central to what I call guerrilla diplomacy.

Our response to globalization will have implications for all elements of the diplomatic ecosystem—including, among many constituent elements, the principal structures and institutions of international policy: diplomacy, the foreign ministry, and foreign service. The three are inextricably intermeshed and best treated organically. All require major reform and reconstruction. To understand the *ecology of diplomacy*—which is to say the interlocking relationship among diplomatic methods, agents, and institutions—it is necessary to operate unconventionally, outside the usual scholarly confines of data sets and exclusive theoretical frameworks, while maintaining the vantage point necessary to survey the findings generated by many different disciplines. These largely unexplored frontiers are our destination.

The Diplomatic Agenda: Globalization in Context

Globalization—the historical process that is shaping our times—carries enormous implications for diplomacy, development, security, and international policy. In the context of globalization, none of the latter are usefully viewed in isolation. New actors drawn from civil society, tribal and religious groups, supranational bodies, and the private sector now play major roles distinct from those of governments. A different constellation of challenges and threats has emerged, in tandem with multiplying media and unexplored possibilities.

Old-style, state-to-state relations, with all of their associated conventions and rigidities, remain in the diplomatic mix, but as the center of gravity has shifted, their relevance has diminished. The erstwhile global village has come to resemble something more akin to a corporation of gated communities surrounded on all sides by sprawling, seething shantytowns. As a result, diplomacy, too, has dispersed: the front lines are frequently far from the chancellery. The encounters that matter often occur in dangerous and faraway places and the issues are almost unimaginably complex.

Unlike some, I do not glamorize globalization—but neither do I dismiss it, as has lately become fashionable.[1] Instead, I maintain that the central task of analysts is to grapple with its manifold and continuing implications.[2] Where these are negative, the development of remedial strategies will be required.

Although driven primarily by economic forces, globalization often conditions and sometimes determines outcomes across an expansive array of human activities. Thus it has produced a very mixed picture, featuring both winners and losers, beneficiaries and victims—providing comfort and choice for some, misery and hardship for many. Globalization is nothing if not complex and paradoxical. Even where levels of absolute poverty and deprivation are diminishing, the relative gaps—and the media-fueled perceptions thereof—are at all levels increasing, while the spaces left for shared goals and common identity are shrinking.[3] Notions of difference—ethnic, religious, cultural, and political—rather than similarity, are ascendant everywhere. These are particularly manifest in the many expressions of political Islam.

One of the most interesting but frequently overlooked aspects of globalization is its tendency to deterritorialize social, economic, and political spaces.[4] While not happening at the same pace or intensity everywhere, time and distance, as barriers to human interaction and exchange, are disappearing; shared identity and a sense of community are no longer dependent upon physical proximity. The advent of the Internet and wireless communications has made possible the creation and extension of virtual communities—jihadis among them—but also widely dispersed and numerous groupings of overseas Chinese, South and Southeast Asians, African tribes and clans, and many others. This carries largely unexamined implications not only for national and international security but also for the potential for enlisting the aid of newcomers in the project of nation building.

While globalization compresses geographic space, the connectedness that it engenders expands the possibilities for contact and cooperation. Diplomats need to learn how to operate in these amorphous horizontal spaces, but at present diplomats are more attuned to and adept at working in the familiar vertical mosaic of the apparatus of the state, where official designations and hierarchic social relations are the norm.

The combination of exploitation and inequality with a sharpened awareness thereof has created fertile ground for extremist causes, especially religious ones. In the globalizing world, more people have more access to more information, much of it visual as well as textual. In these circumstances, perceptions of growing inequality and inequity, however relative, become both sharper and more widely held. The ever-expanding use of information and communications technology has encouraged intense feelings of exploitation and suffering to become vicarious.[5] And it is that destabilizing development which brings concerns about addressing its underlying causes front and center.

Shifting precariously, the globalized world is at the same time monolithic and fractured. If it had a texture, it would be uneven. By imposing the ethos of competitiveness and polarizing the creation and distribution of wealth, resources, and opportunities both within and among states, globalization aggregates at some levels as it fragments at others. By expanding markets for goods and ideas and extending networks, globalization enlarges the scope for democratization even as it cheapens its content and corrodes the broad cultural base upon which democracy depends, in part through the promotion of values originating in the metropolitan center. By disseminating vast quantities of information, it undermines monopolies previously enjoyed by governments and corporations, while it concentrates and reinforces the power of a smaller number of key players ranging from international financial institutions and celebrities to private charities and philanthropic organizations. By subverting repressive, authoritarian structures, it contributes to political liberation, even as its tendency to sharpen economic inequalities undermines the delicate social contract upon which all representative institutions ultimately depend.

Globalization generates wealth, but not for all. It churns out ever cheaper consumer goods, at least for those who can afford them. It contributes to capital accumulation but also to instability by inflating speculative bubbles and then bursting them. Highly prone to serious disruption, it creates efficiencies but breeds insecurity, particularly in the volatile zones found between integrating cores—OECD countries and other beneficiaries of globalization—and disintegrating peripheries, where the standard of living is declining. These zones are sometimes referred to collectively as "the gap."[6] Globalization, whatever its virtues, has become a primary source of disaffection and, as it weakens the machinery of government while exacerbating inequity, a major contributor to state failure. Weak states seem to be multiplying; according to the World Bank, the number of fragile states has grown recently from seventeen to twenty-six in only three years.[7]

These powerful currents are responsible for much of the violence of our times. Today, the animus of most conflict originates not in the kinds of proximate political, ideological, and territorial differences that have traditionally given rise to interstate warfare. Rather, the causes are rooted in the essential dynamic of globalization, which generates threats of a sort best addressed not by counterinsurgency or a so-called war on terror,[8] but instead, I believe, by agents of diplomacy in the strategic pursuit of equitable, sustainable, and human-centered development.[9]

International Policy and the "New Security"

Searching for good, or at least better, governance in a world faced with deteriorating international relations, severe economic instability, a worsening physical environment, and grinding, systemic violence (especially prevalent where chronic poverty and underdevelopment exist) is stimulating to some, wearying to others. There is, however, one overriding objective shared by all: an interest in survival. However basic, this connection could usefully be built upon.

During the Cold War, the management of interstate relations was the centerpiece of international relations. Globalization, however, has brought transnational issues to the forefront and has made security and development mutually inclusive and indivisible—two sides of the same coin fused by diplomacy and international policy.

This fusion is unprecedented, yet the magnitude and complexity of the impact have tended to induce a sense of powerlessness, hopelessness, and anesthesia, particularly at the level of the lowest common denominator. This apathy must be resisted, especially by those responsible for the framing of international policy, who face steep challenges as a result of globalization's winnowing effects. The delicate balance between the promotion of values such as human rights, democracy, religious freedom, and social justice and the pursuit of interests such as trade gains, capital inflows, commercial advantages, and resource access has become even harder to achieve.

Finding this balance is the province of *international policy,* a term I use broadly to describe most everything that national governments officially do outside of their borders. It refers to activities undertaken by a variety of departments, agencies, and institutions—for example, trade and investment promotion, immigration, development assistance, military intervention, and environmental action. Partners (or targets or adversaries) may include other levels of government or nonstate actors. The term stands in contrast to an older and more familiar term, *foreign policy,* which was transacted almost exclusively between states and was primarily the domain of foreign ministries and heads of state or government. This terminological evolution reflects both the blurring of the lines between the domestic and international spheres and the shift from the Cold War era that of globalization. It is also suggestive of the reality among many countries that diplomatic missions abroad are staffed by representatives from a variety of central government departments, and sometimes by representatives from other levels of government and civil society as well.

Development and security are key international policy objectives, and I view them as inseparable. Both feature prominently in the thinking on human-centered development, which is premised on freedom of political, economic, social, and cultural expression; the provision of reasonable access to the basic necessities of life, both material and knowledge-based; and the absence of chronic threats. Action to address the causes of fear and want—a central pillar of what has come to be known as the *human security doctrine*—is considered germane to human-centered development.[10]

Within this rubric, I have tried to synthesize one especially critical cluster of issues surrounding the opportunity to access and use the burgeoning political economy of knowledge. Developing this capacity will involve harnessing the power of science and technology to bridge strategic R&D gaps both within and among populations, countries, and regions. Not least because of their present state of neglect in the realm of international policy, recognition of the pivotal role of science and technology in international relations and in the achievement of human-centered development is essential for fashioning a better, more secure tomorrow.

In terms of real threats to humankind, terrorism does not make the A list. It is in a different league than climate change, pandemic disease, the scourge of chronic underdevelopment, and, for that matter, such problems as transportation safety and the explosive growth of tobacco use in underdeveloped countries. Nonetheless, the placement of counterterrorism at or near the very center of the foreign policy frameworks adopted by many Western countries since 9/11, secured by the fear-mongering of the mass media, renders the treatment of such issues indispensable to this analysis. Though not a panacea, a thoroughly reconstructed approach to diplomacy, at present significantly undervalued and underresourced, will be crucial in mobilizing the support necessary to achieve global development and security over the longer term. In the meantime, however, a world in which suicide bombing has become commonplace, fundamentalist Islam has been branded as the religion of the oppressed, and terror has been embraced as the weapon of choice by the weak and the disenfranchised desperately requires innovative response. Diplomats, as I will show, can add value here too, not least in conflict situations, using methods not available to soldiers, aid workers, or the representatives of nongovernmental organizations (NGOs).

Diplomatic Deconstruction

If international relations address the *why* in the assessment offered here, and international policy the *what,* then diplomacy is about the *how.* As understood and practiced today, diplomacy is a relatively recent addition to international relations. As part of the lexicon of statecraft, it has come into common usage only in the eighteenth century. Since then, the ends of diplomacy have not changed: the nonviolent resolution of differences through negotiation and compromise, the promotion of cooperation for mutual gain, and the collection and analysis of information related to the advancement of national interests.[11] Dialogue, however, cannot flourish in the absence of a commitment to development or in a violent climate wherein large-scale insecurity is treated mainly by the application of force.

Simply put, security is no longer best understood as a dimension of defense. Instead, in this world of organized militaries pursuing irregular militants, vulnerability has become mutual, and the use of conventional arms is frequently counterproductive. To find the best route to a more pacific future, the fundamentals of security need to be rethought, and the intellectual foundations reconstructed. Only then will public diplomacy and nation branding emerge as vital instruments.

At the highest level of analysis, public diplomacy involves efforts by governments to promote their policies and interests abroad by influencing international public opinion through interaction with other polities, forging partnerships with civil societies, and using the media strategically. The approach is noncoercive and based on the use of "soft power"—the attractive rather than coercive power to make others want what you want and to harness public opinion in support of particular interests.[12] In other words, public diplomats use the tools and tactics of public relations to connect with populations abroad, and they count on that connection to produce intelligence and to move host governments toward desired ends. This is very different from classic diplomatic practice.[13] Agents of public diplomacy and branding move the goalposts, enlarge the playing field, and rewrite the rules of the game in a manner not fully captured even in the literature that has attracted renewed attention to these subjects post-9/11.[14]

In liberal democracies generally, and in major cities such as London, Tokyo, New York, and São Paulo, public diplomacy works well. Globalization has produced a cultural commonality, and, especially in democracies, audiences are both accessible and influential. But the model needs to be pushed when applied to underdeveloped areas and areas of conflict and insecurity. What I call guerrilla diplomacy offers a formula for as much, particularly in response to some of the more exigent challenges posed by globalization.[15] In developing that concept and putting the focus on adaptability, agility, self-sufficiency, intelligence, and technology, I stress the importance of tapping into both mass and elite sources of fact and opinion. Clearly, if you are to connect with the population among whom you are operating, you must first devote a great deal of effort toward understanding deeply what your interlocutors are all about. That is precisely why some lines of thinking about public diplomacy and counterinsurgency are converging.

For this reason and others, we must also fundamentally reconsider our approach to the generation and analysis of foreign intelligence by asking ourselves where, how, and for what purpose it is gathered and what is done with the product. I am not talking here about spying, or running agents, or any of the various forms of espionage, subversion, and skulduggery. Au contraire, in my view, among the most promising of recent developments has been the move away from an exclusive, discreet if not secretive, boutique type of diplomacy catering mainly to the tastes of the pinstripe set toward something much closer to the ideals of Main Street—something that operates at the grassroots to take diplomacy to the people. With an ear to the ground, much can be heard.

As a network builder and knowledge worker, the public diplomat, and even more so the guerrilla diplomat, becomes an agile agent with access to critical information sources, connecting directly with populations and navigating pathways of influence others can't chart or maneuver through. Boring deep into the interstices of power and operating unconventionally—often outside of their traditional metropolitan comfort zones—guerrilla diplomats can negotiate both the drivers of globalization and the consequences of change.

This kind of diplomacy is most effective when meaningful exchange is translated into policy development and action. It goes well beyond the work done by public affairs offices found in most embassies—which typically seek more to inform than to persuade—and has more in common with dialogue than propaganda, which is a one-way flow of information often characterized by inaccuracy and bias in support of a particular cause. But neither public diplomacy nor its more radical variant, guerrilla diplomacy, can work in a vacuum.[16] To ensure that they deliver on their full potential, we need a much larger, more comprehensive, and in many respects more complicated package of structural and institutional changes. Here we must examine critically the other two elements of the diplomatic ecosystem: the foreign ministry—and especially its role in the formulation of development policy and aid programs—and the foreign service, which is in desperate need of reform. That said, in the era of globalization it is precisely diplomacy, the foreign ministry, and the foreign service that remain the most efficient tools with which to identify and, ultimately, address the daunting range of economic, social, and political needs worldwide, and, in so doing, make the planet a more secure place.

Geodiplomacy: The World in Five Uneasy Pieces

Where in the world are we going? How might we best chart where we've been, where we are, and where we would like to arrive? A reconsidered grand strategy would set out basic principles, policies, and instruments; analyze the threats and obstacles to be broached; and identify the objectives sought. Uniting them under the general heading of *geodiplomatics,* I summarize here the central issues to be treated and principal arguments to be advanced in the pages that follow.[17]

1. Globalization is a profound historical process that works very well for some, affording them comfort and choice—but at the direct expense of many others. Because globalization generates insecurity, its management must be moved to the top of the diplomatic agenda. To accurately apprehend the nature of that agenda and of the environment in which international policy is formulated and implemented, diplomats will need an explanatory and predictive world order model—one that takes full account of the impact of globalization, highlighting especially the dialectic between security and development.

2. As we have moved from the Cold War era to that of globalization, development has displaced defense as the most secure foundation upon which to build a common future. The range of threats and challenges generated by this epochal shift are best addressed not through armed force, a global war on terror, or the militarization of international policy[18]—which has resulted in a severe misallocation of resources—but through the strategic pursuit of human-centered development. Particular emphasis must be placed by diplomats on the role of communications, culture, nonstate actors, and the implications of the deterritorialization of political space.

3. Many of the key challenges for international policy in the twenty-first century—the quality of life in megacities, the existence of weapons of mass destruction, the depletion of energy supplies, pandemic disease, climate change—are fundamental to both security and development and are rooted in and driven by science and technology.[19] To address these issues, diplomats will need to develop new skills that reflect their understanding of the emerging political economy of knowledge. I refer to this strategic capacity to bridge R&D gaps by connecting local problems to global understanding as *souplesse.*

4. Diplomacy is not a cure-all for the ills of globalization, but compared to the alternatives—especially defense—it is an undervalued, underresourced, and cost-effective asset with which much more could be done. Public and especially guerrilla diplomacy are uniquely attuned to the challenges and threats generated by globalization. But diplomacy's structures, principles, and practices must be rethought from the ground up, with special attention dedicated to the relationship between development and security, not least in the context of counterinsurgency. If states are allowed to fail, insecurity will deepen and widen.

5. To better support a transformed international policy agenda, we must consider the machinery and institutions of diplomacy together—constituting as they do the aforementioned ecology of diplomacy—and revamp them in tandem. The foreign ministry and foreign service are not predicated upon the need to connect with populations, to construct and maintain networks of contacts, or to generate the intelligence required to understand and deal effectively with complex, crosscutting issues. If institutional performance in the pursuit of peace and prosperity is to be improved, the entire diplomatic ecosystem must be restored.

Diplomacy matters, but it is in crisis because it has not adapted to globalization, it lacks a functioning world order model, and it is in large part divorced from development as well as science and technology. It is, in short, in need of a systemic makeover. The challenges are great. But the potential for progress is greater still. The Internet—the flagship of globalization—is both changing diplomatic practice and empowering individual diplomats by giving them access to a vast amount of knowledge and the ability to communicate to a worldwide audience. Even so, diplomats will need new tools, both heuristic and practical, if they are to act effectively in response to the challenges of the twenty-first century, underdevelopment foremost among them. Success will turn on both political leadership and, at the senior bureaucratic level, a determined effort to avoid further reductions and acquire new resources. In many governments, each has been notable mainly for its absence.

With so much to do, we must take time to reflect. To reconsider. To think things through. Diplomacy was largely frozen out of the Cold War, and it has been shunted to the sidelines in the global war on terror. Government spokespeople are fond of saying they "don't negotiate" with the Taliban, militants, Al-Qaida, extremists, terrorists, and so on. That must change. Communication in itself is neutral. To engage in it is not necessarily to support or in any way condone the actions of the other party to the exchange.

War is the antithesis of diplomacy, and reliance upon armed force as the international policy instrument of choice is costly. When the fighting starts, the negotiations intended to avert recourse to violence stop. Diplomacy may continue, or resume, but for purposes of conflict resolution rather than prevention. The willingness to compromise wanes, especially on the part of the side that's winning. The scope of useful diplomatic enterprise becomes limited. Yet as a tool used to treat the afflictions characteristic of globalization, the military is both too sharp, which is to say damaging, and too dull, which is to say imprecise. When states lead with the sword, they forfeit the predisposition to grapple with complex differences through meaningful political communication. That is guerrilla diplomacy's forte.

Amid the din of plowshares being beaten into swords, I believe that it is time to commit to talking, not fighting. The next twelve chapters explain why and how. But getting from here to there will involve formulating the right questions at least as much as proffering any answers.

A Thumbnail Sketch of This Book

Part 1, The Evolving Context of Diplomacy, lays the conceptual and historical foundations necessary for understanding the shift from the freeze that characterized the Cold War period to the flux so evident in the era of globalization—a transition upon which the rest of the volume is constructed. Chapter 2, Cold

War Comfort, offers a survey of the profoundly changed environment in which international policy is being planned and executed in the postmillennium. In Chapter 3, Globalization and Empire, I examine some of the essential cross-currents generated by the shift from the Cold War to the age of globalization and identify those elements that are consequential for diplomacy. Chapter 4, Understanding World Order, pulls together some of the principal strands of the ragged transition and weaves them into a new cloth, in part using thread provided by dependency theorists. My emphasis here is on the interactions at all levels among an integrating core, a vast disintegrating periphery, and those who find themselves in the interstices.

Part 2, Drivers of Change, moves to an intermediate level of analysis at which I consider issues of security, including its relationship to development, and the impact advances in science and technology have had on it. In Chapter 5, Persistent Insecurity, I make the case that the prospect of equitable, sustainable, human-centered development—as opposed, for instance, to power balancing, deterrence, or the war on terror—represents the only durable basis for international security. On that premise, I examine the ideological and strategic baggage carried over from the Cold War past—as well as the luggage that was, perhaps mistakenly, left behind. Chapter 6, Development Revisited, compares conceptions of development and evaluates the record of progress to date. In Chapter 7, Science and Technology, I explore a vital but rarely assessed characteristic of globalization: the rising significance of science and technology as a component of international policy. Much more than terrorism or religious extremism, I argue, the challenges rooted in science and driven by technology—from climate change to pandemic disease—threaten human survival. That these generators of epochal change are frequently overlooked or understated by analysts, or ineptly managed by policymakers, may be attributed to their near-complete absence in the contemporary diplomatic mix.

In Part 3, Diplomacy Unbound, we shift from an analysis of past and present trends in international relations to a consideration of the future and the ways in which we can prepare for what may be in store. Here I move from the poetry to the plumbing, zooming in on issues and institutions (the foreign ministry, the foreign service, and the diplomatic business model) that constitute the core of diplomacy's ecosystem and analyzing how states and their representatives might best equip themselves to respond to the challenges of globalization—professionally, organizationally, and administratively. Chapter 8, The Global Political Economy of Knowledge, examines the potential use of science and technology by diplomats in bridging the digital divide that maps onto the global development gap. In Chapter 9, The Foreign Ministry, I review the myriad bureaucratic challenges facing diplomacy, the range of problems and preoccupations that confront international policy managers, and some of the responses attempted to date. I propose that a reformed foreign ministry, one attuned to the uncertainty engendered by the flux of globalization, is the sole body capable of integrating action and making sense of it all. But success will require a commitment to administrative and cultural transformation; we must refashion the foreign ministry from a formulator of narrow foreign policy and a manager of interstate relations into an international policy entrepôt and a nation's storyteller and interpreter, addressing both domestic and international audiences. In the final chapter in this section, Public Diplomacy and Foreign Service, I inquire as to how diplomatic practitioners' methods, skill sets, and professional organizations might be realigned to address the requirements of the twenty-first century.

Part 4, The Way Ahead, considers the future of diplomacy and its institutions and integrates many of the main arguments and themes presented earlier in the volume around the consideration of guerrilla diplomacy. In Chapter 11, International Policy Instruments, I propose a mantra—*relevance, effectiveness, transformation*—for the reinvention of the foreign ministry, diplomacy, and the foreign service. I also assess the possible costs of coasting for too long on a seriously outdated image and reputation. Could branding assist policymakers in limiting the vulnerabilities associated with a growing credibility gap? Chapter 12, Guerrilla Diplomacy, etches a portrait of the diplomat as guerrilla that reveals his or her personal qualities, use of technology and intelligence, and role in the management of counterinsurgency. The guerrilla diplomat is above all effective—swimming like a fish in the sea of the people, making and maintaining networks of contacts, communicating politically, mastering new media, and generating both tactical and strategic advantage. I argue that guerrilla diplomats, as a key subset of public diplomats, are uniquely suited for dealing with the contemporary constellation of security threats. They are equipped to address feelings of resentment, humiliation, alienation, anger, and fear in ways the old Westphalian school of diplomats could not begin to contemplate. By taking them from hearing to listening, from looking to seeing, and, even more important, from transmission to reception and from broadcast to exchange, guerrilla diplomacy allows its practitioners to build relationships on the basis of critical personal and situational elements—confidence, trust, and respect—rather than positional power.

In the concluding chapter, I summarize the principal findings that have emerged from the research, analysis, and personal experience that inform this book, and I also indicate some areas of possible future scholarly interest. The volume wraps up with a discussion of five abiding paradoxes associated with globalization and international policy, suggesting some implications and possible options for policymakers.

The upshot? In the age of globalization, security, development, and world order have become inseparable, and diplomacy is the key to treating the new range of threats and challenges rooted in science and driven by technology. Better performance with respect to shaping our common future won't take a miracle, but it will require an accurate understanding of the world we live in, the will to learn new skills, and a commitment to realign grand strategy and address global priorities. In that calculation, diplomacy, rather than defense, must occupy a central place, for it has the crosscutting applicability all other international policy instruments lack. Public and especially guerrilla diplomacy can restore the relevance and effectiveness of the world's second oldest profession in the face of the threats and challenges globalization presents. First, however, we will have to find ways to correct the crippling imbalance between the exploding demand and diminishing supply of all forms of diplomacy in an insecure world. A substantial reallocation or injection of new resources is a sine qua non.

Notes

1. Thomas Friedman (1999; 2005) has been perhaps foremost among the cheerleaders. For a positive institutional perspective, see assessments prepared by the IMF. For the other end of the spectrum see, for instance, John Ralston Saul (2005). The onset of economic crisis in mid-2008 has produced many obituaries attesting to the end of globalization; I believe them premature.

2. In seeking ways to find virtue in necessity, or, at minimum, to make the most of a very daunting set of circumstances, see Stiglitz (2002 and, especially, 2006). His transformation from the voice of orthodoxy as chief economist for the World Bank to a darling of the global justice movement has been epic.

3. See World Bank (2005b: 55–69).

4. See Scholte (2005). This might also be termed *denationalization* and is related as well to the reduced regulatory and mediating power of states.

5. What motivates those young Muslims, Sikhs, Jews, Hindus, Christians, and others to turn to violence to express their disaffection? Some commentators emphasize that those who become attracted to terrorism or radicalism are often relatively well-to-do members of the working and middle classes or citizens of middle-income or wealthy countries. I find that unsurprising. You don't have to have lung cancer to get upset about the efforts of tobacco companies to develop new markets, you don't have to have been hit by someone under the influence to be an advocate for stronger drunk-driving laws, and you don't have to be suffering personally from structural violence and systemic injustice to feel empathy for the victims, especially if it appears that members of your ethnic or religious group are being afflicted disproportionately.

6. See Barnett (2003; 2004). The 2003 reference appeared in *Esquire* and is a preliminary encapsulation of the book's more fully developed thesis.

7. On the increasing number of fragile states, or "low-income countries under stress," see World Bank (2006). Vinod Thomas, principal author of the Bank's report on this subject, notes: "Neglecting the fragile states—home to 500 million people, half of whom are living in extreme poverty—risks worsening their misery, in turn feeding regional and global instability." For an introduction to some of the many issues and competing assessments associated with state failure, see Zartman (1995), Rotberg (2003), Chesterman (2005), and Chomsky (2006).

8. The war on terror has been justified by what has been coined the Bush Doctrine of preemption, unilateralism, and military preeminence. See White House (2002; 2006). The approach codified in these documents was developed mainly by a loose alliance of neoconservatives exiled from the center of power during the Clinton years. Founded in

1997 by William Kristol and Robert Kagan, this group, which came together as the Project for a New American Century, advocated a defense buildup, a confrontational foreign policy, and the aggressive promotion of their version of liberty and democracy. Its members, including Dick Cheney, Donald Rumsfeld, Paul Wolfowitz, Richard Perle, Richard Armitage, Lewis "Scooter" Libby, and Jeb Bush, were especially prominent in high places during George Bush's first term. See http://www.newamericancentury.org.

9. See the World Commission on Environment and Development (1987).

10. The main lines of the human security doctrine are set out in the UN Development Programme's Human Development Report 1994, which fuses conceptions of development with those of security. Since the report's release, interpretations have become so broad that the concept has lost much of its precision, permitting its appropriation by the proponents of the use of armed force as the favored international policy instrument. In important respects, NATO's intervention in Bosnia and Kosovo, including its so-called human security bombing of Belgrade, has served to keep the militarization of international policy acceptable and has opened the door for subsequent interventions. I have accordingly tried to minimize my use of the term.

11. Surely one of the more curious aspects of diplomacy is that so few of its practitioners can actually define the term—or even think much about its meaning.

12. See Nye (1990; 2004b).

13. See, for instance, Nicolson (1980). For a historical perspective, see Anderson (1993) as well as Hamilton and Langhorne (1995). On diplomatic theory, see Berridge (2005). The classic vocational text is Ernest Satow's *Guide to Diplomatic Practice* (1979). A more contemporary perspective is offered by Barston (2006). See also Bull (1977) for the so-called English School's assessment of the role of diplomacy in international relations, Marshall (1999) for a practical guide, Freeman (1997) on tools of statecraft.

14. See Jönsson and Hall (2005).

15. See Copeland (2004: 165–175).

16. Public diplomacy or, to put it more broadly, the new diplomacy emphasizes the need to move beyond the idea of conducting traditional state-to-state relations through designated channels like foreign ministries and envoys toward that of connecting directly with populations. For an assessment of what this might mean for Canadian foreign relations, see Copeland (2005).

17. The term *geodiplomatics* was coined jointly by former British diplomat Sir Peter Marshall and Nabil Ayad, director of the Diplomatic Academy of London at the University of Westminster. It is used in the same global and strategic sense as *geopolitics* or *geoeconomics*, often in the context of image projection and reputation management. Professor Ayad and I agreed to the definition of geodiplomacy as "the effective management of the global strategic nexus." Personal communication with the author, January 18, 2008.

18. For a broad treatment of this theme in the US context, see Herr (2008).

19. Since 2004, there has been some controversy concerning which of these issues is most pressing and whether a preoccupation with one (such as climate change) might come at the expense of attention to another (for example, the AIDS pandemic). See, for instance, Lomborg (2007). My point, however, is that all of these challenges share a common source in science and technology.

PART 1

The Evolving Context of Diplomacy

Cold War Comfort: The World We Knew 2

A handful of retired generals, the odd remnant dictator, a diminishing number of Russian pensioners, and diehard fans of films like *Dr. Strangelove* and *On the Beach* might feel nostalgic about the passing of the last political ice age.[1] Beyond them, it is hard to find many who miss living in the perpetual shadow of nuclear annihilation.

From the Big Chill . . .

The long superpower standoff did offer more scope for diplomacy than hot war would have—but not much. From the late 1940s to the early 1990s, the military superpowers in question—the United States and the USSR—were locked in a heavily armed standoff predicated upon the suicidal logic of massive overkill and the doctrine of mutually assured destruction. Terrifying prospects—from urban incineration to radioactive clouds and black rain to endless nuclear winter—were more than enough to ensure that most people could not "stop worrying and love the bomb."[2] First strike, throw weight, launch on warning: power was measured in the kilotonnage of warheads and influence calibrated against numbers of hardened silos.

Bertolt Brecht famously likened love to war—both would "always find a way." With its purges, parades, and powerful imagery, the Cold War occupied vast tracts of the collective imagination. How could it not? In North America, just beneath television's happy, suburban, make-believe world of *Leave It to Beaver, Loretta Young,* and *Father Knows Best,* there were air raid sirens, basement and backyard bomb shelters, "duck and cover" exercises in public schools, and regular headlines warning of the Communist Menace and fomenting the Red Scare. Rabid finger-pointing reached an apogee during the McCarthy hearings, and fear-mongering attained levels not to be seen again until after 9/11.

Subtle it was not. Yet as the Cold War ebbed and flowed, with periods of détente interspersed with moments of intense drama—the Berlin blockade, the Cuban missile crisis—there developed a certain degree of familiarity. Not too far beneath the gleaming surface of missiles, warheads, and intercontinental bombers on twenty-four-hour standby, the world order model that outlined agreed strategic geography and followed rules was collectively understood. It was usually characterized as bipolar—but it was in the contested lands beyond those poles that much of the action occurred. Through it all, plenty of blood was drawn and a hoard of treasure squandered. Death squads and rebel groups were armed and trained. Nasty regimes were propped up, elected ones subverted, and whole generations deprived of their most basic rights. But many places and events seemed part of a script: Checkpoint Charlie, the crossing point between East and West Berlin made famous by popular spy novels and films; the capture of US navy vessel the USS *Pueblo* during an intelligence mission off the North Korean coast; the alleged attacks by the North Vietnamese against US destroyers in the Gulf of Tonkin.[3] As captured so vividly in John Le Carré's novel *The Spy Who Came in from the Cold,* it was all there: the stark contrasts, the irreconcilable objectives, the dramatic confrontations. From time to time, sparks flew around the perimeters of spheres of influence and conflicts threatened to escalate into something larger and more dangerous—particularly in Korea, Cuba, and Vietnam. In the end, however, the confrontations abated and lids were one way or another eventually screwed back on.

During the Cold War, the superpowers were generally interested in signing up copycat conscripts or junior partners in the pursuit of their respective causes. Each side treated security as largely unrelated to development. Aid was usually tied to larger political or ideological objectives—primarily to reduce susceptibility to blandishments by the other side—and security was assumed to be the responsibility of those in uniform.

In the end, the Cold War was not actually a war at all but a heavily armed peace—a political and ideological struggle punctuated occasionally by military flare-ups. Still, defense ruled the roost: military and weapons programs almost always took priority over social welfare and international development assistance. The human costs of underdevelopment barely registered in the collective mind of the public.[4] One of the greatest ironies of this period was that both sides built up their military forces mainly so that they would never have to use them, especially against each other. That was the essence of deterrence—the basis of international security as it was then understood.

The Cold War era was very much a time of governments and states, formal alliances and international organizations. Interstate diplomacy was mainly set-piece and predictable. Sovereignty, territorial integrity, and noninterference were sacrosanct, if not in practice then at least at the level of rhetoric. Corporations and NGOs assumed roles throughout the crisis, yet their activities were secondary to the titanic political and ideological struggles that played out on center stage. Intranational sectarian fissures were ensconced within larger geopolitical or federal constructs. And while the Cold War occasionally produced bizarre results—Cubans fighting South Africans in the Angolan civil war in 1975, the US invasion of Grenada in 1983 and the Manuel Noriega fiasco in Panama later that decade, the selling of US weapons to Iran to fund the pro-US contras in Nicaragua, the seating of the murderous Khmer Rouge in Cambodia's chair at the UN General Assembly—the routines by and large went uninterrupted and fundamental interests were respected.[5]

This exploitive and self-serving arrangement did evoke resistance, as antiwar movements began in the late 1960s and continued through the early 1970s. There were the Students for a Democratic Society (SDS) in the United States, which splintered into the more militant Weathermen, who aimed to overthrow the US government; the dissidents in Russia and the uprisings in Hungary and Czechoslovakia; the antinuclear campaigns and occasional barricades in Europe. There were the violent Baader-Meinhof group and Red Army faction terrorists in Germany and the Italian Red Brigades, who kidnapped and killed Prime Minister Aldo Morro in 1978. Che Guevara and Ho Chi Minh became iconic in the West—you could (and still can) get the T-shirt even if you weren't really up for the revolution.

But none of it was enough to fundamentally alter the worldviews held in Moscow and Washington. On the whole, bloc members followed the rules of the game. When differences arose, they were resolved through diplomacy, deterrence, and, sometimes, surrogate war. Grievances, when they arose, tended to be territorially fixed, mainly by national borders often delineated by colonial cartographers with little reference to the realities on the ground. Whatever the outcome of the dispute, respect for the inviolability of secured political space was unchanging on the part of the principals.

That was not so long ago, but it seems very far away. For more than forty years, the superpowers had the board to themselves. China and India, which even then accounted for a third of the world's population, were for the most part internally preoccupied or engaged in various attempts at triangulation vis-à-vis the superpowers. On the other side of the globe, the great integration project planned in Western Europe was stuck in the deep freeze.

In short, moments of terror notwithstanding, international relations and their attendant crises were, for the most part, manageable. That was the essence of Cold War comfort.

When the end finally did come, it was more with a whimper than a bang. The USSR exhausted itself trying to keep pace with the US arms buildup during the 1980s, while Gorbachev's policies of *glasnost,* or "openness," and *perestroika,* or "restructuring," opened political floodgates and produced consequences that proved impossible to reverse—above all the demise of the Soviet Union itself.[6] Still, so ingrained were the habits and so deep the mistrust of many in the West, especially those who had made their careers as Cold Warriors, that at first they simply refused to believe that it was happening.[7]

As it happened, the initial euphoria that accompanied the crumbling walls and receding curtains was quickly supplanted by uncertainty over the speed of the Soviet implosion and, in many cases, by instability. Long-buried but deeply

Magical Realism: Vignettes from the Edge

Despite its established conventions and unwritten rules, the Cold War was far from dull. Working in the Horn of Africa as a political officer in the late 1980s reminded me of being assigned to a theme park designed by the four horsemen of the apocalypse.

Ethiopia, Somalia, and, eventually, Sudan were nasty dictatorships of varying political and religious hue, and all were in play as outlying pieces in the great ideological and geopolitical game. There was famine, drought, floods, and plagues of locusts. There were coups. The civil wars in Eritrea, Tigray, the Ogaden, and southern Sudan meant that huge tracts of each country were off-limits. Addis Ababa, however, was cosmopolitan—in a Cold War kind of way. It thronged with emergency humanitarian relief administrators, not to mention Polish pilots, Cuban doctors, East German secret police trainers, and all manner of Russians who found the shopping in the Mercato district of the capital to be surpassing.

The sprawling and heavily guarded US diplomatic compound buzzed with activity, more than a little of it associated with the activities of consular officers seconded from the CIA. Several of the buildings that lined the shady avenues inside the walls were festooned with antennae, towers, and satellite dishes. Among other things, they had the best television reception in town. And the pub operated by the Marine security detachment was always busy.

As the only African country—with the exception of Liberia, which is a special case—to successfully resist colonization, Ethiopia was chosen as the site for two pan-African multilateral organizations, the Organization of African Unity (now the African Union) and the UN Economic Commission for Africa. The fleets of Volvos and Mercedes seemed strangely out of place amidst the famine relief activities and omnipresent images of starving children.

While Addis Ababa was awash with visitors, the mighty Awash River, home to colonies of hippos, flowed down from the central Ethiopian highlands, only to disappear, mysteriously, before ever reaching the Red Sea. For years, no one had an explanation. Several expeditions were dispatched to find the answer. None returned—the indigenous Afar and Issas tribes apparently did not take kindly to uninvited visitors. It was eventually learned that the Awash poured into the Danakil depression—below sea level and one of the hottest places on earth—where it dispersed and evaporated completely.

Prior to being deposed in 1974, Emperor Haile Selassie, the Lion of Judah whose appeal to collective security fell upon famously deaf ears at the League of Nations in 1936, kept several lions on the grounds of the Imperial Palace. This became the Presidential Palace under Colonel Mengistu Haile Miriam, and the new leader decided to spare the lions. One was still alive,

continued

Magical Realism (Cont.)

barely, when I arrived, and it paced, forlorn and emaciated, in a small cage in a dusty park. It struck me as particularly poignant.

Prior to his coronation as emperor in 1930, Haile Selassie was known as Duke (or Ras) Tafari Mekonnen. With a little help from Jamaicans like Marcus Garvey, Ethiopia came to be seen as the *promised land*, and the emperor as the incarnation of God by the founders of a new religious sect, the Rastafarians. When the emperor paid a state visit to Jamaica in 1966, he was greeted at the airport by over 100,000 ganga-smoking true believers who saw his arrival as the second coming and prostrated themselves on the ground when he embarked. The emperor later announced that Jamaican pilgrims would be welcomed as settlers and be granted parcels of virgin land hived from huge tracts of royal reserves in the south. Thousands came, and although many also left after the Derg seized power (and recovered unused property previously controlled by the Ethiopian Orthodox church and the aristocracy under their "land to the tiller" program), hundreds nevertheless stayed on. They could regularly be seen in the small, remote town of Sheshamane, dreadlocks flowing under their red, yellow, and green rasta caps, reggae music pulsating, the scent of burning spliffs wafting into the street. Rastaman vibration in the Great Rift Valley.

Irregular warfare was pioneered in Ethiopia in the early 1940s by British Major Orde Wingate and his Gideon Force. This ragtag group successfully waged a hit-and-run campaign of unconventional war against the Italian occupiers, who had moved to take over the entire country from their base in Eritrea. Among Wingate's officers were Laurens van der Post, later to become a famous author, and Wilfred Thesiger, an explorer who later walked across the "empty quarter" of the Arabian peninsula and solved the mystery of the disappearing Awash River. Later Wingate went on to develop the techniques of what has come to be known as asymmetrical conflict while leading the *chindits* against the Japanese in Burma.

One of the biggest cultural events I attended in Addis Ababa was the performance by a precision marching troop from North Korea. One sunny Sunday afternoon it was the headline act at the national stadium. Rock stars associated with the "We Are the World" campaign for famine relief passed through the country for photo-ops, but never stayed or played. A permit would have been hard to come by, and ticket sales pretty miserable. There was also a midnight curfew, enforced at roadblocks by unfriendly soldiers from small villages carrying large guns. If you were out past 11:30, it meant staying all night, wherever you happened to be. There was never any shortage of duty-free alcohol. Party central.

continued

Magical Realism (Cont.)

With their thousands of years of recorded history, culture, language, and mythology, the Ethiopian people have tremendous pride, dignity, and a strong sense of themselves and of their country's place in the world. I often encountered the phrase "never kneel down," and in all of my dealings with Ethiopians I never experienced any of the neocolonial types of social interaction that remain pervasive elsewhere in Africa. In the midst of every conceivable kind of adversity, Ethiopians would look you straight in the eye and tell you exactly what they were thinking. Bracing, and welcome.

During those few years in the Horn of Africa the final acts of Cold War played out. For me, the time was formative, powerfully moving, and more than a little zany. Sometimes, life imitates art. I recall thinking that Gabriel García Márquez might have felt right at home.

rooted tribal, ethnic, and religious differences quickly sprouted to the surface, while information and communication technologies facilitated the development of new types of virtual communities, many with exclusionary and sometimes virulent identities.

The rigid, hierarchical command-and-control mechanisms were being enveloped and, in some cases, overtaken by more supple, adaptable networks. Nonstate actors with a preference for direct action—from Greenpeace to the global justice movement—became independent players in the international arena. And the much anticipated peace dividend, which was to have been created by the diversion of now unnecessary military spending into social programs and aid, never materialized.[8] It was largely sideswiped by the first Gulf War, overtaken by the costs of reintegration in Europe, and otherwise lost in the fin-de-siècle shuffle. Had the massive demobilization been matched by the initiation of an equivalent of the Marshall Plan for the less developed countries of the Economic South, the world might now be a very different—and, in my view, much better—place to be.

As fading memories take on a rose-colored hue, the Cold War period is starting to seem rather quaint. Although those years offered many lessons, most of them, as we will see in Chapter 5, remain unlearned—and those that were brought forward might better have been left behind. For most of those years, as both sides adhered to the theory of deterrence and the doctrine of mutually assured destruction, they valued the possession more than the practice of military power. In the globalized twenty-first century, by contrast, grievances have become transferable and disputes portable, especially when involving violent nonstate actors. If one party to an asymmetrical dispute wishes to retaliate, it may strike anywhere, anytime, either directly at its enemy or at its enemy's interests. The restraints, which had traditionally given pause to states, are gone. In the age of globalization, a rash of irregular, low-intensity conflicts have sparked calls for the judicious application of arms for peace. Yet the record of their use is spotty; the world's most powerful militaries remain characterized by force structures designed to fight the last war.

When the blocs dissolved, governments and resistance movements in many of their former client states found themselves at a loss politically and, often, economically—as the deals cut with their former patrons fell apart. Much of Africa was erased from the list of geopolitical priorities and drifted off into obscurity. Yugoslavia, no longer the star of the delicate balancing act between East and West, fissured. The newfound independence for the states of Central Asia and the Caucasus proved largely empty as key indicators of social and economic progress in the regions started to point south.

In Latin America, as in Russia, Eastern Europe, Africa, and Southeast Asia, the World Bank and the International Monetary Fund (IMF) doled out the bitter medicine of market liberalization, interest rate and currency "reform," and structural adjustment.[9] By 1983, Latin America's cumulative debt exceeded US$315 billion, or 50 percent of the region's gross domestic product (GDP). The worldwide recessions and low commodity prices of the 1970s and 1980s combined with spikes in the price of oil to reach a breaking point for many countries in the region. In response, most nations abandoned their Import Substitution Industrialization (ISI) models of economic development and adopted an export-oriented industrialization strategy, usually with the full encouragement and support of the World Bank and IMF.[10]

The social costs associated with the program cuts were enormous. Adjustment programs typically involved interest rate increases, currency devaluations, deregulation of the financial sector, market liberalization, and cuts in social spending. Massive capital outflow, particularly to the United States, further depreciated the affected currencies, thereby raising real interest rates further as well. The real GDP growth rate for Latin American economies was only 2.3 percent between 1980 and 1985, but in per capita terms, they shrank by 9 percent. Africa's experience with imposed adjustment policies was as bad or worse because base levels of development were considerably lower.[11]

In other places, events were precipitated by more overtly political factors. The negative consequences of covert espionage operations led Chalmers Johnson to coin the term *blowback* to refer to the unintended price of imperialism.[12] Analysts have described the events of 9/11—which occurred in the same year that Johnson's book was published and vindicated its contents—as the most significant single example of blowback, attributing the attacks in large part to anger over US policies toward the Middle East and Afghanistan, where the Reagan administration helped fund and organize opposition to the Soviet occupation in the 1980s. When the USSR withdrew from Afghanistan, that graveyard of empires, the Najibullah government was left—like the Thieu regime in

Vietnam—to fend for itself. But there was to be no comfortable retirement in exile for Najibullah; he was strung up on the grounds of the UN compound in Kabul and left, quite literally, twisting in the wind. With the collapse of this government, factions of the mujahedin, deprived both of their Western sponsors and a common enemy, turned on each other. The ensuing civil war was in the end resolved largely in favor of the Taliban—which in turn hosted Al-Qaida.

During the Cold War, the diversion of scarce resources toward the global competition for influence had left populations either in need of or, at minimum, with an appetite for an enormous array of goods, services, and technology. When the Cold War ended, large corporations—mainly American, Japanese, and European—whose international operations had been to some extent constrained by the crisis found suddenly that the whole world was their oyster. Faced with an opportunity of historic proportions, big business went to work.[13]

The stage was set for new contests and, in turn, a reframing of the very nature of security. While still pervasive, conflict was about to become less predictable, more complex, more diffuse, and, above all, asymmetrical. In no time, the arms race gave way to what some would characterize as a "race to the bottom," whereby competing states progressively lowered regulatory standards to make operations easier and cheaper for business. The suspension of legal obligations that leads to lowered labor standards, taxes, and trade barriers, ostensibly in order to sharpen competitiveness, tends to increase poverty within states, particularly those unwilling or unable to provide the vulnerable social or environmental protection in order to remain competitive.[14] Chronic instability results. Welcome to the age of globalization.

. . . To Brave New McWorld

Globalization has been expedited over the past half century by revolutionary technological change—first in transportation and communications, then in electronics, computerization, semiconductors, and software. Advances in information technology have reduced costs dramatically, and extensive databases, satellite and fiber-optic transmission, and connections between networks have compressed time and space. As is typically the case, however, many of today's political contours were shaped by the same tectonic plates that underlie the immediate past. Like glaciation, however, the effects are not always immediately obvious. In other words, the transition from freeze to flux, from the Cold War to global war, left some tracts of the geopolitical landscape unchanged and others altered almost beyond recognition.

The first ninety years of the twentieth century were marked by conflicting attempts to, on the one hand, make room for and, on the other, suppress the emergence of new powers: Germany, Japan, the Soviet Union, the United States. Two world wars and a cold war later, one might be forgiven for concluding that this passage was not, for the most part, well managed. By and large, diplomacy failed; when negotiations did succeed, the results were usually temporary. Think of Chamberlain's claim to have secured "peace in our time" in Munich. When the British prime minister's best efforts were betrayed by Germany, the pact was vilified by Churchill as "appeasement," and hawkish hard-liners have been dining out on the episode ever since.[15] Negotiation was equated with weakness and splattered with disrepute; in some respects, the image of diplomacy has never fully recovered. It remains to be seen whether we can do a better job in the twenty-first century, accommodating China and India as they come to assert their own growing power as the dynamic centers of the world economy and, indeed, that of the Asia-Pacific region more generally.[16]

In other, more mundane respects, however, much about the basic state of modernity remained constant, or nearly so. Early in the twentieth century there were trains, boats, planes, and automobiles. There were high-rise buildings, elevators, public utilities, telephones, radio, and, later, television. But, interestingly, the end of the Cold War corresponded with the advent of the digital age of new media—the Internet and wireless communication.[17] Not only was everything suddenly faster, cheaper, and generally more connected, but new sources of information began to proliferate, ranging from highly particularistic jihadi websites to direct broadcast satellite news services such as Al Jazeera, to blogs, personal websites, and a host of social networking facilities, including Facebook, LinkedIn, MySpace, Twitter, and YouTube. The full impact of the much-heralded and still-accelerating information and communication technology (ICT) revolution has yet to be felt, but it would be difficult to overstate.[18]

In combination with scientific breakthroughs in areas such as genetic engineering and the development of alternatives to the carbon economy, it has quickly become clear that however superficially similar much of the physical world might still look, we are nonetheless moving toward somewhere, toward something, quite distant from the familiar present. The world has become much smaller and more connected, but that is no guarantee of intimacy or goodwill. Indeed, the combination of population increase and resource scarcity has convinced many analysts that we are on a collision course with the future.[19] The dire predictions of imminent resource shortages articulated by the Club of Rome in the early 1970s may have been premature, but there can be little question that sooner or later the trend lines that highlight finite resources against infinite demand will cross. Peak oil, whenever it comes, seems poised to make this point emphatically.[20]

Unlike the Cold War, with its starkly lined, ominously shaded blocs casting dark shadows across the world atlas, the era of globalization is giving us borderless nations, stateless firms, infirm states, and a new frontier—one without frontiers. That's the *Reader's Digest* version, anyway, popular especially with the cocktail party cognoscenti and those who imagine themselves attending the

World Economic Forum in Davos, Switzerland.[21] The solid blocs have given way to the paradox of simultaneous integration and fragmentation; globalization has rendered the world a much more complicated place.[22]

Globalization in its present form began well before the end of the Cold War, but has come into its own only since. Some have suggested that globalization is itself now somewhat passé.[23] While there has certainly been some reaction against some of the more extreme aspects of *globalism*—which might best be defined as the ideological expression of globalization—I believe that the historical process of globalization continues unabated. It remains the defining historical phenomenon of our time, transforming structures and conditioning outcomes across an expansive range of endeavors.

That is not to suggest that continuation is inevitable; the depression of the 1930s brought the last period of globalization to an abrupt halt, and something similar may be under way at the beginning of the 2010s. For the moment, however, there is scant reason to doubt that the world operates according to the globalizing paradigm, which is, in turn, a work in progress, a new order under construction, an expression of power relationships. Greater commercial interchange and technological capacity; the increased mobility of most factors of production; higher levels of market integration and liberalization; and deregulation, privatization, and reduced state control are reshaping the international political economy.[24] Given the continuing activity of its multiple drivers—the relentless diffusion of new technologies, the mass media, and entertainment industries; the volatile capital flows and levels of trade and international investment, travel and immigration, education and communications—it seems likely that there is much more to come before we can close the curtain on the globalization age.

As an active and comprehensive process in which a critical range of activities—political, economic, social, and cultural—occur on the global scale, globalization is creating a world society of sorts. But it is one that not everyone can join, and certainly not on the basis of equality. Its effects are highly uneven, contributing to insecurity in some places and posing a threat to democratization in others. Those with a limited tolerance for ambiguity or uncertainty, however, should be forewarned. Multistranded and asynchronous, globalization has no single narrative or common face.[25]

Loved or loathed, globalization can be resisted, but it can't be ignored.[26] It is the backdrop against which the links among diplomacy, security development, and international policy are best apprehended.

Shaking It Up

As the industrial age is supplanted by the information age, first in the OECD countries and then beyond, many of the economic constructions, political relationships, and diplomatic conventions established in the wake of World War II have been or are being overtaken by events. The triumph of transnational structures and forces has shifted much of the action beyond the purview of governments. The exchange of goods among countries is being dwarfed by foreign direct investment, trade in services, and the exchange of both goods and services within and between corporations: over one-third of world trade now occurs among units of the same firm.[27] This metamorphosis of the global political economy is affecting the lives of individuals, the balance sheets of businesses, and the survival prospects of governments. Few have emerged unscathed.[28]

The spirit of globalization is corporate, its mantra is the marketplace, and its creed deregulation. As the highest cosmopolitan expression of capital, globalization is the apotheosis of the neoliberal imagination.

Indeed, globalization is founded and dependent on the interrelated constellation of macroeconomic policies known as *neoliberalism,* a term used to designate the strain of international economic policy that seeks to minimize the role of government. This school of thought focuses on the "opening" of foreign markets through free trade and reduced government intervention. Known as *structural adjustment* in the 1980s and policy *conditionality* in the 1990s, this policy course has been aggressively promoted through multilateral channels and international financial institutions—especially the World Bank and IMF—as well as by many bilateral aid donors. Its reputation took a large hit during the Asian financial crisis of 1997 and 1998, which spread to Brazil, Russia, and elsewhere with devastating effect. Countries that had refused to "liberalize" according to someone else's timetable, like China, India, and Vietnam, or had chosen to impose additional controls, such as Malaysia and Chile, were able to mitigate the damage substantially. Only since 2002, especially post-2008, however, has the received macroeconomic wisdom been challenged, and mainstream institutions continue to resist the criticism.[29]

Multinational corporations in particular tend to be keen on neoliberalism, being the primary agents of globalization.[30] They control information, markets, investment, financial flows, and employment practices. At the outset of this century, their weight and presence were huge: 51 of the 100 largest economies in the world are corporations; Mitsubishi generates more annual economic activity than Indonesia; and sales by the 200 largest firms exceeded the combined economies of 182 countries.[31] But globalization relies as well on a complex of political institutions and conditions such as regional integration, international trade negotiation, and the continuing conviviality of multilateral organizations. The muscle of the United States or the UN Security Council is still exercised from time to time to compel the uncooperative and quell intra- or interstate conflict, but with respect to restructuring the world political economy, look to the World Trade Organization (WTO) rather than the General Assembly for the key indicators of change.

In the era of globalization, the international community tends to stumble around crises like those in Afghanistan, Darfur, or Haiti just as it did around Rwanda and the former Yugoslavia—at least in part because these are not the kinds of places that attract much corporate interest. Where core interests are not at stake, performance is unlikely to improve. On the other hand, if access to strategic energy or mineral supplies is introduced into the calculation, then intervention becomes a near certainty. The invasion and occupation of Iraq, the creation of new military commands for Africa and North America, and the prepositioning and forward deployment of US armed forces worldwide are the obvious examples here.[32]

The bid to secure profitable or strategically essential parts of the world for business heralds a whole new era in which world wars are out and world markets, world sourcing, and world product mandates are in. Geopolitics has given way to geoeconomics. At its core, globalization is far from neutral or value-free. It is about profitability, efficiency, competitiveness, individualism, and consumerism.[33] Fitting within the neoliberal framework, globalization includes winners and leaves out losers.[34] That helps to account for some of the opposition to it, especially prior to 9/11, when it was at times quite prominent.

The end of the Cold War removed the last, slender constraints on globalization. A decrease in aid flows and other forms of support has contributed to the overuse or degradation of dwindling resources across broad tracts of Africa and South and Central Asia as well as parts of Latin America. Under the banner of economic liberalization and reform, a new international division of labor has emerged.[35] It clearly separates those who play from those who pay. Military budgets have recovered from the reductions made in the aftermath of the Cold War; in the case of the United States, each year has set a new record. Spending on development assistance and diplomacy, however, expressed as a percentage of GDP, is at nowhere near the levels of the early 1990s. In Canada's case, for example, real spending remains at about 55 percent and 70 percent of previous levels, respectively.[36]

Whatever qualities one might wish to associate with the powerful efficiency of the global economy, the distribution of wealth is increasingly skewed.[37] Unfettered markets and corporations accountable only to investors may have their virtues, but equity is not among them. For this and other reasons, the peace, such as it is, remains mightily armed and punctuated by low-intensity conflict, an inordinate and increasing reliance upon private security contractors, and the occasional enforcement action.[38] With gaping inequalities now an essential element of what is sometimes referred to as the "new world disorder," in many places neither security nor development has ensued.[39]

Inclusion, of Sorts, for the Comfortably Numb . . .

At the international level, and notwithstanding the recent readiness of some to apply coercive force, guns are not, by and large, globalization's instruments of choice. Instead, beyond the constraints imposed and the opportunities afforded by economic integration, globalization's most obvious and possibly most powerful impacts are cultural and psychological, manifest in technology, popular entertainment, and the media. In his 1983 film *Videodrome,* director David Cronenberg probed the assertion that "video is the retina of the mind's eye." His vision of the dark fusion between man and machine, like that of Ridley Scott in 1982's *Blade Runner,* was disturbing, but it resonated to the extent that both films have since become cult classics.

Since the release of these films, the scale, intensity, and penetration of global society by the avatars of technological homogenization have exploded. The Internet and other digital new media are on the leading edge of the current wave, but with the satellite-enhanced penetration of wireless and television services, the images of a global consumer society are everywhere. An international community united by similar lifestyles and appetites is being forged. At the most fundamental level, what is most remarkable about all of these media—from Bollywood movies to Filipino hip-hop to the ads in the Moscow subway—is that they share a look and a feel deriving from common production values.

One might ask: What kind of culture is being created and what kinds of norms are being imparted as a result of constant saturation by the latest in broadcast and information technology? What can be said of the health of democracy when, in the United States, 43 million more people watched the Super Bowl than voted in the 2004 presidential election?[40] This is especially worrisome because what happens in the United States usually happens elsewhere; in cultural terms, with some exceptions, globalization and Americanization have become largely indistinguishable. This may account for some tensions that have found expression as the rising tide of anti-Americanism.[41]

Television has long been recognized as a potent medium of cultural influence: part fifth column, part narcotic. Now, with ever more people spending ever more time tapping on keyboards and gazing into monitors, millions upon millions are being drawn deeper into cyberspace and further away from the reflective habits of the Gutenberg galaxy. And the websites, like the billboards, the music, the television shows, and the films, look much alike. From Tunis to Tokyo, Santiago to the Seychelles, Melbourne to Madrid, places and people are losing their distinguishing characteristics. Aspirants to the emerging world class drink Coke, drive Toyotas, shop in malls, and don the United Colors of Benetton. But while membership may well have its privileges, not everyone can afford to pay the price of admission. To a large extent the values transmitted are those associated with the uninhibited pursuit of self-gratification and commercial interest.[42] This is seen by many as a form of cultural aggression, and that, in turn, can be used to generate antipathy toward the West.

Among the newly affluent and their increasingly numerous wannabes, having the means for personal consumption and a business-class lifestyle is of greatest importance. Engagement in public affairs—be it community service or political action—just doesn't fit into their plans. The disadvantaged—those ill equipped to protect, defend, or even effectively express their interests—are given barely a thought. Weakened civic consciousness, it should be added, whether in North America or elsewhere, makes the promotion of diplomacy and international policy on the home front—and hence the likelihood of achieving support for whatever is being attempted abroad—much more problematic.

. . . For the Rest, the Picture Is Mixed

On the margins—both within developed countries and on the periphery of the North America–Europe–East Asia axis—billions have never surfed the Internet, unable to afford a computer or even a pair of Nikes (or, for that matter, Nike knockoffs). Still others opt deliberately for locally produced sandals. For some, NGOs provide loci of resistance as grassroots organizations addressing labor, environmental, human rights, and development issues.

NGOs, however, can often be accommodated within power structures; indeed, with the help of governments and cash-laden foundations, they can be co-opted entirely. A growing number of those stuck on the outside looking in have turned to the identity politics of ethnic nationalism or found voice in fundamentalist religious movements. These mass-based political and cultural alternatives tend to run more directly counter to the mainstream and were significant even when they were not highly visible. Since 9/11, their influence has become obvious.[43]

Events in the margins will rarely receive protracted prime-time attention. If vital interests are not at risk, coverage will be limited to disasters or conflicts, which will be treated as unfortunate sideshows, instantly terrifying and just as soon forgotten. If the scale of the tragedy is sufficiently overwhelming—like the December 2004 tsunami in the Indian Ocean—or if the news media happens to be fully engaged as a result of domestic political implications, as during Hurricane Katrina in August 2005, then the popular resonance may linger. For the most part, however, while mass suffering in Darfur or the disintegration of the Congo may merit episodic coverage, much of what happens outside of the metropolis (or at least outside of areas in which it has a stake) commands about as much serious or sustained international attention as did the long-running civil war in Sri Lanka or the continuing struggle of the Sarahawi people for independence from Morocco in what was once the Spanish Sahara.

Though the signal emanating from the margins may at times be faint, stay tuned. They are a primary source not just of threats but also of alternative approaches and creative responses, from liberation theology to appropriate technology. Moreover, as the lack of coverage of the events unfolding in Rwanda, Bosnia, or the former Soviet Union prior to its disintegration illustrated with some force, the judgment of the international media as to what is worth watching can be highly fallible. Change often begins at the fraying edges of the status quo, and the new order is full of surprises.

Both doctrinal certainty and international security—at least of the type guaranteed by nuclear weapons—ended with the Cold War. But its successor, globalization, has generated its own uncertainties and insecurities by elevating communications and culture to the level of politics and economics. In so doing, it has exacerbated differences and fertilized extremism. Across societies, and especially on their peripheries, alienation appears to be growing. In more than a few former neighborhoods, ethnic, religious, and political resistance has been articulated through violence.

Diplomats must be better attuned to events occurring in the margins of globalization. Before getting to that, however, we must inquire more fully into several key issues: How, exactly, does globalization operate? What are some of its defining features? And what do the answers to those questions mean for development, for security, and, especially, for those who are being left behind?

Notes

1. In *Dr. Strangelove or: How I Learned to Stop Worrying and Love the Bomb,* a 1964 film directed by Stanley Kubrick, an insane US general orders a first-strike nuclear attack on the Soviet Union. *On the Beach,* a 1959 film directed and produced by Stanley Kramer, is based on a Nevil Shute novel in which the Northern Hemisphere has been devastated by nuclear war and the radioactive fallout, carried by global air currents, threatens the remaining survivors in the South. For key historical and political facts related to the Cold War, see Grogin (2004), Gaddis (1997).

2. A compelling account of the effect that nuclear weapons could have on civilization is offered by Schell (1982).

3. This purported incident led to the Gulf of Tonkin Resolution, which authorized the US president to assist any Southeast Asian country whose governments were jeopardized and became Lyndon Johnson's legal validation for sending US troops into the Vietnam War.

4. There were, as always, a few notable exceptions. See, for example, George (1976).

5. Following its declaration of independence from Portugal in 1975, Angola descended into civil war among three principal factions: the Popular Movement for the Liberation of Angola (MPLA), the National Liberation Front of Angola (NFLA), and the National Union for the Total Independence of Angola (UNITA). The MPLA, nominally a Marxist force, was supported by the USSR, which airlifted Cuban forces to fight against the NFLA and UNITA, supported in turn by the United States and South Africa. In the wake of a coup in 1983 that brought pro-Soviet, Cuban leader General Hudson Austin to power, Grenada was invaded by US forces, ostensibly to protect foreign nationals enrolled at St. George's University. Leaders of the coup were arrested and handed a death sentence, which was later commuted to life in prison, where they remain today. The Iran/contra affair, the largest political scandal in the United States during the 1980s, involved the sale of weapons to Iran by several US officials, who used the proceeds to fund an anticommunist guerrilla organization in Nicaragua called the *contras*. The Khmer Rouge governed Cambodia between 1975 and 1979 and was

responsible in that time for the deaths of an estimated 1.4 million citizens. Despite its association with one of the worst genocides in modern history, the Khmer Rouge enjoyed Western support as it retained Cambodia's seat in the United Nations General Assembly until 1993.

6. See Grogin (2004).

7. From 1989 to 1992, I worked as the Canadian foreign ministry's intelligence analyst for South, Central, and Southeast Asia. Despite both satellite imagery and human intelligence to the effect that the Russians were pulling out of Afghanistan and abandoning Vietnamese in the deep-water port of Danang, many of my colleagues, especially in the military, were for months convinced that it must be an elaborate ruse.

8. See Barnaby (1992: chapter 22).

9. Many developing countries had soaring economies in the 1970s and borrowed heavily from international creditors for industrialization and infrastructure projects, only to find themselves vulnerable when growth slowed and interest rates took off.

10. There are some exceptions, such as Chile and Costa Rica, which adopted alternative strategies.

11. See Copeland (1989a).

12. C. Johnson (2000). The public was unaware of secret or "black" operations; hence their consequences came as a surprise, producing the hostile reaction that was blowback. See also Franko (2003).

13. World inflows of foreign direct investment, for example, grew 652 percent from 1990 to 2000, compared to 251 percent throughout the 1980s. See World Bank, "Foreign Direct Investment, Net Inflows," World Development Indicators Database, http://publications.worldbank.org/WDI/.

14. See Vogel and Kagan (2004), Jensen (2006).

15. I am indebted to Robert Johnstone, professor of history at the University of Toronto, for drawing this aspect to my attention.

16. For an introduction, see Sachs (2004). We will return to this theme in greater detail later in the analysis.

17. On the implications of this epochal shift, see Castells (2000).

18. Ibid.

19. For a resource-related history of collapsed cultures, see Diamond (2005), Homer-Dixon (1999; 2006b).

20. On the inevitability of demand for oil outstripping supply, see, for instance, Deffeyes (2002).

21. In the era of globalization, the marketing of ideas is at least as important as the marketing of goods. On "faculty club culture" (or Western intellectualism), "Davos culture," and "McWorld culture" (or Western corporate ideology), see Berger (1997).

22. See Fergusson and Mansbach (2004), Rosenau (2003), Gaddis (1991).

23. See, for instance, Hobbs (2000).

24. See Maswood (2000), Rupert and Solomon (2005), Harrison (2004), Gilpin (2001).

25. See Mittelman and Othman (2001).

26. The literature on globalization is vast and varied. For a sampling of the arguments in favor of the process, see Bhagwati (2004) and Wolf (2004); for an introduction to those opposed, see Klein (2002; 2004) and Tabb (2002).

27. UN Centre on Transnational Corporations (1993).

28. Outsourcing decreases the overall number of jobs within the domestic labor market. The threat of outsourcing contributes to job insecurity and undermines the ability of organized labor to respond. See Uchitelle (2006).

29. See Stiglitz (2002; 2006).

30. For a popular take on this theme, see Klein (2000).
31. See Anderson and Cavanagh (2000).
32. The arrival in Washington of a relatively progressive Democratic administration in January 2009 augurs well for "change," a word that figured centrally in the 2008 US presidential campaign. Yet the damage inflicted as a result of eight years of neoconservative influence will not be easily overcome; the wounds will heal, but the scars will show for years, both within the United States and throughout the world. Moreover, the healing will be slowed by the economic crisis, which threatens, among other things, to create an "expectations gap" for the new administration that will be difficult to manage, let alone to bridge.
33. See Hurrell and Woods (1999).
34. See World Bank (2005b).
35. See Lal (2006), Alam (2000).
36. See Copeland (2006).
37. See World Bank (2005: 55–69).
38. Privatization is a key theme of globalization. Nowhere is this more evident than in the booming security sector, which contracts out armed force of all sorts. It is also a defining feature of the war on terror, and the outsourcing of state-sponsored violence has created grave problems of control, regulation, and accountability. See Singer (2007), Verkuil (2007), Pelton (2007), Chesterman and Lehnardt (2007), Avant (2005).
39. See Todorov (2005). See Halliday (2000), Brzezinski et al. (1992).
40. Super Bowl XL, for instance, commanded 141.4 million viewers, numbering more than the voters in any presidential election (122 million in 2004).
41. On the end of the US empire, see Zakaria (2008). See Pew Research Center (2006).
42. On the decline of the public spirit in the United States and for an elaboration on some of its potential causes (including modern broadcast media), see Putnam (2000).
43. On the detriments of ignoring these sentiments, see the 9/11 Commission Report, particularly chapters 11 and 12, and Clark (2004).

Globalization and Empire: The World We've Got 3

Inclusive, participatory development is impossible without durable security and grassroots democracy. Although development prospects are conditioned by history, geography, demography, and ecology as well as technology and resources, the advocates of globalization worship only at the altar of growth, which is now almost undisputed as the primary indicator of national achievement and business acuity. National governments who preside over growth are awarded the international Good Housekeeping Seal of approved policy and governance by the World Bank and IMF. While globalization and development are not opposites, neither is their relationship one of cause and effect. Yet there are inherent tensions, which can produce flashpoints and full-blown crises, as we will see upon examining more closely the linkages between the two in Chapters 5 and 6.

Memories of Development

It was not until the 1970s that matters related to development and underdevelopment became prominent political issues in the international community; they would remain so throughout the 1980s. In 1974, the UN General Assembly passed a resolution calling for the establishment of a so-called New International Economic Order that would reform investment, financial flows, trade, debt, and commodity pricing. That same year, the United Nations Educational, Scientific, and Cultural Organization (UNESCO) called for a "New International Information Order." Both initiatives were backed strongly by the Group of 77 (G-77), a league of developing countries that attended the 1981 North-South Summit in Cancun in force. This event was the high-water mark of a movement favoring fairer international rules, a more level playing field, and distributive justice. Apart from a token recognition of the desirability of "global negotiations" (which never happened), the adoption of the voluntary Restrictive Business Practice Code, and the establishment of the Common Fund for Commodities—which has been only modestly successful at stabilizing prices—very little came of this decade-long campaign for a fairer world.

That much-vaunted North-South dialogue fell victim to competing East-West priorities, including the arms race and other preoccupations of the Cold War. Its last gasp was the 1992 Rio Summit on Environment and Development. In a compelling historical parallel, the development prospects of many of the G-77 states have been similarly affected by globalization, which has led the international community to once again drop many of their concerns from the negotiating agenda.

Donor countries and agencies, the World Bank, the IMF, and regional development banks backstopped client economies during the Cold War and today play a central role in the globalization process through their enthusiastic promotion of growth-centered national strategies. These are based on a worldwide expansion of trade and investment.[1] Although this brief treatment can't do justice to the manifold implications of the role played by multilateral financial institutions and trade negotiating bodies, we should note that many analysts have expressed second thoughts about the sorts of advice tendered by the likes of the Washington Consensus in response to, say, the Asian financial crisis of 1997.[2] Yet the strict policy conditions attached to aid packages and loans remain a powerful instrument for advancing international economic integration. This highly intrusive aspect of globalization represents a significant change from the Cold War era, whereby the opposing powers simply propped up regimes on the sole condition that they declare their allegiance to the proper bloc.

Because the consequences are mainly situational, it is impossible to rank categorically the drivers of change. Yet with a few major exceptions such as Iraq and Afghanistan, I would argue that economic activity—with all of its attendant cultural, social, and environmental impacts—has largely displaced political and/or military intervention as the engine of international transformation. Equipped with heavy machinery, informed by maps derived from infrared satellite imagery, and unimpeded by the burden of government controls, from the rain forests to the seabed to the tundra, Adam Smith's modern-day disciples are exacting a heavy toll. The ethics of environmental stewardship and sustainable development seem irreconcilable with the central elements of globalization. Much of the present instability seems to result from the collision of values and interests.

For those concerned with growth alone, there are success stories, especially in parts of Asia and Latin America.[3] But even their progress is beginning to bump up hard against environmental limits. Decades of unconstrained and frequently double-digit growth in much of East and Southeast Asia have given rise to environmental pressures that are beginning to exceed tolerable limits. Whether manifested by street children with symptoms of lead poisoning; sharply deteriorating soil, air, and water resources; or unparalleled pollution and congestion, degraded environmental conditions are increasingly the rule rather than the exception.[4]

The gritty truth of life in many areas supposedly celebrating economic success does not jibe with the naive boosterism of neophytes who mainly report on the wonders of growth. A single visit to a coastal city in southern China or to the capital of any Southeast Asian economic miracle should be enough to raise major questions about the ecological costs of the present course. Under present conditions, the earth's ecosystem cannot tolerate a significant increase in the number of people living at anything close to developed-country levels of consumption.[5] In any scenario, constraints, be they imposed or voluntary, are almost certainly coming; perhaps that was the more profound message embedded in the Asian currency crisis and stock market meltdown of 1997 and 1998.[6] Until the global crisis struck at the end of the first decade of the postmillennium, few dwelt for long on any lessons derived from the calamitous global stampede that triggered the episode of a decade before. Memory is short.

Finance Is Flowing . . .

As governments have become preoccupied with managing the decline of the state, the multinational corporations and banks that drive globalization have succeeded in avoiding both intranational and supranational control. Without much supervision, they have generated substantial amounts of international capital, some of which qualifies as "hot money"; technology and the integration of world financial markets allow them to move it about with great ease and speed.[7] This raises critical issues about speculative flows of short-term investment and flight capital and calls into question the continuing effectiveness of the Bretton Woods financial institutions. Record bank profits added to the growing body of empirical evidence that the financial sector benefited most from the liberalization of financial markets.[8] Tax and revenue authorities were not able to keep up. So the questions are: Whose interests were served by deregulation? Can the consequent instability be managed? These questions loom large.

Arbitrage and the global trade in cash have become major features of the world economy. About US$1.9 trillion in foreign exchange is traded daily.[9] Whether in search of speculative opportunities or spooked by rumors of instability, traders move capital among national economies with striking speed, often in pursuit of the slightest margins. Such movements can be tremendously destabilizing. A given nation is seen as an attractive investment destination one day and faces a run on its currency and a spike in interest rates the next, as was the case for Mexico in 1994 and Thailand in 1997. Korea and a raft of Southeast Asian countries were widely praised as success stories in the 1980s and most of the 1990s, yet, with the exception of Malaysia, were later that decade made to swallow the IMF's bitter prescriptive pill of currency devaluation, interest rate increases, and cuts in social programs.[10] What kind of system turns prodigies into basket cases and then back again into hot prospects almost instantly?

In the absence of effective regulation, global financial markets will remain volatile and hazardous. In 2009, the market meltdown initiated by the collapse of several venerated Wall Street investment houses caused many to forget the Barings Bank failure, the Orange County bankruptcy, the Mexican peso crisis, and even the runs on the economies of Russia and Argentina. If the financial system is at risk, governments act. And who benefits from the terms of the so-called rescue packages? In the savings and loan crisis of the 1990s, depositors were spared; in the string of corporate failures attributed to bad investments in subprime mortgages that occurred in 2008, negligent senior officers of the derelict companies came out ahead of investors. Taxpayers and ordinary citizens were left on the hook.

Extreme volatility has become the exception rather than the rule, but just how many more corporate or national bailouts can be financed is anyone's guess. Ad hoc responses and a measure of luck seem (barely) to have sufficed to date, but—even if the calamity of 2008–2009 can somehow be managed—what if the next crisis is larger? The repercussions of a wholesale international loss of financial confidence in the United States would be catastrophic.[11]

What, then, is the message when money itself becomes one of the most traded commodities in the world? And how can weakened states cope with the power of markets whose increasingly predatory and destructive agents depreciate the value of human capital and dismantle the social infrastructure? The answer is that they can't do it very well, and the results have given rise to great resentment wherever conditionality or shock therapy, as in Indonesia or Russia, respectively, in the 1990s, has been applied. It is not surprising that when many in those countries or Mexico or Argentina faced falling living standards, they concluded that globalized finance led to globalized insecurity, and that so-called interdependence came at too high a price.

. . . While National Affiliation and Sovereignty Ebb

Corporations have become increasingly cosmopolitan and sophisticated, able to respond to challenges and exercise influence with subtlety.[12] Circumstances may still dictate the occasional hiring of mercenaries or subverting of governments; more often, however, corporate power is effectively wielded through local consultants, sympathetic national or international organizations, or blue-ribbon panels of distinguished elder statesmen who proffer high-toned recommendations—and who just might hold stock options and a corporate directorship or two as well.

The conventional wisdom is that corporations have become stateless and that the location of the head office is incidental to a company's priorities and objectives. The internationalization of production, in combination with the lure of tax avoidance, has largely brought an end to corporate affiliation with countries of origin—except, perhaps, when foreign assets are threatened or when it suits marketing objectives. Patches depicting the US flag, for example, became a popular ornament on denim when the international prestige of that country was flying high under President Clinton—though much of the apparel was not only made but sold offshore. Since the invasion of Afghanistan and Iraq, there are no longer many stars and stripes to be seen on apparel worn outside of the United States, except on the shoulders of the many thousands of soldiers serving abroad.[13] Yet symbols and images, as we will see in the chapter on nation branding, are important vectors of power and influence in the age of globalization.[14]

For the most part, major corporations raise capital in international financial centers, do their design work in places where creative expertise is abundant, assemble products where labor market conditions suit, pollute where regulation or enforcement is weak, market where demand is strong, and so forth. With the exception of demands related to trade policy negotiations and to the policing of intellectual property rights, it is in the interest of multinational corporate managers to retain at most an arm's-length association with host governments. No sinister plots underlie their lack of allegiance, just rational responses to objective conditions. The same could be said for the recent espousals in an increasing number of boardrooms of the notion of corporate social responsibility (as long, that is, as it fits the business plan).

By way of example, in the 1990s, BP, an energy company, adopted a stylized flower as its logo and announced plans to invest US$8 billion over ten years in a new business: BP Alternative Energy, which would aim to be the world leader in the production of solar, wind, natural gas, and hydrogen power as well as in the promotion of cleaner electricity worldwide through education.[15] The vast majority of BP's operations, however, remained dedicated to oil and gas production and sales. Such cases have given rise to the highly evocative play on the concept of whitewashing: *greenwash*.

Corporate goodwill and public relations are generally context specific, as illustrated by the fact that Wal-Mart recognizes the All-China Federation of Labor Unions but ardently refuses to accept North American unionization.[16] Meanwhile, big-box stores have hollowed out downtowns and bankrupted family business; low wages and minimal benefits are all part of the high cost of low prices.

The global negotiating agenda in recent years has also reflected the interests of big business. Dreams of a North-South dialogue and a new international economic and information order have receded into distant memory, and in their place stand the WTO, Asia-Pacific Economic Cooperation (APEC), and a host of regional trade liberalization agreements. Successive rounds of trade talks have brought widening agreement on measures intended to facilitate competition, while *protectionism* has become a bad word. In such areas as terms of entry, access to technology and intermediate goods, and the treatment of investment capital and remittances, most barriers are down. The Multilateral Agreement on Investment (MAI) promised to level the international economic playing field yet further—for certain players. It was derailed by an especially effective and unprecedented Internet-based campaign mounted by the antiglobalization movement.

But such an effective public intervention in a multilateral negotiation was very much an exception. When differences do arise, reference can usually be made to one or another of the dispute-settlement mechanisms that are standard features of most trade agreements. These tribunals, however, tend to meet behind closed doors, and neither their responsiveness to the public interest nor their accountability is well established.

Defenders of free trade and investment argue that the transition to a rules-based system has brought a measure of order to a world that would otherwise be subject to anarchy. Agreed rules are supposed to enhance accountability, improve performance, and curb the worst unilateral impulses of the strongest players. Be that as it may, compliance with the provisions of international agreements has translated into significant intrusions into the business of many state governments, with broad implications for domestic management and national identity. And rules and procedures, as well as institutional outcomes, must remain closely aligned with the underlying interests of the powers that be; if not, they are met with antipathy or dismissal.

Maximum efficiency in a global economy requires an unprecedented degree of policy uniformity among states, which in turn involves a substantial surrender by governments of their decisionmaking control, mainly to the private sector.[17] In many OECD states—the United States, the UK, Canada, Australia, and New Zealand, among others—one need look no further than the explosive growth in private health care and education as the public systems run down. To some observers, such developments can be attributed to the inevitable friction between dichotomous systems—public/private, national/international, social democratic/neoliberal. Others see it as a new imperialism. Whatever your preference, the impact of globalization on sovereignty, popular and national, is enormous.[18]

For some states—again, mainly the advanced, OECD countries—the surrender of a degree of sovereignty in exchange for prosperity and security may seem a reasonable trade-off. For others—mainly the underdeveloped countries—the value proposition is less clear-cut. But in either case, when sovereignty decreases, so do the domain of traditional diplomacy, the relevance of the foreign ministry, and the indispensability of the foreign service.

Public Service . . .

The policy consensus required by globalization often translates, for practical purposes, into agreement on setting international standards at the level of the lowest common denominator. This erodes social progress in advanced industrial countries and takes a greater human toll elsewhere. No one should defend duplication or waste, but responsible social spending—for instance, on education and health care—is an investment in human capital and an essential component in any effective development strategy. Quality of life, which is a much more useful indicator than quantitative measurements alone, is becoming a critical comparative advantage, particularly in the efforts of some states, such as Switzerland or Sweden, to attract investment in high value-added enterprises. Nonetheless, the apostles of the marketplace have triumphed even in public-policy circles. With few exceptions, the siege of the public sector has continued. This trend has implications across the board, especially in terms of regulatory capacity.

So markets have ruled. Markets can perform many useful functions, especially with respect to the rapid allocation and deployment of resources. But they also have inherent weaknesses: above all, they are driven primarily by greed and fear, and they respond to opportunity rather than need. Timing and chance are hugely significant. If they behaved rationally, markets would be predictable, and everyone would be rich. Instead, a cautionary word or ineptly expressed comment from the chair of the Federal Reserve Bank in the United States can result in chaos.

To paraphrase Oscar Wilde, the problem with relying on markets is that while they can put a price on anything, they put a value on nothing. The ethic of universal and equitable access to services is giving way to private contracting, cost recovery, and user payment. This has occurred at the same time as service reductions, regulatory rollbacks, and a transfer of the burden of taxation from companies to wage earners, leading some analysts to conclude that globalization is tantamount to the enforcement of a corporate agenda: the accumulation of private power under the guise of an attack on intrusive government.

Study after study has shown that most government programs benefit middle- and upper-income groups, that tax expenditures benefit wealthy corporations and individuals, and that wealth, in the absence of progressive mechanisms to redistribute it, tends to accumulate upward.[19] Even so, with little debate and less defense, government has been saddled with the blame for all economic ills and has been evicted from large areas of its former jurisdiction in transportation, communications, environmental protection, resource management. and health care. Except for foreign affairs, defense, finance, and a few other core policy areas, the apparatus of the state has been stripped and public services have been repackaged as business opportunities and corporatized, privatized, or simply vacated.

This reduction in the legitimacy and domain of state activity has produced both policy paralysis and a revision of the popular notion of government. Elites who once championed the state as the embodiment of shared convictions, arbiter of competing demands, and agent of distributive justice now hold probusiness, antigovernment values. The social investment in welfare—predicated on the belief that the state has a duty to protect certain services and the constituents thereby served from market forces—has given way to the capitalist imperative of competitiveness. The scramble to deregulate in most places has continued unabated,[20] and while corporations have largely outgrown state control, there have been few commensurate moves to establish standards or regulate behavior globally.

Despite rhetoric to the contrary, governments have largely given up on distributive justice as they struggle less to provide for the disadvantaged and more to attract investment and create suitable environments for business through, for instance, tax holidays, zoning exemptions, and loan guarantees. Such priorities are not propitious for either democratic development or security. Unchecked by either effective policies or proper regulation or legislation, globalization foments insecurity and is difficult to manage in the public interest. For these and other reasons, diplomats need to become globalization managers.

Private Interests . . .

Just about everywhere, previously autonomous actions such as the establishment of interest and exchange-rate levels have become, in large part, a function of international capital markets. Indeed, in an integrating world economy, national financial well-being is increasingly conditioned, if not determined, by international monetary and investment flows and by the perceptions of those who control them. Could the fate of nations be decided by a 28-year-old MBA in red suspenders whose responsibilities include the assessment of sovereign creditworthiness for a major Wall Street bond-rating agency? Though many of these self-appointed masters of the universe have fallen upon hard times lately, it is not inconceivable.

Nor is it hard to understand why there is a growing sense of powerlessness and anxiety among those struggling under globalization. Capital and technology are highly mobile. Labor, however, is much less so, and governments—repeated attempts by the United States notwithstanding—cannot legislate beyond their political territory. Neither parliaments nor trade unions have much leverage when faced with a run on their nation's currency or the threat of corporate relocation to a sweatshop in some export zone in the economic South. And as the number of homeless people grows along with the pressure on food banks, globalization is bringing more and more aspects of underdevelopment—economic, social, political, and cultural—home to the industrialized world. Many member states of the OECD face continuing high unemployment and underemployment, which exerts downward pressure on wages and incomes and is helpful to the employer in collective bargaining.[21]

Meanwhile, professionals, senior managers, entrepreneurs, and knowledge workers have enjoyed prosperity beyond the wildest dreams of those stuck in McJobs (or stuck without them). Many young people and a growing corps of the downwardly mobile face a difficult and uncertain future. And all of this preconditions the public response to outreach by foreign ministries and their willingness to support the development of international policy.

. . . and the Insecurity of the Residual State

Governance and security are relative concepts, but ultimately they turn on economic well-being, social justice, and the absence of conflict. Achieving these, along with articulating national values, policies, and interests at home and promoting them abroad, has for centuries been a central goal of the state as such. But just when individuals, and especially working people, need the most protection—namely against the worst excesses of globalization—the state is abandoning them.[22]

The prevailing political culture has delivered more enterprise, less governance. We are now facing the consequences. In OECD member states—and even more in less developed countries—the severe shocks, backlashes, and social divisions that constitute the side effects of globalization have impaired the structure and function of representative institutions. As the reach and wherewithal of government have been diminished, durable security has proven elusive, and democratic development, especially where it has not taken firm hold, has been jeopardized.

While globalization will affect virtually everyone and everything one way or another, it heralds particularly tough times for states.[23] In capitals around the world, governments seem too big to do the small things and too small to do the big things. Power is flowing upward to multilateral bodies, outward to corporations and NGOs, and downward to other levels of provincial and municipal government. Even within the state, institutional elements of national governments are forming associations with similar elements elsewhere, and these new global coalitions have contributed to the further dismantling of the state apparatus.[24]

For diplomats, the vast majority of whom work for national governments, the weakening of the state is generally bad news. On the one hand, their old domain—the management of relations between states—is no longer the centerpiece of world politics. On the other hand, however, heightened instability in the international system may broaden the scope and underline the need for negotiation and cooperation.

But is the end of the state near? Not quite. Hollowed out from within by ethnic, religious, and regional uprisings; washed over by waves of supranational force; and undercut by subnational currents, governing has perhaps never been more difficult. Having lost much of their ability to defend the interests of their citizens on the one hand and their monopoly on the means of force on the other, an increasing number of states are frail if not actually failing.[25]

Still, at the end of the day, it is for states to ensure the security of the people, which is the highest calling of government. Even (or especially) as it awards massive subcontracts to the likes of Blackwater and Wackenhut, it is clear that government can best resolve certain basic questions—involving war and peace, taxation and expenditure, policy priorities and legal sanctions—politically, through public administration, rather than by privatized proxy, through corporations or markets.

Some roles for government will go unchanged, while others may of necessity be enlarged. Trade liberalization, macroeconomic policy reform, and structural adjustment tend to concentrate wealth. Neither the gains nor the losses from globalization are evenly distributed. As polarization leaves increasing numbers economically distressed and politically disenfranchised, governments may have to shift their attention from creating incentives for business to a more fundamental activity: maintaining control. Look not for national daycare but for the continued expansion of the criminal justice system, as correctional facilities proliferate and more heavily equipped security forces emerge. What some have called the residual state may be closer to an actual police state—or, à la Singapore, a *virtual* police state, where social problems and violence decrease as strictly enforced limits on the freedom of association and expression increase. The twenty-first-century version of the national security state—including the so-called homeland security state modeled by the Bush administration—does not augur well for democratization anywhere.

Civil Society at Risk?

How, then, to reply to claims that globalization has forced authoritarian governments in Latin America, Southeast Asia, Taiwan, South Korea, and elsewhere to become more democratic? Looking backward, Gwynne Dyer, Francis Fukuyama, and others are convinced that the triumph of democracy over dictatorship looms as one of the major historical themes of the late twentieth century.[26] A more searching assessment might conclude, conversely, that globalization has narrowed political options in countries with long-standing democratic traditions and complicated the transition to genuine democracy—which implies much more than the orchestration of successful elections—most everywhere else.[27] The penchant of the international community to intervene, organize a vote, declare victory, and get out—call it *ballot and bolt*—has done a disservice to genuine democratic development in places like Cambodia, East Timor, Liberia, and Sierra Leone.

Indeed, the greatest impact of globalization may be the extent to which it has engendered a palpable dissonance within and among existing forms of economic and political organization. On the one hand, multinationals have leapfrogged ahead of any countervailing form of authority and are accountable only to their shareholders, many of whom are other firms or large investment funds with little or no interest in corporate responsibility. National leaders, on the other hand, remain accountable to electorates even as their ability to control outcomes diminishes rapidly. When power without accountability meets accountability without power, it seems a safe bet that volatility will result.

The Industrial Revolution provided the tools and resources to transform countries into nation-states and then welfare states. To a greater or lesser extent, these modern political constructs accommodated heterogeneity by imparting a sense of common civic culture based on shared values and interests rather than on ethnic, linguistic, or religious particulars. In developed countries, the historic compromise between capital and labor—expressed as social democracy and seen by some as one of the greatest achievements of the past century—is disintegrating under the pressure of global competition and shifting factors of production, which favor employers, investors, and others who control capital. This narrowing of the middle ground has proven especially profound in the United States and Britain, but it is also increasingly seen in Canada, the countries of the European Union, and Japan.[28]

In both public and private sectors, globalization has brought massive job cuts as companies downsize, rightsize, and so on. In the name of restructuring—which does not necessarily maximize efficiency or increase productivity—OECD countries have experienced a staggering loss of salaried positions (and with them decent benefits packages) to relocation, outsourcing, and contract labor.[29] Whose interests are served by such measures? Even legendary financier and investor George Soros has come to recognize that the rush to competitiveness, which has rehabilitated social Darwinism, exacts painful social costs. In its latest incarnation the struggle of each against all extols the survival of the fittest in a laissez-faire environment marked by an abiding absence of commitment to the common good.[30] This represents a substantial retreat from the set of more cooperative principles previously accepted as the hallmarks of contemporary civilization and advanced human development. Social justice requires deliberate moral and political action; globalization is conducive to neither. Rising pressures at home—ironically often linked to globalization—are forcing the implementation of defensive, inward-looking measures. This, too, is a problem for diplomacy, which is more concerned with looking out.

Since the late twentieth century, democracy has been spreading, but its representative structures and institutions everywhere seem weak, hollow, or dysfunctional.[31] In many countries—from Italy to Kazakhstan to Zimbabwe—elections seem little more than meaningless rituals or light entertainment. This is disheartening in itself but also insofar as it is just one more symptom of the manufacture of consent and the insidious erosion of real choice.[32] The media, especially the free press, is to the democratic process what wind is to sails. Yet one of the effects of convergence is a shrinking number of independent media voices; one need look no further than Canada, a country dominated by CBC, CTVglobemedia and CanWest, for a convincing case in point.[33]

The result is another paradox. Coverage of emancipating political change can bolster resistance to arbitrary authority and kindle the spark of rebellion—even as the concentration of media ownership and control limits the diversity of opinion and stifles dissent elsewhere. Shrinking horizons, stock perspectives, and the sonorous op-eds of the like-minded are not conducive to the diverse and pluralistic debate by which open and democratic societies flourish.[34]

As the consensus breaks down and economic disparities grow, social peace will surely be tested. Remarkably, in most places, the various stresses and strains have not yet propelled alternative political options. On the contrary, political parties throughout the Western world have lost most of their distinctive ideological identity, and now vary mainly in the extent of their enthusiasm in cheering for free enterprise. In the political mainstream of most countries, there is no longer a discernible distinction between right and left—except, on occasion, in rhetoric.

Beyond spin control and sloganeering, politics has been reduced to an empty shell.[35] That this has more to do with the changing needs of elites than with any general shift in the disposition of the polity is an interesting likelihood, but the point is that the very nature of the political process has changed. Thus globalization has had a debilitating impact on the amenability of the domestic public environment to international policy deliberation.[36] Who benefits? Certainly not diplomats.

The Gathering Gloom . . .

Throughout the industrialized world, globalization has created enormous challenges. At the same time, the ability of underdeveloped countries to deal with the consequences of neoliberal reforms—welfare reductions, program cuts, privatization, marketization—has lessened. The imposition of these so-called reforms in the context of structural adjustment, aid conditionality, and the like has contributed to the desperate circumstances that, in combination with population pressure and resource scarcity, give rise to currents of extremism. As we have seen in the former Yugoslavia, Afghanistan, and all around the edges of the Russian Federation as well as in Algeria, Egypt, and still elsewhere, those on the losing end of the global competition seek shelter or meaning in political extremism, religious fundamentalism, and virulent forms of ethnonationalism. The alienated and marginalized are likely to try to construct a new identity, one founded on the compelling vision of a brilliant but often utterly unattainable future or on shared but often dreadfully distorted memories of an idyllic past. Intolerance and demagoguery thrive in a climate of exclusion. They stifle popular sovereignty and preclude the development of an open and inclusive political culture. In their absence, insecurity is inevitable, and democracy cannot take root or grow.

Capital Accumulation, Social Dislocation

For a few weeks in early 2008, six months after completing the first draft of this book, I visited Russia for the first time. I returned almost a year later to find my impressions reinforced. The rich historical and cultural dimensions of Moscow, St. Petersburg, and two ancient capitals from the pre-Muscovite period, Suzdal and Vladimir, left me reeling. So did the fact that—along with China, Brazil, India, and perhaps a few other countries—Russia finds itself on the raw frontier of globalization.

Signs of the ultimate victory of the counterrevolution against Bolshevism were everywhere in the form of a prominent display of globalization's defining characteristics. Within the cities, the gaps between the pulsating, world-class central business districts and their dismal, disintegrating peripheries—where broken-down industries and monotonous, shabby apartment blocks stretch beyond the horizon—were palpable. The glossy lifestyle magazines distributed for free in the better neighborhoods—in first-class train compartments and business-class lounges—extolled the virtues of conspicuous consumption; from cars to cognac to jewelry, the trappings of excess were worshipped as gods.

Beyond the cities—in December 2008 I visited Tatarstan, the Urals, and western Siberia—the divides are even more pronounced. Many are without indoor plumbing and heat their homes with wood. Some are without electrical service. Moscow seems even further away than it is, which is to say very far.

It is all there: The energy. The edginess. The dynamism. The unbridled appetite for the good life. The revival of Mother Russia as a symbol of nationalist pride. The restoration of Orthodox Christianity in conjunction with a crackdown on minorities. The rehabilitation of the reputation of Solzhenitzyn as a prophet of Russian greatness and voice of traditional values. The increased pressure exerted on the recipients of gas supplies as resource access becomes a strategic asset.

These days, the new Russia is looking and acting a lot like the old one from the nineteenth century—flexing its muscles, demanding consideration, playing hardball. The bear has come out of hibernation.

For the winners gliding around in fine cars and making deals, life has never been better nor the future more bright. It's the oligarch's ball. For the losers—pensioners, the unemployed, the rural poor—the triumph of the acquisitive ethic is a sharp reminder of how much has been lost since the collapse of the USSR. For them, the future looks bleak. Such tensions are what globalization has wrought not only in the former Cold War colossus but everywhere.

In short, despair is the mother of fanaticism, and hopelessness often gives way to violence. As state after state fails, those with the wherewithal are often left by default to deal with both the causes and the consequences through conflict resolution or peacekeeping ventures—or, with increasing frequency, through heavy-handed security measures, including foreign invasions, designed to protect potential targets at home. Herein lies another irony: by embracing globalization as the only world order model, the international community contributes to the very problems that it must then address. If the much hyped "interdependence" associated with globalization was more equitable, then everyone might indeed have a stake in the system. Instead, because interdependence translates into dominance for a few and dependence for many, it is widespread insecurity rather than collaboration that flourishes.

. . . Is Not Entirely Unremitting

Combined, all these images reveal a big picture not of a globalized cultural landscape so much as a rather desolate, dark tunnel. But there is a glimmer of light at its end that may be something other than an oncoming train. Globalization is driven less by political conspiracy than by the consensus of the market's beneficiaries. Hybrid motor vehicles, handhelds, fast food, slick blockbusters, glitzy apparel—multinationals do what they can to manipulate markets and shape demand, but in large part they give at least some people what they want. Or think they want.

I suggested at the outset that we may be caught in some kind of temporary lag that presages passage toward a more balanced future. Indeed, there may already be some early signs of institutional catch-up. In the 1990s, serious consideration was accorded a proposal by Yale University economist James Tobin to tax international financial transactions, assigning a higher rate to short-term speculative flows.[37] Although this was an idea whose time had yet to come, over a decade later there is renewed interest. Implementation could produce revenues in the range of US$100 billion a year, which could be applied toward . . . capacity building and debt reduction for the poorest? Hope springs eternal.

There have, in any case, been more concrete developments. Labor and environmental subagreements, however imperfect, were retrofitted into the North American Free Trade Agreement, are raised in discussions within the WTO, and—along with provisions for human rights—are finding their way into a variety of other international negotiations. Discussions of fair trade, working conditions, and debt have become mainstream. Trade unions, aboriginal confederations, human rights organizations, and ecological advocacy groups attend the World Social Forum in Porto Alegre as a counterweight to the World Economic Forum in Davos. They are all working to internationalize their operations and, in so doing, provide some alternative to the status quo. It's a start.[38]

At the most elemental level, if globalization is the contemporary expression of a more familiar form of economic and political organization—empire—then it may, in the classic pattern, be the source of its own undoing and thus of the next phase of world history.[39] Reference has been made, for example, to the crucial role information technology plays in the globalization process. Falling prices, growing market penetration, and the impossibility of imposing effective controls have combined to expand greatly all manner of national and international communications. Anyone with access to a computer and the Internet can communicate with anyone similarly equipped, anywhere. Electronic publishing is the equivalent of a vast informational ventilator, and the fan speed is being cranked up daily.

Although access remains extremely uneven, the diffusion of information and communication technologies (ICT)—globalization's circulatory system—is profoundly subversive of hierarchy and control, supportive of the ethic of democracy, and conducive to the exchange of ideas. In the classic pattern of the dialectic, similar countervailing phenomena might well be adduced for other disturbing aspects of globalization.

Is globalization ultimately cause for celebration or lament? Should we buy the world a Coke, or use the bottle for a Molotov cocktail? The answer will be based mainly on personal values. For many, the private accumulation of capital is still the greatest good. Since the 9/11-induced chill on public protest, the antiglobalization movement has become less visible—especially in the streets, as patriotic rallies replaced public protests and the pitched battles in Seattle, Quebec City, and Genoa gave way to speaking tours and book promotions by now-complacent movement leaders. For many, though, including some in the global justice movement, increasing poverty and inequality remain unacceptable.[40]

Globalization does create wealth, but not for all. It fosters dynamic efficiencies, but not everywhere. It generates new economies of production but it also exerts downward pressure on wages and working conditions. It makes national economies—or at least what is left of them—more internationally competitive, but it renders currencies and financial markets chronically unstable. And its price tag carries significant implications for good governance, democratization, development, civil society, and security.

Globalization's critics are finally infiltrating the mainstream, a trend that will doubtless accelerate as the economic crisis triggered in 2008 continues to unfold. The World Bank, for instance, has released a detailed analysis highlighting the growing inequalities, labor market pressures, and threats to the common global interest that combine to underscore the need to "manage" globalization.[41] On November 15, 2007, Foreign Secretary David Miliband of Britain delivered an address to the College of Europe in Bruges, Belgium, on this issue. Titled "Europe 2030: Model Power Not Superpower," it set out

Miliband's vision of a Europe that leads the way in responding to the challenges of globalization.[42] It seems, then, that globalization will be with us for a while yet.[43] Though down, it is far from out—there are simply no alternative models waiting in the wings.

If globalization had a symbol, it might be the two-edged sword, cleaving in all directions. As its ability to create wealth and produce goods and services is matched by its ability to exacerbate poverty, developing ways to manage the ensuing discord—salving wounds and averting conflict, in large part by emphasizing development and security—is *the* issue of our times.[44] Though the McWorld is still young, it is not too soon for its inhabitants to contemplate how best to address the emerging contours and currents of its economic and political landscape.

If progress with respect to security and development is to be made, diplomacy and international policy will have to figure centrally. But policy planners and analysts, in foreign ministries and elsewhere, will need better tools. How can the structures and processes of the new global order be more fully grasped and better managed?

Notes

1. See Woods (2006).

2. See Best (2003). The term *Washington Consensus* was coined by John Williamson (1993) to describe the economic worldview that prevailed in the 1980s. For the side effects of these policies, see Yergin and Stanislaw (2002).

3. Some obvious success stories include "the Chinas" (PRC and Taiwan), South Korea, Chile, and Singapore, among others—all of which are confronting significant environmental problems. For information on economic development and environmental concerns, see the country analysis website of the US Department of Energy's Energy Information Administration.

4. See Raven and Berg (2006), Sindermann (2006), Naidu et al. (2006).

5. The exact extent of the earth's carrying capacity and the size of humankind's ecological footprint are subjects of some debate. The World Wildlife Fund estimates that consumption now exceeds capacity by 25 percent. See World Wildlife Fund (2006).

6. For different perspectives on the Asian financial crisis, see Hunter, Kaufman, and Krueger (1999).

7. Stiglitz (2002: 65–66).

8. See Campell, Pal, and Howlett (2004: 166) and Sandbrook (2003).

9. See Bank for International Settlements (2005).

10. Stiglitz (2002: chapter 4).

11. The United States has by far the largest debt in the world, 44 percent of which is held by foreign residents and banks; see White House (2005: 269). The latent danger is that international investors could lose confidence in the dollar and sell their holdings, thereby setting off a financial stampede. See Sennholz (2002).

12. An excellent documentary treatment of several of these themes is offered in 2005's *The Corporation*.

13. For a current assessment of US foreign policy with particular emphasis on the impact of globalization, see Pickering and Crocker (2008).

14. The stunning decline in the international image and reputation of the United States, following a peak in the immediate aftermath of 9/11, is as unprecedented as it is disturbing. For details, see Pew Research Center (2004; 2006); for analysis, see Fouts (2006).

15. For a contextual analysis of BP's rebranding efforts, see Center for Media and Democracy, http://www.sourcewatch.org/index.php?title=BP.

16. See Meyerson (2004).

17. There is a large and expanding body of literature on this issue. For accounts of declining sovereignty, see Strange (1996). For an alternate perspective, consult Gilpin (2001) or Garrett (2003).

18. One commonly cited example of the power that vested interests and business now have over government is Chapter 11 of the North American Free Trade Agreement. Chapter 11 allows investors to sue a state when actions taken by the state adversely affect their investment. The US-based Ethyl Corporation argued that Canada's 1997 Fuel Additives Act had that effect, as it banned methylcyclopentadienyl manganese tricarbonyl (MMT)—a product that Ethyl manufactured. The Canadian government lost the case and paid US$13 million to Ethyl in compensation, even though the environmental and health hazards of MMT remain hotly debated. See Environmental Defense Fund (1996).

19. Manuel Castells, for example, cites numerous studies showing that although the overall trend is toward income inequality, it is less marked in the several East Asian countries where governments resisted wholesale deregulation. See Castells (2003: 434–435).

20. See Scharpf (1999: 374).

21. See World Commission on the Social Dimension of Globalization (2004: 19–20), Rodrik (1997: 379–380).

22. See Kapstein (1999).

23. The archetypal account of the decline of the state under globalization can be found in Strange (1996). More contemporary sources generally see globalization as a challenge that states must confront rather than as an absolute detriment to their survival. See also Saul (2005), Fukuyama (2004: chapter 2).

24. The idea of the disaggregation of states is elaborated in Slaughter (2004).

25. See R. Cooper, who refers to such states as existing in a "premodern world" (2003: 16–19).

26. See Dyer (1996), Fukuyama (2004), Huntington (1991).

27. On the difficulties of developing stable democratic institutions under globalization, see Fukuyama (2004: chapter 2).

28. For the effects globalization has had on Canadian politics, see Marden (2003).

29. Commission on the Social Dimension of Globalization (2004: 19–20).

30. See Soros (1998; 2006).

31. This trend of democratic enlargement may recently have peaked and even be reversing. See Freedom House (2008), "Freedom in the World," January 16, http://www.freedomhouse.org/template.cfm?page=395.

32. Noam Chomsky (1988) has written widely and is a pioneer on this subject.

33. For a critique of Canadian mass media, see Barlow (2005: 12–13).

34. On disturbing trends within the United States, see Naomi Wolf (2007), who offers a ten-point historical perspective on the corrosion of open society.

35. See J. Klein (2006).

36. We will return to an assessment of the complexity of the public environment in the final chapter.

37. See Patomaki (2001).

38. There are many avenues of response to globalization. For a media-focused analysis, see Sosale (2003). On the changing concept of sovereignty and the growing use of intervention to prevent human rights violations, see Eberwein and Badie (2006). On the growing need for distributive justice and religious pluralism, see Barber (2002: 245–262). On the rise of international networks of activists, see Keck and Sikkink (1998: chapters 1 and 3).

39. For one of the more original formulations of globalization, see Hardt and Negri (2000). At press time in 2009, as the 2008 meltdown of global financial markets continued, this kind of shift seems increasingly probable.

40. Joseph Tulchin and Gary Bland (2005) present a very useful introduction to the issue of inequality—perceived and real, absolute and relative—as central to the globalization debate; Milanovic (2005) considers the challenges of measuring inequality.

41. The World Bank (2006b) argues that globalization remains the context in which all other aspects of international relations must be understood.

42. See Miliband (2007).

43. Fareed Zakaria (2008) argues that whatever the fate of globalization, the world is clearly moving beyond Americanization, and anti-Americanism is giving way to indifference.

Understanding World Order: The March of History 4

In the Preface, I tried to make a distinction between *looking* and *seeing*, and in subsequent chapters I have made reference to the tide of afflictions rising worldwide. If policymakers and decisionmakers are to chart a new way forward, they must be able to both look and see. Yet doing either has become more difficult in the absence of effective navigational tools. Indeed, there exists a desperate need for new thinking about the nature of the current predicament—before the temptation to proceed to the nearest landfall without first determining the location of the reefs and shoals or, worse yet, to plot the course of least resistance grows any stronger. This is especially true for diplomats, who are supposed to be managing global issues and who require more accurate maps than those with which they have recently been equipped.

Meanwhile, as these tides rise, not all boats are staying afloat. Snagged anchors, heavy seas, restive crews, and leaks in the hull are pulling them down. The Mayday calls are growing louder; if the vessels in peril stand any chance of rescue, then, at minimum, the drafting of a new set of charts with revised points of reference will be imperative. How, then, to find our bearings?

The View from Above

The transition from the Cold War to the globalization age has created myriad challenges and ambiguities for diplomacy, security, and international policy. The Cold War decades produced deeply ingrained habits of both thought and action that must be examined. First, however, we must return to elements of the analysis presented in Chapters 2 and 3 in order to conceptualize both the Cold War and globalization—to present them in a way that advances our sense of the contemporary scene. One way to view the economic and political landscape rising up through the mists of the new century is through world order modeling.

World order modeling requires that we shift to the highest plane of analysis by identifying the defining characteristics of a given historical period and then mapping these qualities such that the details do not obscure the elemental patterns. Think of the view afforded from an aircraft circling the world at 10,000 meters. The major geographical features stand out beyond the minor ones. If the altitude is increased about tenfold—to satellite orbit—it is possible to produce an even more essential picture.

The Peace of Westphalia, which in 1648 codified a system of international relations based on the premise of the sovereign equality of states, represented what might be considered the first world order model. State interactions—and later the machinations of colonial empires—were based on the idea of the balance of power among the parts. The Westphalian model was subverted by World War I and collapsed completely after World War II. It was replaced by a new global framework based on the reality of two dominant superpowers. The ideological and territorial divisions between them found expression in the notion of so-called first, second, and third worlds. The present global order, characterized by the ready flow of people, ideas, and capital, has yet to find cogent expression in a model that adequately reflects its defining features.

All models, or course, are flawed insofar as they oversimplify or obscure detail, but their flaws do not make them useless—quite the opposite. By revealing basic forms, world order modeling allows us to clarify and crystallize—to reach a level of abstraction that transcends that of political science or international relations theory. It will then be our task to construct a new framework in which to place some of the strategic issues treated in subsequent chapters.

Cold War World Order: How Two Blocs Became Three Worlds

During the Cold War the world was divided, through both formal and informal means, into two main blocs—each organized under the patronage of one superpower and each with its own ethos and extensive international network of clients and associates. This arrangement was encapsulated by the discourse on a nuclear weapons–based "balance of terror" between the United States and the Soviet Union. The prospect of massive retaliation and mutually assured destruction deterred rash behavior by either party or by the members of their blocs. This equilibrium was reinforced by a series of arms control agreements, formal treaties and informal understandings, and other tight controls over the transmission and use of fissile materials. However much these arrangements have come to resemble some form of collective insanity, their existence did ensure that for the better part of half a century wholesale conflagration was avoided.[1] There was even an element of continuity with the immediate past: the legacy of colonialism—boundaries, alignments, essential political and trading relationships—was adapted so neatly that it was necessary to coin a new term: *neocolonialism.*

Individual countries and intergovernmental organizations—seen by many analysts as the agents of neocolonialism—were the main actors, and international relations were largely considered the exclusive domain of states. There was a widely shared belief in the principles of national sovereignty, territorial integrity, and noninterference in others' internal affairs. The two superpowers did engage in a formulaic kind of rivalry, both ideological and geopolitical, but with a few exceptions early on—such as the Berlin blockade and the Cuban missile crisis—the contest took place according to the rules endorsed by both parties. As decolonization spread in the 1950s and 1960s, the newly independent states formed their own sub-blocs while still aligning themselves, to a greater or lesser extent, with one or the other superpower.

The unity of the worldview held by governing elites was striking; within the global condominium, the armed peace continued, order prevailed, and predictability ruled. There were periods of slight warming or *détente*—often indicated by increased trade or cultural and scientific exchanges—but by and large the two blocs functioned independently. Deterrence guaranteed that major conflict between the principals was averted (however narrowly); thus, those conflicts that did exist were mainly between proxies, whether states, nongovernment actors, or even terrorist groups. During the Korean War, for instance, the Soviet Union assisted the North Korean communists without actively engaging the UN forces led by the United States. In Angola, the protracted and bloody struggle between the National Union for the Total Independence of Angola (UNITA), which was backed by the United States and South Africa, and the Popular Movement for the Liberation of Angola (MPLA), which was backed by the USSR and Cuba, provided a case study in limited war between proxies.

Modeling the Cold War was quite straightforward because during that period much of the world fit rather neatly into one of three "worlds." Migration between them, and to a considerable degree within them, was limited. For comparative and review purposes, it is worth summarizing the principal attributes of each, especially since the terminology remains in wide usage.

This concept of the first, second, and third worlds developed after French demographer Alfred Sauvy coined the term *third world* in the early 1950s. For Sauvy, it designated regions marked by underdevelopment. However, in the Cold War environment, the term became synonymous with the nonaligned nations or those unaffiliated with either bloc.[2]

The first world consisted of developed market economies. Members were industrialized, capitalist democracies whose affinity for each other found organizational expression in the OECD and NATO. They were led by the United States. Also known as the Western Bloc, this was the dominant group in economic and military terms, but the maintenance of global geopolitical competition served the most powerful interests in all groups.

The second world or Eastern Bloc consisted of centrally planned economies that were also developed—but arguably less so than those of the first world. Members were industrialized (specializing in heavy industry more than consumer goods), nominally communist, and led by the USSR. This group found organizational expression in the Council for Mutual Economic Assistance (COMECON) and the Warsaw Pact.

From 1950 to 1990, the United States adopted what came to be known as the Truman Doctrine.[3] Under its auspices, the superpower offered political, economic, and military aid to states who would assist in containing or otherwise preventing the spread of communism.[4] Those with an economic interest in fueling the arms race or a political interest in protecting defense-related jobs in their legislative districts always made the most of this doctrine, citing the need to confront communists everywhere and on every level in order to keep the dominoes of the free world from falling down. But the actual threat was almost always exaggerated.[5]

The third world essentially consisted of what remained beyond the blocs—nominally independent and recently decolonized countries featuring both planned and, more typically, free-market economies. Compared to the first or second worlds, the third world was less developed by virtually any measure, especially industrialization, per capita income, and human development. It found representation in the Non-Aligned Movement, the UN, and the G-77 and was led, at various times and to varying degrees, by Indonesia, India, China, Brazil, Ghana, and Egypt. Governments tended toward the authoritarian; dictatorships were common. It was in these vast expanses of what would come to be known as the Economic South that the superpowers played a latter-day version of the Great Game between the British and Russian empires in Central Asia in the nineteenth century.

The third world was where the United States and Russia exploited interstate, intrastate, and ethnic rifts, maneuvered for geopolitical advantage, fought proxy wars, and competed for client states, especially in Africa (Ethiopia, Somalia, Angola, Mozambique), Asia (Afghanistan, Cambodia), and Central America (Nicaragua, El Salvador). The toll in lives was staggering.[6] Countries of interest to one or the other superpower—and that usually meant to both—sometimes tried to play one suitor against the other to maximize the terms of a given bargain. Various states had stronger or weaker negotiating positions, but between the lines there was some margin for maneuver.

Globalization and World Order: Cream Floats

This tripartite division suited the imperatives of the Cold War, but massive changes have since rendered that model dated if not irrelevant. Most obviously, the demise of the USSR has made the term *second world* obsolete; COMECON and the Warsaw Pact have folded while the Central and many Eastern European countries have joined NATO, the European Union (EU), and the OECD to effectively become part of the West.

Equally if not more significant changes have occurred in what used to be the third world. It is here that entire countries, such as South Korea, Qatar, the United Arab Emirates, Kuwait, and Bahrain, as well as city-states such as Singapore and Hong Kong, and near countries such as Taiwan, have for all economic intents and purposes joined the first world.[7] Certain cities, moreover, seem well on their way toward development; among them are, arguably, large chunks of Santiago, Montevideo, Buenos Aires, Cape Town, Kuala Lumpur, São Paulo, Mexico City, and Bangkok.[8] Conversely, the profusion of homeless and destitute persons in major Western cities suggests that the significant cuts to social programs in the 1990s created conditions of impoverishment in the first world usually associated more typically with the third. As is characteristic of globalization, the distinctions, once clearly defined, are blurring.

At the other end of the spectrum, the increasing frequency of state frailty and failure has expanded the size of what some analysts have described as a fourth world of least developed countries.[9] This extremely impoverished and highly unstable group—whose strategic value and resources may be of limited interest—is found mainly, though not exclusively, in sub-Saharan Africa: Somalia, Sierra Leone, Sudan, Democratic Republic of Congo, and Liberia, to name a few. Parts of Central Asia might also qualify, as could Afghanistan—although it, like occupied Iraq, is a special case.

Just as it has mitigated the significance of boundaries between individual states, globalization has erased the lines that were once so clear between these formerly distinct worlds. Accordingly, we need a post–Cold War model that captures the most prominent characteristics and flows of today's world. That challenge is steep—much steeper than before. Flux, it seems, is more difficult to model than freeze. Still, if diplomats and international policy planners are to be more effective, they will need to face that challenge.

New Patterns Are Emerging . . .

This need is not easy to express, and it is even more difficult to meet. In the preceding chapters, we observed that globalization has splintered the previously steadfast blocs, giving rise to a contradictory duality of integration and fragmentation complicated further by the politicization of ethnic and religious differences. It might be argued, however, that in some respects the former first and third worlds nonetheless remain much as they were. Indeed, with the expansion of the EU and the rapid development of parts of Asia, the first world seems, if anything, to have grown—even as the gaps between it and most of the rest of the planet appear to have widened.[10]

Still, the problems associated with trying to salvage the upper (first) and lower (third) strata of the old model are serious. The Cold War order does not accommodate the dynamic complexity of globalization; thinking in terms of static divisions is too reductionist. The old model does not account for the growing disparities *within* OECD countries or for the emergence in some of these countries of what appears to be a permanent underclass whose relative well-being has diminished following, for instance, the removal of once widespread social safety nets. Furthermore, the old model does not reflect either the relative economic success achieved by certain countries in the former third world, for example in Southeast Asia, or the first world–like development in sometimes large areas of China, Brazil, India, and others.

Because it is premised on place rather than people, on territories rather than relationships, the Cold War model has outlived its usefulness. Clearly, its emphasis on the state as the essential unit of power and influence in the world is out of sync with present conditions. While most states have seen their relative power and influence decline, nonstate actors—ranging from individuals like Bill Gates and Bono, to NGOs like Greenpeace, Doctors Without Borders, and Oxfam, to evangelical Christian groups like Pat Robertson's Christian Coalition and James Dobson's Focus on the Family, to Islamic extremist networks like Al-Qaida—now play a much more significant role in world affairs.[11] At the same time, intergovernmental organizations like the UN and its agencies have become less influential, and the institutions of global governance whose arrival was once widely anticipated have not, for the most part, materialized.[12]

The principles of national sovereignty, political territory, and noninterference are no longer sacrosanct. The number of weak or collapsed regimes that cannot enforce their sovereignty, protect their territories, or provide services to their people has grown in proportion to the rise of rogue states, kleptocracies, and in extreme cases, anocracies marked by the absence of rule.[13] In such circumstances, something akin to Hobbesian conditions often arises, characterized by pillage, plunder, massive human rights violations, and the warring of each against all.[14] With the exception of a few brief interludes, much of Somalia has been in just that situation for almost twenty years.

In addition to the growing number of failing and collapsed states that benefited little from investment during the Cold War and that were cut loose after it ended, there are fewer strong states.[15] As a result, according to some analyses, the world is now composed of "rule makers and rule takers," such that levels of inequality are increasing and attention to issues of international social justice are decreasing.[16] Where order is maintained, it tends to be by force rather than by agreement.

The formal and informal understandings, familiar patterns of behavior, and general orderliness of the Cold War era have given way to a more volatile environment marked by the widespread incidence of intrastate conflict, a tendency toward ethnic and cultural partition, and the possibility of unprecedented mass migration.[17] Arms control is no longer the centerpiece of international cooperation: the Comprehensive Test Ban is languishing, the ABM Treaty has been repudiated, and the UN Committee on Disarmament has been unable to agree even on a program of work since the mid-1990s.[18] Old alliances based on the idea of collective security, such as NATO, are having to make way for newer ones, including free trade bodies and the likes of the Shanghai Cooperation Organization, which is loosely consultative and structured around the challenge of internal more than external threats.[19] New forms of informal association are cropping up regularly, such as the group of countries—Nicaragua, Ecuador, Cuba—that has attracted the generous attention of Venezuela's president Hugo Chavez.

Another trend emerging in the wake of US support for the mujahedin in 1980s Afghanistan is the propensity for states to back religious militants in other countries: Iran aids Shiite militias in Iraq and Hamas in the Palestinian territories, the Saudis assist various Sunni groups, Syria supports Hezbollah in Lebanon, and so forth. We shall return to this theme in Chapter 5.

. . . As the Mutation Continues

Much has understandably been made of the notion of *unipolarity,* or the existence of a single superpower, namely the United States, especially as regards its military dominance and willingness to act preemptively to maintain its hegemony into the indefinite future. Whether they revered or reviled the United States as the world's leader, all other members of the international community had little choice but to deal with it. Some had concluded that unipolarity is itself the new world order model. Certainly in the immediate wake of the Cold War, US power, both hard and soft, seemed unassailable. There has been much debate about whether the superpower was in fact an empire and, if so, whether it is inclusive, liberal, and benevolent or exclusive, authoritarian, and predatory.[20]

In any case, the fleeting unipolar moment—however unconvincing in economic terms—is already ending in a spectacular starburst of military violence (in the form of foreign wars) and economic collapse (beginning in 2008 with the Wall Street crisis).[21] As they grow ever more integrated, European nations will increasingly resist division over issues like Iraq, and sooner or later Europe will exercise international political influence in keeping with its economic clout. So, sooner or later, will Japan, an (eventually) resurgent Russia, and (still) rapidly rising Brazil, India, and China.[22] If the Washington Consensus on neoliberal political economy played a crucial role in changing the post–Cold War world, it may be that a new Beijing Consensus, based on sovereignty, innovation, and "asymmetric power projection," is emerging in its place.[23]

The full implications of the rise of these developing states are much too vast to be summarized here. That said, if power is in fact shifting across the Pacific, the first indications could be more symbolic than substantial. The sequence would be something like this: the Beijing Consensus displaces the Washington Consensus, the Shanghai Cooperation Organization displaces NATO, and the East Asian Summit (composed of regional members only) displaces APEC (membership in which is open to all countries with a Pacific coastline). Assuming all that transpires, the rapid diffusion of economic power, in tandem with the ever-increasing scope and intensity of transnational relations, is likely to produce a new kind of international equilibrium by the midcentury at the latest—

one that is dynamic rather than static, as hegemonic nationalism cedes to something more akin to "multilateral globalism."[24]

In the meantime, however, the interventions in Afghanistan and especially Iraq—and the policy pronouncements used to justify them—have led to the widely held impression that the United States is leading a Western crusade against the Islamic world. This has in turn contributed to a precipitous decline in the reputation of the United States throughout much of the world.[25] People in many nations who once shared American values and goals now sense a growing distance.[26] It remains to be seen whether or not, and if so, how quickly, the Obama administration can reverse this trend. If the nature of cabinet-level and senior bureaucratic appointments suggests more continuity than change in US foreign policy, the recovery of lost ground may be slower and less dramatic than anticipated.

Diplomacy, in any case, has not managed to keep up with such changes; the amount of conflict and the number of looming threats around the world are but two indications. One explanation for its failure is that it lacks a model that accounts for the changing circumstances. How, though, to build one?

Success Will Depend . . .

With a view to better conceptualizing these complexities, I propose we begin with a brief review of dependency theory. Though now largely forgotten, it contains, I believe, critical insights into the workings of globalization.[27]

Dependency theory was formulated by Raul Prebisch, and further shaped by more radical proponents such as Andre Gunder Frank and Samir Amin, as well as the more pragmatic Fernando Cardoso, Enzo Faletto, and Osvaldo Sunkel.[28] These academics developed their model based on the Latin America of the 1950s through the 1970s.[29] Especially resonant in the age of globalization is dependency theory's emphasis upon active center-periphery relations, a concept that has recently been revisited in an especially provocative manner by Thomas Barnett.[30] Barnett's analysis and model are supported implicitly by the approaches to international relations taken by the likes of Robert Cooper, Benjamin Barber, Robert Kaplan, and, for that matter, Samuel Huntington.[31]

While very popular in its heyday, *la dependencia* is barely mentioned today.[32] I argue that many of its central elements nonetheless remain as (if not more) relevant on the cusp of the postmillennium's second decade as they were more than thirty years ago. How so? Because, anticipating one of the major aspects of globalization, the model emphasizes the importance of external influences (corporations, world markets, terms of trade) and actively links the growing prosperity of the center—which is to say the first world—to the persistence of poverty on the periphery, which is to say the third world. This process of imbalance is seen as ongoing, indeed ever intensifying.

For dependency theorists, then, underdevelopment was not the result of isolation from the global political economy but rather the result of denial of the benefits of participation therein. Underdeveloped countries, in other words, found themselves locked into structurally subservient positions. Their dependence was a function less of exclusion than of disadvantageous integration and an undue financial and political reliance on the vagaries and constraints of commodity exports.

Dependency theorists focused on the linkages between underdevelopment on the global periphery and development in the metropolitan center as two sides of the same coin. Although the focus was on the role of the United States specifically in terms of US–Latin American relations and, more generally, those of the then first and third worlds, most of the world's states could similarly be located either in the center or on the periphery. Underdevelopment in this conception was not a natural or accidental condition but, at the end of the day, the inevitable result of the expansion and consolidation of global capitalism.

While *interdependence* was the term of choice on the part of liberal analysts who sought to justify the status quo, *dependency* was seen by its adherents as more accurate insofar as it referred to an organic, dialectic, and, especially highly asymmetrical process that functioned at multiple levels. Dominance on the part of the few who controlled the world's capital, technology, skills, and markets contrasted with dependence on the part of the many who provided the labor, raw materials, and secondary markets under conditions that ensured their dominant partners would benefit at their expense. This pattern was established during the colonial period via mercantilism, but during the second half of the twentieth century it evolved into neocolonialism, which was seen to serve mainly the needs of multinational corporations and their political patrons in the metropolis.

It might be argued that dependency is a necessary if difficult step toward development—a preliminary form of integration into the global political economy.[33] That may be so, but dependency distorted the political economies, social and cultural relations, and state apparatuses of peripheral countries such that their development became subject to the requirements of the center. Reflexive rather than autonomous, dependent countries were seen by the theorists to be riddled with intractable structural and functional problems that tended to worsen over time. Their domestic economic sectors were unintegrated. National output was organized to satisfy metropolitan needs rather than to correlate with domestic demand, which was often met by imports. Income distribution was enormously skewed and accompanied all of the expected quantitative and qualitative disparities.

In the dependent countries, the elites, or *comparadors,* enjoyed a symbiotic relationship with those counterparts in metropolitan states who shared similar tastes and goals, forming transnational ties and networks.[34] These were not conspiracies, but consensuses among those with common objectives; nevertheless, the comparadors were complicit in the extent to which the interests of their states were subordinated to those of the center, not just in economic terms but also politically and culturally. Years of underdevelopment in these states yielded legacies of authoritarian government that was as notoriously unstable as it was unrepresentative.[35] One need only look at any number of South American governments during the late 1970s and 1980s (for instance, Chile under Pinochet or Argentina under Videla) and even the 1990s (like Peru under Fujimori) to see how dependency reinforced authoritarian regimes.

In short, dependency theory remains strikingly apt in the postmillennium, bringing many useful insights to bear on underdevelopment. Why, then, has it almost disappeared from the contemporary discourse? Many of the policy directions advocated or implied by the dependency model either were actively discouraged by foreign investors and the international financial institutions (that is, the IMF, the World Bank, and regional development banks), were overtaken by events, or were simply—like the proposal to delink individual national units from the global economy—impractical or unappealing. Autarkic, isolationist policies pursued in Albania, Burma, and North Korea illustrated that point with some conviction. Perhaps more to the point, though, is the fact that such policies, usually under the pejorative label of *protectionism,* were inimical to the neoliberal approach to economic organization that evolved from laissez-faire to structural adjustment and finally to the highly prescriptive package of policy conditions provided by the Washington Consensus and promoted by those favoring free trade and unimpeded commerce.

Still, compared to the prescriptions offered by Western-style modernization, the dependency approach was commendable.[36] Reference has been made to its usefulness in advancing our understanding of the central tenets of globalization. Moreover, some of the remedies its theorists proposed for dependence were actually field tested—and met with some degree of success. These include the promotion of national and collective self-reliance, especially regarding food production and manufacturing (for instance, through regional economic integration like that codified in the Andean Pact), import-substituting industrialization (which worked well in the 1960s and 1970s), and South-South cooperation.[37]

Dependency theory is largely based on a reading of global economic relations, and it is not surprising that some of its main lines of argument have been echoed by supporters of the antiglobalization movement.[38] That said, perhaps because Latin America was considered in large part to be within the US sphere of influence during the Cold War, the *dependencia* model is not especially forward-looking, lacks a strategic dimension, and makes scant reference to either national or international security from a non-economic perspective.

Beginning in the 1970s, the proponents of the multidisciplinary *world-system school* pioneered by Immanuel Wallerstein rejected both conventional modernization and the two-tiered, bimodal approach of dependency theorists as overly state-centric and simplistic. Proponents of the world-system likewise emphasize the relationship between development/underdevelopment and the expansion of capitalism but propose variants on the themes of core, periphery, and, additionally, a new (and growing) buffer zone they call the semi-periphery.[39]

Another trimodal model has been developed by Robert Cooper, who sees three types of states: premodern (chaotic and failed or failing), modern (interest-based, sovereign, and functioning) and postmodern (globalizing, integrating, peaceful, and prosperous).[40] In my view, however, the dependency model still provides the most useful insights into the dynamics of power and influence in the twenty-first century.

. . . On Adapting the Foundations . . .

The dependency theorists' emphasis on perpetual motion and active global bifurcation—between metropolitan states and satellites, winners and losers—is particularly apt for analyses of the nature of globalization. That said, much like the formulation of the first, second, and third worlds, dependency is mechanistic and rooted in defined political and economic space. It does not take adequate account of the existence of worlds within worlds, as illustrated by the four key observations that follow.

First is the increasing incidence of culturally and technologically sophisticated individuals, groups, cities, and regions located within states that would otherwise be labeled "underdeveloped." Examples of what we used to call the first world within what we used to call the third could include the rise of superwealthy industrialists in Cairo, the many thousands of prosperous software developers in South India, and the more prosperous parts of cities like Capetown and Caracas, or those of coastal China.

Add to this consortium the similar, although larger and more prevalent, constellations of globalization's beneficiaries found in the OECD countries, and we can call this the *A* or *advancing* category, which aligns closely with the dominant or metropolitan groups described in dependency theory. What is especially noteworthy and distinctive about this category are the strength and prominence of the transnational ties that bind all of those affected.

Second is the appearance on the world stage of a class of individuals, groups, cities, regions, and countries that, if not fully developed, certainly does not any longer fit the underdeveloped category. Examples could include the front desk staff at a world-class resort in Kenya; the cloth merchants of Old Delhi; entire countries like Malaysia, Turkey, and Algeria; and regions such as the southern cone and northern tier of Latin America. This group has not been effectively captured by or incorporated into any of the former models; it can be referred to as the *C* or *contingent* category.

Third is the widespread emergence of individuals, groups, regions, and settlements characterized by conditions resembling those in what we used to call the third world but located within the first or second. Examples include some aboriginal communities within North America and Russia, the uninsured poor in the United States (such as those who suffered in the aftermath of Hurricane Katrina), the Roma (or gypsies) in Europe, temporary workers, and the chronically unemployed and angry residents of social housing projects in many major cities—such as the rioters in Paris in the spring of 2006. For appalling third world–like living conditions among aboriginal peoples, one need look no further than many reserves in Canada.[41] Add to this the world's dependent, underdeveloped countries, previously referred to as the third world, and call it the *T* or *tertiary* category.

Finally, although only the most primitive and remote peoples—including, for instance those (rarely) found in the New Guinea interior or Amazonia—have remained almost completely unaffected by globalization, significant numbers have nonetheless been largely marginalized or left out. Examples here would include subsistence cultivators on a South Pacific island, the hill tribes of Southeast Asia, the populations of significant areas of sub-Saharan Africa and Central Asia, and the chronic homeless in metropolitan areas. Place those who find themselves of little or no interest to the beneficiaries of globalization in the *E* or *excluded* category.

. . . To Construct Something Different

How might such diverse and shifting categories be incorporated into the construction of a new world order model? Jorge Nef has suggested that "a fresh way of looking at the world could offer the kind of analysis and policy prescriptions capable of breaking the present cycle of self-reinforcing dysfunctions."[42] To that end, I would propose moving beyond the now-obsolete categories of first, second, and third world as well as beyond the elementary center-periphery model and its variants to adopt the four broad categories of people and places affected by globalization we have just set out: the *A-world,* whose economic and political advantage is advancing; the *C-world,* whose prospects are uncertain and will be contingent upon future developments, positive or negative; the *T-world,* whose relative position is subservient or dependent; and the *E-world,* which finds itself largely excluded from globalization's matrix. Put the four categories together and voilà! We have a user-friendly and adaptable world order model, the ACTE.[43]

Each category may contain individuals, social or cultural groups, cities or parts thereof, states or parts thereof, and regions in multilateral combinations. This hybrid formulation, which is transnational rather than geopolitical, combines the utility of labels with the dynamic assets of the dependency analysis. It avoids adherence to fixed national and political boundaries, thus allowing for constant movement upward, downward, and sideways within and among the principal groups associated with globalization.

The point here is that it is no longer useful or even possible to put entire countries, regions, and/or groupings into this or that particular intellectual or geographic box. The circumstances are simply too complex. In the age of globalization, deterritorialization—of power, agency, nationality, language, even ethnicity—has become a key concept. While it is very difficult to avoid completely the use of spatial and geographic terms, economic and political relations in the era of globalization are less and less territorially based and more and more socially constructed—among individuals, classes, and other groups of various description. It is these billions of people—almost one half of whom are under twenty-five and live in cities—rather than the countries they inhabit that experience development and underdevelopment.[44]

The situation of BRIC (as Brazil, Russia, India, and China are collectively called) is illustrative. These resurging or aspiring powers contain within their borders very large examples of A-, C-, T-, and E-worlds. There are also elements of each in the United States, although in its case the A-world is the largest, the E-world is smaller, and the C- and T-worlds are perhaps more fluid. In 2009, at all levels, most of the mobility is downward, and this carries implications that remain unclear.

Admittedly, proposing an alternative model to the dominant worldview is bold and quite possibly futile. I further recognize that I have provided but a sketch, which I will leave to my critics to rip apart. Nonetheless, I do hope that the ACTE model might prove useful in identifying, illuminating, and assessing the trends associated with globalization that are not easily accommodated within the current parameters. Although the viability of any new construct should be supported by further research and detailed empirical analyses that I must leave to others, I will, by way of hypotheses, make a couple of fundamental points at the outset.[45]

As we move from the A- to the C-, T-, and E-worlds, we see an increase in vulnerability to threats anchored in science and mobilized by technology combined with a decrease in the capacity to use science and technology remedially. This is a defining feature of the model, with major implications for diplomacy to be discussed in later chapters.

With regard to the population size of each category, I would postulate that the A-world is growing gradually, the C-world rapidly (especially in Asia), and the T-world steadily. The E-world is likely getting smaller as globalization extends its reach into the farthest corners of the earth.

However, the economic distance between the A and T/E groups, real and perceived, is increasing. It is this phenomenon which has given rise to polarization, and it is in large part attributable to the aforementioned ICT revolution.

It must be stressed that the combination of rising literacy rates and accelerated media penetration has resulted in a growing appreciation of the gaps between the four categories, especially that between the A-world and all the others.[46] In a connected world, everything becomes known and everything becomes relative. Perception then becomes critical, especially on the part of those whose position is slipping; even if the absolute conditions in the C- and T-worlds are improving, their inhabitants may feel as though they are falling ever further behind.

We encounter a similar dynamic when we try to explain how it is that some relatively better-off members of the working and middle classes, as well as some people from middle-income and wealthy countries, become attracted to extremist causes or fundamentalist religions and turn to terrorism. This fact is adduced frequently by those seeking to discredit so-called root-cause arguments—who are often inclined toward military solutions.[47] Yet their logic is false. In the globalizing world, more and more people have access to more and more information. In these circumstances, perceptions of abuse or of growing inequality become both sharper and more widely held. Offering vicarious experiences, the new media obviates direct experience as a prerequisite for shared sentiment, which can then shift from personal and local to virtual and universal.[48] All of which brings concerns about the root causes of insecurity front and center.

We will return to the ACTE model as an organizing framework and analytical tool. As a reconceptualization of the way we see the world, it provides a foundation for the new diplomacy—a subject to which we shall return in Chapter 10. First, however, we will examine the relationship between the A-, C-, T-, and E-worlds, paying particular attention to how we might encourage progress toward the indispensable and interdependent diplomatic objectives that are security and development.

Notes

1. See Bottome (1986).

2. The Non-Aligned Movement was created after the Bandung Conference in 1955.

3. See Freeland (1972).

4. Containment was codified in *NSC 68: United States Objectives and Programs for National Security.* See National Security Council (1950). The doctrine had its origins in US diplomat George Kennan's oft-cited "long telegram" from Moscow, and was elaborated further in Kennan's famous article "The Sources of Soviet Conduct," published under the pseudonym Mr. X. Kennan (1947). In his later years, Kennan complained bitterly that his advice had been misinterpreted and co-opted by those supporting military responses, that he never saw the USSR as a military threat, and that he had wished to advocate "containment" of the Soviet Union primarily through political and economic means.

5. On October 2, 1957, the launch of the Sputnik satellite prompted fears that the United States was falling behind the Soviet Union in technological achievements. Soon after the launch, a *missile gap*—an imbalance between the size of US and Soviet nuclear arsenals—was allegedly discovered. These events heralded the beginning of both the space race and the arms race. See Preble (2004).

6. Estimates vary, but the figure of 25 million is frequently cited.
7. See Glatzer and Dietrich (2005).
8. Kuala Lumpur and Bangkok, for example, have better rapid transit connections from the city center to their international airports than do Toronto and Montreal.
9. See World Bank (2006a). This report also notes that "low income countries are fifteen times more susceptible to internal conflict than countries in the OECD." See also Rotberg (2003; 2004). See Brenner and Keil (2006), Mirovitskaya and Ascher (2002).
10. On the shift of power to Asia, see Mahbubani (2008a; 2008b), Steingart (2008).
11. See S. Smith (2002), Held and McGrew (2003: introduction), Willis (2006).
12. See Mendes and Ozay (2003).
13. See Weart (1998).
14. Without the rule of law or the provision of even minimal security, it is not surprising that there has been newfound interest in doctrines of humanitarian intervention, such as the Responsibility to Protect (R2P)—a mechanism designed to end gross and systemic acts of violence in nations whose authorities are either unwilling or unable to protect their populations. The principles that inform R2P have found wide acceptance and were formally recognized, in a slightly diluted form, at the UN Millennium Summit in September 2005. Yet suspicions linger that the doctrine will be invoked only by the strong—and then only when convenient or coterminous with their interests. For critiques of the R2P doctrine, see Lu (2007), Brunnee and Toope (2006).
15. See Fukuyama (2004).
16. See Hurrell and Woods (1999), Robertson (2004), Thomas (2001), Hurrell (2003).
17. See Fearon (2004), Rudolph (2003).
18. See Sands (2005).
19. For proponents of collective security, an attack on any one ally is considered an attack on all.
20. On unipolarity since the Cold War, see Bacevich (2004), Fukuyama (1992), and Ikenberry (2002); on benevolent imperialism, see Boot (2002), Ferguson (2004), and Ignatieff (2005); on globalization as empire, see Hardt and Negri (2000); and on exclusivity and predation, see Lens (1971) and Kinzer (2006).
21. See S. Smith (2002).
22. For a sampling of the economic implications, see "The New Titans: A Survey of the World Economy" (2006).
23. See Ramo (2004).
24. The essential characteristics of globalization, including the separation of state from economic power and the new interlinkages among states, are captured well by Nye (2004a) and Slaughter (2004). These developments are considered by some analysts to be contributing to the creation of a "postinternationalist" world of "multilateral globalism." See Mansbach (2000), Harris (2005).
25. See, for instance, the Pew Research Center, *Global Attitudes Project,* available at http://pewglobal.org. The so-called soft power of a nation, particularly that of the United States, is partly contingent on the conduct of foreign policy. See Nye (2004b).
26. On the psychological gaps caused by socioeconomic differences, see Fergusson and Mansbach (2004).
27. We will return to dependency analysis when we examine the ethic of development in Chapter 6.
28. Dependency theory constitutes a large and amorphous body of literature that dates from the early 1960s, blossoms in the 1970s, and tapers off in the 1980s. The ear-

liest articulation of its core tenets can be found in Prebisch (1962). The substantial legacy of the dependency school is considered in Chapter 5. For key works, see Prebisch (1962), Frank (1969), Amir (1977), Griffith-Jones and Sunkel (1985).

29. Prebisch was also a bureaucrat in the UN Economic Commission for Latin America (ECLA), and Cardoso went on to become a two-term president of Brazil, holding office from 1995 to 2003.

30. See Barnett (2004). On US grand strategy post-Bush, see Barnett (2009).

31. See Barnett (2004), R. Cooper (2000; 2003), Barber (2003), Kaplan (1994; 2000), Huntington (1997).

32. For an account of the many failings of dependency theory and a brief record of its decline, see Velasco (2002).

33. I am indebted to my colleague Michael Taylor for this observation.

34. *Comparadors* is the term favored by the theory's originators; it refers to those who owe their elite status to an association with foreign corporate or political interests. See Baran (1957).

35. See Franko (2003).

36. For a classic defense of neoliberal economics, see Dollar and Kraay (2002).

37. The Andean Pact began in 1969 as a deliberate but largely unsuccessful attempt to reverse dependent underdevelopment through regional economic integration. In 2004 it merged, partially, with another Latin American trading bloc, Mercosur. The remaining members—Colombia, Bolivia, Ecuador, and Peru—have kept the organization on life support, although its fate seems uncertain.

38. See, for example, Dowlah (2004), Harris and Seid (2000), N. Klein (2000; 2007).

39. On the world-system, see Wallerstein (1974), Nef (1999).

40. See Cooper (2003), Barnett (2004).

41. On conditions in the now infamous Kashechewan community, see CBC (Canadian Broadcasting Corporation) News (2006a). On aboriginal child poverty, see CBC News (2006b).

42. See Nef (1999: conclusion).

43. Although I think its rationale is compelling, mine is undoubtedly an imperfect formulation. I tried many different key words (for example, *A* for *acquiring, C* for *conditional,* and *T* for *tributary*) and letter combinations. Suggestions for better alternatives will be enthusiastically welcomed.

44. Barnett (2004), with his emphasis on a spatial representation of the "functioning core" and the "disconnected periphery," largely misses this point. One of the key attributes of globalization is the deterritorialization of political and military space; thus his attempt to map and hence territorialize the new world disorder is, I think, misguided. Mapping is visually impressive, but it can be misleading, especially when based on assumptions, often state-centric, that have been overtaken by events. Barnett suggests that economic and technological connectedness is the best path to peace and prosperity. Yet higher levels of connectedness tend to intensify sensations of difference, which can quickly turn into anger; they also facilitate the formation of virtual communities, jihadis among them. A second weakness resides in Barnett's attempt to use the invasion and occupation of Iraq to illustrate his thesis. In my estimation, that experience better illuminates what can happen when the approach he advocates is ignored.

45. Excellent globalization statistics are regularly provided in the UN Development Programme's annual *Human Development Report* (http://hdr.undp.org) and the World Bank's annual *World Development Report* (http://publications.worldbank.org/

ecommerce/catalog/product-detail?product_id=5424413). Their interpretation, however, can be controversial. For a brief introduction to the debates surrounding globalization statistics, see Castells, Wade and Wolf, and Steans in Held and McGrew (2003); see also Dollar and Kraay (2002).

46. Graham and Sukhtankar (2004) have found that individuals in Latin America with greater access to the Internet are more likely to feel that the unequal distribution of wealth in their countries is unfair. On growing inequality, see Rogers (2002), Thomas (2001).

47. This phenomenon was alluded to in Chapter 1; see also Radu (2002), who maintains that terrorism is a response to asymmetries of power rather than poverty, injustice, inequality, or the like.

48. I refer to this phenomenon writ large as *global empathy,* which is discussed further in Chapter 6.

PART 2
Drivers of Change

Persistent Insecurity: Lessons Unlearned 5

Not long ago I attended a concert at one of my favorite local venues, the Black Sheep Inn in Wakefield, Quebec. For the first time that I was aware of, a Make Poverty History campaign banner was displayed onstage. Its three main messages were "More and better aid—Trade justice—Cancellation of debt."

Like anyone else who watches television or has been exposed to viral marketing on the Internet, I was well aware of this international campaign, with its finger-snapping motif so effectively supported by stylized black-and-white images of music celebrities from North America and Europe. I was delighted to see that the campaign organizers were managing to think and act locally.

What struck me even more, though, was the choice of objectives highlighted on the banner.[1] There was something in small print near the bottom about child labor, but otherwise it focused only on fairly conventional aspects of development. There was no reference to stopping violence or ending conflict, no reference to security either as it is traditionally understood—involving states—or in its broader and in some respects more contemporary iteration, centered on people.[2]

This curious lacuna, minor in itself, may indicate a larger anomaly. For instance, there was no reference to security, in the UN Millennium Development Goals either. Go back to 1992 to the Earth Summit's Agenda 21: you'll note a similar absence.[3]

If no obvious link appears when we view issues of security through a development lens, what if we reverse the glass and view development through the prism of security considerations? Suddenly, the picture changes. The much publicized study *A More Secure World: Our Shared Responsibility: Report of the Secretary General's High-Level Panel on Threats, Challenges, and Change,* for example, offers near-encyclopedic coverage of the usual insecurity suspects—terrorism, conflict, organized crime, weapons of mass destruction—but also emphasizes the central roles played by poverty, infectious disease, and environmental degradation within the broader context of development.[4]

A Kinder, Gentler Machine Gun Hand

Neil Young's totemic anthem "Rockin' in the Free World" suggested that we were on a collision course with the future. In the 1990s, Thomas Homer-Dixon found a direct relationship between the incidence of conflict on the one hand and resource depletion, population growth, and environmental degradation on the other.[5] The broader connection of these security concerns to development, however, did not stick. Ten years later, one might add to this list pandemic disease, climate change, and a variety of other challenges—most related to science and technology—that together represent the greatest threats to human survival. Militaries, for their part, often speak of the need to provide security in the form of counterinsurgency operations so that development can take place, but the two goals are otherwise treated, for the most part, separately.

Is there a pattern here—a partial disconnect, an analytical inconsistency? Could it be that those who situate development within a primarily economic and social context are missing the vital connection to security? Indeed, a review of the literature indicates that even many experts see development and security as largely unrelated.[6] And many of those who work in the development field exhibit a visceral antipathy toward anything associated with security, let alone defense and the armed forces.

Insecurity arises from unchecked threats and unmet needs; the popular conception of security, and hence the response of states to insecurity, are flawed. Since at least the time of Hobbes, it has been clear that without peace, order, or the rule of law, progress in other areas of national life are impossible. If diplomats are to improve their performance with respect to avoiding wars and negotiating peaceful settlements to all manner of disputes, then they will need a more powerful analysis than that suggested by the likes of the Make Poverty History sloganeers, however well intended.

Is Security a Martial Art?

Security today is widely understood to represent the condition of protection from danger, damage, or loss. Under that vast umbrella, the variations are almost endless. They include human security (as discussed earlier); national security and state security (respectively, the integrity of the nation-state and that of its government apparatus); international security (concerning matters of war and peace among states); collective security (the basis of formal alliances, whereby an attack on one member is considered to represent an attack on the entire alliance); common security (the conceptual basis of the UN Charter and its determination to avoid the "scourge of war"); cooperative security (multilateral and preventative); and a raft of more particular types, including economic security, environmental security, food security, and energy security. For the purposes of this analysis, suffice it to say that security (broadly defined) and development are considered mutually inclusive and indivisible.

During the Cold War, it was not security and development that most saw as part of the same package but security and defense. Development for its own sake? That was someone else's responsibility—quite possibly someone who was soft on communism. When I first became interested in international affairs, the field of security studies was dominated by those—usually men—with an interest in defense issues and the military. Many of the principal players were either in uniform or closely associated with those who were. They were comfortable with a world whose borders were delineated by imperial cartographers. In government, the public servants who were responsible for so-called security policy had a similar orientation. It was a small world: generals, admirals, and their counterparts in the academy and bureaucracy pretty well had the run of the roost.

Much of this was attributable to the Cold War context, which was conducive to fixation on matters of hard security—the order of battle, comparative armament, territorial integrity, and the ability to project power. Over the past fifteen years, however, the security discourse has undergone an inversion. Especially significant has been the shift in emphasis from the security of states (that is, traditional, defense-related security) to the security of individuals, populations, and groups. This formulation, as we have seen, is popularly known as *human security,* and although the term is not in vogue to the extent that it was in the 1990s, many of its underlying assumptions have continuing applicability and as such have survived intact—for example, in the form of the R2P doctrine discussed earlier.

Evidently our understanding of security and its relationship to development is evolving. What do we now identify as the core elements of security? And how does their dialectical relationship with development play out in terms of the discussion presented in the preceding chapters?

To begin that inquiry, it may be useful to return to a comparison of some of the critical components of the Cold War past and the globalizing present. There are several similarities: the leading role played by the United States, for instance, or the endurance as concepts of the former first world or center (per my model, part of the A-world) and the third world or periphery (which I have referred to as the T- and E-worlds). The essential differences between the two eras, however, outweigh the similarities. Indeed, just about every pundit of note has held forth on the significance of the changes that have occurred since the end of the Cold War, elaborating upon US unipolarity and military dominance, the clash of civilizations, even the end of history.[7] Contemporary conflicts are by and large asymmetrical—often involving nonstate actors on at least one side, they are no longer conducted mainly among countries, governments, and formal armies. Beneath these obvious shifts, however, lie some additional and largely unappreciated parallels. Few analysts, for example, have focused on the weight of the baggage carried over from the Cold War to the era of globalization. This carryover, I maintain, is critical to understanding that in the twenty-first century, development has, in an important sense, actually become the new security. But the metaphor of luggage requires some unpacking.

My Mujahedin: The Tote Bag from Hell

In the transition between the two eras, perhaps the most striking element of continuity has been intellectual or conceptual. Here I refer to certain aspects of the dominant international political ethic or worldview of each period, the legitimacy of which must be upheld to ensure that domestic public opinion remains in favor of the national government in question. The propaganda disseminated to that end is considerable.

In the United States, the persistence of the Cold War mentality may be attributed in large part to the ongoing influence of the neoconservative movement, often acting in concert with the evangelical Christian right. During the 1980s, this group (which included future powers in the George W. Bush administration like Richard Cheney, Donald Rumsfeld, Paul Wolfowitz, and Richard Perle, plus a gaggle of polemicists like Irving Kristol and David Frum) helped convince the Reagan administration that the USSR was intent on global domination, and would have to be resisted universally, through force. It was the Truman Doctrine on steroids. After a period of exile during the Clinton years—about the same time, ironically, that Islamic fundamentalists were suffering serious reverses in Egypt, Algeria, and elsewhere—these neoconservatives set to work on the Project for a New American Century.[8] Their influence was restored under the George W. Bush administration, especially after 9/11—as illustrated by the 2002 National Security Strategy, by which the decision to embark on the global war on terror and send troops to Afghanistan and Iraq was made.[9] Now it was the terrorists and Muslim extremists rather than the communists who had to be "contained" and "deterred," in the recycled parlance of the Cold War.

In Afghanistan since the 1980s, the effects of this mentality transfer have been especially pernicious. Under Reagan, rebuffing Soviet expansion meant joining forces with and providing military support to those Islamic fundamentalists, warlords, and opium traders who were willing to oppose the Soviet occupation that had begun in 1979. Operating both directly and through intermediaries in Pakistan and Afghanistan, the CIA unified, armed, and nurtured this disparate group, which came to be known as the *mujahedin,* or "holy warriors." This resistance movement consisted of many factions—including, as they became known during the civil war that raged after US support was withdrawn in the early 1990s, the Taliban and the Northern Alliance. When the Soviets departed Afghanistan in 1989 and the USSR imploded in 1991, both the neocons and the mujahedin took credit. A decade later, deprived of a common adversary, these former allies each saw the other as the real enemy.[10]

Some of the Things We Carry . . .

There are at least three characteristics germane to our understanding of security and the conduct of international relations as they have been carried over from the Cold War onward into the twenty-first century. These are now so familiar that they seem almost congenital to the prevailing worldview, and so embedded are they in the discourse of mainstream media and government that for the most part they are now simply accepted. Related yet distinct, these aspects deserve more analysis if we are to better understand just how we arrived at the present (dis)juncture.

During the Cold War, the stage was set for the global contest of us against them—capitalists versus communists, the free versus the oppressed, democrats versus totalitarians. "The other" was out there, plotting our downfall, scheming for advantage. But *it* was also among *us,* as the venomous antics of Senator Joe McCarthy and the House Committee on Un-American Activities revealed so clearly.[11] The enemy could be found on many distant shores, but it was also right there in our own backyards.

At the end of the Cold War, the United States had a variety of strategic options, but in the end it chose primacy.[12] As a result of that choice, the defining feature of international relations in the twenty-first century, particularly post-9/11, is the war on terror, accompanied by a return to the rhetoric of "us against them."[13] Then it was the communists; now it is the terrorists. Like the former, we are often cautioned, the latter are not just "out there" but are lurking among us—whether "homegrown" or imported as immigrants, for example students or guest workers.

In just over a decade, terrorism has come to fill the void left when communism was vanquished. The costs to diplomacy and development, from which scarce international policy resources have been diverted, have been colossal. And while there have been many arrests of suspected terrorists, there have not been nearly as many convictions.[14] Meanwhile, the imposition of draconian controls on civil liberties, the suspension of civil rights, and a litany of other antiterrorist measures—ranging from extraordinary rendition to the establishment of so-called black sites for interrogation to the legitimization of torture—have had far more impact.

The second carryover from the Cold War to the present is the characterization of the threat. During the Cold War, the Red Menace was seen as global and undifferentiated. Western interests were believed to be at risk in Central Europe, in Northeast and then Southeast Asia, in Africa, in the Middle East, in Central and South America. Dominoes were poised to fall—apparently everywhere. To contain the widespread threat, the West in large part set aside any concern for human rights or democratic development and chose instead to support or even install some very unsavory figures—most of whom, in retrospect, resemble cardboard cutouts of right-wing dictators: Thieu in Vietnam, Pinochet in Chile, the Shah of Iran, Mobutu in Zaire, a slew of Central and South American caudillos, and all too many more. It was a rogues' gallery, but they were our rogues.

During the first decade after the end of the Cold War, it was difficult to single out a threat as pervasive as that posed by communism. China and a host of lesser players such as North Korea, Iraq, and Iran were being sized up as possible stand-ins for the now defunct USSR. Attention was devoted, if fleetingly, to political Islam and the dangers of fundamentalism. Many, like Harvard professor Samuel Huntington, examined cultural and religious cleavages and saw entire civilizations embarking on an inevitable collision course.[15] In general, though, despite brief interludes such as Operation Desert Storm and the Balkan wars, the 1990s constituted a rough patch for threat conjurers; none of their demons or bogeymen captured the public imagination.[16] Although no peace dividend was to be paid, defense budgets began to shrink: world military spending declined 35 percent from 1989 to 1999.[17]

September 11 changed all of that. Suddenly, the West was again at war, this time against terrorism, and that threat, too, was spun as global and undifferentiated. I recall a comment by James Der Derian of Brown University at the March 2002 meeting of the International Studies Association (ISA) in New Orleans. He opined that although he discounted the various conspiracy theories that had sprung up around the attacks on the Twin Towers and Pentagon, there was nonetheless no doubt in his mind that the events of that day had been manipulated to advantage by those with a clear agenda, an abundance of ideological drive, and a calculated understanding of political opportunity. The costs would be great.

My own report on the 2002 ISA conference echoes Der Derian's observation.[18] It concludes:

> Though not likely a conspiracy, 9/11 nonetheless played into certain agendas, perhaps especially that of the military-industrial complex, [which] until [then] faced a desperate absence of credible threats against which to pitch requests for support and resources. For [its members], 9/11 and the new international terrorist menace represent manna from heaven and can be expected to reliably serve the same open-ended structural purposes as had the Cold War for almost half a century previously. This new threat, however, has been conjured at a great domestic price.[19]
>
> The executive [branch] has been vested by the Senate with vast new powers, and has been given a carte blanche authority, roughly equivalent to the Tonkin Gulf Resolution, to respond vigorously—if unaccountably—to the new situation. Racial profiling and new police powers are disturbing. Meanwhile, civil defense preparations are not advancing, with states and municipalities going off madly in all directions, while civil liberties have taken the pipe. Tom Ridge, the first cabinet secretary for Homeland Security, ha[s] been awarded a dysfunctional homeland security mandate, disconnected from any authority other than moral and nominal.

> In the absence of a coherent central strategy, every other level of government ha[s] jumped on the bandwagon or waved down the gravy train, bidding on the new money for every pet project in an utterly chaotic fashion. Emergency preparedness and civil defense planning require a high degree of central control; the new reality is exactly the opposite, and valuable ground has been lost. This may not be widely appreciated, unfortunately, until after the next incident.

Few suspected that it would be a natural disaster, rather than a terrorist attack, that would prove my point. Yet it dramatically foreshadows the events that unfolded in the wake of Hurricane Katrina, when the existence of the T- (tertiary) and E- (excluded) worlds were revealed under the belly of the A- (advancing) world.

The third similarity between the Cold War and the era of globalization involves the preference for confrontational responses to undifferentiated threats through use of the military, leading to "an endless string of conflicts, crises, containments, and battles in the frontier lands of what used to be called the third world."[20] While a confrontational stance and an inaccurate characterization of the threat at hand might themselves be harmless in and of themselves, the militarization of international policy has proven deadly.[21]

During the Cold War, containment meant going to war in Korea and Vietnam, threatening to do it over in Taiwan or Cuba, garrisoning Western Europe and East Asia, building up the mujahedin to fight the Soviets in Afghanistan, and so on. The global war on terror has been used to sideline diplomacy and justify, among many other things, the intervention in Afghanistan; the invasion and occupation of Iraq; the establishment of new military bases in Central and Southeast Asia, the Horn of Africa, and the Middle East; and an enormous increase in military expenditures overall.[22]

A noteworthy side effect of the current emphasis on military solutions has been the rehabilitation and even celebration of martial culture evident in the mass media, especially in the United States. In the wake of the disaster in Vietnam (1975), the failed attempt to rescue diplomatic hostages in Iran (1980), and the Black Hawk Down episode in Somalia (1993), the tendency to valorize the military lessened (except perhaps during Operation Desert Shield and Operation Desert Storm in 1990 and 1991). As we have observed earlier, however, it was strengthened during the buildup to and throughout the invasion of Iraq, reaching its apogee on May 1, 2003, when President Bush, standing in a flight suit on the USS *Abraham Lincoln,* proclaimed the "end of major combat operations" as a banner reading "Mission Accomplished" draped the deck.[23] As of press time, with the situation in Afghanistan deteriorating and the occupation of Iraq alternating between a simmer and a boil, the glorification of the military may again wane.[24] If so, a strategic political opening for the consideration of international policy alternatives might be in the offing.

. . . Are Best Left Behind

When expressed as policy translated into action, these three tendencies have the familiar, even comfortable quality of inherited traits, as if part of the DNA of international relations. But they are not part of the genome of the species. Instead, in ways that recall Noam Chomsky's observations on manufactured consent, the legitimacy of at once maintaining a binary worldview, diagnosing the threat as undifferentiated, and favoring lethal response has been established because it serves larger purposes, foremost among them the interests of those who benefit most from the militarization of international policy.[25] It also preempts any attempt to implement alternative international policy options and priorities such as human-centered development or environmental stewardship.[26] Indeed, by continuing to divert budgetary resources away from aid or diplomacy in favor of defense, underdevelopment and insecurity are being exacerbated.[27]

The persistence of this trio of traits helps explain why the world remained in the rut of the Cold War for almost fifty years. If we wish to avoid becoming mired in a similar predicament for the next fifty years, then it follows that we will have to find a way to break free from these philosophical manacles. Doing so will involve not only a significant broadening of our understanding of security and its underpinnings but also a change in orientation and direction. Neither of these changes is too difficult to imagine. First, the ethos of us versus them will have to be jettisoned in favor of a single, unified formulation: us. All of *us* on this small, fragile planet need to work together to meet the challenges to our collective survival.

This brings us back to the second piece of inherited luggage, the assessment of the threat. It is not terrorism—at least not as we have known it so far—but climate change, the uncontrolled spread of weapons of mass destruction, nuclear proliferation, pandemic disease, resource scarcity, and environmental degradation that represent the greater threat to humankind's long-term prospects.[28] These threats—and a raft of others—are not universal and undifferentiated but specific and identifiable. What's more, they can be addressed without recourse to the third carryover, violence, mainly through concerted political and economic action.

Thus, I suggest we replace these Cold War carryovers with three new, linked goals: strategic advances in science, technology, and R&D; a massive program of global resource reallocation (as a means of distributive justice); and the encouragement, through both public and guerrilla diplomacy, of an entirely more communicative, cooperative approach to international relations. In short, more talking, less fighting.

The Costs Are Mounting . . .

The present focus on counterterrorism among elites in the A-world is sharp and narrow. Anyone seeking to broaden the investigation of terrorism to include an examination of its root causes is accused of being unpatriotic or soft on terrorism. It often causes discomfort in respectable company to simultaneously condemn terrorism and ask why it occurs.[29] Should there not be room in the mainstream for the accommodation of alternative concerns and perspectives? Have the believers in the one true path led all others to the precipice?

The answer to each of these questions is yes. Debate and criticism are signs of a healthy polity; those who have silenced them have brought the world to the brink. Their open-ended, nonnegotiable declaration of war on terror has been costly and counterproductive. Today, as a result, the world is less rather than more secure; warnings about the possible spread of terrorism have become self-fulfilling prophecies. One need only look at the skyrocketing rates of terrorist incidents, especially in the Middle East, to see the world is becoming less secure.[30] The cost of the war in the form of military and civilian casualties has been unacceptably high.[31] Much of the world has been alienated from the United States and the UK, from their traditional allies in what Donald Rumsfeld called "the old Europe," to governments in Latin America, China, India, to ordinary people on the Arab and Islamic "street." Colossally expensive in every respect, the militarized option represents a massive misdirection of resources and has inflicted dreadful damage across the board.

The power and influence of the United States eroded precisely because the government ideologues behind the war on terror misunderstood the nature of the threat and miscalculated their response.[32] Contributing to this miscalculation is the fact that foreign policy is in large part an outward reflection of the domestic political economy, and here the pervasive influence of the US military-industrial complex is not to be underestimated.

These arguments should be convincing enough. But even if we viewed security from the defense perspective, our assessment of the success of the war on terror would not be much different. Indeed, many mainstream security analysts have concluded that the militarized response to 9/11, the 7/7 bombings in London, and related incidents has further degraded national and international security.[33]

How so? With the end of the great military confrontation in Central Europe, world wars are unlikely to recur. Small-scale, irregular wars, however—such as those being waged in Afghanistan and Iraq—and asymmetrical wars such as the war on terror have pitted state militaries against unconventional opponents. These types of conflict are becoming more common, yet success—that is, greater security—has not been achieved.[34]

Irregular, asymmetrical warfare has become the new normal in global conflict and has given rise to different approaches to conflict and its management, including the so-called three block war—a triple-headed or "3-D" approach to international intervention—and the revolution in military affairs (RMA).[35] This so-called revolution, however, has not produced the results its proponents predicted. Instead, we can observe the following:

- The technologically strong cannot always defeat the militarily weak, especially if the latter have the support of the local population.
- Insurgent forces can inflict significant (politically speaking) casualties against a much-better-armed opposition; vulnerability has become mutual.
- When organized militaries, regardless of their notional capacities, pursue irregular militants, victory is by no means assured; indeed, blowback is likely.
- Tactical, real-time intelligence plus precision munitions can destroy targets but cannot replace boots on the ground if longer-term impacts are being pursued.
- Victory, even if it can be achieved, is costly.

If the conflict is based on cultural, religious, tribal, or ethnic differences, then the use of force may backfire.[36] The increasing reliance on impregnable bases, airpower, and high-tech weaponry—which reduce infantry casualties but tend to increase collateral damage—has further fueled feelings of humiliation and resentment and has thus only contributed to the intensification of a generalized, anti-Western backlash. The examples of Vietnam, Lebanon, Palestine, Iraq, and Afghanistan have made clear that the application of overwhelming force is much more effective in winning battles than it is in winning wars. Diplomacy, by contrast, has lower costs, fewer downsides, and greater potential.

If you fight your enemies where they live, any victory—unless accompanied by a massive, long-term occupation and an immediate, broad-spectrum reconstruction—will be extremely costly, if not impossible. Foreign troops are on their opponents' turf; their enemy is not invading but lives there, has better intelligence, and can't be driven out. Furthermore, it can access an inexhaustible source of new recruits as long as the conditions that gave rise to their movement persist. Outsiders cannot distinguish friends from foes, and the latter will outlast them, waiting until their casualties produce a political crisis at home and they are forced to withdraw. Victories in these circumstances are pyrrhic.

I am not seeking to trivialize the threat represented by terrorism, especially that involving the possible use of weapons of mass destruction—for example, according to some analysts, the possible detonation of a dirty bomb in a large urban area.[37] Terrorism has often been described as the war of the weak against the strong; it certainly brings T- and E-world grievances to the immediate attention of the A-world even if it doesn't legitimize them. That is why I advocate working to detect, deter, and defuse immediate threats while maintaining a longer-term, global perspective.

And there have been some indications, however belated, that those of us who favor a less derivative, more contemporary approach are beginning to be heard. I detect the glimmer of an understanding that any military action, if it is to succeed, must be part of an overarching political and strategic framework, firmly founded on local conditions.[38] This revelation, while a long time coming, is not without antecedents.

In 1989, a group of serving and former members of the US military, mainly marines, released a very focused paper about insurgency titled "Fourth Generation Warfare."[39] These authors maintained that the essence of warfare had evolved from massed manpower, to massed firepower, to maneuver, to asymmetry. The old linear, hierarchical, and orderly doctrines and practices must be replaced by an appreciation of the loosely networked and disorderly conditions so prevalent in battle today—particularly in the T- and E-worlds where most of the conflict occurs. In October 2008, the US Department of Defense released documents on the subjects of counterinsurgency and stability operations that take account of many of these points. Robert Gates, defense secretary under both George W. Bush and Barack Obama, has promoted them publicly and often.[40]

This reawakening to the ever-evolving nature of war has perhaps been captured most eloquently by retired British general Sir Rupert Smith in *The Utility of Force*.[41] Smith argues that the all-out struggles of the twentieth century—the epic trials of strength that he terms "industrial war[s]"—were made obsolete with the invention of nuclear weapons and were replaced by a battle of wills or "war among the people," the outcome of which would ultimately have to be settled by political rather than military means. This was the case in Northern Ireland, Cyprus, Algeria, and Vietnam, and it will be in Iraq and Afghanistan.[42]

Most of these observations, sadly, could have been made just as aptly in the 1980s, or indeed in 1969, when the US military victory in Saigon, Hue, and elsewhere in the aftermath of the Tet Offensive actually accelerated the superpower's political defeat in Vietnam.[43]

. . . While Few Are Counting

By any reasonable measure, the military path to supposed global security does not lead to any kind of destination that most people would like to visit, let alone live in. Quite apart from its onerous curbs on civil liberties, the aggressive pursuit of the global war on terror has involved a gross and systemic violation of internationally recognized human rights—from extraordinary rendition, torture, the use of the highly contested designation illegal enemy combatant, and the limiting of habeas corpus—to selective but sometimes mistaken assassination. The publicizing of these aspects of US policy and officially condoned behavior has undercut the government's rhetoric about the importance of promoting democracy and civil liberties as an antidote to terrorism.[44]

The oratory rings particularly hollow when the inconvenient results of free and fair elections are ignored or undermined—as happened, for instance, when Hamas won in the Palestinian territories in 2006, or when Hezbollah won as part of the Resistance and Development Bloc in Lebanon in 2005. Similarly corrosive to fledgling or would-be democracies are elections that have been orchestrated as ends in themselves in the absence of broader political development—as we have seen at various times in Iraq, Afghanistan, Bosnia, Haiti, East Timor, and Cambodia.

None of which is to say that security, even in its traditional form, has ever been unrelated to development. Indeed, their relationship is always revealed in periods of conflict, when human and financial resources are diverted to defense, powerful military elites reduce civil liberties, and long-term investments in social and economic infrastructure are jeopardized, as are existing levels of infrastructural development. As the World Bank reported on the increasingly frequent phenomenon of civil war, "[It] usually has devastating consequences: it is development in reverse . . . generating or intensifying a significant part of the global poverty problem."[45]

Perhaps it is obvious that any kind of war is inimical to advances in human welfare, but lately some attention has been devoted to the linkages, especially those involving so-called conflict resources such as diamonds, timber, and fossil fuels.[46] Especially insofar as it has led to explosive economic growth in China and India, globalization has engendered a tremendous increase in the world's demand for and the prices of primary resources. This has been good news for some resource-extracting countries, but in insufficiently developed areas—for example, Democratic Republic of Congo, Nigeria, Angola, and Sierra Leone—it has led to conflict and instability.

Evidently, conflict hinders development and reflects its absence. Similarly, the likelihood of conflict decreases markedly with increases in per capita GDP.[47] At the same time, the prosperity and access to information and advanced technology spawned by globalization have functioned—by simplifying travel and communications, encouraging the growth of virtual communities, and expediting fundraising and recruitment—to ironically facilitate terrorism. So the overall situation as regards cause and effect is complex. It is not, however, entirely unintelligible.

Clearly, the incidence of poverty can be shown to encourage extremism. In Pakistan, for instance, the sad state of public education and high cost of private secular education have contributed to the popularity of Islamic madrassas, which are often financed from abroad. Some of these have been used to incubate religious extremists. Poverty also appears to correlate with the fragility and failure of a given state, which can then become a permissive environment for terrorist organizations, as we have seen in Afghanistan, Iraq, Somalia, and Sudan.

In any case, bombs and guns are unlikely to provide lasting solutions. But neither is the abolition of the military, although I would advocate a wholesale rethinking of defense policy and a reallocation of defense resources in support of other public policy objectives. At issue here are our definition of, goals and priorities for, and approach to security; how do we deal with certain types of issues, and with which tools? For the armed forces, there will always be important roles: protecting sovereignty, surveilling resources, enforcing and keeping peace, denying sanctuary, and providing the security necessary to permit emergency humanitarian relief and/or longer-term development assistance.[48] Unwelcome occupations (as with the United States in Iraq) and interventions in support of one side in a civil war (as with Afghanistan), however, would not qualify as legitimate security measures according to the new understanding of the role of defense in security I have proposed here. Rather, they represent a misallocation of resources that could have been deployed, for example, in support of UN missions or converted into budgetary savings and used for other purposes.

Over the longer term, it seems clear that if security is largely a function of development, then an emphasis on education will be required to foster an environment in which civil society and commerce can flourish and the capacity of human resources and public institutions can be augmented. These issues and others related to development will be the focus of the next phase of our investigation.

In the meantime, however, it must be emphasized that a broader conception of the nature of security is warranted. For inhabitants of the T- and E-worlds, and indeed for those in the A- and C-worlds as well, the creation of conditions conducive to lasting security will have more to do with development than with defense, although it is the latter that remains the A-world's preoccupation. For that reason and others, it is time to more meaningfully involve diplomacy in the quest for both security and development and to reconstruct our thinking about each for the era of globalization.

Notes

1. These objectives, it is worth noting, are almost identical to those promoted by economist Jeffrey Sachs, who—apparently as a result of the efforts of Irish rock star Bono—has become closely associated with the campaign. Sachs's prescription includes a fourth element: access to technology. See Sachs (2005), including Bono's introduction, and Sachs (2008). The former prophet of radical, laissez-faire shock therapy in postcommunist states has come a very long way.

2. As mentioned, the UN Development Programme has long championed human-centered development and was among the first governmental body to focus on human security, beginning in 1994. See http://hdr.undp.org/en.

3. These documents can be accessed at http://www.un.org/millenniumgoals and http://www.un.org/esa/sustdev/documents/agenda21/index.htm, respectively.

4. See UN (2004). To this list of threats might be added global warming and resource scarcity. Any one of these is significant enough to give rise to an even greater calamity: mass migration.

5. See Homer-Dixon and Blitt (1998), Homer-Dixon (1999).

6. There are encouraging signs that this may be changing, and that some analysts are adopting a comprehensive view of security. Chris Abbott (2008), for example, has prepared an assessment of the implications of climate change from a security perspective, and Kearns and Gude (2008) have authored a major report that identifies globalization and power diffusion, poverty and state failure, climate change and resource scarcity, political Islam, and socioeconomic vulnerability as the main drivers of insecurity in a changed strategic setting.

7. Significant contributions include works by John Ralston Saul, Robert Kaplan, Thomas Friedman, Paul Kennedy, Niall Ferguson, Michael Ignatieff, Samuel Huntington, Francis Fukuyama, Robert Cooper, Benjamin Barber, and others too numerous to mention.

8. See Project for the New American Century, http://www.newamericancentury.org.

9. Text of the 2002 National Security Strategy is available at http://www.globalsecurity.org/military/library/policy/national/nss-020920.htm.

10. A persuasive but largely overlooked interpretation of this twisted chapter of history, which considers the use of the politics of fear to restore authority to government, is found in a three-part 2005 BBC documentary by Adam Curtis, *The Power of Nightmares.* (2005). Curtis argues that both the neocons and the Islamic fundamentalists promoted fantasies that, when acted out, failed miserably.

11. Joseph McCarthy was a prominent senator and anticommunist who, in the early 1950s, accused several government institutions—including the State Department and the US Army—of employing communists. He headed the Senate's Permanent Subcommittee on Investigations. The aggressive tactics he pioneered are now often referred to as acts of McCarthyism, among them slander. For more on anticommunism in the United States during the Cold War, see Fried (1990).

12. An overview of options is offered in Posen and Ross (1996–1997).

13. Among the countless writings on what is wrong with the Long War, as it is also known, my personal favorite is Rogers (2007). See also Schur (2004), Gurtov (2006). For a diverse compendium of background materials on many aspects of the global war on terror, see Hoge and Rose (2005).

14. See, for example, testimony by Right Honorable Charles Clarke before the Home Affairs Committee on Tuesday, October 11, 2005, especially question 73, available at http://www.publications.parliament.uk/pa/cm200506/cmselect/cmhaff/515/5101101.htm.

15. There have been many effective ripostes to Huntington's thesis, which owes much of its characterization of the Islamic world to the work of Bernard Lewis. Huntington's description of a "civilizational clash"—a term he borrowed from Lewis (1990)—enjoyed renewed popularity in the wake of 9/11. Perhaps Huntington's most persuasive critic was Edward Said, who faulted his sweeping generalizations and "belligerent and dishearteningly ignorant" reading of history. See Said (2002: 71). An alternative but similarly powerful counterargument is found in Sen (2006). For a critique of what Lewis (1990) referred to as "Orientalism," see Alam (2003).

16. At a colloquium hosted by the CIA in 1991, I attended a presentation by an analyst from the US Defense Department warning of the immanent threat posed by North Korea's nuclear weapons and missile programs. Great hostility was showered upon my suggestion that a country whose people were starving and that could not even manufacture a decent farm tractor was unlikely to be much worth worrying about. Fifteen years later, it is still not entirely clear who was right.

17. US State Department (2002: 1).

18. Retrieved from the personal records of the author.

19. On working the domestic politics of fear, see Gardiner (2008).

20. See Chernus (2006: 4).

21. There are indications that this tide is turning. Since late 2007, US Defense Secretary Robert Gates has been calling publicly for increased spending on the "civilian instruments of national security," including diplomacy, development, governance, and strategic communications. See Gates (2007).

22. See C. Johnson (2008), who also makes the point that "military Keynesianism"—using domestic military spending to stimulate growth, generate jobs, and encourage innovation—amounts to voodoo economics and is bankrupting the United States.

23. In 2003, the mainstream media may have hit rock bottom in their failure to provide balanced, objective, and accurate coverage of major events. The froth and foam were enough to induce a feeling of nausea. Criticism was absent almost entirely.

24. While the balance could shift at any time, in the summer of 2008, monthly coalition casualties in Afghanistan began to exceed those incurred in Iraq, despite the far lower number of soldiers involved.

25. Chomsky (1988).

26. Over the longer term, this displacement of alternative international policy objectives can be seen as a more significant dimension of preemption than the narrower if more aggressive aspects emphasized in the National Security Strategy.

27. According to data derived from the Stockholm International Peace Research Institute and the OECD databases, the amount of official development assistance from twenty-one rich countries was a fraction of the amount spent on the military in 2003. In Canada, it was one-fifth. In the United States, it was about one–twenty-fifth. See Global Policy Forum, http://www.globalpolicy.org/socecon/develop/oda/tables/milvsaid.htm. The opportunity costs have also been felt in a number of Western countries, especially in conjunction with the serious erosion of civil liberties and the rule of law. In the United States, for example, it has been calculated that "with just the amount of the Iraq War budget for 2007, US$138 billion, the government could instead have provided Medicaid-level health insurance for all 45 million Americans who are uninsured. . . . or added 30,000 elementary- and secondary-school teachers and built 400 schools." See Pollin and Garrett-Peltier (2008).

28. Terrorism's toll pales in comparison to more common killers like cancer, heart disease, car accidents, etc. The Memorial Institute for the Prevention of Terrorism's (MIPT) Terrorism Knowledge Base cites 35,877 terrorism-related fatalities between January 1, 2000, and February 13, 2007; see http://www.terrorisminfo.mipt.org/incidentcalendar.asp. By contrast, cancer alone killed 67,423 people in Canada, with a population of 30 million, in 2003. See Statistics Canada (2006).

29. On this continuing debate, see Homer-Dixon (2006a).

30. See Glasser (2005), the Memorial Institute for the Prevention of Terrorism Terrorism Knowledge Base, available at http://www.terrorisminfo.mipt.org/incidentcalendar.asp, and the declassified key judgments of the 2006 National Intelligence Estimate, available at http://www.dni.gov/press_releases/Declassified_NIE_Key_Judgments.pdf.

31. See Johns Hopkins Bloomberg School of Public Health (2006). Estimates of casualties in the Iraq War vary greatly according to who is counting and what is being counted. On October 11, 2005, the Johns Hopkins Bloomberg School of Public Health released a study finding that almost 655,000 more Iraqis had died during the war than would have been expected under prewar conditions. More conservative estimates of civilian deaths for that period are between 56,122 and 61,840. See Iraq Body Count (2007). Coalition deaths prior to 2008 exceeded 4,000, and, though the rate has been reduced since, the numbers continue to mount. See Iraq Coalition Casualty Count, http://icasualties.org/oif/default.aspx.

32. Among many critiques, see especially Bacevich (2008) and Mayer (2008).

33. See, for example, Gregory and Wilkinson (2005).

34. The declassified 2006 US *National Intelligence Estimate* noted, for example, that the Iraq war has become a "cause celebre for jihadists."Available at http://www.dni.gov/press_releases/Declassified_NIE_Key_Judgments.pdf.

35. The term *three block war* was coined by US General Charles Krulak and refers to three levels of engagement: aid and assistance, stabilization efforts, and, last, high-intensity battle. This formulation is closely associated with the so-called three Ds of Canadian international policy (development, diplomacy, defense). See National De-

fence Canada (2006), Foreign Affairs and International Trade Canada (2003). The RMA is a theory originating in the United States and was very popular with the Bush administration. Adherents suggest that changes in technology and organization have transformed the ways in which wars can and should be fought. See Rumsfeld (2002). Widely hyped in its heyday, the term is falling into disrepute.

36. For a critique of the RMA as deficient in its recognition of the human factors of warfare, see McMaster (2008).

37. See Allison (2006).

38. Many interesting articles and blog discussions on counterinsurgency may be found in the *Small Wars Journal*; see www.smallwarsjournal.com. For practical, experience-based advice on the role of diplomacy, see especially postings by Amend (2008) and Green (2007).

39. Lind et al. (1989), Lind (2004), Hammes (1994).

40. See US Army Field Manual 3-24, *Counterinsurgency,* available at http://usacac.army.mil/cac/repository/materials/coin-fm3-24.pdf, and also "The Paradoxes of Counterinsurgency," *New York Times,* October 5, 2006. For an assessment of these themes in relation to the theories of Karl von Clausewitz, see van Creveld (1991) and the very useful interpretive update, with particular reference to militant Islam, by Corn (2006). More sweeping yet are Philip Bobbitt's historical analyses of military strategy, politics, and the law in *The Shield of Achilles* (2002) and *Terror and Consent: Wars for the Twenty-First Century* (2008), wherein Bobbitt argues that the nation-state is being superseded by the market-state and proposes counterterrorism strategies. In each of these works, the need to situate military action within a political and strategic framework is considered germane. In this respect, among others, the war on terror fails utterly. See US Army Field Manual 3-07, *Stability Operations,* available at http://usacac.army.mil/CAC2/Repository/FM307/FM3-07.pdf. This document, released October 6, 2008, elevates stability operations (namely military support for public safety, economic development, and governance) to the same level as conventional offensive and defensive operations; somewhat remarkably, then, it is premised on an appreciation of soft power. It still begs the question, however, as to whether the military is the most suitable instrument for such operations. See, for example, Gates (2008).

41. See R. Smith (2005).

42. The sad case of Haiti provides a different angle for consideration: there, military intervention by a variety of outside forces, followed sometimes by internationally supervised elections, has not proven a successful substitute for development.

43. Just as the relationship between war and politics has attracted renewed attention, so too has the parallel relationship between diplomacy and counterinsurgency, about which there will be more in Chapter 12.

44. On these points, see Caruthers and Ottaway (2006).

45. World Bank (2003: ix).

46. On the role diamonds play in conflict in Angola, see Fowler (2000). His "Report of the Panel of Experts on Violations of Security Council Sanctions Against UNITA" is considered a landmark.

47. Humphreys (2003: 2).

48. It is impossible to generalize about the relationship—including whether or not there should be one—between formal military establishments (or private security contractors) and aid workers (or diplomats). Some humanitarian relief agencies have complained that armed protection impugns their neutrality, while some diplomats resent that they are not free to mix with the population. The debate continues.

6 Development Revisited: No Justice, No Peace

I have argued that to address the fundamental drivers of insecurity, decisionmakers must break the habit of attempting to contain or vanquish adversaries and instead move toward engaging them while acting on the most pressing needs of humanity. They must reduce the use of armed force in favor of diplomatic approaches to achieve economic and political objectives, which will entail stowing the Cold War baggage, substituting dialogue for battle, and embracing human-centered, equitable, and sustainable development as the long-term basis for the new security.

A Better Way?

It is powerfully ironic that even as globalization drives insecurity, it provides the knowledge and tools required to address the challenges of broad-based development. To date, however, this potential has gone largely unrealized because, as illustrated in Chapter 5, many in the West remain constrained by outdated habits of thinking.

How then to break free from the debilitatingly simplistic mindset of us versus them, whereby global threats are perceived and responses are militarized? At the highest level of analysis, it will have to start with the relocation of development from the margins to the mainstream of international policy. Development must be both made a top priority and understood in relation to security.

During the Cold War, development tended to be situated mainly in an ethical and humanitarian context; it was seen by opinion-shapers and decisionmakers—especially those of the A-world—as secondary to security, especially with respect to the defense of sovereignty and territorial integrity. In the era of globalization, the number of inputs into the security calculus has multiplied; among them are elements related to the health, welfare, and prosperity of whole populations. Moreover, the very meaning of the word *territory* has morphed; it has come to include the realms of the intellectual and the virtual at least as much as those of the geographical and political.

In the era of globalization, development can no longer be seen as some minor candidate for inclusion on a second-string wish list. Instead, it has become a vital strategic imperative in the quest for global security. It is becoming increasingly difficult to avoid the conclusion that "underdevelopment is a threat and therefore a security issue."[1] The next step—however giant—is to give force and meaning to that conviction.

Days of Future Past

Millennia ago, Plutarch observed that "an imbalance between rich and poor is the oldest and most fatal ailment of all republics." And so it remains.

Development is an elusive concept: it means different things to different people in different settings, institutional and otherwise. In our discussion of world order models as built on the global political economy, I argued that there is much to be learned from the dependency theorists of the 1960s and 1970s. I would make the same case for development, which dependency theorists conceived of as very broadly defined. Inspired by the likes of Paulo Freire and Frantz Fanon, genuine development was understood to affect quality of life and was seen as a process at least as much as a condition.[2] This expansive conception could not be measured merely quantitatively, via the usual economic indicators—employment rates; GDP growth; financial, trade, and investment performance—of standards of living. Rather, demonstrable progress toward social justice and civic progress was seen as critical—as the UN Development Programme's Human Development Index, for instance, and the Millennium Development Goals illustrate today—as was a liberating and transformational ethic that would suffuse the entire enterprise.[3] Aid in the form of disaster relief or humanitarian assistance might from time to time be required and international cooperation on mutually beneficial terms would be welcomed, but development per se was seen as primarily a matter of comprehensive and long-term domestic concern. Building essential infrastructure and satisfying the basic needs of the population were necessary, but so too was a socioethical means of advancing the human prospect, both individually and communally. People were at the center of this vision. They were at once the agents and the beneficiaries of their own development, articulating and adjusting their goals and values for and among themselves rather than having them imported or imposed by outsiders.

What else might be said of this vision of development? It had become clear that the dominant development paradigm, based on notions of modernization and trickle-down economics, was not going to deliver as advertised—if at all. Trade and foreign investment were not ruled out as part of the new equation, but the focus was on national or regional markets and domestic capital formation. To qualify as genuine, development would have to do more than enrich local elites and foreign corporate interests. At the national level, there would have to be progress toward poverty alleviation, including an equitable redistribution of opportunity, wealth, and resources; a democratic dissemination of power, involving a mode of popular sovereignty that would go well beyond elections to include the establishment of responsible and accountable as well as representative institutions (this is widely referred to today as "good governance"); and respect for basic human rights and freedoms.

Rather than just a restatement of motherhood issues or an endorsement of someone else's ideas, this was an inclusive and progressive articulation of development, one that reflected the realities of persistent poverty, social marginalization, economic exploitation, and political exclusion. It was founded on the conviction that the primary source of development-related thought and action must be indigenous and that progress could never proceed from "trying to be like" others, however successful they were.[4]

The concept of development constructed by members of the dependency school was not only relevant in its day but, in my view, helps explain the widening gap between the A- and the T- and E-worlds today. Caused by globalization, that chasm is the source of a good deal of contemporary insecurity. Addressing that insecurity effectively and eschewing the militarization of international policy in favor of equitable, sustainable, human-centered development will require a large-scale revision of priorities and a significant reallocation of resources, not by imposing "justice" on the uncooperative but by pursuing a more cooperative, less violent, and fairer world order. Such a goal could serve to unite people from all ethnic groups, cultures, and religions behind a shared set of objectives.

A Reality-Based Strategy . . .

Dreamy idealism this is not. It is based on an analysis of the world we live in, a world transformed by globalization and facing a multiplicity of challenges. Globalization has been debilitating for many of those in the T- and E-worlds. During the Cold War, the then third world had representation (in the forms of the Non-Aligned Movement, G-77, the UN Conference on Trade and Development or UNCTAD, and the South Commission) for its cause, the New International Economic Order. Little of that remains in evidence.

Though it has been considerable, absolute poverty reduction does not mean much if inequality and inequity are left festering like open sores, giving rise to resentment and hence sympathy if not subscription to extremist causes. Such extremism may or may not in itself threaten the world order, but terrorism is much more likely to take root in an environment of grinding hardship, oppressive social relations, weak institutions, and political repression. Fragile or failed states with little or no capacity to provide public security—for example, Somalia, Afghanistan, Sudan, and Iraq—serve as magnets for extremists of every stripe.[5] To address these issues, donor countries will not only have to coordinate their assistance efforts but take the long view toward building state capacity, without which development and security will remain unrealized.

Foremost among the objectives here will be the construction of effective institutions for governance: broad-based deliberative and decisionmaking bodies; a public sector characterized by competence and probity rather than corruption; an independent judiciary dedicated to the rule of law; and a standard of public services, personal safety, and physical security sufficient to permit economic and social progress and guaranteed by state regulation of access to the means of violence. Generous international financial assistance—funded with savings in defense expenditures and directed especially toward education, health, and the building of public institutions—will have to be accompanied by ample reserves of patience and good faith.[6]

What does not work—and indeed proves perniciously counterproductive—are ballot-and-bolt interventions on the part of the so-called international community. The 1990s were littered with such ventures—as in Cambodia, Haiti, and East Timor—that kept UN officials busy, flooded small economies with foreign currency, disgorged fleets of SUVs, and produced a bonanza for high-priced consultants and international NGOs. Shipping companies, the vendors of duty-free goods, and the proprietors of luxury hotel chains are among the main beneficiaries when the representatives of global power and wealth, to whom the term *international community* is euphemistically applied, pile in and do their business—be it electoral assistance, peacebuilding, or disaster relief. Ironically, it is the very governments who are supposed to benefit from the "foreign assistance" that often end up as the biggest losers. State-run services such as education and health care can be gutted as skilled personnel get lured away by the higher salaries and better working conditions offered by aid agencies, private contractors, and international NGOs. This debilitating side effect of aid—nation unbuilding—is frequently overlooked.

And when they depart? In their wake, they leave graft, inflation, corrosive social relations, crime and prostitution, the spread of globalized values, and the denationalization of local elites.[7] Whether it is a photo-op of rock stars touring an Ethiopian famine camp or a newsreel of Western immigration officials pencil-pushing in air-conditioned comfort in the midst of squalid refugee camps, there is something fundamentally wrong with this picture of international aid—which I have heard described in terms ranging from "unhelpful" to "obscene." The patterns it reveals, moreover, are deeply ingrained. To see how they are perpetuated, look no further than Afghanistan under the influence of the NATO countries and the International Security Assistance Force. With its profusion of new bars, clubs, restaurants, and escort services, Kabul is showing every sign of becoming another Saigon. Former British diplomat and soldier Rory Stewart, who walked across Afghanistan three months after the defeat of the Taliban in 2003, offers some telling insights on all of this. Comparing contemporary expatriate "state builders" in Afghanistan to the frequently maligned yet often respectable performance of district officers in the colonial era, he remarks:

> Most . . . knew next to nothing about the villages where 90% of the Afghan villagers lived. They came from postmodern, secular, globalized states with liberal traditions in law and government. It was natural for them to initiate projects on urban design, women's rights and fibre-optic cable networks; to talk about transparent, clean and accountable processes, tolerance and civil society; and to speak of a people "who desire peace at any cost" and understand the need for a centralized, multi-ethnic government. . . . But what did they understand of the thought processes of Seyyed Kerbalahi's wife, who had not moved five kilometres from her home in forty years? Or Dr. Habibullah, the vet, who carried an automatic weapon in the way they carried their briefcases? . . . Postconflict experts have got the prestige without the effort or stigma of imperialism. . . . Their policy fails but no one notices. . . . Their very uselessness benefits them.[8]

The 1990s and the first decade of the postmillennium have brought unprecedented prosperity to the A-world, which had the means to improve its record and to accomplish what is necessary in the T- and E-worlds. Yet it failed to summon the will. Foreign aid has in the twenty-first century become almost passé, and its relative place in development has been shrinking. In many countries, official development assistance inflows have been eclipsed by the value of remittances received from abroad and by private sector philanthropy. Among the problems with this trend is that in mid-2009, many foreign workers—be they Mexicans in the United States or Filipinos, Bangladeshis, or Sri Lankans in the Gulf states—are losing their jobs. Remittances are drying up and workers returning home, where they may place additional strains on already limited public services. Meanwhile, budgets for both ODA and corporate charity are typically among the first to be cut, and these flows, too, are certain to diminish. The dependency theorists warned of an overdependence on outside sources of finance, either public or private. The net effect of the across-the-board reductions, at least in the short term, will be to set development prospects back further.

What happens, then, in the absence of a commitment to long-term, human-centered development? During the Cold War, small states were propped up and large states issued threats. Today, with the sometime exceptions of the United States and Russia (to return to our discussion of Cold War carryovers), most large states are concerned mainly, although by no means exclusively, with using peaceful means to advance their interests. It is now smaller states that are the main source of violent extremism.

In the era of globalization, weaker states can become so dysfunctional that they become sources of insecurity for their own populations, and hence for ours as well. It is estimated that 14 percent of the world's population and 33 percent of its poor now live in fragile or failed states; these, along with a number of particularly fertile threat incubators located mainly in the Middle East and Central Asia, should become the immediate focus of A-world development-policy planning and activity.[9] However, because globalization has rendered security indivisible from development, it is inevitable that in the not-too-distant future, many in the T- and E-worlds will need to be similarly engaged. .

. . . Must Scrutinize Results

The staunchest defenders of globalization tend also to be the most determined detractors of the structuralist critique in international political economy and, especially, of the dependency school discussed previously. The globalizers are typically quick to dismiss complex interpretations of insecurity. Instead, we hear a twisted litany to the effect that "they hate our freedom" and "detest what we stand for." Accordingly, "they" have had to be killed, captured, or otherwise "brought to justice"—at Guantánamo Bay, Abu Ghraib, the Bagram air base outside Kabul, or any number of other destinations of "extraordinary rendition."

When it comes to development, the indicators adduced by those subscribing to this viewpoint are often statistical or based on an interpretation of quantifiable trends. In aggregate terms, however, the reliance upon numbers to demonstrate development gains leads altogether too easily, I believe, to the conclusion that significant strides are being made.

Let's look at some of these indicators of global development progress:

- The proportion of the world's population subsisting in absolute poverty—living on less than US$1 a day—has declined by one-half over the past twenty years, from 40 to 21 percent; in absolute terms, the number of people living in poverty fell from 1.5 billion to 1.1 billion.[10]
- Life expectancy has doubled; for example, between World War II and 2001, it rose from 30 to 63 years in South Asia, from 40 to 70 in Latin America, from 30 to 47 in sub-Saharan Africa, and from 56 to 78 in the industrialized world.[11]
- The percentage of people living in countries where food supplies per capita are under the recommended 2,200 calories per day fell from 56 in the mid-1960s to 10 by the 1990s.[12]
- Infant mortality has decreased.
- The incidence of chronic malnutrition has been reduced, and access to clean water has increased.
- Many types of disease have been controlled or eradicated.
- Literacy rates are increasing, especially for women.
- Fewer children are in the workforce or the army and more are in school.

Impressed? The problem is that these kinds of facts and figures can be deceptive. They mask the fact that even as levels of absolute poverty recede in some areas, the relative distance between incomes and living standards is increasing both within and among countries. The numbers also ignore the social content of growth—or the lack thereof—which is key. I have tried to avoid an undue reliance on statistics because they can be used to support almost any point of view.

Consider, in contrast, this material, based on the period from 1990 to 2004:[13]

- The number of people living in extreme poverty has increased by 100 million people.
- Average per capita incomes have declined in at least 54 of 191 countries.
- Every year, 11 million children die of preventable diseases, and over half a million women die during pregnancy or childbirth.
- In Latin America, the income of the wealthiest 20 percent of households is thirty times greater than that of the poorest 20 percent.
- In sub-Saharan Africa, where poverty and malnutrition are increasing, life expectancy has declined from 50 to 46; a comparable decline has occurred in Russia.[14]
- In sub-Saharan Africa, one in ten children die before reaching age five, compared to one in 100 in the developed world.
- Fifty percent of the world's children are living in poverty, while 3 billion people are living on under US$2 a day.[15]
- The world's 500 richest people have a combined income of over US$100 billion, which exceeds the combined income of the world's poorest 400 to 500 million people.[16]

Although these numbers don't directly contradict those presented in the first dataset, they certainly leave a different impression. Again, carefully chosen statistics can be used to "prove" almost anything. Like so much else in life, where you stand depends in large part on where you sit.

In examining the aggregate global figures, we can see that much of the total progress has occurred in South and East Asia—especially in China, India, and the "baby tigers" of Southeast Asia, where the numbers have been impressive. With the notable exceptions of Pakistan and Sri Lanka, these are not the sources of today's global instability. However, most of the world's poor still live in Asia, and the economic and political, cultural and religious, ethnic and linguistic divides within many Asian countries continue to pose great challenges that may yet develop into political crises and jeopardize those gains that have been made.

Examples? Xingjian, the largest province in China, is the homeland of the Uighur people. A group of Uighur Muslims have for years been contesting Chinese control of the province. In 2001, China declared the group to be terrorists. Similarly, on the Indian-controlled side of the disputed territory of

Kashmir, secessionist campaigns and numerous acts of terrorism have been countered with harsh police and military repression since Kashmir's incorporation into India following the British withdrawal in 1947. Likewise, in the tiny northeast Indian state of Assam, numerous organizations are agitating for independence. The most prominent is the United Liberation Front of Assam, which as of the late 1990s has accelerated its terrorist activity in the region. In Ache, Indonesia, an uneasy accommodation is now in place after years of violent (if episodic) agitation for independence organized by the Free Ache Movement. Meanwhile, in the Pattani region of southern Thailand, a nominally Islamist insurgency has created a climate of violence and instability that has transformed social relations in three southern provinces.[17] These conflicts are real but likely to remain obscure—unless and until the violence spreads. Al-Qaida, after all, began as a small faction of the Afghan resistance against the Soviet occupation.

The economic and social statistics for North Africa, the Middle East, and West Asia tell a different story yet again—and these are the very regions that have been exposed to Western military and political intervention since the end of the Cold War. Here the presence of Western interests in countries characterized by low levels of political, economic, and social development has produced calamitous results, expressed in particular as religious extremism.

The same intersection of underdevelopment with foreign economic and/or political interest is not found in Africa, where the development indices are lowest and where intervention has been less frequent, smaller in scale (as with the French and British incursions into West Africa), and often multilateral (such as has occurred in Somalia, Sudan, and Angola). In Africa, however, uneven development, compounded by epidemic mismanagement and corruption, has exacerbated ethnic and tribal as well as religious differences; Kenya and Nigeria serve as especially potent examples.

What, then, might be said of the actual global record? According to one usually reliable source, the international community committed in 2005 to increasing development assistance expenditures to US$130 billion by 2010.[18] Instead, aid flows actually declined 13 percent from 2005 to 2007 to a total of about US$104 billion, or about 28 percent of GDP. The prospect of improved access to OECD markets evaporated with the collapse of WTO negotiations in Doha, Qatar, in 2008. A total of 1.4 billion people in the developing world were living in extreme poverty in 2005; 20 percent of children under age five are underweight, and their mortality rate is 14 times that of children in the developed world. Again, numbers can be used to show just about anything, but even so, this catalog does not provide grounds for celebration.

I have advanced the case that it is not who we are in the A-world that has so angered much of the C-, T-, and E-worlds, but what we do—and that anger is only reinforced by the spread of negative perceptions about what we have and how we got it. It is also fed by globalization's polarizing tendencies, which, coupled with the relentless diffusion of information and communications technologies and their often culturally offensive content, facilitate its translation into acts of violence.[19]

Underdevelopment generates a set of insecure conditions that are easily manipulated by extremists to advance their own ends. It follows that while a comprehensive program of development cooperation should start with a focus on growth and poverty reduction, it should also be designed to go well beyond these objectives over time.[20]

The Role of Religion . . .

Given the routine attribution of religious motivation to violent acts, consideration of the role of religion in the relationship between security and development, as well as of its function in providing some sense of certainty and order in a rapidly changing world, is inescapable. While evangelical Christianity (implicated deeply in the persistence of unconditional support for Israel, particularly in the United States), Hindu extremism (leading to attacks on the mosque at Ayodhya and elsewhere), and extreme Orthodox Judaism (leading to support for partition and settlement in the occupied territories) would, among other examples, all merit mention, for reasons of its sheer preponderance it is Islamism that is most relevant to this inquiry.[21] Though it will be impossible to pursue in any depth the many complicated issues involved, I hope that a political analysis will produce some helpful insights.

The debate over the political and security issues surrounding the extreme expression of Islamism, or Islamic fundamentalism, speaks to a set of circumstances whose antecedents long precede the events of 9/11.[22] Since at least the 1970s, there has been a growing sense in the Muslim world that Islam is under sustained attack from the West—not just physically, in the form of what is interpreted as consistent US-backed Israeli aggression, but also culturally and intellectually, in the form of what is seen as a new crusade. Extremist movements have provided collective voice and outlets for active resistance to those who feel helpless and unheeded.

To understand insurgency it is sometimes necessary to think like an insurgent. Yet most of what has been written about the Islamist threat is predicated upon the idea of "us" responding to "them." What if that were reversed? How might "they" be thinking about "us"? From the perspective of a Muslim encountering the West—not in history or literature but through experience and over the course of a lifetime—what kind of picture might emerge?

For starters, Europeans or North Americans might be remembered as imperialists who as often as not failed to deliver on promises of postcolonial independence. Next, they'll be identified by their thirst for oil, whereby they back corrupt and unrepresentative but pro-Western regimes that benefit from the status quo and profit from exploitive economic relations. Their thirst is unquenched, their support for the status quo is unremitting, and the benefits flowing from the resource they exploit remains quite unknown to many of those toiling on the land above it.

Long before the so-called liberation of Kuwait or the occupation of Iraq, there were many other illustrations of Western self-interest. In Afghanistan, the mujahedin were created and then cut loose when their purpose had been served. The Camp David Accords were negotiated and then allowed to collapse. Various road maps to Middle East peace have materialized and disintegrated. Highly visible military bases have been established, and occasionally closed all over the Middle East and Central Asia. A blind eye has been turned to Russia's vicious suppression of Chechnyan rebels and Israel's invasions of Lebanon and, in early 2009, Gaza. Electoral victories by Hamas in Palestine, Hezbollah in Lebanon, and, in 1991, the FIS in Algeria was ignored or subverted. Every day there are stories in the media about the plight of the Palestinians, arbitrary restrictions on the movement of people and goods, outrages associated with the construction of the so-called security barrier in the Israeli-occupied territories, political assassinations, retaliatory raids, dead schoolchildren, closed borders, bombed UN compounds—the list goes on.

Set in this context, the wounds of twentieth-century history open directly into the running sore of the postmillennium in a causal chain of pain that looks something like this: imperialism = modernization = Westernization = globalization = submission, humiliation, betrayal, and underdevelopment. That is an inflammatory equation, and if it does not add up to justifiable extremism, it might at least make the miscalculation more explicable. It has also occurred to me that Islamism is in many respects demand driven. It appears to have filled the political space left by the disappearance of secular socialism, militant Marxism, and pan-Arab nationalism. Islamist parties have stepped into the void created by corrupt and unrepresentative governments—one marked by the absence of public services and civil-societal alternatives.

One of the defining features of contemporary Islamism—which I see more as a symptom than a cause of insecurity—is a strong desire for domestic opportunity and empowerment, international respect, and a more audible voice and equitable place in the world order. Yet Islamism represents something of a special case—one in which the religious dimension has, for various reasons, been overemphasized by all sides.[23] The anger and resentment so often vented through violence may in fact be due less to ascendant religious fervor than to the absence of options between perceived Western decadence and oppression on the one hand and the hardships associated with rule by corrupt, unrepresentative local governments on the other. Faced with those choices, rebellion begins to appear a rational option.

In this context, it is important to stress that most terrorists (including suicide bombers), while likely angry and looking for vengeance, are neither insane nor even seriously unstable.[24] It is worth recalling as well that it was not any group affiliated with Islam but instead the Tamil Tigers of Sri Lanka who have popularized suicide bombings. People volunteer and train for this sacrifice. Prospective suicide bombers may be attracted to the idea of martyrdom, the desire to receive compensation for their families, or both. But most reach the decision to act as they do through rational means. The upside? If rational, suicide bombing may be susceptible to a policy fix.

How to begin a discussion about the political dynamics of this phenomenon? I would begin by reiterating that it is not necessary to be victimized personally in order to feel the pain of others who are. In the not-too-distant past, news traveled slowly, access to information was limited, and cultures were less inclined to mix. Now, news travels instantly, access is becoming universal, and migration and immigration are widespread. Before the explosive growth and diffusion of information and communications technologies, it was simply not possible to identify personally with events taking place on the other side of the planet; there was no way to know what may have been occurring. Today, the acquisition of knowledge about what happens elsewhere is virtually inevitable, affecting almost everyone almost everywhere. This development has given rise to something previously unimaginable: near-simultaneous mass experience, however vicarious.

Of many examples, especially notable is the widespread reaction to the publication of a caricature of Muhammad in a Danish newspaper (see Chapter 10). In August 1998, television news covered a US cruise missile attack, authorized by President Clinton, on a factory making infant formula in Khartoum. The US military claimed the facility had been used to manufacture nerve gas for a terrorist group suspected of bombing the US embassies in Tanzania and Kenya, but later investigation raised serious doubts about that claim. Negative reaction was both strong and worldwide. The stunning impact of the televised "shock-and-awe" bombing of Baghdad and the online dissemination of graphic images from Abu Ghraib and Guantánamo Bay are just two more examples among many.

This kind of shared experience gives rise to the development of a potent new phenomenon: *global empathy.* Fueled by the Internet, cell-phone technology, and satellite television, global empathy, I believe, is among the more significant, if less obvious or appreciated, by-products of globalization. In the context of Islamism, global empathy is yet another driver of insecurity.

Let me try to put this metaphorically. In the constant flux of globalization, many in the T- and E-worlds feel as if they have been swept overboard to find themselves adrift in a hostile and dangerous sea. For people who feel as though they are drowning—under waves of poverty, government oppression, persecution and injustice both real and perceived, and despair—a common condition in the T- and E-worlds—the natural reaction is to reach out and grab anything that floats by. For many Muslims, Arabs, and members of related diaspora communities around the world, that floating object often takes the form of radical Islam—especially its most extreme iterations: Wahhabism, Salafism, and others based on fundamentalist interpretations of the Quran. From the preachings of the fiery local imam to the jihadi websites streaming videos and selling DVDs of suicide bombings or posting graphic images of abuses committed against Muslims—the bombing of a wedding party, a dead child, a door being kicked in, a community leveled—the pressure to grab on to *something* with a modicum of explanatory power is intense.

It stands to reason that those who have felt themselves rescued are grateful to their saviors—like survivors hauled into a lifeboat. If that gratitude is accompanied by camaraderie with other survivors and a sense of being a part of something larger, so much the better from the point of view of those interested in attracting recruits to their cause. Thus do cells mutate and movements grow. But if this is an even partly accurate portrayal of the radicalization process that is evident in so many parts of the world, then the question must be asked: what might be done to provide alternative flotation?

. . . Requires Attention

The acquisition of state power by a majority of moderate Islamists could do much to weaken the radicals, but as the road to representative government is blocked in many places, violent detours are understandable.[25] To choose rather than to accept, to oppose rather than to support, is to empower oneself. Resistance to Western influence and interests seems to arise from the reading of Islam as political narrative and inspirational myth. This combination has helped turn Islam into Islamism, and it has proven very effective in providing meaning, mobilizing opinion, and initiating action. For many poor and disaffected Muslims today, Western policies appear to amount to little more than excuses to torture Arab prisoners. Joining Al-Qaida can seem an attractive response to domestic oppression and international subjugation.

The prevalence of under- and unemployment, especially among the huge numbers of educated youth, ensures there is even more time to dwell on insults and feelings of degradation and helplessness. Bombarded by the aforementioned relentless procession of inflammatory images, the jobless may make for particularly willing conscripts.

Consider the case of Afghanistan in 2003 and 2004, when Taliban members and those suspected of membership were rounded up by the Northern Alliance (composed of warlords, drug traffickers, and the otherwise disaffected) and turned over, in exchange for bounty payments, to the invaders. Those who evaded capture might well have concluded that they had little to lose by joining the anti-NATO resistance, at least relative to the risk of being picked up off the street and sent to a black site, maybe one on the other side of the planet, for "interrogation." Even among the better-off, the success and notoriety of Al-Qaida have commanded admiration along with a sense of pride and belonging.[26] In this regard, Al-Qaida has in some circles been conflated with an Islamic renaissance and credited with the restoration of Muslim respectability.

For those dealing with the hard core of violent militants, there will always be a place for counterterrorism and the application of conventional force in a selective, strategic manner. Armed intervention—never a preferred option—can be used to initiate change, but if plans are not in place for an immediate economic and political follow-up, then Iraq War–style calamity is likely to ensue.[27]

To improve results significantly, we must place a renewed emphasis in the short term upon intelligence and patient police work. Terrorism is a crime, and dignifying criminals by referring to them as enemies in a war is mistaken.[28] In the longer term, addressing the motivation for and underlying conditions of terrorism will be essential.[29] It may involve a comprehensive reconsideration of Western policies toward the Muslim world.[30] Equally if not more important, reversing the violent backlash against Western countries will require some real changes on their part—not just in policy but in behavior. Richard Farson argues convincingly for the need to transcend cultural boundaries, demonstrate more sensitivity and respect, show an openness to ideas other than our own, and find a way to communicate in noninflammatory terms—avoiding, say, "Islamo-fascist."[31]

Serious, sustained, bidirectional engagement with Muslims as individuals and with the Islamic community as a whole would be an essential first step not just in defusing anger and mistrust but also in dislodging some of the longstanding obstacles to Middle East peace. Were that to occur, as eventually it must, the world's chances of breaking free from the debilitating constraints imposed by the Cold War would increase markedly.

Where might such a critical path lead? To a place very far from where we find ourselves today, where a host of possibilities might come into view—including an enlarged program of long-term, targeted development assistance and the acceptance of a form of Islamism that reflects the beliefs of the majority in the Middle East—one critical of the West but nonviolent in nature. As Michael Hirsh, a senior editor at *Newsweek,* has remarked: "The best alternative may be some kind of hybrid . . . a moderately religious democracy . . . conceived with a nuanced federalism . . . [that] uses its distinctly Islamic character, and concomitant anti-Americanism and anti-Westernism, as ideological glue."[32] An emphasis on improved socioeconomic conditions and political prospects in the Arab and Islamic quarters of the T- and E-worlds, especially for young people, could produce dramatic improvements in international security. These would only be compounded if combined with the more effective integration of a new generation of Muslims into the A- and C-worlds and greater progress toward lessening, among other grievances, Israeli-Palestinian differences.

In sum, if the immediate threat of Islamic and other forms of religious extremism is to be blunted, then it is imperative that the West replace strong-arm tactics with more sophisticated ones.[33] Religious fundamentalism in general and Islamism in particular have provided the alienated with a locus of resistance, and a sense of both connectedness and renewed dignity in a hostile and alienating world. The popularity of the jihadi archetype, disseminated ever more widely over television and the Internet, has given rise to a virtual community of holy warriors who are repulsed by what they perceive as the moral decay of the West and the influence of that decadence in their home countries.[34] In overcoming such perceptions, the widespread creation of compelling, credible options for those with economic aspirations—the local entrepreneur, the small-businessperson, the farmer who produces a surplus for market—could make a world of difference. In this regard, providing incentives to offer microcredit, technology transfer, and direct foreign investment on terms favorable to all parties will be key. So, too, will a degree of cultural congruity and compatibility with local belief systems via innovative forms of partnership among international organizations, the private sector, NGOs, and recipient and donor governments.[35]

Only when the marginalized are offered tangible reasons for developing an alternative sense of purpose that could lead to inclusion in a vibrant middle class will the goal of nation building seem credible. Diplomacy can prepare the ground and development assistance can fertilize it. But in this globalized setting, it will be the employment-generating, income-distributing, profit-spinning private sector that will, over the long haul, have to take root and grow.

We cannot overemphasize that such progress must be achieved on terms favorable to and supported by those directly involved. Simply trying to convince or compel the rest of the world to do what it is told or to act like us will never produce the desired outcomes. Existing Western policies, often self-serving and antithetical to cultural sensitivity, have provided a focal point around which their opponents have found it all too easy to organize. They have thus boosted the power and popularity of both regimes and nonstate actors bent on violent retribution against, and deepening the isolation of, the West.

So the clock is ticking. Under attack are not just Western interests, power, and influence but also Western political will. Indeed, significant damage has already been wrought in that respect. If our resolve is to be restored, we will need something more morally defensible and inspiring than the global war on terror to rally around. This is where diplomacy, with its dedication to effective political and cross-cultural communication, and development, namely as an antidote to insecurity, come to the fore.

What of Al-Qaida?

None of my argument is intended to suggest that the symptoms of deeply rooted problems, especially those involving violent extremism, do not require treatment along with the causes. Clearly, there are some whose antipathy toward Western countries is so entrenched and their alienation so profound that no amount of dialogue is going to convince them to make nice. Occupation and the use of armed force, however, tend to exacerbate the very difficulties they are supposed to address, and hence they are not among the preferred countermeasures.[36] Granting that the persons who kill indiscriminately and foment hatred must indeed be brought to justice, I propose rejecting the military option in favor of a strategy of nonviolent neutralization and radical disempowerment, combined with measures to increase society's resilience to terrorist attack.[37]

Since its dispersion post-9/11, Al-Qaida has by all accounts become the embodiment of an idea more than an organization—a loosely federated network of autonomous cells that together represent the incarnation of extreme Islamism.[38] Highly dependent upon the sophisticated use of technology and the new media, Al-Qaida today is less effective as a revolutionary structure than it is as a brand; the leadership—now effectively brand managers—has adapted well to the conditions of globalization. In other words, Al-Qaida is now beating the West at one of the West's best games—marketing and public relations.[39] It is time to tarnish the Al-Qaida brand, instead of merely "killing or capturing," to use the parlance of the Bush administration, its membership.

Al-Qaida has proven adept at reinventing itself; its franchises and affiliates have benefited. Al-Qaida's reliance upon wireless and Internet-based media may more than compensate for the post-9/11 disruption of its integrated command structure.[40] Today, its most powerful promotion and recruitment tools are often provided by the West—in the form of graphic images of the destruction its armed forces have wrought. In the era of globalization, the most compelling narrative wins. Combined with such horrific illustrations, the story Al-Qaida tells—charged with vengeance and vitriol but often containing just enough truth that it cannot easily be dismissed—is uploaded onto websites, attached to e-mails, and otherwise dispersed by every method from listservs to the latest in viral marketing techniques. Meanwhile, producers of Al-Qaida's slick, digitalized training videos have turned suicide bombers into iconic action heroes who appear capable of addressing universal grievances by protecting and avenging the faithful. Often set to an Islamic rap soundtrack, these videos glorify martyrdom and portray the doomed jihadis as courageous, even hip, defenders of Muslims everywhere, whose actions will enrich their families and ensure their place among the virgins in heaven.[41] No wonder neither Western public diplomacy (PD) nor agents of counterterrorism have kept up.

Make no mistake: the best way to undermine this media strategy is to change the behavior that makes the pictures possible. But in the meantime, the point seems to have been lost that opposition to Western policy toward the Middle East is not necessarily inconsistent with opposition to Al-Qaida, its techniques, and interpretation of Islam. There is much more to be done if a small minority is to be isolated from the Islamic mainstream and stopped from turning impressionistic young minds against the world.

It must be assumed that Western security and intelligence agencies have spared nothing in their attempts to penetrate and subvert Al-Qaida through deception, espionage, and other covert means. It may also be the case that they are fully engaged in efforts to suppress Al-Qaida's media strategy and to spoil its brand. But if not, then clearly it is time to move these goals to the top of the short-term priority list. Countermeasures could include hacking, virally infecting, and crashing networks; jamming and intercepting communications as well as identifying and arresting webmasters and production and technical staff members on hate-crimes charges; and producing and disseminating graphic and emotionally laden materials illustrating the collateral damage to innocents caused by suicide bombings and other terrorist tactics.[42]

According to US Secretary of Defense Robert Gates, "It is just plain embarrassing that Al-Qaida is better at communicating its message over the Internet than America . . . Speed, agility, and cultural relevance are not terms that come readily to mind when discussing US strategic communications."[43] To summarize, Al-Qaida may no longer represent the prime-time television threat it once did, but it has sustained a degree of popular support by projecting an image of successful resistance, by casting its messages within a version of Islamist ideology, by emotionally charging its communiqués, and by availing itself of the full possibilities associated with the Internet. In other words, and perhaps without knowing it, Al-Qaida has turned to soft power and branding to advance marketing and recruitment objectives. However, unlike Hamas in Gaza, Hezbollah in Lebanon, the Taliban in Pakistan and Afghanistan, or the Shia militias in Iraq, Al-Qaida is not as connected to a defined population, and this may ultimately affect its staying power. With that in mind, if the Web-based component of the violent Islamist enterprise can be shut down, or at minimum seriously degraded, then the prospects for improved performance—political, diplomatic, counterterrorism—in the contest against Al-Qaida could brighten considerably.

The Steeper Challenges That Remain

Religious extremism, therefore, is part of today's threat environment—but only one part among many. I have lingered on the issue of religion and especially Islamism because it is emblematic of the kinds of complex challenges and responses we face in the age of globalization. If international policymakers are to deal effectively with the problem of insecurity over the longer term, they will have to conceive it in much subtler terms than former US president George W. Bush's pronouncement that "you're with us . . . or with the terrorists." That type of response, especially in combination with the roiling effects of globalization, will serve mainly to generate another set of grievances that will in turn serve as a rallying point for opposition, some of it undoubtedly violent.

Addressing these issues will require, at minimum, the following:

- A real commitment to democratic reform that goes well beyond electoral cherry-picking or ballot-and-bolt interventions
- The opening of markets and a balancing of equity-based considerations against economic growth
- The universal (rather than selective) promotion of development, good governance, human rights, and the rule of law
- Real action on global issues such as climate change, resource scarcity, public health, energy use, urban quality of life, and the environment
- A commitment to applying the tools of science and technology in general and ICT in particular to the problems of underdevelopment[44]

I would add that there is a more profound question here. Can development cooperation and assistance, however well intentioned, contribute to nation and state building? That is something the dependency theorists might have doubted. It seems to me, however, that even if the empirical evidence is not clear, it is certainly time to find out, since the costs of doing otherwise are incalculable. As a result of the war on terror and the global instability it has exacerbated, the United States, once regarded widely as a beacon of progress and enlightenment, is no longer seen by many as admirable, invincible, or deserving of the trust required to exercise international leadership. A 2006 poll of international experts revealed that over 80 percent of respondents believed the United States was losing the war on terror and that the world was now a less safe place for US citizens. The most popular alternative, favored by 87 percent, was greater emphasis on diplomacy (as opposed to defense) by increasing the budget of the State Department.[45]

Otherwise, what's next? If we recall our earlier discussion of the links between underdevelopment and insecurity, we can think of numerous dire possibilities: Imploding cities. Advancing deserts. Dying oceans. Pandemic disease. Epidemic poverty.[46] Mass migration. Collapsing states. Occurring in conjunction with the consequences of imperial overstretch, such calamities would result in a level and intensity of conflict that could be nearly impossible to manage.

Terrorism, not to mention a host of other threats, originates not mainly in the poorest countries per se but in those marked by chronic inequality, political repression, rigid social divisions, and the absence of good governance, democratic development, and respect for human rights. Action on all of these problems, however daunting to undertake, will be essential if we are to make real progress in defusing international insecurity. As Mike Duffield puts it, "The threat of an excluded South fomenting international instability through conflict, criminal activity, and terrorism is now part of a new security framework. Within this framework, underdevelopment has become dangerous."[47]

The fundamental, long-term threat is complex; it does not just involve terrorism—which is symptomatic of larger grievances in any case—but also underdevelopment, a condition closely related to not only the economic aspects of globalization but the highly contextualized political, cultural, social, and psychological ones as well. This is precisely why I have identified the need for deep comprehension and concluded that in this most intricately interconnected world, development itself, in large part, is the new security.

Acceptance of that premise could be a key component in something that is desperately lacking on all sides: the formulation of grand strategy. When planning how the big picture might be redrawn—and the time to start that process is now—those organizations and countries with special capacities will have to think through their roles with some care, in the full light of what is known about specific development needs in particular places. All of this will be necessary but not sufficient if we are to find a common and more peaceful way forward.

I turn to these matters, and especially to the implications for international policy of repositioning science and technology, R&D, and innovation at the nexus of development and security, in the next chapters.

Notes

1. Pugh (2007: 482).
2. See Fanon (1965), Freire (1970).
3. See UN (2000). This project, managed originally by Jeffrey Sachs and still of inconclusive consequence, has eight development objectives: (1) eliminate extreme poverty and hunger; (2) provide universal primary education; (3) promote equality between men and women; (4) reduce infant mortality; (5) reduce maternal mortality; (6) reverse the spread of diseases, especially HIV/AIDS and malaria; (7) ensure environmental sustainability; (8) develop a global partnership for development.
4. I am indebted to Randolph Gherson for this observation, offered at a sounding board session organized by the Ottawa chapter of the Canadian Institute of International Affairs. See Defense Science Board (2008), available at http://www.acq.osd.mil/dsb/reports/2008-01-Strategic_Communication.pdf. See also Paul (2009), http://www.rand.org/pubs/occasional_papers/2009/RAND_OP250.pdf.
5. On fixing failed states, see Ghani and Lockhart (2008).
6. Collier (2007) argues persuasively that aid alone can never work unless underdeveloped countries can overcome obstacles related to public administration, market access, resource scarcity, and conflict.
7. These themes are discussed more fully in Chapters 2 and 3.
8. Stewart (2006: 246, 248).
9. Cited in Lockhart and Maxwell (2006: 12).
10. Visit the World Bank's Poverty Database, PovcalNet, at http://iresearch.worldbank.org/PovcalNet/jsp/index.jsp.
11. Pfeffermann (2002).
12. Bailey (2005).
13. UN (2004: 24).
14. See World Bank (2005a).

15. These figures, cited in Kearns and Gude (2008:18), are for 2005.

16. See "Global Inequality," one of the "Nine New Realities" identified by *Canada's World,* http://www.canadasworld.ca/learnmor/ninenewr.

17. I was a frequent visitor to southern Thailand in the early to mid-1980s. The region was then peaceful and quite prosperous, at least compared to the northeastern regions. A weak political center, government ineptitude, and mismanagement of the continuing insurgency (based on a preference for crackdown over compromise), combined with the 2004 tsunami, have jeopardized continued development progress.

18. All figures in this paragraph are cited from "A Fast-Fading World of Good Intentions," *International Herald Tribune,* September 25, 2008.

19. On the destabilizing effects of the Western-sponsored spread of markets—which tends to concentrate wealth (often in the hands of ethnic minorities, such as the overseas Chinese) and exacerbate inequalities—and so-called democratization, which can empower the majority but also generate ethnonationalism, see Chua (2004).

20. See Ellis (2008) and the related Overseas Development Institute briefs (2008a; 2008b; 2008c), which provide an excellent summary of the pro-poor approach to underdevelopment.

21. I use the term *Islamism* here to refer to Islamic political activism in the sense promoted by Hugh Roberts of the International Crisis Group (personal communication, October 26, 2006). Pan-Islamism—now attracting many Southeast and Central Asians—has picked up where pan-Arabism left off.

22. Islamic fundamentalists subscribe to a literal interpretation of the Quran and believe that their understanding of its teachings, including *sharia* law, should be accepted as the political and legal basis for societal organization. See Siddiqui (2006), Lewis (2005; 1997; 1992), Said (1978).

23. On the long-standing misunderstanding of Islam in the West, see Said (1978); for the counterargument that there is something inherently debilitating within Islam that accounts for its present status, see Lewis (1990; 1997).

24. See Hudson (1999), Morgan (2001).

25. The establishment of and access to new, Arab-language direct broadcast satellite television services (Al Jazeera and Al Arabya) have done much to open up and encourage political discourse in many Middle Eastern countries that would probably prefer otherwise. Egypt, Saudi Arabia, and Syria come immediately to mind. For a fascinating assessment of the effect of Al Jazeera's possible role in mediating conflict, see el-Nawawy and Powers (2008). For a broader survey of the impact of the military-industrial-media-entertainment network, combining international relations theory with popular culture, see Der Derian (2001).

26. See Shishani (2006), Wike and Samaranayake (2006), Emerson (2003).

27. For an up-close and personal take on the contemporary presence of the US military on the ground, see Kaplan (2005).

28. See Chatham House (2006).

29. See Patman (2006).

30. See the excellent analysis offered in the Princeton Project on National Security, Ikenberry and Slaughter (2006).

31. Farson (2007).

32. Hirsh (2004).

33. No amount of public diplomacy can compensate for actions and policies observed to be hostile. See Slavin (2005), L. Jones (2005). Hoffman (2002) focuses on the shortcomings of US public diplomacy in the Muslim world. See also Khouri (2004). The longer reports prepared by the Council on Foreign Relations (2003), the Defense Science Board (2004), and Armitage and Nye (2007) are especially useful.

34. For more on the appeal of the jihadi identity as well as on the pressing need to address differences through political engagement, see Barkawi (2006).

35. Those who are able to operate effectively across class, cultural, linguistic, and religious divides are few and getting fewer, as the assassination of Benazir Bhutto in December 2007 illustrated. Her book, released posthumously, sets out a vision of reconciliation, one that may be harder to achieve without her participation. See Bhutto (2008).

36. On the effective use of police, intelligence, and political inclusion in counterterrorism, see Jones and Libicki (2008).

37. Robb (2007) argues this case persuasively. He proposes that instead of attempting to protect everything at the risk of becoming a police state, all while trying to remake the world, policymakers should take a systems-based approach to increase resilience and in so doing defeat open source warfare.

38. On terrorist networks and especially the roles played by alienation, kinship, and loyalty in their formation, see Sageman (2004; 2008).

39. In other respects, there is some evidence that the Al-Qaida brand is losing some of its luster in the Islamic mainstream. See Bergen and Cruikshank (2008).

40. See Kimmage (2008), who in an excellent survey of jihadi new-media production, distribution, and strategy argues that Al-Qaida may not in fact be ready for the interactivity of Web 2.0 and beyond.

41. Al-Qaida reportedly controls a production company called Al-Saheb, which is responsible for the creation of many of their videos. See CBC-TV (2008).

42. Recruiting from the West's huge pool of online gaming aficionados, software designers, and computer geeks would offer a significant advantage.

43. See Gates (2007). The literature on the new "war of ideas" is growing. See, for example, Phares (2008), Waller (2007a), Lord (2006).

44. See UN Conference on Trade and Development (2008). Science and technology issues will be examined more closely in Chapters 7 and 8.

45. See Foreign Policy/Center for American Progress (2006).

46. See Overseas Development Institute (2008a; 2008b; 2008c).

47. Duffield (2001).

Science and Technology: Black Hole or Silver Bullet? 7

Science. Technology. To most readers this pair of terms will seem very familiar. It crops up daily in the mass media, sometimes as a generator of mind-melting threats, at others as the source of wondrous remedies. Both are intimately associated with the principal building blocks we have covered thus far: globalization, security, and development. Yet even the lightest analytical scratch reveals that just below the surface of recognition, much remains unclear.

Nowhere is this ambiguity more marked than in the distant relationship between the world of scientific discovery and technological development (S&T) and that of international policy.[1] Where one might have expected to find close ties, there instead seems to be a surprising degree of alienation. Although S&T issues have long been features of the more specialized discourse on defense and development issues, neither that discourse nor a more general consideration of the relationship of S&T to international relations has percolated into the mainstream of international policy. A broad survey of some of the issues associated with international S&T is thus overdue—although the difficulty of finding language adequate to the task of producing it is greater still.

The Elephant in the Room . . .

In the age of globalization, S&T has emerged as both a defining characteristic and a curious contradiction, a fulcrum both for problems and for their solution. Depending upon the setting and specific application, S&T can furnish terrorists with the blueprints for explosive devices, improve people's economic prospects, promote the appeal of extremist causes, and increase agricultural yields. From the invention of catapults and gunpowder to the proliferation of missiles and nuclear weapons, S&T has, as a force (and risk) multiplier, one way or another been present in international relations from the outset, but in the era of globalization its prominence has been magnified.[2] It warrants a much closer look.

Traditional drivers of the international policy agenda such as politics and ideology are deeply rooted in subjectivity and perception. Not so S&T. Although for the purposes of this analysis S&T will be treated, for the most part, as a unit, it should be understood that the two are distinct, especially at the level of interplay with international policy.[3]

The scientific enterprise is predicated upon the empirical method of rigorous experimentation and the demonstrable repetition of results. Although no activity initiated by humans can be completely objective, science proceeds from the premise that all effects have a cause and, moreover, that these causes can be determined. Addressing and often answering fundamental questions about the nature of things, science plays a critical part in pulling back the curtain of history, explaining the natural world, and illuminating the road ahead. It reinforces the hope that misery is not fated and that even the most daunting challenges can be met. It makes discoveries that enlarge our understanding of the workings of the world. Crucially, it also provides the means with which to change them.

Science and indeed the scientific community tend toward the universal. Scientific activity is long-term, bottom-up, and peer reviewed. National affiliations are not determinant, research is often collaborative, and the fruits of scientific research are usually widely shared. The scientific vocation is conservative insofar as it does not easily accept radical changes in theory.

Technology, meanwhile, is applied knowledge and as such does not always result directly from science. Like international policy—to which it is more closely related than is science—technological development tends to be more competitive, short-term, and directed. To the extent that government sets the priorities, decisions are top-down. Where the private sector is involved, commercial considerations are paramount since technology can confer competitive advantage. In both cases, advanced technology, although it may be licensed or sold, is rarely given away.[4] Economic, military, and/or security concerns tend to ensure as much.

One of the recurrent strands in the work of Marshall McLuhan is the notion that science shapes and technology transforms both communications and their environment.[5] Science is a vector of international communication; technology is an international (and economic) policy tool. It follows that scientific and technological activity, like many other indicators of international power and influence, reflects trends in the global political economy. Notwithstanding recent surges in countries like China and India and long-standing scientific enterprise in Japan and Korea, it is not surprising that the center of S&T is still the A-world—that is, the OECD countries, especially the United States and the UK.[6] What's more, much of this scientific development evolves from the pursuit of defense and military objectives. Consider the origin of the Internet in the 1970s with the US Defense Department's ARPANET or the diverse achievements in science and technology that grew out of the space race between the United States and the USSR.[7]

The research focus on defense rather than development reflects the militarization of international policy carried over from the Cold War and discussed in preceding chapters.[8] Yet when a product of scientific endeavor results in the kind of technological innovation that responds not only to commercial opportunities but also to the challenges of global development, it can function as a powerful agent of emancipating and progressive change. For example, S&T carries enormous potential to address the major issues associated with agricultural production, health, engineering, and information technology in the T- and E-worlds. The realization of this potential would be critical not only to development and economic competitiveness but also to nation building; the actual lack thereof is therefore particularly problematic.[9] The ratio between the per capita GDP of OECD countries and that of low-income countries, for example, was about 64:1 at the end of the twentieth century. Yet the ratios of scientific achievement (scientific publications per population of 100,000), technological output (patent applications per population of 100,000), and high-tech exports per capita were 331:1, 1,260:1, and 730:1, respectively.[10]

It is not just the research and technological outputs of scientific activity that are significant. The influence of scientific enterprise on the formation of intellectual culture and values is also underappreciated. In its methods, scope, and remedial possibility, scientific experimentation per se plays crucial roles in developing creativity, informing current analysis, and educating inquiring minds. The ethos of trial and error and the values embedded in objective analysis have broad appeal; the scientific process promotes merit (through peer review), openness (through publication), and citizen empowerment (through respect for diverse perspectives). These kinds of values, as much as or more than any quantifiable advantages, represent the building blocks of progress.[11]

For all of these reasons and more, scientific and technological activity is best understood not as an abstraction or an expensive pastime for the well endowed but rather as something germane to the advancement of humankind. It accordingly should be a preoccupation for the agents of diplomacy. The reality, however, is otherwise.

. . . Is Invisible

That fact leaves us with a central problem. If we are to realize the full potential of S&T as a progressive source of new knowledge, we must find ways to liberate it from rigid commercial and institutional confines. Governments and international organizations will have to work harder to ensure that knowledge is shared or, better yet, developed via cooperative effort. At a global level, this will involve not only active collaboration but the assignment of S&T to a catalytic role in international relations.[12] Notwithstanding a degree of lip service to the contrary, however, the role it has thus far been given has been minor and/or misunderstood. The fact that funding for the creation and commercialization of new technologies is mainly in the hands of large corporations has complicated matters further.

The central place of science and technology in not only matters of defense and development but world affairs more generally has not yet fully registered. Within the diplomatic establishment and among experts in international policy, the lack of consideration for S&T is even more pronounced.[13] To make matters worse, the links between those engaged at the knowledge-development end of the spectrum—the scientists, engineers, technologists, and medical researchers—and those charged with the evaluation and management of said knowledge for international policy (among them diplomats, politicians, and senior officials) are, at best, tenuous.

This failing might be attributed to the perennial difficulty of making scientific and technological information widely accessible to the appropriate audience; most scientists and technologists are notoriously poor mass communicators and inept at tapping into anything but their own highly specialized media, which are not usually monitored by the international policy elite.[14] Moreover, the events of 9/11 in the United States and 7/7 in the UK introduced a chill into international scientific relations, whereby information was securitized and cooperation in areas considered sensitive was discouraged even as research self-sufficiency was encouraged by the two countries best able to achieve it.

These two problems—to reiterate, the absence of institutional linkages and the need for procedural restructuring—require urgent attention and indeed are the focus of much of the extant prescriptive literature.[15] To be sure, strengthening cooperation among specialized, science-based multilateral institutions, governments, universities, research councils, think tanks, and elements of the private sector will be essential. But the top priority is not just a matter of finding better ways to join up the dots. In fact, with a few exceptions, there are no dots.[16]

A Disconnect

One reason that the alienation of S&T from the popular international policy discourse is not widely appreciated may be that there *appears* to be much interaction. In 2004, for example, the OECD's science ministers issued a declaration pledging support for the exchange of information about effective methods to promote sustainable development through S&T, research cooperation, and international dialogue.[17] And in May 2007, a colleague of mine made a presentation to the Annual Forum on Science and Technology Policy, organized under the auspices of the American Academy for the Advancement of Science.[18] He highlighted a series of headlines to underscore the rising prominence of S&T in world affairs:

- African Union Summit on S&T; African Development Bank Adopts Landmark Science Strategy
- Islamic Countries to Fund Science Development Network

- China Embraces Nanotechnology
- Indian Science to Aid Tanzania
- S&T Partnership Fund Established to Cement Opportunities in India, China, and Brazil
- Plan Afoot to Mobilize G8 Domestic R&D in Support of International Development Needs

Within some international and scientific communities and even in the public mind, then, there appears to be a growing awareness that S&T knowledge is "the new currency for development."[19] Is that understanding, however, finding expression in policy and action? Is the world on the cusp of something new and better?

Sadly, not yet. In 2003, UNCTAD launched its Science and Technology Diplomacy Initiative. In setting out the terms of the project, the organizers observed that

> new and emerging technologies . . . have the potential to assist developing countries to "leapfrog" entire stages of development. However, there is a considerable concentration of technology and technological know-how in a limited number of countries and large transnational corporations. . . . [W]ithout a greater focus on the transfer of technology and its links to international trade and foreign direct investment, and without a more determined strategic approach by governments, the private sector, [and] regional and international organizations, technology may . . . perpetuate development gaps.[20]

Despite the increasing amount of token acknowledgment, then, belief in the central place of S&T in international affairs is not yet widely shared by decisionmakers. Meaningful expression of the capacity of S&T to contribute to development and thus to a more secure world—especially as measured through demonstrable results rather than recommendations in scattered reports—is therefore scarce.[21]

One powerful indication of this disconnection is the relative paucity of published research relating S&T to specific elements of international policy. By way of illustration, here is an experiment. Enter these key words into your favorite Internet search engine, in any selected order: science, technology, research, development, diplomacy, security, international policy, globalization. The search results will almost certainly surprise you: the variety of sources offering either analytical insights or useful data is amazingly limited. One project that does come up is GLOSPERA, a landmark study of globalization and international-research cooperation funded by the European Commission. The findings, however, serve mainly to underscore the dimensions of the problem in question: "National policymakers have not generally sought to address global problems through international research cooperation. International agencies lack the resources and the political power to take up such initiatives.

. . . [G]lobalization is not yet a major factor in the growth of international scientific *cooperation*" (italics mine).[22]

Another good illustration of this curious oversight can be gleaned from a glance at the home pages of the websites of the World Bank and IMF. Any mention of S&T is conspicuously absent.[23]

A telling if not widely appreciated indicator of international policy priorities may be found in the program of the International Studies Association's annual conference. This international gathering features thousands of participants from around the world, mainly academics specializing not just in international relations, economics, or political science but other aspects of international affairs as well. Over the course of four or five days, some 600 to 700 panels and presentations are offered. I have enthusiastically attended this sprawling brain-food buffet most years since 1997. However, one enduring quality has been the almost complete lack of discussion related to S&T. For example, at the 2008 gathering in San Francisco and the 2009 event in New York, only a handful of the hundreds of panels made any reference to S&T, although that was more than in most of the previous years. [24] Those who specialize in the history of ideas may have some sense of just how this chasm between international relations and S&T developed. In any case, the import is clear: for some reason, from the perspective of diplomacy, science and scientific knowledge exist in a bubble, however shiny, expansive, and attractive it may be. Science, like Esperanto, should be a common language uniting a diverse community of players and group of interests. Instead, like Esperanto, it remains largely exotic, even obscure.

Certainly it is often far removed from both international policy and public administration. Although the job packages of some trade commissioners, aid officials, and science counselors have S&T content, it is not generally linked to fast-breaking developments in the wider field of diplomacy or woven into the fabric of diplomatic life. How often do scientists and diplomats mix? How many diplomats are scientists? Universities, the private sector, and specialized institutes conduct most of the basic scientific research. Corporations produce the commercial innovations and own the technology. Trade and industry departments and certain specialized agencies of government play roles in promotion and regulation. Yet in the international sphere, where, day after day, the workings of globalization serve to underscore the inherent importance of S&T, little critical attention is devoted to understanding the nature and consequences of that relationship. Ultimately, if they were to be queried about the role of S&T in their work, all too many envoys would ask that the question be repeated.

Dim Light of the New Dawn

One might expect that diplomacy, which is concerned with the management of international relations and global issues by nonviolent means, would figure meaningfully into this picture. After all, one of the most salient characteristics of diplomacy is its worldliness. While there has always been a place for theory, at the end of the day diplomacy is mainly about practice—finding amenable solutions to the very real problems that afflict members of the international community.

Traditionally, diplomacy has been employed in service of resolving questions of war and peace, mediating territorial disputes, negotiating international law and treaties, and otherwise engaging in the many other sorts of issues that arise among states and peoples. During the Cold War era, however, less familiar elements began to appear in the diplomatic mix, and globalization, as has been illustrated, began to extend the boundaries of diplomatic activity. It therefore seems inevitable that the world's diplomats and their institutions will sooner rather than later have to confront more directly than they have the looming S&T agenda.

Science has long been associated with defense policy and weapons programs, and scientists played a crucial role in the drafting and negotiation of the Treaty on the Non-Proliferation of Nuclear Weapons; the Convention on the Prohibition of the Development, Production, and Stockpiling of Bacteriological (Biological) and Toxin Weapons and on Their Destruction; the Chemical Weapons Convention; and the Comprehensive Nuclear Test Ban (opened for signature in 1996 but not yet in force).[25] But the working relationship between science and diplomacy has not been as close. By the time of the 1987 Montreal Protocol on Ozone Layer Depletion and the 1991 Canada–United States Acid Rain Pact, for instance, interstate conflict was declining, but intrastate violence was increasing.[26] There began to appear some telltale signs that something new was going on.

Indeed, we saw them a few years later in 1992, at the Rio Conference on Environment and Development. The Earth Charter, Agenda 21, and the Biodiversity Convention provided powerful testament to the changing nature of international relations.[27] Granted, as is the case in all transitional periods, the more traditional sorts of files did not and have not disappeared from the diplomatic agenda: free trade pacts and open-skies agreements, the Dayton Accords, the establishment of the International Criminal Court, and the Treaty to Ban Land Mines come immediately to mind.[28] Business between states remains a substantial part of international relations. Yet with the turn of the millennium, many of the largest, most pressing issues appear different in kind. More and more concern science, and the solutions in many cases involve both targeted research and the application of appropriate technology. And this trend is, I believe, accelerating.

In Chapters 2 and 3, I remarked upon the rising importance of S&T in the context of the shift between the Cold War era and the era of globalization. Whether directly or indirectly, S&T issues today are coming to dominate substantial parts of the global political agenda. The big picture is being redrawn, but its implications have yet to be fully appreciated by international policymakers. Diplomatic practice and doctrine have remained, in large part, unresponsive. That is all the more troubling when the following catalog of concerns is considered:[29]

- Climate change and global warming[30]
- Public health issues, including pandemic diseases such as SARS, BSE, HIV/AIDS, and avian flu
- Environmental degradation and ecosphere collapse, affecting fisheries, forests, the air, soil and water quality, deserts
- The spread of weapons of mass destruction and nonproliferation agreements[31]
- The endangerment and extinction of species, leading to diminished biodiversity
- The development of alternative energy sources and environmental technology
- Scarcity of resources, including food, fuel, and water
- Emerging science, technologies, and platforms: biotechnology, nanotechnology, genomics, new materials, information and communications applications

What can be said about this list? First, it reads like a collection of daily news headlines, tracking closely the leading edge of the globalization age. Second, it bears little similarity to the litany of concerns conventionally associated with diplomacy. Each of these issues is deeply rooted in science and propelled by technology. And third, each is of global import, affecting not just governments and states but the lives and livelihoods of virtually all people everywhere.

This catalog, I argue, represents an inventory of the principal threats and challenges likely to face humanity hence decisionmakers, over the medium to long term. Long after the intervention in Iraq, the strife in Darfur, and the carnage experienced in 2008 in Georgia have faded from memory, these types of international S&T issues—as well as many yet to be manifest—will undoubtedly still be with us. Moreover, notwithstanding significant economic and political preconditions having mainly to do with the creation of partnerships between the public and private sectors, capacity building, and the development of scientific and research infrastructure, most of these matters are also open to S&T remedies—remedies based on empirical findings, unlike those prescribed for the international conflicts arising from differences in religion, culture, and ideology.

Now is the time to develop and put into place adequate policy and planning mechanisms, hopefully well before full-blown crises in one or several of the listed areas of concern force action. To cite just one example, in 2005 there was a series of documentaries and reports on the possibly catastrophic consequences of an avian flu pandemic—whose development is not a question of *if* but *when*. It was headline news. Are governments ready? Not even close.[32] Yet fashioning a common response to these sorts of global issues could unite the world community. Providing, that is, that it can find a basis on which to proceed. And that is the province of diplomacy, not defense.

Science Diplomacy?

In December 2002, the journal *Science and Public Policy* dedicated an entire edition to the issues of globalization, science, technology, and policy. In her introduction, editor Josephine Anne Stein noted:

> Globalization is changing the interplay between science, technology, and international affairs. While national sovereignty is being eroded in even the largest countries, science and technology is becoming central to a growing number of international issues. These trends have implications for the conduct of S&T-related public policymaking in the international realm. Yet there is little evidence of "joined-up thinking" between foreign ministries, economics ministries, and bodies responsible for S&T cooperation policy.[33]

This is a message worth remembering—and one that is being heard more frequently. A 2005 report by Japan's Council for Science and Technology recommends that in "the era of intense international competition for knowledge" about an "increasing number of issues common throughout the world," efforts in support of the "strategic promotion of international activity in science and technology," which will "strengthen the foundations" and "build a network of international research personnel," should be undertaken urgently.[34] Scientific journals note that scientists can serve as "ambassadors of goodwill" and advocate that "it is time for the scientific community to increase its role in diplomacy."[35]

Diplomacy in general, and science diplomacy in particular, could play a critical role in bridging the digital divides that separate the A- (and to a lesser extent the C-) from the T- and E-worlds and in so doing facilitate the search for solutions to the afore-listed catalog of global threats.[36] Even so, finding workable solutions will certainly be difficult; it is one thing to call for change, but it is quite another to effect it.[37] At the very practical, vocational level, most diplomatic practitioners inhabit a universe remote from that of the scientists and technological entrepreneurs of Silicon Valley or the software incubators of southern India. Diplomats do not generally have the requisite S&T skills or experience.[38] Nor are they typically familiar with S&T's organizational machinery. Foreign ministries, for their part, tend to be compartmentalized and hierarchical rather than fluid; they aren't well networked among centers of S&T research in their home countries, let alone those abroad, and they aren't organized to access or assess crosscutting S&T developments.[39]

The decisionmakers of international relations, for the most part, lack the expertise and, often, even the interest to adequately manage S&T-driven issues. High-level scientific advice is difficult to obtain. Foreign Service training institutes do not usually teach the role of S&T in international policy. When they do, it is most often in a commercial context—that is, the primary question raised is how best to sell national S&T products and services that will guarantee returns on investment for the owner of the intellectual property rights. In discussions geared toward a better understanding the origins of insecurity and underdevelopment, S&T rarely comes up.

The foreign ministries of the UK, which have set up a Science and Innovation Network, and the United States appear to have advanced further than most. The latter has produced a raft of reports on the role of science in foreign policy, and that theme can be found in a number of high-level statements and speeches.[40] Still, the post–Cold War history has been mixed. Immediately after the Cold War, the US State Department dismantled its science "cone" (specialist grouping), cut the number of science counselors abroad, and downgraded the department's most senior scientific advisory position. Since then, however, the State Department has reversed course. It has launched a significant science internship program, expanded its network of science counselors, initiated global dialogues and partnerships on S&T as well as series of S&T conferences, and reelevated the status of its science adviser.[41] State Department spokespeople make a point of emphasizing the place of S&T in foreign policy generally.

But when we consider the ground that has already been lost and the magnitude of the challenges ahead, especially in light of the marginalization of diplomacy in international policy more generally, we may doubt whether such steps are sufficient. Although S&T issues are referenced more frequently in statements and speeches, particularly in those from the United States and the UK, I would argue that S&T per se now represents an even smaller portion of the overall content mix of international policy and practice than it did during the Cold War years.[42] In that period, scientific and educational exchanges, technical cooperation, and academic relations were prominent features both of the day-to-day business between the superpowers and of their efforts to woo clients elsewhere, especially with respect to technology transfer.[43]

With the advent of the era of globalization, much of this type of activity stopped or was reduced dramatically. Intense S&T collaboration continues on some projects within the A-world—for example, joint weapons programs within NATO, or research on HIV/AIDS and global warming among G8 members. More significant, however, are the multiple institutional and professional disconnections, and especially those between the A- and T-/E-worlds and between diplomats and scientists everywhere. Negotiations on S&T agreements between states remain a popular pastime, but the discussions they engender are often a pale substitute for more concrete cooperation.

All of this has left international decisionmakers perilously ill equipped to respond effectively to the S&T threats and challenges generated by globalization. To the extent that S&T issues do find their way onto the international policy agenda, they tend still to be framed in competitive, adversarial, Cold War terms, thus reinforcing the patterns identified in Chapter 5. The quest for control over oil supplies eclipses collective action on limiting greenhouse gas emissions, encouraging conservation, and developing alternatives to the carbon economy. Electrical power generation is a key vector of development, yet in the field of nuclear energy, the emphasis remains on disarmament and nonproliferation rather than technical cooperation.[44] Defense continues to be a huge item in national budgets, with government spending on weapons research outstripping expenditure on health research.[45]

Almost twenty years after the end of the Cold War, the defense programs pursued by A-world powers continue to exert inordinate influence over the S&T agenda.[46] Even more troubling, this pattern has been mirrored in key countries elsewhere; India, Pakistan, Iran, and North Korea, to name a few, have all allocated inordinate percentages of scarce budgetary resources in support of nuclear weapons programs at the expense of developmental priorities.

All told, the S&T file clearly requires more attention from foreign ministries and international organizations. This must go well beyond attempts to address the intellectual property issues that have limited the spread of innovation and transfer of technology or promote the sale of technology to those who can afford it. Instead, S&T should be used to help construct the still-missing spans between diplomacy, development, and security.

An obvious riposte would be to suggest that these sorts of challenges might one day be addressed in diplomatic circles through recruitment, professional development, and organizational reform. Indeed they might, but the challenges need meeting now. Nor would bureaucratic remedies alleviate an even more deeply troubling problem: the general lack of attention directed toward S&T on the part of both analysts and practitioners specializing in foreign policy and international relations. This intellectual and cultural obstacle is formidable.

In most foreign ministries, notwithstanding the S&T dynamic that propels so many twenty-first-century issues, the S&T dimensions of international policy are neither systematically brought to bear on decisionmaking nor treated as priorities by most senior officials. A survey conducted for the US Congressional Research Service, for example, cites concerns about (1) the lack of S&T expertise, presence, and global engagement in the Department of State; (2) the decline in support for S&T activities at the United States Agency for International Development; and (3) the lack of coherent and integrated S&T policy direction and federal coordination.[47]

These observations are both indicative and representative. To better understand the near-invisibility of S&T in international *policy,* it will be necessary to examine more closely the dynamics of S&T within the political economy of international *relations,* and from there to consider how S&T concerns might be more integrally reflected in the practice of diplomacy, the operations of the foreign ministry, and the activities of those in the foreign service.

Notes

1. For example, the Canadian government barely mentioned S&T in the comprehensive, multisectoral, five-volume international policy review it released in 2005. Literature on international development, conversely, is replete with such references. See, for example, Hoekman and Javorcik (2006), Bar and Galperin (2006).

2. Consider, for instance, the case of a biotechnologist who uses genomics to create a pathogen capable of causing an epidemic for which there is no vaccine.

3. I thank my colleague, Trade Commissioner Thierry Weissenburger, for elaborating and underscoring the importance of this point.

4. In 2007, with particular support from Germany, the G8 established the Heiligendamm Process, a forum for discussion between G8 members and five important developing countries: China, Mexico, India, Brazil, and South Africa. The objective is to tackle, among other issues, those related to innovation and intellectual property rights in a nonconfrontational manner. A report is to be tabled at the 2009 G8 summit in Italy. See http://www.g-8.de/Content/EN/Artikel/_g8-summit/2007-06-08-heiligendamm-prozess_en.html.

5. See McLuhan (1964), McLuhan and Powers (1989). For more seminal work on this key theme, see also Innis (1950), Grant (1969).

6. A cogent visualization of the world centers of R&D can be found in Dufour (2007).

7. Defense research has had profound impacts on the social sciences as well. See, for example, Amadae (2003).

8. See Singer (2007).

9. On the nature of the relationship among knowledge, innovation, and development, see UN Conference on Trade and Development (2008).

10. These figures exclude India, which is considered a special case. Cited in Bezanson and Segasti (2005: 28–29).

11. On the broad relationship between science and society, see International Council for Science (2005).

12. One example of the international community's efforts to engage S&T in this respect was the designation of 2007–2008 as International Polar Year. There is no doubt that activities on the part of governments and NGOs in the Arctic and Antarctic regions are being stepped up, but whether this will result in increased cooperation or new sources of conflict remains to be seen. See http://www.ipy.org/.

13. In 1999 the US National Research Council prepared one of the few major studies to look comprehensively at the relationship among science, technology, and foreign policy. That report and its recommendations, many of which were accepted, may be found at http://www.nap.edu. By way of comparison, a recent strategy document prepared by Canada's Advisory Council on Science and Technology did not even address the question, commenting only that "there is no effective mechanism for coordinating our foreign policies with . . . international S&T activities." See Advisory Council on Science and Technology (2007).

14. A quarterly dedicated to the analysis of the global implications of developments in S&T would be a useful addition to the existing literature.

15. Many of the sources cited in this chapter deal in some respect with the structural weaknesses in international S&T linkages and relationships. See, in particular, publications by the InterAcademy Council (2004a; 2004b; 2005) and the International Council for Science (2002–2003; 2005).

16. For a more upbeat take on the dynamics of global science and the evolving role of institutions, see Wagner (2008).

17. See Organization for Economic Cooperation and Development (2004).

18. Information on this event is available at http://www.aaas.org/news/press_room/forum/forum_2007.shtml.

19. Dufour (2007).

20. UN Conference on Trade and Development (2003). UNCTAD has been at the forefront of linking S&T issues to those of development. See, for instance, its *Information Economy Report* (2007–2008).

21. While a few exceptions do not a rule make, several are certainly worth noting. The Bill and Melinda Gates Foundation has made priorities of global health (http://www.gatesfoundation.org/global-health/Pages/overview.aspx) and science (http://www.gatesfoundation.org/global-development/Pages/overview.aspx); the US National Institutes of Health has successfully encouraged transnational research and the formation of global consortia around issues related to human health and biodiversity and has been a pioneer in ensuring public access (http://publicaccess.nih.gov/); Canada's McLaughlin-Rotman Centre for Global Health helps researchers and companies get their life sciences technologies to those who need them in the developing world (www.mrcglobal.org). These initiatives and others like them are encouraging, but relative to the scope and intensity of the need, they are just a start.

22. See University of East London, http://www.uel.ac.uk/ssmcs/research/funded_projects/glospera.htm. This and many other reports highlight the need for more S&T partnerships, capacity, and cooperation. There is not much evidence that their advice is being heeded.

23. S&T content can eventually be found. From February 13 to 15, 2007, for example, the World Bank, in association with various partners, organized a Global Forum on Building Science, Technology and Innovation Capacity for Sustainable Growth and Poverty Reduction and has posted a number of papers and presentations. Without diligently searching for this kind of content, however, casual visitors to the site would be unlikely to access it. See World Bank (2007).

24. Conference programs can be viewed at the International Studies Association website, http://www.isanet.org/conventions.

25. "Treaty on the Non-Proliferation of Nuclear Weapons" (July 1, 1968); "Convention on the Prohibition of the Development, Production, and Stockpiling of Bacteriological (Biological) and Toxin Weapons and on Their Destruction (April 10, 1972)" (1992); Chemical Weapons Convention (1992).

26. This treaty was opened for signature in 1987 and entered into force in 1989. Montreal Protocol on Substances That Deplete the Ozone Layer (1987). The Human Security Report Project tracks trends in armed conflict and publishes its findings in an annual report. See Human Security Centre (2005).

27. Convention on Biological Diversity (June 5, 1992).

28. For example, the Agreement to Amend the Air Transport Agreement (1992). See Bond, *Aviation Daily* (2001: 3). *Rome Statute of the International Criminal Court* (1998). See the Convention on the Prohibition of the Use, Stockpiling, Production and Transfer of Anti-Personnel Mines and on Their Destruction (September 18, 1997).

29. This compendium is illustrative only. For more information on climate change and global warming, environmental degradation and ecosphere collapse, alternative

energy sources and resource scarcity (including water), and endangered species and diminishing biodiversity, see UN, http://www.un.org/climatechange, which provides links to many relevant international organizations, groups, and networks. For more on public health and pandemic disease, see the World Health Organization, http://www.who.int/csr/disease/avian_influenza/en/index.html; on weapons of mass destruction and nonproliferation, see International Atomic Energy Agency, http://www.iaea.org/OurWork/SV/index.html, and International Atomic Energy Agency, http://www.iaea.org/OurWork/SS/index.html; on emerging science, technologies, and platforms, see UN Conference on Trade and Development, http://stdev.unctad.org/themes/ict/docs.html and http://stdev.unctad.org/themes/biotech/docs.html.

30. The Intergovernmental Panel on Climate Change is a highly respected and crosscutting group of experts organized under UN auspices. When it released its *Fourth Assessment Report* in 2007, the authors distilled their detailed findings into a Synthesis for Policymakers, available at http://www.ipcc.ch/pdf/assessment-report/ar4/syr/ar4_syr_spm.pdf. It is encouraging that these findings, and the publicity they attracted, seem to have put an end to the debate about the veracity of the science behind climate change. It is discouraging, however—even if supportive of the arguments offered in this chapter—that so little has been achieved politically.

31. See Weapons of Mass Destruction Commission (2006).

32. See, for example, Osterholm (2007).

33. Stein (2002: 402).

34. See Japan Ministry of Education, Culture, Sports, Science, and Technology (2005).

35. See Lord and Turekian (2007: 769–770).

36. A promising nongovernmental initiative intended to help bridge the digital divide is the One Laptop per Child campaign launched by Nicolas Negroponte at MIT. See http://laptop.org/en/.

37. On the security implications of S&T in US policy toward the Islamic world, see Brookings (2005).

38. Those with the skills and experience, moreover, rarely think of careers in the foreign ministry. As Nina Fedoroff, administrator to the US Agency for International Development and science and technology adviser to the secretary of state, remarked, "The notion of becoming a science diplomat . . . is just not on the radar screen for most scientists and engineers." See Fedoroff (2009).

39. This is one area in which partnering with transnationally networked NGOs with an interest in S&T issues could be of great benefit to foreign ministries. See, for instance, Keck and Sekkink (1998).

40. See, for example, the National Research Council (1999; 2006) and the US State Department (2000). See Atkinson (2007), Marburger (2005).

41. The Jefferson Fellowships program brings scores of postdoctoral science scholars into the US diplomatic service each year as interns. See the US Department of State, Office of the Science and Technology Adviser's website, http://www.state.gov/g/stas. It is also worth noting that former secretary Rice's science adviser, Nina Fedoroff, has been retained by Secretary Clinton.

42. These are the two countries that are also the most advanced in terms of S&T and R&D capacity. As noted, both have begun to take account of this advantage in the organization of their foreign ministries.

43. See Dizard (2004), Richmond (2003), and Schweitzer (1989) for accounts of the Cold War origins of US public and technological diplomacy and the effect they had on the Soviet Union.

44. Nonproliferation is one area that has managed to engage the interest of the international community. Yet even here, widely held resentment over the fixation by the founding members of the nuclear club on arms control at the expense of international collaboration on civilian concerns such as power generation and transportation has, if anything, contributed to the standoff in North-South scientific coöperation. See, for example, the continuing dominance of nuclear weaponry–related topics among those covered in the programs of the annual Pugwash Conferences on Science and World Affairs; see Pugwash Conferences, http://www.pugwash.org.

45. A telling analysis of world military expenditure can be found in the Stockholm International Peace Research Institute's annual yearbook. See Stockholm International Peace Research Institute (2006: chapter 8). An excellent overview is provided in Shah (2008). Global expenditures on health and health research are harder to quantify. For statistics on US spending ratios, see the Center for Arms Control and Non-Proliferation's data on past discretionary spending at http://www.armscontrolcenter.org. For national percentages of GDP for military expenditures, see the Central Intelligence Agency's World Fact Book, available at https://www.cia.gov/library/publications/the-world-factbook/rankorder/2034rank.html. National health expenditures as a percentage of GDP can be found at the World Health Organization's National Health Accounts website, http://www.who.int/nha/en.

46. For an account of the influence the military has had on science and technology in the UK since the Cold War, see Langley (2005).

47. See Deborah Stine (2009), *Science, Technology, and American Diplomacy: Issues for Congress*. Congressional Research Service. February 3, at http://www.fas.org/sgp/crs/misc/RL34503.pdf.

PART 3
Diplomacy Unbound

The Global Political Economy of Knowledge: Working Smarter

8

In the previous chapter, the case was advanced that as they face looming S&T threats and challenges—most tied one way or another to globalization—the world's foreign ministries, decisionmakers, and diplomats are largely unprepared and ill equipped to respond effectively. This new set of issues—ranging from pandemic disease to weapons of mass destruction, climate change to energy supply, nanotechnology to genomics—has to a considerable degree displaced the Cold War preoccupations over matters such as territory and ideology. Yet science remains largely outside of the concerns of international policy or the day-to-day workings of international relations. By the same token, as a product of R&D whose application has cultural and social impact, technology plays a critical role in conditioning international relationships—but little attention has been devoted to either examining or managing this issue either. Meanwhile, the various digital divides between the integrating cores and the disintegrating, underdeveloped peripheries are widening, with significant implications for both development and security.

Thinking Things Through . . .

If S&T's potential as a progressive, liberating force is to be more effectively harnessed, then its role and place in international relations will have to be recognized in practice as well as in prose. The S&T knowledge and network gaps that afflict diplomats and plague foreign ministries are serious, but they pale in significance to the widening S&T chasm between those individuals, groups, cities, and regions that comprise the A-world and are part of the integrating core (consisting, to reiterate, of OECD countries, global centers, and other growth nodes) and those relegated to the T- and E-worlds.[1] Owned and controlled by the powerful and employed in service of their interests, scientific knowledge and technological innovation tend to exacerbate inequality. This growing divide—both institutional and in terms of capacity and resources—must be bridged, or it will further global instability.

To better grasp the important political, economic, and geostrategic implications of this increasing concern, the relationship among science, technology, security, and development has to be contextualized. Treating these issues will require inquiry at a somewhat more abstract level than was necessary for considering the specific challenges presented in the last chapter.

In the age of globalization, with its transformed threat environment, I have suggested that equitable and sustainable, which is to say human-centered, development is fundamental to the new security. In that regard, the generation and application of S&T knowledge to R&D challenges has become key for development—and hence for security.

S&T capacity and accessibility do not well reflect global need. To cite one report, "The global technology divide is large. In 2004, 75 percent of Americans had access to the Internet. In Africa, Internet penetration is below 1.2 percent. . . . Only 10 percent of the world's pharmaceutical R&D resources are focused on the 90 percent of diseases that afflict the poor; the same ratio holds for crop science budgets and tropical agriculture."[2] In other words, while the scientific and technological advances that helped drive globalization have afforded policymakers many new avenues and instruments for action, they have also contributed to the exacerbation of global inequality and created a host of new threats and challenges. These issues, especially in light of the sets of power relationships that underlie them, must be confronted if global development that supports the new security is to be expanded rather than diminished.

In Chapter 4, I identified the need to bring our thinking about the world into the globalization age and to that end proposed the ACTE framework. I then explained the structure and characteristics of that model but did not focus in any detail on the nature of the relationships among the four worlds. One way to broach the connections across the digital divides that separate the A- or advanced, C- or contingent, T- or tertiary, and E- or excluded worlds is by examining the emergence of what we have termed the *global political economy of knowledge*.[3]

The political economy of knowledge and the digital divide represent two essential—hence in my view underappreciated—elements that animate and define the sets of relationships inherent in the ACTE framework. A capacity to connect to the political economy of knowledge is a prerequisite of economic and political success, a contemporary reflection of the old axiom that knowledge is power. In the twenty-first century, many of the leading indicators and benchmarks associated with the political economy of knowledge are scientific and technological in nature. Networked, deterritorialized, and interconnected as the global political economy of knowledge is, we must gain access to it and understand how it works if we are to advance our national interests.

The second element, the digital divide, represents the challenge upon which appropriate know-how and tools must be brought to bear. We must tap into the political economy of knowledge in order to harness S&T in service of bridging the digital divide and working toward broad-based development.

. . . With *Souplesse*

Souplesse may be defined in this context as the ability to connect with the *global political economy of knowledge* for the remedial application of scientific and technological capacity in order to engage specific threats and challenges, typically in support of security and development.[4] The approach I have proposed uses *souplesse* particularly to improve prospects in the T- and E-worlds. It would be embodied in diplomatic practice and assist in catalyzing activities of the private and public sectors. Considerable skill will be required to use souplesse effectively; one must be familiar with the global political economy of knowledge and be culturally and technologically literate in the context of both public and guerrilla diplomacy—two related prescriptions for the management of international relations, to which will be returning.

Knowledge powers the integrated global political economy. Scientific research creates new knowledge, and technological development converts this new knowledge into useful innovations. Higher education and continuous learning programs build on the foundations provided by basic science; investment in both is critical for broad-based development. Simply put, as produced, absorbed, and applied, knowledge creates jobs and growth. This in turn generates tax revenues through which public goods may be provided, public institutions strengthened, and the public interest served. Through R&D, the new knowledge is tested and applied to specific problems or challenges—urban quality of life; alternative energy sources; pollution control and abatement; high-yield, disease-resistant grains; and so on. One very common and practical contribution of the new technology involves the profusion of free satellite imagery available on the Internet.[5] A decade ago, only the intelligence community and its political masters could access this type of high-resolution photography. Today it is available for free to anyone with broadband service. For resource managers, land use planners, farmers, and many others (including those with darker purposes), access to services such as Google Earth has changed everything.

Inserting S&T inputs into primary product production can rapidly and strikingly improve profitability, especially in the agricultural sector, where access to timely information on markets, techniques, and crop varieties can make all the difference. And from the R&D process come the technological innovations intended to redress identified problems. These technologies can be disseminated and put to work through foreign direct investment, aid, international trade and commerce, institutional linkages and partnerships, and diplomacy and international policy, among other means.

In sum, S&T activity results in knowledge creation, technological innovation, and economic development, which are all primary engines of prosperity and progress. India, for example, has done a noteworthy job of connecting knowledge to commerce, and in so doing has attracted a growing share of foreign direct investment. China has achieved similar results by connecting commercial opportunities, most notably in manufacturing, to technology and labor. Thriving commerce, however, can create its own problems. Indian agricultural self-sufficiency, for example, is threatened by soil degradation—the result of an overuse of fertilizers and pesticides. The green revolution must therefore give way to the evergreen revolution—and, some would argue, perhaps even to the gene revolution.[6]

To be sure, markets and corporations will continue to figure centrally in the allocation of the benefits of scientific and technological advances, but governments, international organizations, and civil society will play an important role in ensuring that human needs are matched with economic opportunities, particularly in the T- and E-worlds. In many cases, these needs and opportunities are mutually inclusive and can result in a win/win combination.

Understanding the Global Political Economy of Knowledge

In the age of mass travel and communications, more and more people are able to exchange more and more data and ideas.[7] This has the effect of breaking down barriers and creating a shared consciousness that is beginning to shape values and inform culture. One promising area of research in the relationship between communication technology and collectivity that brings together elements of globalization, S&T, and the political economy of knowledge involves the concept of the *noosphere,* developed by French theologian Pierre Teilhard de Chardin in his posthumously published *The Phenomenon of Man* (1959).[8] Teilhard de Chardin detected the emergence of an integrated, transhuman sphere of awareness that he believed represented the final stage in evolution from the inanimate (geosphere) to the animate (biosphere) to the collectively cognitive (noosphere). He conceived of a global mind, or shared world of ideas, that in many ways prefigured our flight into cyberspace. Some of the more instrumental implications of Teilhard's ideas, particularly in relation to soft power and public diplomacy, have been addressed under the rubric of *noopolitik,* which bears some relevance to our discussion of the global political economy of knowledge but which I must leave for others to develop further.[9]

On the ground, at the working level, the global political economy of knowledge is bidimensional.[10] The term itself is used in reference both to the emergence of a world economy in which knowledge as such supports critical productive and power relationships and to the growing importance of transnational networks consisting of public- and private-sector organizations, NGOs, and individuals engaged in the production, manipulation, and/or use of knowledge. Sometimes these various players are working collaboratively; sometimes they are competing. In all cases, however, a premium is placed on information access, collection, analysis, and application. Together, these represent the value added by *intelligence*, a much-misunderstood commodity that will be explored more fully in subsequent chapters.

In the conventional wisdom of international political economy, and especially critical political economy, political and economic relationships are dichotomous: there are the haves and the have-nots, owners and workers, landlords and peasants, and so forth. Although the relationship between one group and another can be complex and multifaceted—as it would be for, say, the landed aristocracy, the state, the bourgeoisie, and the peasants in a period of social revolution—of primary concern is the point at which those with directly opposing interests meet.[11]

International policy and relations as practiced throughout the Cold War era used to reflect this kind of traditional thinking about political economy. The ideological universe was binary. There were two broad political camps, one democratic, one autocratic; two broad economic systems, capitalism and communism; and two principal players, the United States and the Soviet Union. They were, to varying extents and intensities over time, engaged in direct competition with each other.

As has been shown, however, this world has been replaced by an order that is too fluid to characterize even as multipolar, never mind uni- or bipolar. Instead, it is something more akin to *heteropolar* and is differentiated according to whatever is being measured, be that military might, economic power, or cultural achievement. No one state is likely to dominate across the board. Just as globalization has undermined the polarity of world politics; deterritorialized social, political, and economic space; and disaggregated the hierarchical, top-down model of the bureaucratic state, so too has it affected the dichotomous relationship between the haves and the have-nots. By dissolving the polar edges of the old model and stretching the remaining pieces apart, globalization has diffused, dispersed, and transformed the roles of individuals, groups, countries, and regions. What had been an epic, if relatively straightforward, struggle between the first and second worlds that was often played out in the third has become murkier and vastly more complex, featuring an ever wider range of actors and agents. It reflects, in a word, ACTE.

Charting the Digital Divide

In Chapters 5 and 6, I argued that development is a major feature of the new security. For this reason, international policy and development assistance goals are—or in any case should be—converging, especially with respect to S&T.

In the emergent global dispensation, both the political economy of S&T knowledge and the digital divide that has opened up in the absence of that knowledge are fundamental influences on the components of the ACTE axis. The complex of relationships among and between these components can be best understood as constituting a global supply chain of S&T knowledge production and distribution. The functioning of this chain would be optimized and its benefits better distributed if the digital divides were bridged, which is why doing so must become a priority for those in international diplomacy and development.

The levels of development found in each of the digitally divided A-, C-, T-, and E-worlds are defined in large part by their relative accumulation of knowledge and level of connectedness. Simply put, this divide separates those who know how to use and have access to or even own digital technology—principally information and communications technologies—from those who don't. The design and control of this technology and the science that underpins it reveal and reflect the global dissemination of power and resources at any given time.

The digital divide is not the immediate product of S&T developments but instead mirrors as much as it magnifies existing social, economic, and class divisions. Thus the digital divide is inherently political, reflecting the polarizing effects of globalization. Not coincidentally, this divide parallels the democratic deficit—both the unequal distribution of political and economic power and the extent to which democracy exists in name only, if at all, in many areas of the world. The digital divide is of course newer than those it reflects and affects, but in any case the influence of technology, especially in conveying economic and educational advantage, is pervasive.[12]

The centrality of science and technology to the specialized discourse on international development, as opposed to its relative scarcity in international policy discussions, has received increasing attention in recent years.[13] In the context of development, S&T is typically considered not a cure-all but a major piece of the puzzle. A 2006 UN report on this matter, for example, notes, "The technology gap is the divergence between nations and communities in their abilities to *access, diffuse,* and *use* scientific and technical knowledge" (italics mine).[14] While this statement, which defines the digital divide, rings true, it is nonetheless incomplete. Although the report accurately points to the many different conditions required for partnerships among participants in the global political economy of knowledge, it ensconces them within the traditional rubric of states and communities. It does not take account of the multifaceted and interacting tiers of development represented in the ACTE model. What's more, it neglects to consider fully a very significant class in the global knowledge economy—the owners of knowledge: "Most intellectual property rights and patents in the life sciences are controlled by companies in industrial countries, which in turn restrict the ability of poor countries to develop and commercialize products for their markets."[15]

When considered in light of the proprietary control of intellectual capital, the distribution of the political economy of knowledge across the digital divide comes to resemble more clearly the patterns identified in Chapter 4. At the top are the owners and investors, ranging from states or groups of states, to corporations, to organizations and associations, to individuals. These inhabitants of the A-world make the crucial international investment decisions. They create and sell S&T knowledge. Worldwide patent-distribution statistics, for instance, in keeping with state rankings across a wide variety of different measures, clearly illustrate the divide between S&T-producing members of the A-world and everyone else.[16]

One step down, in the C-world, are found members of a larger group of agents who have access to S&T, can use it effectively, and play a vital role in distributing it throughout their organization, community, or society. However, they are neither forerunners in the creation of S&T knowledge nor its primary beneficiaries. More specifically, although they may rent or license S&T from the A-world, those in the C-world do not own the rights to it or derive maximum profit from its use. With its technological and scientific know-how, however, the C-world notably does have a stake in the industries that produce knockoffs for a burgeoning black market.[17]

The third tier, the T-world, is peopled by those for whom the terms of S&T trade are generally disadvantageous—and whose ability not only to access but apply S&T knowledge is typically limited, often by a lack of educational and institutional infrastructure. Although this tier straddles the C- and E-worlds, it is characterized neither by the intermediary function of the C-world in relation to S&T nor by the exclusion from the benefits of S&T typical of the E-world. Examples might include certain parts of the Middle East, Africa, and South America in which access to the benefits of S&T is hindered by both structural and institutional capacity barriers. On the T-world's dark side, military technology is acquired from the C- and A-worlds, as has been the case with Pakistan and Iran in their pursuit of nuclear programs. The role of members of the T-world in the creation of scientific knowledge and the transfer of technology is often that of passive recipients upon whom are imposed fees, conditions, and terms decided elsewhere.

The last tier, the E-world, holds the remainder of the world's population but has minimal or no access to cutting-edge S&T. Members of the E-world are effectively excluded from active participation in the global political economy of knowledge; benefiting the least from S&T's liberating potential, they are nonetheless the most vulnerable to S&T-related drawbacks and disasters.

Examples of this tier would include New Orleans's poorest neighborhoods, which suffered disproportionately following Hurricane Katrina in August 2005; the millions of impoverished inhabitants of South and Southeast Asia whose lives were rent asunder by the December 2004 tsunami in the absence of early-warning systems and evacuation plans; and much of the nation of Bangladesh, which cannot afford to construct dikes to control devastating seasonal flooding. The list goes on.

The political economy of knowledge, the digital divide, and the dynamics that characterize activity in the interstices among the four tiers of the ACTE model can doubtless be further elaborated. For the present, however, suffice it to say that the advancing A-world owns the knowledge and the tools. The contingent C-world has the ability to use the knowledge and the tools but is largely prevented from ownership. Those in the tertiary T-world are treated as objects rather than subjects, with limited access to and little control over R&D or technology transfer. And the excluded in the E-world are, well, excluded.[18] Until or unless a way is found to liberate the ownership and control of technology from the highly commercial, proprietary, and competitive network formed and operated by those in the A-world, none of this is likely to change.

A Virtuous Cycle for the Privileged

The A-world combines the main sources of accumulated global capital (banking services, financial acumen, venture and investment pools) and head-office business expertise with access to advanced R&D, making it possible for surplus profits to be invested in innovative processes and products. This in turn leads to the generation of more profits, more investment in R&D, more tax revenue available to support basic science, and so forth. Those in the A-world—be they in London, São Paulo, Shanghai, or a regional center somewhere in the hinterland—are the beneficiaries of the virtuous cycle. Conversely, as one moves downward and outward through the C-, T-, and E-worlds, the patterns of underdevelopment are reinforced. There are lower levels of median education and connection to advanced R&D, innovations are fewer and further between, and dependence on external sources and producers increases.

Because the terms of R&D trade generally favor the A-world, so do the resolutions to most disputes, thus reinforcing and sometimes exacerbating the knowledge gap. A particularly cogent example of the monumental human impact of the R&D divide, in all its complexity, is the comparative lack of access to pharmaceutical products among the world's poor and excluded.[19] Remarkably little attention, even compared to other neglected areas of international policy, is devoted to attracting and retaining S&T-related investments and technology transfer in the health sector, especially where resources are scarce and strategic value insignificant.

The UN report on international science cooperation cited earlier emphasizes the importance of network building, which, as we have seen, is a central feature of globalization. It is networks that give form to the global political economy of knowledge, facilitating and using the linkages that define—although certainly not on the basis of equity—each tier of the digital divide. These multipronged connections play a critical role in keeping the global political economy functioning and intact. However, with continuing economic polarization, the gaps between the tiers are widening, a situation that in my view accounts for much of the instability we are seeing—in the contrast between booming coastal China and the impoverished interior, or between rural and urban Brazil or India, and in the migratory pressure along the border between the United States and Mexico.

If we are to address these gaps, we must not only put greater emphasis on S&T issues generally but make a substantial effort to identify the critical points at which A-world knowledge, C-world skills, and T- and E-world needs intersect. This, in turn, will involve the application of souplesse. Mutual interest, after all, is the mother of successful international cooperation. By focusing on these strategic points of intersection, many of which are located in the C-world, it may be possible to seize hold of latent opportunities and chart a path into a brighter future.

Rebooting

On the basis of the assessment presented above, we can see that the interests of all four tiers converge around security and development. While it will not be possible to delve into specific issues in detail, the following set of priorities might warrant closer examination—for example by policy planners in foreign ministries:

- Establishing partnerships in education and training programs to upgrade human capital and increase absorptive capacity
- Focusing on emerging technologies and platforms (bio- and nanotechnologies, information and communications technologies, genomics, new materials)
- Developing and implementing strategies to strengthen national innovation systems, networks, and infrastructure
- Collaborating with the private sector on developing new approaches to technology transfer (foreign direct investment, small and medium-sized enterprises, private philanthropy, venture capital) and leveraging global value chains and investment partnerships
- Building domestic capacity and fostering institutional linkages (between public and private, national and international)
- Addressing the most pressing issues of development (urbanization, environment, water and food supply) at the points of intersection among local needs, S&T capacity, and commercial opportunities

In large part because of its (at least superficially) apolitical nature, S&T, like cultural relations, is a natural arena in which countries looking to expand bilateral ties and bridge ideological rifts can engage. Unfortunately, it has been my experience that bilateral S&T agreements are often of mainly symbolic value, and serve frequently as a substitute for more pressing, controversial, or comprehensive issues on which consensus is lacking. Such agreements, moreover, will never compensate for a lack of commercial incentives for S&T-based direct foreign investment.

It is clear that much work will be required to identify additional points where interests intersect; the prospect of mutual gain provides a durable basis for international cooperation. Direct cooperation in S&T among governments, corporations, and functional bodies such as universities and research institutes also offers much promise as a means by which to circumvent problems of local corruption and ineffective governance, especially if the necessary coordination can be achieved multilaterally.[20]

Recognition of the centrality of S&T in the global political economy of knowledge and digital divides could be expressed in the formation of a given country's international policy and the character of its institutions (foreign ministry, foreign service, development agencies) as well as in its diplomacy. Relying on communication and running as it does on soft power, public (or, as we shall see in the following pages, guerrilla) diplomacy is ideally suited to give voice—and wheels—to an S&T-driven agenda in ways a more militarized version of international policy cannot. And, as we shall see, technology in general and ICTs in particular have transformed the way that diplomats work.

But here, again, is the rub. However obvious the agenda may be, most diplomatic practitioners cannot play the required role of catalyst and conduit for S&T knowledge. They do not know what they need to know; they do not know where or how to get the knowledge they need; and they would not know what to do with it if they got it. Although it is true that the more S&T drives the international policy agenda, the more knowledge of relevant developments could provide a real edge in various international negotiations, those charged with managing the international S&T files are, for the most part, either ill informed, inadequately directed, or otherwise unprepared to do what's necessary.

As always, there are exceptions, but they do not prove the rule. I have already referred to encouraging S&T developments in the US State Department and the UK's Foreign and Commonwealth Office. Elsewhere, the picture is quite different. Despite many attempts, for example, Canada's Department of Foreign Affairs and International Trade has never managed to appoint a science adviser, and the position of National Science Adviser has been moved out of a central agency—the Privy Council Office—and into a line department, Industry. In the C-, T-, and E-worlds, science is typically even further removed from the political and bureaucratic center.

Can this somehow be fixed? We noted in Chapter 5 that the literature on security still deals predominantly with issues of defense rather than development. Similarly, except for references to the relatively specialized area of technology transfer,[21] discussion of the antecedents and preconditions for development has omitted the more nuanced analysis of the dependency school; participants have returned again to a more orthodox focus on trade, investment, and capital flows. The 1980s and 1990s were characterized by a shift in development-oriented thought and practice from the problems of dependency to the neoliberal focus on market solutions examined in Chapter 3.[22] With this shift, neither the international political content of S&T nor the need to create cross-cutting linkages has received much attention.

Inside Out, Outside In

Black hole or silver bullet? S&T is a bit of each, I suppose. According to a recent report commissioned by the Rockefeller Foundation, "the ability to effectively participate in an increasingly competitive world and to acquire the surplus to make necessary investments in human capital and infrastructure will depend more and more on the ability of nations to achieve an appropriate level of science, technology, and innovation capacity."[23] For those with the access and the resources, developments in S&T will result in longer, richer, better lives. Those without such wherewithal are likely to fall further behind, in keeping with the polarizing tendency of globalization. Without the institutional, planning, and policy instruments so clearly required, uncontrolled globalization will produce the kinds of S&T-driven crises that will be most difficult to manage. Moreover, if the essential cooperative work required to begin fashioning S&T-based remedies is delayed further, the costs will inevitably be greater.

How might the progressive potential of S&T better be realized in service of equitable and sustainable development, which offers the best prospect for global security? Foreign direct investment has proven reliable for technology transfer, but the achievement of lasting benefits requires effective demand, absorptive capacity in education and infrastructure, functioning markets, and viable regulatory structures to ensure reasonable terms. Here, as with facilitating cooperation between appropriate institutions and organizations, there is no substitute for government leadership. As a start, training in S&T issues should become an integral part of the curriculum at diplomatic academies, and the importance of S&T files should be reflected in the organization of foreign ministries and the foreign service.

To borrow again from Josephine Anne Stein, "The diplomatic landscape is littered with scientific cooperation agreements. . . . It is curious, therefore, that international science policy and 'mainstream' foreign policy have remained so heavily segregated. . . . The scientific and diplomatic professions are today still structured differently, around scientific rationality and the universalism of Mertonian science, in contrast to the human-centered notions of history, identity, and nationalism. Can this dualism be allowed to persist?"[24]

I think not. Yet more reports and ministerial declarations will be of great benefit to no one but the recycling industry; ministers do sometimes exhibit a tendency to conflate exhortation with real action. For instance, the OECD Ministerial Declaration on International Science and Technology Cooperation for Sustainable Development issued in January 2004 contains all the right language. But instead of committing new resources, it concludes with only a call to "take this declaration into account."[25]

Providing the means for us to address a range of the most pressing threats and challenges as we leapfrog from land lines to cell phones and from blackboards to desktops to BlackBerries, S&T may be, from the standpoint of international policy and relations, the missing link between development and security. In ways that go well beyond theories of comparative advantage and product life cycles, that potential for linkage alone should be enough to warrant the deliberate repositioning of S&T both within the firmament of diplomacy and as an essential element of human progress in the age of globalization.

Complex challenges demand innovative responses, and S&T needs a more accessible, user-friendly interface with the everyday working world. This is precisely where the conceptual meets the practical and where elements of international public administration, far from being boring, become indispensable. Specifically, a closer examination of the aging infrastructure and brittle institutionalism of diplomacy, the foreign ministry, and the foreign service is essential. That often staid, stuffy world is our next destination—and an assessment of how it might be revived with entrepreneurial savvy, an understanding of the global political economy of knowledge, and the capacity for souplesse is our goal.

Notes

1. There is a growing body of literature on building S&T capacity for development. See, for instance, Watkins (2008), Third World Academy of Sciences (2004), InterAcademy Council (2004a), UN Millennium Project (2005).

2. Rockefeller Foundation (2006: 10). The report goes on to note that the "Internet and all phone technologies offer poor countries new 'leapfrog' possibilities: they allow these countries to rapidly upgrade the skills of their workers . . . offer producers and consumers timely market information, break government control over news, and provide a platform for political and social action." In the meantime, Africa's Internet penetration rate is increasing rapidly—but only to 5.3 percent as of 2007. See Miniwatts Marketing Group, http://www.internetworldstats.com/stats1.htm.

3. The *global political economy of knowledge* may be defined as a collaborative, heuristic, and virtual body of the world's information and expertise that pervades and supports critical transnational, productive, and power relationships.

4. I struggled somewhat with the choice of language here. My original selection for a term to encapsulate these related strands was *smart power,* by which I referred to the capacity of diplomats to apply particular knowledge strategically in support of human-centered development. Unfortunately, that term has now become too closely as-

sociated with the recent work of Harvard scholar Joseph Nye, who advocates the careful blending of hard and soft power in a US foreign- and defense-policy context. For a summary of those arguments, see Nye (2006). See also Armitage and Nye (2007).

5. Consider, for example, the interactive maps available online at sites like Mapquest.

6. For more on the so-called evergreen revolution see Swaminathan (2001), who is known as the father of the green revolution. See his website, http://www.mssrf.org.

7. Jon Husband has coined the term *wirearchy* to refer to "an emergent organizing principle based on interactivity and listening to the voices of people connected by online capabilities and social media." See http://www.wirearchy.com.

8. See Teilhard de Chardin (1959).

9. See Arquilla and Ronfeldt (2007; 1999).

10. I am indebted to James Gaede for his comments regarding some of the material presented in this section.

11. See Moore (1966).

12. Canadian communications theorists Harold Innis, George Grant, and Marshall McLuhan wrote about these issues. Grant's work considers the detriments of technology in modern society (1969); for analyses of the relationships among media, technology, and human society, see Innis (1950), McLuhan (1964), and McLuhan and Powers (1989).

13. The UN's Millennium Development Goals highlight S&T issues and are generally accorded considerable priority in the literature. On the role of science and technology in meeting development goals, see reports by the InterAcademy Council (2004a; 2004b; 2005), the International Council for Science Series on Science for Sustainable Development (2002–2003), and the UN Millennium Project (2005).

14. UN Economic and Social Council (2006: 3). China, India, and some other destinations are attracting ever larger and more significant shares of global R&D investment. See Doz (2006: 2–5). These figures do not take account, however, either of who owns the R&D product in question or to what uses it is directed.

15. Rockefeller (2006: 10).

16. See World Intellectual Property Organization (2007: 13–17).

17. While in many instances the fake products are inferior but harmless, they are also sometimes unsafe—as has been the case with certain pharmaceuticals, manufactured goods, children's equipment, accessories, and toys. That said, it is also possible that the fakes could one day be not only less expensive but as good as or better than their legitimate counterparts. See Koeppel (2007).

18. While I have emphasized the nonnational, nonterritorial aspect of the ACTE model, most of the literature continues to speak in terms of states. Not surprisingly, it has been observed that in both relative and absolute terms countries such as China, India, and Korea are quickly enlarging their share of global scientific research, technological development, and commercial innovation. See Steinbock (2007), Organization for Economic Cooperation and Development (2006), and Demos's *Atlas of Ideas*, http://www.demos.co.uk/projects/atlasofideas/overview. This trend reflects the broader pattern of transpacific power shift, wherein the dynamic center of the global political economy is increasingly Asia.

19. On the issue of intellectual property rights and their implications, see Joseph (2003). On R&D spending in developing countries, see Keller (2002).

20. In the 1990s, the International Development Research Centre funded Science, Technology, and Innovation Audits for the governments of Chile and Vietnam. See Mullen et al. (1999), Bezanson et al. (1999).

21. UNCTAD maintains an excellent list of key documents on technology transfer; see UN Conference on Trade and Development, http://stdev.unctad.org/themes/tot/docs.html.

22. See Williamson (1993), Nef (1999).

23. Rockefeller Foundation (2006: 11).

24. Stein (2002: 402).

25. See Organization for Economic Cooperation and Development (2004).

9 The Foreign Ministry: Relic or Renaissance?

The role of the foreign ministry, like that of diplomacy and the foreign service, might not be familiar to most readers. When we think about who copes with the S&T issues set out in Chapter 8, who manages the blowback from globalization, or who achieves the necessary preconditions for international security and durable development, diplomats seldom come to mind first. In fact the subject of diplomacy might seem boring, its institutions outmoded, its practitioners dinosaurs. But that's not—at least not necessarily—so.

The Setup

Foreign ministries are knowledge-rich information producers with an integrating, catalytic role to play in all national governments. But they tend to be among the oldest institutions of state, and, on the surface, they are both too foreign and too ministerial.[1] Thus studying the myriad interactions of people, policies, processes, budgets, and programs upon which these institutions are built can yield critical insights; there is much more to large organizations than might be gleaned from a glance at the lines, boxes, and titles found in their organizations' diagrams.[2]

Diplomacy, the foreign ministry, and the foreign service represent more than, respectively, the spirit, the machinery, and the face of a nation to the world. All are closely related, in fact interdependent—a change in any one of the constituent parts effects changes in the others. Together, these organs represent what we have called the *ecology of diplomacy.* This is an interlocking and organic whole, the framework of international policy, the place where new ideas live, or—too often and frequently for the wrong reasons—die. Indeed, a cascade of adversity is now jeopardizing the health of this ecosystem like so many others.

Due to the relentless dwindling of resources, diplomacy and its supporting institutions are facing difficult times. Initiative has passed to other actors, leadership has waned, and creative international proactiveness has given way to reaction to external demands (and not especially effective reaction at that). Diplomats are leaving the field in droves.[3] As none of this will stand, the moment has arrived to embrace comprehensive, full-bore reform.[4]

As an alternative to the militarization of international policy, governments need, I am convinced, to rely on the art of diplomacy and science of public administration to meet the new constellation of unconventional and asymmetrical threats. This assertion holds true everywhere but perhaps especially in the A-world, where the apparatus of the state is most developed and the remedial potential greatest.

I argue that the triad of the foreign ministry, diplomacy, and the foreign service offers a promising approach to resolving many of the complex issues that fuel instability and find expression in violence. Constructive action will involve harnessing the triad's inherent remedial potential and addressing not only the proximate causes of conflict, but also the more difficult and longer-term structural issues, such as the need to bridge the R&D gaps that divide the beneficiaries of globalization from those it excludes or constrains. This, in turn, will require expertise—the combination of a nuanced understanding of the political economy of knowledge with its strategic application through dialogue, engagement, and the orchestration of concerted action (*souplesse*).

Diplomats will always have business to do in the A-world. It is in the other worlds, however, especially those left behind by globalization—be they ridden with poverty, wracked by conflict, or ignored by international business—where special efforts on the part of foreign ministries will be necessary. If this is to occur, governments will need to get busy; none of them can go it alone, nor can they achieve the necessary results with the tools—or, in some cases, the personnel—they are using.

The Game

Whereas international policy is substantial and the foreign ministry organizational, diplomacy is mostly about process. As the part of the triad concerned less with *what* gets done than *how,* diplomacy relies on style. But it also involves far more than that—from forming new partnerships, collaborating widely, and connecting meaningfully with citizens at home and abroad to demonstrating effectiveness by producing tangible results.

Doing diplomacy and managing the foreign service—that cadre of employees whose professional time is divided between work at the headquarters of their home state and diplomatic missions abroad—are the principal responsibility of the foreign ministry.[5] As I have already noted—and notwithstanding the exclusivity imposed by individual academic disciplines—my experience suggests that it is impossible to fully consider any one of these components without making integrated, interdisciplinary reference to all of them.

For instance, a foreign service will not be able to develop innovative international policies or provide effective diplomacy in difficult environments if it is managed by a dysfunctional and underresourced foreign ministry disconnected from those who control the levers of domestic power or led by distracted or inexperienced ministers. Similarly, a foreign ministry that is constantly overshadowed by the defense department—former Canadian foreign minister Lloyd Axworthy, for instance, speaks of the "serious displacement going on between the influence of the military and DFAIT"—will never be able to deliver on its mandate.[6]

In the complex and dangerous world of the early twenty-first century, extracting from this intricate conglomerate the kinds of results that advance national interests is no simple task. A dizzying array of global threats and transnational challenges call for a strategic and holistic rather than a piecemeal response. The foreign ministry must be redesigned if it is to deliver.

The ends of diplomacy, and hence the writ of foreign ministries, have not changed a great deal since international politics first coalesced around the relations between states a few hundred years ago. Nor, in certain respects, do they need to. The search for the nonviolent resolution of differences through negotiation and compromise is a constant, as is the promotion of cooperation for mutual gain. Yet if the ends are immutable, the practice of diplomacy—the means—are certainly not. Most everywhere, these are being subject to thoroughgoing review within an evolving context.

As observed in the preceding chapters, ours is a crosscutting and highly interdependent era, one characterized by a global economy (with its markets, sourcing, and value chains), global issues (such as the environment, climate change, pandemic disease, and weapons of mass destruction), and the global war on terror (whether labeled as such or not). New actors drawn from civil society, other levels of government, and supranational bodies—terrorists, zealots, and criminals among them—now play major roles distinct from those of government representatives.

The global geopolitical and diplomatic landscape has been altered radically, and the operating environment is roiling. Much of this upheaval, as I have argued in Chapters 2 through 4, can be attributed to globalization—the totalizing force that has become the defining historical process of our time, breeding insecurity, exacerbating underdevelopment, and driving state failure.[7] How have foreign ministries, diplomacy, and the foreign service—in my view all significantly underappreciated international policy assets—adapted to these challenges? Not well enough. In this volatile and edgy world, S&T is racing forward, fundamentalist Islam has been branded as the religion of the oppressed, and terrorism has been embraced as the weapon of choice by the weak and disenfranchised. Thus far, the response of foreign ministries to these issues has been inadequate and the results—if measured by the incidence of violence and conflict—discouraging. To mobilize the support necessary to avoid costly military interventions and achieve peaceful change, they, along with the agents of diplomacy and the foreign service, must embrace innovation. Among the most promising of recent developments has been the move away from the exclusive, discreet, boutique style of diplomatic practice we discussed earlier to something much more public, even grassroots. Progress in this respect, however, has been halting. Foreign ministries and diplomatic practice are notoriously resistant to change. In my experience, in most large organizations, half the decisions that really count can be attributed to factors perhaps best described as personal and situational: career ambitions, working relationships, and everyday contingencies. Another 30 percent or so of all decisionmaking turns on matters of chance and timing. That means only about 20 percent of decisions are made primarily on the basis of public interest, objective circumstance, or the strength of an analysis or business case.[8] If these statistics are even close, it is little wonder that performance has been less than optimal. Meritocracy in bureaucracy is not unknown, but nor is it as commonplace as might be wished. The injunction to speak truth to power is honored mainly in the breach.[9] What I have seen, moreover, has taken place mainly in the A-world, which prides itself on excellence in governance. Add the nepotism, cronyism, and other forms of corruption more common in the C-, T-, and E-worlds, and the prospects for reform become even bleaker.

Going Public—but Not Just Like Old Times

In this age of uncertainty, formal state-to-state relations are still necessary, but they are no longer sufficient to obtain the kinds of international policy outcomes required. If governments are to be effective, they must connect directly with foreign publics, whether by engaging them through the new as well as the conventional media, opening storefront operations, or negotiating joint ventures with civil society—whatever works. The days of near-universal reliance upon standard operating procedures have passed. Diplomacy may still begin and end with interstate relations, but the effective exercise of influence is related increasingly to forging partnerships, managing networks, and shaping opinions. Few foreign policy objectives can be achieved in the absence of initiatives designed to engage, understand, advocate, and influence. Whether a country needs to build international coalitions, cooperate to protect the ecosphere, or compete to attract foreign investment as well as skilled workers and students, the cultivation of a broad cross section of civic support is essential to its success.

For these reasons and more, foreign ministries everywhere are concluding that the doctrine and practice of public diplomacy seem best suited to meeting the challenges of the era of globalization. How, then, should today's diplomats be spending their time? Building project-based networks both conventional and virtual, negotiating alliances based on mutual interest, working on media strategy, leveraging private-sector activity—in sum, privileging cooperation over coercion and exercising influence through dialogue and relationship building.[10]

Public diplomacy and nation branding will be examined more closely in the next chapter. For now, suffice it to say that the interconnectedness of today's world means that most political entities—including but not limited to states—*are,* in important respects, the image they project abroad. In this information-saturated age, all countries—but especially those without significant economic and military power—have come to depend on their images and reputations, which is to say their national brands, to achieve vital objectives. A nation's brand has become its strategic equity, a key vector of influence, and a source of legitimacy. The competition to project a recognizable and credible image internationally—that is, to have an effective brand—has become acute, while the costs of failure, of projecting a poor or inaccurate image, have grown exponentially. Instability only drives them up further.

If a country has a good reputation, its representatives should use that to advantage, especially if other options are constrained. Public diplomats can develop and manage the national brand, wielding its soft power in order to leverage resources and advance interests. That said, the practical and institutional implications of so doing are far-reaching and achieving results can be difficult. Progress has been fitful and halting. Anyone who has worked in a foreign ministry for more than a decade can attest to that.[11] As recently as the early 1990s, a diplomat from a typical OECD country would usually begin a working day by reviewing a raft of encrypted messages, received via telegraph from headquarters. Some were instructions, stamped with the word "ACTION" in bright red; most, however, were copies distributed for information purposes. These messages typically were carefully crafted, benefiting from multiple levels of sign-off. Whatever the particular content, more often than not the action in question involved a meeting with a colleague at the appropriate level of the foreign ministry of the receiving state. A car and driver would be booked, a démarche undertaken, notes made, a record left (be it in the form of a diplomatic note, aide-mémoire, or other device), and a report drafted. This was usually done by hand, because most foreign service officers (like most white-collar workers in those days) didn't type. A secretary would prepare the reply on a special carbonized form. After suitable approvals had been received and amendments made, the missive would again be encrypted and a telegram dispatched. At that point the officer would attend to other duties and await further instructions.

Just a few years later, it seems little short of amazing that such rituals passed for interstate relations, Westphalian style. It was a laborious, usually predictable set piece that, by postmillennial standards, seemed to happen almost in slow motion. Public affairs and cultural programs existed, but they

Learning by Doing

Diplomats are finally beginning the task of professional reconstruction. While the extent differs from case to case, especially for smaller countries, the rise to prominence of public diplomacy or PD in Canada is, I think, quite telling. At times PD has come to dominate the agenda, though at others obstacles to further progress have appeared.

In Canada, the relationship between mainstream diplomacy and public affairs (or public information) began to change, along with most everything else, around the end of the Cold War. Among the early examples of broad-based civil-society partnerships in support of policy objectives are the campaign within the Commonwealth against apartheid in South Africa, which lasted from the mid-1980s to the early 1990s; the negotiation of the Montreal Protocol on Ozone Layer Depletion in 1987; and the effort to secure indefinite extension of the nuclear nonproliferation treaty (NPT) from 1993 to 1994. Even more extensive was the international political tapestry woven in cooperation with NGOs and like-minded states prior to the drafting of the Rio Declaration, Agenda 21, Biodiversity Convention, the Framework Convention on Climate Change, and the Statement of Forestry Principles at the Rio Summit on Environment and Development in 1992.[12] NGOs were included in the official delegation, and funding was even provided for the organization of an alternative event, the People's Summit, which in some respects prefigured the establishment of the World Social Forum in Porto Alegre, Brazil.

In my recollection, however, the defining moment for public diplomacy came during Canada's dispute with Spain over North Atlantic fisheries in 1994. Canada's position and actions—in particular the pursuit and attack on the trawler *Estai* in international waters—were predicated on tenuous legal grounds. Some even called the attack an act of war. It was recognized almost from the start that standard diplomatic practice would not be sufficient. A decision was therefore made to move the contest as far as possible into the court of public opinion.

A major global campaign was orchestrated out of Ottawa, one based largely on the principles of public relations and particularly the notion of earned media. On the day the Spanish were to present their case in New York to a UN conference on straddling and migratory fish stocks, the Canadian fisheries minister, Brian Tobin, stood in front of the international press on a barge in the East River opposite UN headquarters, holding up a fishing net with illegally undersized mesh seized from the Spanish trawler. Tobin's brash stunt made for brilliant visuals and produced headlines everywhere. It amounted to an ambush of the Spanish government and effectively preempted Spain's

continued

Learning by Doing (Cont.)

attempt to make a case against Canada before the UN. It also completely undermined the position of the Spanish fisheries minister, Luis Atienza, who had to withdraw an op-ed in the *Wall Street Journal* setting out Spain's position. To top it all off, a few days later, Canada's high commissioner to the UK, Royce Frith, posed against a sea of Canadian flags displayed by supportive Cornish fishers who were similarly riled over Spanish fishing practices. Again, the photo-op received massive coverage. The court of public opinion had been so sufficiently conditioned that when Spain approached the World Court in The Hague with their complaint, the justices balked.

In short, Canada orchestrated a vivid, news-making global campaign, backed up by briefings and presentations on overfishing and resource conservation. It worked, and people noticed. As the 1990s rolled on, Canada led the diplomatic world in forging coalitions with like-minded states and NGOs, for example in support of the (ultimately aborted) humanitarian intervention to assist refugees in Rwanda and Zaire in 1996. During the tenure of then foreign minister Lloyd Axworthy, the new diplomatic style was honed to a fine edge via successful partnerships with civil society and state allies in campaigns leading to, for instance, the signature of the Treaty Banning Land Mines in 1997 and the establishment of the International Criminal Court in 1998.[13] Both were orchestrated over the opposition of the United States and other major powers.

More or less the same approach was taken toward initiatives to limit the proliferation of small arms, curb the use and abuse of child soldiers, and restrict the sale of conflict diamonds via the establishment of the Kimberly Process. Canada also sponsored the International Commission on Intervention and State Sovereignty, whose final report, *The Responsibility to Protect,* though initially forgotten in the aftermath of 9/11, resurfaced and was adopted in principle at the UN Millennium Summit in September 2005.[14]

These examples are intended to illustrate that the diplomatic paradigm, as it were, is shifting.[15] Public diplomacy is geared, in the first instance, toward connecting with a population rather than a state; conventional diplomacy may still be necessary, but it is no longer sufficient to influence foreign governments. That influence is best brought to bear through their publics as well as through international public opinion, especially if recourse to hard power is not an option and in an era when democratization has expanded the scope for exercising influence indirectly. This, in turn, requires the cultivation of opinion leaders, locally and globally; the strategic use of the media; the founding of partnerships with business, NGOs, scholars, and the like-minded; and as much technological sophistication and savvy as can be mustered.

were mostly considered to be, like communications, supplemental rather than integral to the real business of diplomacy. Thus they were always the most vulnerable when resources were reduced.

For its many virtues, PD is not yet part of the cultural mainstream in foreign ministries; changing the way that diplomats work also requires changing who does the work.[16] Recruiters of public diplomats and especially guerrilla diplomats (of whom more in the chapters to come) will have to start emphasizing the need for demonstrated excellence in cross-cultural communication, networking, language skills, advocacy, negotiation, and more. Think knapsacks and BlackBerries rather than Guccis and limos, denim and khaki rather than suits and ties. The upshot is that diplomats will start to look less like decorous messengers—envoys of the sovereign, extraordinary, and plenipotentiary—and more like streetwise lobbyists whose experience as world travelers may be at least as useful as a sheaf of prestigious degrees. And this new, more public style of diplomacy is not just for designated officers; it's for everyone at the embassy, and indeed, for many beyond—providing, that is, that the activities have some direct connection to governance and the goals of international policy. Otherwise, they amount to international public relations.

If forging relationships with citizens in other countries is now at least as important as engaging in dialogues with their governments, then certain countries will be better positioned than others to exercise influence on the world stage. Globalized countries with diverse, multicultural populations such as Brazil, Canada, and Malaysia may find it easier to make connections beyond their borders than those whose cultures are more isolated and/or whose populations are more homogeneous, as is the case with Japan and Korea. A global network of diplomatic missions will help by providing a suitable platform. Membership in multiple international organizations has obvious advantages. A robust, competitive economy, an advanced technological capacity, and a sophisticated infrastructure can help finance and otherwise enable public diplomacy. Being known as, say, a national content creator for the mass media, especially television, and (even better) being liked and admired help, too. How can governments best gain these advantages? Is it just a matter of budgeting or tweaking the international policy machinery? If only.

The Way We Were

The points I have just raised bear directly on a country's ability to gain popular advantage in a competitive and insecure world. Yet the general public rarely if ever dwells on thoughts of foreign ministries, the foreign service, or diplomacy per se. If the subject does come up, it tends to evoke images of the arcane if not irrelevant: top hats and tails, stately receptions, crystal and chandeliers, the tact and discretion of dignified emissaries, and so on. Diplomacy in the twenty-first century retains a bit of all these things, but only a bit. Diplomacy, the foreign ministry, and the foreign service, like all government institutions facing the transformative challenges of globalization, are in a period of profound transition.

Of course, even if the public were to acknowledge such change, it may yet remain deeply uninterested. Diplomacy is a forsaken, even desolate area of international studies, underserviced and undercriticized. Foreign ministries have attracted similarly little examination, even among those in the fields of public policy and public administration, which are themselves considered by many to be among the least dynamic of intellectual pursuits. In the words of diplomatic studies scholar Paul Sharp, "This stuff is so important. . . . I just don't understand why no one pays any attention."[17]

There have been some exceptions. For example, in his superb *Diplomacy and Its Discontents,* James Eayrs writes of "the cronyism of the diplomatic corps, the diplomat's desire to think well of the regime at whose pleasure he remains, the circumspection required by protocol."[18] Much of Eayrs's critique of diplomacy, penned over the course of two decades (from the 1960s to the 1980s), remains strikingly prescient today.

Constructive criticism of foreign ministries is something that the world could use more of. For those interested in the nonviolent resolution of international conflict and the effective management of global issues, foreign ministries, diplomacy, and the foreign service are, however imperfect, far from irrelevant. They're positioned at the juncture where the rubber hits the road. However unlikely it may seem, then, concerns about organizational structure, bureaucratic process, and institutional engineering matter in the context of development and security in the age of globalization. So why has there been so little analytical activity?

Back to Basics

Let's start with a look at the terminology, which is also widely ignored or misunderstood. Diplomacy and the issues with which it deals remain for most people fairly remote, even obscure subjects with limited relevance to daily life. Readers who wish to delve into the subject more deeply will have to wait until the next chapter; for present purposes, diplomacy might best be understood simply as a nonviolent approach to the management of international relations, whereby shared values and interests are identified through political communication and differences are resolved through negotiation and compromise. Influence is managed, policy advocated, and objectives and national interests pursued. In short, diplomats seek to achieve results, and in so doing advance or defend their country's political and economic place in the world. That is the purpose, the essence, of diplomacy.[19]

Of course diplomacy as a tool of international relations does not exist in isolation, even though it sometimes seems that way. It is linked organizationally to the foreign ministry, which provides administrative and policy support, and to the foreign service, which puts the human face on diplomacy. To be sure, foreign ministries are not the only government departments vested with diplomatic agency, and many people outside the foreign service are involved in diplomacy. But this trio is at the core of international policy, which is the necessary starting point.

Faced with a host of challenges engendered by globalization, foreign ministries most everywhere, and especially those in the A-world, have responded in a like fashion. Almost all are attempting to "work smarter" (to use the contemporary parlance) by reconciling priorities with resources, identifying clients and establishing standards of service, and focusing on the core business to determine how best to provide representation abroad.[20] New terms—*crisis communications, accountability frameworks, risk management*—are finding their way into the diplomatic lexicon. Foreign ministries are entering into partnerships with civil societies and are relying increasingly on the Internet and other new media for their communications.[21] Innovation and entrepreneurship, if not yet universally in evidence, are becoming more common.

In practice, available resources and improved results form an intimate dialectic. Resources, when skillfully managed, usually produce results, and results—especially if they can be demonstrated in the run-up to national elections or during the preparation of budgets—tend to produce additional resources. Lately, many foreign ministries have found both to be in rather short supply. In fact, at a time of flat or shrinking capacity, practitioners seem caught in a vise between a constant mandate that includes coordinating international relations, managing global issues, and providing consular services both at home and abroad and an operating environment characterized by increasing demands born of crosscutting transnational forces and the activities of nonstate actors. The final result has been universally predictable: do more, get less.

Since at least the 1970s, when then Prime Minister Pierre Trudeau quipped famously that he could get all of the international reporting he needed from the *New York Times*, Canadian diplomats have had to fight a determined rearguard action to demonstrate their continuing relevance and address negative popular perceptions. Certainly, the advent of low-cost travel has made it much easier to dispatch specialists to problem areas around the world quickly and has thus lessened the need to have generalists on the ground everywhere. But there is no substitute for firsthand observation, local knowledge, or the maintenance of networks of personal contacts.

Managers in foreign ministries—many of whom would gladly trade in their status as senior officials for a suitable appointment abroad—have arrived at a critical moment, and are struggling with variations on a central theme: how best to align the structures, doctrines, and methods of the international policy triad with the new rule set?

Welcome to the Machine

In Canada and elsewhere, the clear trend has been to make the foreign ministry more like any other government department. But in almost every respect, foreign ministries are *not* like other government departments.

Foreign ministries, with their networks of missions abroad, represent the policy and administrative apparatus through which national governments seek to stay in step with, if not slightly ahead of, an ever-changing world. Yet large organizations, particularly ones as venerable as these, typically function according to tradition; they are conservative, predictable, and change-resistant. Hierarchical structures and top-down social relations are defining characteristics. Dissent is generally discouraged, while unquestioning loyalty, unbridled ambition, and faithful service are rewarded. Blessing the received wisdom and running with the herd, often under the guise of team playing, can be the keys to advancement. More than a few successful careers have been forged in the act of making the boss look good. In most foreign ministries, and for all kinds of reasons, progressive human-resource management is not a strong suit.

Globalization, quite apart from its many other impacts, is revealing the high cost of maintaining archaic organizational practices, yet they persist; thus foreign ministries, which are difficult to manage successfully under the best of circumstances, are paying dearly. Compounding the institutional inertia and the pressures of having to cope with an international operating environment undergoing ceaseless evolution, foreign ministries must also take account of developments in domestic politics and public administration. Again, permit a few Canadian examples. Imagine the management challenges associated with the decision to integrate elements of the then Department of Industry, Trade, and Commerce as well as the rotational personnel component of the Canadian International Development Agency into the Department of External Affairs in the first half of the 1980s; the lengthy but ill-fated attempt at reform called Corporate Review that was attempted in the early 1990s and several times since, with similarly inconclusive results; or the spending cuts of 35 percent imposed later in that decade.[22] More recently (in 2003 and 2006, respectively) came the decisions first to bifurcate the department in order to create a separate trade ministry—and then to reintegrate it with Foreign Affairs just after the separation had been completed.

It would be impossible to overstate the anxiety, dislocation, inefficiency, and administrative overhead generated by these sorts of massive reorganizations. But can such crises of productivity and morale be transformed into opportunities? At Foreign Affairs Canada, a strategic decision was made to try, by taking advantage of the 2003 split, to create a foreign ministry (and diplomacy, and foreign service) for the twenty-first century. The process was to reflect no mere clever or convenient calculation of bureaucratic interest; rather, it would entail a disciplined assessment of the best way forward in a changing world.[23]

Although never fully articulated or developed as such, what came to be known as FAC 21 involved the elements of both a strategy and a plan. The strategy? At its center was a significant and sharp redefinition of the foreign ministry's mandate as an interpreter of globalization, articulator of foreign policy, integrator of the international agenda, advocate of values and interests, provider of services, and steward of public resources. And the plan? To identify and address the imperatives for institutional change in the following ways:

- Strengthening policy capacity
- Renewing core professional skills
- Increasing agility, reducing rigidity
- Maximizing assets in the field
- Connecting with wider networks
- Focusing on public diplomacy

But an election intervened, the government changed, new resources were withheld, and the plan to build a contemporary stand-alone foreign ministry that did not contain a trade component was among the first casualties. That is not, however, to suggest that the Foreign Ministry's efforts to perfect the operations of the bureaucratic machinery at headquarters or the methods of representation abroad can or should be set aside. Indeed, these have continued, albeit with more modest intentions.[24]

Meanwhile, another interesting experiment was launched at Georgetown University in Washington, where on January 18, 2006, US Secretary of State Condoleezza Rice set out the Transformational Diplomacy strategy. This initiative was larger in scope and more radical—hence more controversial—than was FAC 21 and its successors. It would dramatically reallocate resources within the US State Department and, especially, within and among diplomatic missions abroad in favor of emerging thematic and geographic priorities. Although prospects are far from certain, the plan is well worth a look.[25]

If only it were the case that all of the major impediments to the transformation of foreign ministries were internal. The authority for much of the key international policy decisionmaking, in the A-world especially, has migrated—to finance and defense departments, cabinet or executive offices, or specialized secretariats. There has been notable centralization, with the prime minister's office (in Canada) and the White House (in the United States) playing particularly prominent roles.[26] The practice of so-called high politics in diplomacy continues, finding expression in summits of various types, from the

G8 and APEC to La Francophonie and the Commonwealth to the EU, the Americas, and North-South. However, the foreign ministry's role in scripting these events or in orchestrating their outcomes is limited. Indeed, the days of near-monopoly control by foreign ministries over international relations are long gone. They have been replaced in the domestic sphere by a free-for-all whose participants include government departments, businesses, NGOs, and individuals—CEOs and celebrities alike.

No Quarter

Foreign ministries everywhere are struggling; indeed, in my view the convergence of past and present developments constitutes a one-two punch. The bout hasn't yet been ruled a knockout, but the foreign ministry is on the ropes.

At the macro level of analysis, the role of foreign ministry has suffered from the emergence of a world characterized by a much smaller place for most states. It features an infertile public environment, with a fragmented international policy constituency on the home front due to the rise of special interests and the concurrent disappearance of any domestic foreign-policy consensus. And, since the end of the Cold War, it has encouraged the continual dismantling of international programs and policy instruments. Microdevelopments—within foreign ministries themselves—are also troublesome. They include the prevalence of rust-out, whereby an aging workforce and decaying physical infrastructure lead to the corrosion of the administrative machinery; a foreign service under acute stress as a result of lateral entries, political appointments, hostility from the executive branch, and a threat to rotationality as the defining attribute of foreign service; and the adoption of business models that are faltering as a result of resource scarcity and requirements to clear all public communications with higher authorities in advance of delivery. As long as its agents are not authorized, as a result of centralized controls, to engage spontaneously in exchanges with foreign and domestic audiences, public diplomacy, considered by many to represent the core element of the "new" diplomacy, is a nonstarter.

In the face of this combined onslaught, diplomats' capacity to perform critical functions such as policy development and analysis, intelligence gathering, and international leadership is limited. But even that is somewhat beside the point if there is little appetite elsewhere in government for the kind of deep area knowledge and policy advice and initiative that might be—and once were—produced by foreign ministries.

What, then, remains? In no particular order, the following:

- The preparation of briefing materials, media lines, routine communications, and question-and-answer documents for use in legislatures
- The planning and execution of incoming and outgoing visits

- Consular assistance—a boom industry in the wake of ever-increasing numbers of nationals traveling and living abroad
- Crisis management (epidemics, evacuations, natural disasters, high-profile kidnapping and hostage cases)
- Maintenance of the physical and IT infrastructure, with special attention paid to security
- Common service provision to departmental employees and those seconded from other government departments—who now comprise a majority of the staff for many missions abroad
- Protocol
- Minimal maintenance of bilateral relations and adherence to multilateral and international legal obligations
- Submission to endless administrative requirements—reorganizations, regulations, audits, performance and publication reviews, freedom of information and privacy requests

It is hardly overcritical to observe that these activities are more a source of busywork than the stuff of statecraft. The more cerebral components of the diplomatic arts are vanishing. And as for S&T? Barely visible.

Yet that's not all. Amid this blizzard of mostly routine demands, diplomats must also reap the whirlwind of new threats: terrorism, genomics, transnational crime, biotechnology, pandemic disease, ecological implosion, and mass migrations. Many of these are generated by nonstate actors, yet foreign ministries are still structured to deal, in the first instance, with states. In short, expectations proliferate while capacities diminish.

The expansion—seen by some as encroachment—of other government departments into areas previously believed to be the exclusive preserve of the foreign ministry has been going on for years, but there has been little compensatory effort to insert the foreign ministry into domestic debates or to underline its relevance to the security and prosperity of those it serves. There has been no concentrated, sustained, or strategic effort to develop a domestic constituency.

The diplomatic ecosystem, then, is facing systemic crisis. The days of diplomats cruising on their vestigial prestige and mystique, faces to the world and backsides to their capitals, have long since passed. Yet to date, most foreign ministries are still struggling to find a suitable new role.[27]

Business Reengineering

What, then, is to be done? To remain relevant, the foreign ministry must develop new forms of representation abroad and establish a headquarters that is smaller, flatter, more mobile, and, not least, more influential and powerful. A foreign ministry that is more attuned to the work of other government departments and to the preoccupations of citizens would be positioned to lead on major international issues across government instead of scrambling incessantly and fighting often ill-fated, defensive actions. A more effective approach to diplomacy—one that eschews dated, state-centric models in favor of a contemporary business model to better connect with foreign and domestic publics—is similarly essential. And the foreign service must be transformed, in part by building a better diplomat. All of these issues are reprised in the next chapter.

On the more practical side—and this cannot be overemphasized—foreign ministries have become, to a disturbing extent, international service providers, spending much more time and money providing for other government officials on missions abroad (furnishing housing, administration and IT support, office space, and so on) than pursuing essential international policy objectives. However necessary, this is not sufficient, for it generates huge administrative overheads and causes an inversion of priorities: picture a giant administrative tail wagging a tiny, emaciated international policy dog that at times seems barely capable of barking.[28]

Foreign ministries need to find a radically different way to manage this anomaly. Dressing common service provision up as stewardship is not enough; after all, that responsibility could be delegated to a special operating agency that would report to the deputy head but function separately. And much greater efforts will be required to improve the terms and conditions of service if a cadre of language and policy experts is to be retained abroad and foreign ministries are to avoid overreliance on local hiring.

In short, it is time to reconstruct the foreign ministry, rethink diplomacy, and reinvent diplomats. More precisely, foreign ministries will need to find ways to accomplish many of the objectives set out in the aforementioned FAC 21 plan.[29] The central elements of that modernization program, though never implemented, seem to me to be of near-universal applicability.

Restoring relevance to foreign ministries means getting beyond the burden of bureaucratic process and organizing for the management of tomorrow's preoccupations—S&T issues foremost among them—today. It means we must fashion a foreign ministry that can interpret, articulate, integrate, and advocate by assessing what the changing world means for its home country. The agents of diplomacy must function as catalysts for their governments, guides for their fellow citizens, and compelling storytellers to the world. To do this, they must maximize assets in the field, connect with wider networks, renew professional skills, and strengthen policy capacity. They must also make much more of the foreign ministry's comparative advantages—notably its matrix of missions abroad and knowledge of the world—as they embark upon a higher level of analysis of such crosscutting issues as governance, sustainable development, the administration of democracy, the rule of law, and peace building, to name a few.

In practice, this will involve a dedication and commitment to intellectual leadership and policy entrepreneurship. It will entail moving beyond the merely transactional and placing a much greater emphasis on planning and deeply analyzing the kinds of broad policy concerns we have already mentioned. Mainly, though, ways must be found to restore the foreign ministry's undervalued and hence atrophying geographic expertise. This overarching understanding of and connection to the world is the foreign ministry's ace in the hole against continuing encroachment by other departments of government.

Most of all, to restore relevance and to secure the transition from relic to renaissance, foreign ministries will have to find ways to realize what I consider to be the single most important potential innovation associated with Canada's abortive FAC 21 experiment: the mainstreaming of public diplomacy. An examination of what, exactly, that might entail is the subject of the final chapters of this volume.

Notes

1. In the United States, for example, the Department of Foreign Affairs was the first agency of government created under the Constitution in 1789.

2. For recent analytical treatments of the foreign ministry, see Rana and Kurbalija (2007), Hocking and Spence (2003), Hocking (1999).

3. See Kurlantzick (2008b).

4. These issues, however, have plagued foreign ministries for some time; see Copeland (1997). An early critique—my first of this sort—was published and distributed internally by the Professional Association of Foreign Service Officers; see Copeland (1989a). The major points still stick.

5. This pool of employees is referred to as *rotational*; it may consist of members drawn from several occupational groups in addition to the foreign service.

6. Personal communication, November, 25 2007. DFAIT stands for the Department of Foreign Affairs and International Trade. In the United States, the Pentagon's influence relative to that of the State Department is proportionately even greater.

7. The implications of such developments for diplomacy and global governance are well surveyed in Cooper, Hocking, and Maley (2008).

8. Chronic resource shortages, low morale, rampant careerism, and a tendency to judge ideas by their provenance rather than by their quality are common complaints. I have written previously on the human-resources problems afflicting foreign ministries and will resist the temptation to repeat myself here.

9. Kafka chronicled the tendency of bureaucracies to bend if not break the will of the people within them. It has been my experience that foreign ministries in particular may fit Kafka's description.

10. A comprehensive survey of the theory and practice of public diplomacy is found in Cowan and Cull (2008).

11. After taking an early lead in the development and application of PD, Canada, ironically, has since moved to the back of the pack in PD practice. DFAIT's PD budget was reduced significantly in 2006 and again in 2008, when international cultural programs were slashed. Whereas one of former US undersecretary for public diplomacy Karen Hughes's enduring achievements was the relaxation of clearance rules for speeches and media contacts, in Canada all outreach, media contact, and publication activity by DFAIT employees is now tightly controlled and scrutinized. And whereas in the United States, the UK, and a growing number of other foreign ministries, employees are allowed to host blogs, in Canada all Internet postings, even purely personal ones, are subject to departmental review.

12. A very good summary of the formidable accomplishments of the Rio Summit on Environment and Development (UNCED) can be found in Cleveland, Kubiszewski, and Miller (2007). Almost twenty years later, it is saddening to realize how little has been achieved in the interim.

13. See Axworthy (2003).

14. See International Development Research Center (2001).

15. They also illustrate the extent to which political leadership can be determinant. The likes of this extraordinary burst of diplomatic energy, all flowing from one minister's insistence on diverting resources toward those arenas in which Canada could, as Minister Axworthy liked to insist, "make a difference," have not been seen since.

16. See Copeland (2008) for a more complete portrait of a public diplomat.

17. Personal communication with the author, March 4, 2007. See also Sharp (1997: 58–78), Sharp and Wiseman (2008).

18. Eayrs (1971) will be revisited in the conclusion. Eayrs's disdain for diplomats, diplomacy, and the foreign ministry has not mellowed much in the intervening years. I discovered this firsthand on June 20, 2007, while attending a dinner to celebrate the release of a special issue of the *International Journal* dedicated to Eayrs's lifetime of scholarship. Special thanks to Denis Stairs for editing that volume and organizing the dinner.

19. A very preliminary sketch of some of the ideas presented here was first presented on March 5, 2005, at a UK conference entitled Diplomacy Today: Delivering Results in a World of Changing Priorities. A more fully developed version of that presentation may be found in Copeland (2005).

20. See, for example, Marshall and Ayad (1996; 1997).

21. On the impact of the ICT revolution on diplomacy and foreign ministries, see Bàtora (2008), Potter (2002), Larson (2004). See also the more complete discussion of IT provided in Chapters 11 and 12.

22. I prepared a critique of this exercise that was published by the Professional Association of Foreign Service Officers under the title *Bureaucratoxis*; see Copeland (1992). A year later, when asked to describe the status of the review enterprise, one senior manager looked down and replied dismally, "We no longer speak of it."

23. Following the political decision to split the departments of foreign affairs and international trade in 2003, efforts to reform Canada's foreign ministry accelerated, reaching an apogee in 2005 and 2006. Amidst much fanfare, former deputy minister Peter Harder and associate deputy Marie-Lucie Morin launched a major organizational change initiative under the slogan "Building a Twenty-First Century Foreign Ministry," which came to be known as FAC 21. There was a series of internal broadcast messages on reform; an intranet site was established; an office of innovation and excellence was created to promote the enterprise among staff under the direct supervision of the associate deputy minister; all geographic branches outside of North America were merged and a global-issues branch created; positions began to be redeployed from headquarters to missions abroad; a special operating agency to provide common services to missions abroad was being examined; and lines of responsibility for some key elements of PD were clarified. Much of this initiative came to a crashing halt when a change in government resulted in a decision to reunite the departments.

24. In late October 2006, some of the essential elements of the 2005 FAC 21 reform program were restyled and relaunched as the New Way Forward: Political Economic Renewal Initiative. That exercise continues in tandem with an omnibus effort to align the department's programs and geographic priorities with those of the government.

25. See Rice (2006). For a critique of the Rice plan as too supportive of military goals, see Herr (2008).

26. Foreign ministries tend to take their direction from presidents and prime ministers, although there have recently been calls to democratize diplomacy by making it and its practitioners more accountable to elected representatives.

27. There is a growing body of critical literature on diplomacy and its relationship to foreign ministries, much of it written by those who have left the service. See, for instance, Ross (2007), Kiesling (2006), and Riordan (2003). John Brown, who resigned from the State Department over the US decision to invade Iraq, now works at the Institute for the Study of Diplomacy and, as senior fellow, reviews PD literature and blogs for the University of Southern California's Center on Public Diplomacy (see http://uscpublicdiplomacy.org/index.php/newsroom/johnbrown_main). See also Brown (2007). An entire anthology by diplomatic dissidents cannot be far off.

28. In Canada's case, by design as much as default, this trend is resulting in the rebranding of DFAIT embassies as service providers for the government of Canada abroad. The trend was described to me by one colleague as a formula not for converting diplomatic missions into service platforms, as is supposedly intended, but for turning diplomats into doormats.

29. Coincidentally, many of the central tenets of the attempted DFAIT reform were set out in Moses and Knutson (2001). It is noteworthy that theorists and practitioners reached similar conclusions and prescriptions independently.

Public Diplomacy and Foreign Service: The Front Lines 10

We have observed how the ever-changing conditions of a world evolving at warp speed have impacted the diplomatic milieu. In Chapter 9, I looked at the struggle tradition-bound institutions like foreign ministries are undergoing to face the challenges of globalization and identified some of the ways in which their performance might be improved. Yet institutional retooling, however comprehensive, will not be sufficient as long as the precepts on which the existing diplomatic business model is founded remain unchanged. In this chapter, therefore, we will examine those elements critical to the transformation of diplomatic practice. In addition to a much closer look at PD and branding, I will include consideration of the often neglected human dimension of diplomacy, which is represented by the foreign service.

Once over Lightly

As we have seen, in 2005, Canada attempted to broaden the effectiveness of public diplomacy by reforming the foreign ministry under the banner of FAC 21 and the so-called new diplomacy.[1] That new diplomacy might be thought of as *public diplomacy plus*—a contemporary, whole-of-government approach based on connecting with populations through networking and advocacy. Its proponents sought to promote values, policies, and interests abroad, both by reforming the machinery of international policy and by attempting to influence public opinion on key issues—from matters of trade, investment, and tourism to support for candidates at the UN. The new diplomacy would use public diplomacy to address four priorities: North America (i.e., relations with the United States and Mexico); global security; multilateralism; and developing bilateral relations with BRIC, or Brazil, Russia, India, and China. It was not a cure-all, but it was a start, and it illustrates the scope and potential of PD.

In this chapter, I will try to demonstrate that in the information-saturated precincts that mark the globalization age—and this cannot be overstated—you are what you seem. Perception very quickly impacts the real world of national interests. And the results can be incendiary, especially if some parties are intent on fanning the flames. When the Danish newspaper *Jyllands-Posten* published twelve editorial cartoons depicting Muhammad on September 30, 2005, Danish Muslim groups deemed the cartoons blasphemous and held public protests to spread knowledge of their publication worldwide. As attention to the cartoons grew, they were reprinted in newspapers in more than fifty other countries, which led to severe protests and even riots. Prime Minister Anders Fogh Rasmussen described the controversy as Denmark's worst international crisis since World War II.[2]

As the Danes learned, image projection and reputation management are now far from optional. Because these are hard to earn and easily lost, public diplomacy, media strategy, and international public relations have become essential to statecraft. Their full potential, of course, can only be realized by the right people doing the right things in the right places. After all, public diplomacy, as will be shown, is at least as much about "them" and their needs as it is about "us" and ours.

Taking Diplomacy to the People

In everyday parlance, the adjective *diplomatic* applies to those who show tact in their interpersonal communications. The noun *diplomacy,* meanwhile, is in the first instance an international activity. Formal, interstate diplomacy is still a big part of international relations. In many parts of the T- and E-worlds, where connecting directly with populations can present significant practical difficulties (for example, language and cultural barriers, inadequate communications facilities, logistics failures), there may be few alternatives to conventional diplomacy. In that respect, it is the default. So, too, in authoritarian countries where attempts by the representatives of foreign governments to engage with local populations on certain sensitive issues could be interpreted as interference in internal affairs.

Strategic and political communications have always been at the heart of diplomacy, but their content, purpose, and practice are evolving.[3] However necessary, traditional diplomacy is often insufficient when it comes to moving foreign governments to act. These days, that is best done through engagement with their publics as well as through influence over international public opinion, both mass and elite. Cultivating this influence requires developing a variety of types of advocacy, reaching audiences and opinion leaders both locally and globally, and forging relationships into networks.[4] In this respect, PD can be thought of as an avenue for activities intended to change people's perceptions in a way that helps sending states achieve their objectives. Employing both government and nongovernment actors to connect with other players at other levels of society, PD reflects the move from the old style of state-to-state foreign policy toward the new style of multimedia, multiparty international policy.[5]

I will concentrate not on policy content but on what I believe to be the general formula for effective PD. The term *public diplomacy* itself, though in widespread use, is somewhat imprecise and disputed. For our purposes, public diplomacy consists of outwardly directed activities by national representatives aimed at identifying shared objectives and potential areas of collaboration with publics abroad. These publics include the general population, special interest groups, the media, civil society, and business and opinion leaders, among others. PD is in the main a tool of triangulation, designed to sway the decisions of foreign governments by influencing their polities.[6] In this respect, related terms such as *branding, advocacy, lobbying,* and *partnership building* are best understood as constituent elements gathered under the umbrella of PD. At its most distilled, this formula is predicated upon the use of mutual interests to find common cause and the recognition that in the era of globalization, action designed to move issues must be distributed and will not only, or sometimes even primarily, involve governments.

Since 9/11 we have witnessed a resurgence of international interest in public diplomacy, which, as noted earlier, played a significant role during the Cold War that diminished after the thaw. Now PD has again begun to preoccupy foreign ministries, particularly in the A-world. Australia and New Zealand have both published PD handbooks, and the Australia Senate has held a public inquiry into that country's PD performance.[7] In the United States, PD has been studied comprehensively by the General Accounting Office and the Office of Management and Budget as well as by various agencies of Congress.[8] Lord Carter of Coles completed a comprehensive review of the UK's PD institutions and activities in 2006.[9] PD also figured importantly in Canada's International Policy Statement of 2005.[10]

Not only foreign ministries but universities, think tanks, and consultants have variously engaged with enthusiasm.[11] A profusion of new programs, courses, books, journals, articles, and conference panels have enlarged a burgeoning body of literature[12] and have sustained the public diplomacy renaissance. Drawing as it does on insights gleaned from the fields of international relations, public administration, communications, political science, and anthropology, to name a few, PD could even emerge as a new academic discipline.[13]

A function of the noncoercive power of attraction—what Joseph Nye has called "soft power"—PD may be focused tactically on a particular issue or objective in the short term or it may be pursued more strategically over time in order to enlarge understanding between peoples.[14] Soft power is something a country doesn't merely wield but earns.[15] As such, it may be gained or lost over time, and it may work best when it is not being employed deliberately. It is based largely on perception—on the response to image and reputation—and is grounded in culture, in demonstrated political values, and in policy as practiced at home and abroad. When the perception is positive, it is easier to make a persuasive case in support of an identified objective, particularly if the ground has been well tilled and the furrows prepared carefully for seeding.[16]

Hard power—armed force, aid spending, espionage, and vigorous conventional diplomatic representation—does not necessarily translate into influence. Indeed, the decrease in US influence and the increase in China's have become defining features of the international scene.[17] There are, however, instances in which hard power can be applied in support of soft power, as with peacekeeping missions or the use of military assets to provide emergency humanitarian relief, as with the deployment of the US Navy to Indonesia in the aftermath of the 2004 tsunami. So, too, can the means of soft power be used to advance the ends of hard power, as when public diplomacy supports peace building or counterinsurgencies (see Chapter 12).[18] In most applications, however, public diplomacy functions as an instrument of soft power.[19]

In order to understand more completely these interrelationships, it may be useful to highlight some of the differences between the nature and agency of hard and soft power. The former is associated principally with the armed forces and the latter with diplomacy, in general, and public diplomacy, in particular. When the two power sources and international policy instruments are compared, the obstacles and constraints to their effective combination become clearer. Following are some of the basic distinctions:

- *Definitions.* Hard power is about compelling your adversary to comply with your will through the threat or use of force. Soft power is about attracting your partner to share your goals through dialogue and exchange.[20]
- *Objectives.* Hard power seeks to kill, capture, or defeat an enemy. Soft power seeks influence through understanding and the identification of common ground.
- *Techniques.* Hard power relies ultimately on sanctions and flows from the barrel of a gun. Soft power is rooted in meaningful exchange and the art of persuasion.
- *Values.* Hard power is macho, absolute, and zero-sum. Soft power is supple, subtle, and win/win.
- *Ethos.* Hard power engenders fear, anguish, and suspicion. Soft power flourishes in an atmosphere of confidence, trust, and respect.

These distinctions can become disjunctures when placed in an institutional setting. That is, while significant enough in themselves, the disconnects are exacerbated by differences within and between the bureaucratic cultures of the military and the foreign service. An institution designed primarily for fighting is not best suited to take the lead on talking. Hierarchy, obedience, and control are part of the DNA of military hard power. The genome of soft power, of public diplomacy, in contrast, turns on relationships, on lateral connectivity, and on the construction and maintenance of collaborative networks. These tasks are better left to diplomats.

That said, traditional diplomacy, whether or not the fact is fully understood within the political establishment, is very often not enough anymore. If your stature in the world is shrinking, you become harder to hear, at least at the official level, and your interlocutors might rather be doing diplomatic business with major or ascending powers. Public diplomacy can help compensate for this disadvantage, working to optimize your international performance by playing up your strengths, such as your positive image and reputation (deserved or otherwise), while addressing the weaknesses associated with your capacity limitations. Many international issues still begin and end with formal interstate relations—for example, UN Security Council membership campaigns or most diplomatic discourse with the developing world. Public diplomacy, however, now accounts for much of the rest of what foreign ministries actually do abroad.

It has been said that public diplomacy is undertheorized—and undercriticized. This may be so, and it is my modest hope here to help correct these shortcomings. Yet in practice, public diplomacy is very commonsense and instrumental. While there is something to be said for more precisely contextualizing and conceptualizing it, PD does not need to be situated in a theoretical framework in order to be intelligible.

Beyond Spin . . .

One way to grasp more firmly this somewhat slippery concept is to eliminate those things that public diplomacy is not. *Traditional diplomacy* involves state-to-state contact through designated channels, principally represented by senior government and political figures, foreign ministries, and envoys. *Public affairs,* as practiced by diplomatic missions, seeks more to inform than to persuade.[21] *Cultural relations* enrich experience and enlarge understanding. *Propaganda* is a one-way flow of information often characterized by inaccuracy or bias; US academic Nancy Snow defines it as "the spreading of ideas, information, or rumor[s] for the purpose of helping or injuring an institution, a cause, or a person."[22] *Domestic outreach* is undertaken by diplomats for purposes of public education on issues of international policy and national constituency building. At the far end of the scale, those engaged in *information warfare* and *psychological operations* (or psy-ops) aspire to dominate communications and to affect thought processes in conflict situations.[23] These are about as far from public diplomacy as political communications can get. They differ in kind from earned media, from partnerships with civil society, from joint ventures with the like-minded, and from the building of enduring relationships based on trust and respect, aspects elemental to my understanding of PD. Crucially, they lack the defining element of genuine dialogue.[24]

Public diplomacy can involve advocacy, or lobbying, defined by educator and consultant Sean Moore as "the daily dynamics of democracy between elections"—that is, the routine business of interacting with elected and government officials for the purposes of influencing decisionmaking and policy on specific issues.[25] The principal difference is that whereas traditional diplomacy (and lobbying) can involve direct engagement with host government authorities, PD mainly establishes agency and achieves its objectives indirectly, through partnerships and collaboration with local actors in civil society, ranging from NGOs to universities to the press.[26] Success will then turn on the ability of these groups to influence the behavior and policies of target governments.

Although predicated on the pursuit of interests, public diplomacy is, in the final analysis, animated more by values, which is to say by what governments consider important, than by ethics, which involve judgments about good and bad, right and wrong. These PD values include two-way communication, transparency, cooperation, respect, and agreement on shared goals. To put it another way, the centerpieces of public diplomacy are empathy and dialogue,

Deception Is Not Public Diplomacy

Occasionally, lobbying can involve disinformation and propaganda. During the run-up to the 1991 Gulf War, the Kuwait embassy in Washington provided a classic case of modern-era propaganda. The embassy hired public relations giant Hill and Knowlton, which arranged for a weeping teenage Arab beauty, known only as Nayirah, to provide wrenching, firsthand testimony before Congress. She shared her pain—the pain, she claimed, of having personally witnessed Iraqi troops emptying incubators in the al-Adan Hospital in Kuwait City and leaving the babies on the cold floor to die. Shortly after this incendiary account, the number 312—the estimated tally of infant casualties—began cropping up in media accounts and was repeated until it became rote.

References to the atrocity appeared everywhere—in presidential speeches, in reports by Amnesty International, on radio and television talk shows. The problem? None of it ever happened. The entire episode was later proven completely false; the witness, who had been coached by Hill and Knowlton, had not even been anywhere near the hospital. Instead, she turned out to be the daughter of Kuwait's ambassador to the United States, Saud Nasir al-Sabah.[27] But the effect her endlessly replayed testimony had on the public was cathartic and helped get Main Street USA behind the administration's plans for war. By the time the charade was exposed, in short, it no longer mattered.

the very antitheses of coercive power. Dialogue is distinct from debate, which can be polarizing and confrontational. In some instances, the best briefing will be no briefing: unscripted exchanges encourage spontaneous understanding, and understanding leads to higher levels of the trust and respect that are cornerstones of security. The proven effectiveness of public diplomacy institutions such as the British Council, the Alliance Française, the Japan Foundation, and the Goethe-Institut, which ply their craft at arm's length from their government sponsors, speaks powerfully to this observation.

The defining ethos of public diplomacy is meaningful exchange guided by the realization that even the best diplomatic practices will not amount to much if disconnected from policy development and political action. Public opinion abroad must be reflected in policy development at home. If the flow is not two-way, PD will be seen as hypocrisy. As they respond effectively to other parties and thereby win the trust and confidence of foreign audiences, public diplomats are indispensible for building bridges between people and in explaining their countries to the world.

Explaining the world to their countries, however, is not within their domain but rather that of domestic outreach, which has only a secondary impact on the management of international relations. It typically involves promoting the role and mandate of the foreign ministry and hence introduces some international content, but it is intended primarily to help educate the public and build constituencies at home. To describe engagement with *both* foreign and local populations as public diplomacy seems to me to complicate the definition and detract from its usefulness.

While messages intended, respectively, for international and domestic audiences must always be consonant, the most obvious but in my view still exceptional application of public diplomacy to a domestic audience would be directed interaction with diaspora communities.[28] Though rarely done, the initiation of exchanges with diaspora communities relevant to international policy makes a great deal of sense.[29] With their dense webs of homeland connectivity, the members of such groups represent a decidedly underutilized political and communications resource. Public diplomats trying to find the best way to engage strategically with, for instance, a faction of the Haitian leadership might start by talking to the Haitian-Canadian communities in Montreal and Toronto—ideally as fellow residents.[30]

Though public diplomacy and outreach are different, they are nonetheless integrated within the foreign ministry; a public diplomacy strategy cannot succeed unless the international messages are relevant and resonate domestically. The support of domestic audiences for public diplomacy is crucial. And other government departments and citizens play vital roles as well in informing and directing the international practice of public diplomacy. Thus diplomats, perhaps more than other officials, need to become Janus-faced, looking and seeing both at home and abroad simultaneously.

. . . To Engagement

The wholesale adoption of a diplomatic business model that is open, participatory, and inclusive is a huge task.[31] Secrecy and information hoarding remain rampant in foreign ministries long after the Cold War. In the words of former diplomat François Taschereau, now director general of the Montreal office of an international public relations firm, "The name of the game today is about giving up control, sharing, exercising transparency to create conversations around subjects of mutual interest. Being at the center of a conversation is what enables one to drive an agenda."[32] In other words, the *act* of communicating is at the heart of public diplomacy.[33] Listening and showing that you are listening are every bit as important as speaking clearly—and more effective than speaking loudly. Active listening is likely to result in a better understanding not just of what those with whom you are communicating want but what they need—as people rather than as mere interlocutors. This aspect of public diplomacy, with its emphasis on identifying human needs and emotions and then acting accordingly, has been largely overlooked.

In that respect I am indebted to communications consultant Rachelle Lamb[34] for drawing the literature on nonviolent communications to my attention. She used the example of negotiating with a suicide bomber. Even in the absence of shared interests or values, if it is possible to identify the bomber's needs, then there might be a basis for nonviolent resolution. Such needs might include solitude, the opportunity to earn a living, control of one's own life, or, crucially, respect. The abilities to overcome mistrust, establish respect, accept personal responsibility, and demonstrate an understanding that what you do affects others are central.[35] As Saul Alinsky has emphasized, a precondition to success in communicating is empathy. Those seeking to initiate a conversation are likely to get further if they are able to situate it within the experience of the other party.[36]

Public diplomats use the tools and tactics of public relations—a commitment to continuing conversation, the identification of shared objectives, and relationship building—to connect with populations at both the mass and elite levels. Kathy Fitzpatrick goes so far as to argue that given public diplomacy's emphasis on relationship management and other matters of public relations, it is itself best understood as public relations as practiced internationally by governments.[37]

To be sure, networking is a prominent element of public relations, and a crucial if underappreciated aspect of public diplomacy. Professor R. S. Zaharna has done pathfinding work in this area.[38] She offers the compelling argument that US public diplomacy is failing in the Middle East because it is predicated upon the idea that simply transferring information and dominating information flows can somehow substitute for using communications as an interactive platform upon which to build social relationships. Slowly but surely, it appears that her argument is gaining traction.[39]

Public diplomats will not be spending much time making démarches at the foreign ministry or following-up with carefully drafted diplomatic notes. Instead, they will count on effective networking in the context of an advocacy strategy and in light of identified objectives. This is seen as a means to shape public opinion and mobilize coalitions, thereby helping propel host governments toward desired ends. In slightly different terms, John Robert Kelly speaks of the centrality of *engagement*—that is, two-way communication as contrasted with, say, information transfer or simple influence seeking—to public diplomacy.[40]

Either way, though its marketplace is global, the territory is cerebral. The unit of currency is the idea. And the public diplomat is part activist, part lobbyist, part street-smart policy entrepreneur. To borrow from a formulation that I have heard articulated several times by US public diplomats, the more practitioners are able to operate *preactively* by conditioning the public environment, the less they will need to do *reactively,* and the more receptive their audiences will be toward *proactive* enterprise. To that it must be added that nothing will work as well as PD that is based on what countries actually do internationally. Credibility is key.

PD works best as an integral part of the policymaking process that reflects core values such as integrity and mutuality (that is, an emphasis on win-win outcomes).[41] For example, a high degree of comfort with the media, both mainstream and new, is essential; personal relationships with journalists and editors, bloggers and webmasters that are based on trust and mutual respect are crucial to success. Effectiveness will increase when positive coverage is earned rather than bought or begged. (Old-style press releases, which many foreign ministries still emit like so much diplomatic effluent, are next to useless unless they address a specific issue that already has currency.) For that matter, when it comes to choosing partners, thought should be given not just to the usual suspects but to strange bedfellows and, where appropriate, local champions. Building such bridges is neither easy nor necessarily approved by the political establishment. Worse, in the absence of due diligence, they can burn down or blow up.

In the general enthusiasm for public diplomacy, it is worthwhile to recall that traditional diplomacy, especially behind-the-scenes negotiations, still produces results, particularly in highly charged circumstances. It often neatly complements public diplomacy—as it has in the ongoing six-party talks on North Korea's nuclear program, which began in 2003, and as it did during the Middle East peace discussions of the early 1990s, which were characterized by the interplay between the public diplomacy–driven Washington peace talks and the more formal Israel-PLO negotiations facilitated by the Norwegian government. The former eventually stalled; the latter resulted in the Oslo Accords. In the post-9/11 period, the highly conspicuous absence of traditional diplomatic activity on the part of the United States in the Middle East is precisely what has undermined the credibility of their public diplomacy efforts there.

The place in diplomacy of confidential negotiations and formal exchanges (often but not always between the designated emissaries of sovereign states) is a bit like the fate of glaciers—shrinking fast but not about to disappear. Still, all of that meltwater is creating new channels for PD. Globalization is causing the center of diplomatic gravity to move, as it were, down the mountain, shifting the action off the peaks and into the populated valleys—out of the chancellery and into the street. Ergo, public diplomacy. And with the increasing democratization of political organization in areas such as Latin America and Africa, the scope for PD is growing.

PD and Branding: A Pair of Aces

Public diplomacy is rooted in issues and characterized by dialogue rather than monologue or information dumping.[42] In this respect it does, as we have noted, have much in common with public relations and even with lobbying. It also bears similarities to branding, a practice that, at its best, seeks to narrow the distance between perception and reality and keeps pace with identities in constant evolution by attempting to fix them, at least for a time, within an adaptable frame.[43] An increasing number of governments seem determined to try to actively manage their country's image and reputation, its global brand.[44] Perhaps because of that determination, however, many of their management strategies involve the one-way flow of information—diktat more than dialogue. In these cases the full potential of PD is unlikely to be achieved.

Using meaningful exchange with public constituencies to exert influence on governments and decisionmakers, public diplomacy is an inherently peaceful form of international relations that has at its center not compulsion but persuasion, an attribute it shares with both branding and public relations. Branding is an import from the private sector, and its corporate origins and provenance may explain its continuing tendency toward the use of paid media to achieve economic and commercial ends. Public diplomacy (which develops networks), public relations (which builds relationships), and branding (which projects an image or manages a reputation) all rely on ideas, intelligence, cultural knowledge, and market research. Yet in my estimation, public diplomacy differs from the others insofar as it receives at least as much as it transmits.[45]

For the purposes of comparative analysis, then, we define public diplomacy as the sum of efforts by governments to promote values, policies, and interests abroad by connecting with populations and influencing international public opinion. A brand, meanwhile, consists of the shared perception of a place, product, or person around which those interested can congregate. It is part projection, part reaction; accordingly, it is more concerned with matters pertaining to image shaping and reputation management than is public diplomacy. The distinction, though, is far from absolute.

Your brand is what sets you apart from others. Good brands are suffused with positive attitude. They have soul and seek to establish or maintain an emotional attachment. Nation branding involves telling a unique story with a clear shape and direction. The resulting brand is the distillation of that story into a form that effectively conveys national values, policies, and interests. It also serves as a mark of national identity for citizens in a confusing and sometimes threatening world. In that way nation branding, even if not especially interactive, is nonetheless a useful tool of political communications both domestically and abroad.

Brands take years to build but are easily damaged and must be protected and promoted constantly. Countries that fail to live up to the promise of their brand risk losing credibility and soft power. National stereotypes can be thought of as a type of shorthand for nation brands. Consider, for example, this old joke: Heaven is a place where the cooks are French, the mechanics are German, the lovers are Italian, the comedians are British, and everything is organized by the Swiss. In hell, the cooks are British, the mechanics are French, the comedians are German, the lovers are Swiss, and everything is organized by the Italians. Whether readers find the characterization insightful, amusing, or even offensive, I offer it to underline the observation that like it or not, nations can and do brand themselves in consequential ways.

Demystifying the Distinction

Engineering a positive predisposition toward a specific nationality is the end of branding; agents of public diplomacy, by contrast, seek support for specific international policy objectives through dialogue. A PD strategy can have a branding component, but individual PD initiatives tend to be more focused and contained; a branding campaign can have a PD component but may also rely on propaganda and other monologic forms of communication. If branding entails consistency, conformity, and staying on message, insofar as its content is paramount, then public diplomacy involves explaining the message, asking for comments, and reporting the response. It privileges form over content, enlarges the communications space by creating a shared frame of reference, and weds talk to action. This is the demonstration effect and without it, credibility will suffer.

Seen another way, if public diplomacy is a nation's story, then its brand is something like a glossy cover, designed to appeal instinctively to the consumers of international policy and encouraging them to buy the book (or visit the country or support the international policy objective). But because the market evolves quickly, the jacket design may need attention even before the book requires revision.

A nation's public diplomacy should support its brand and vice versa. Public diplomacy may be a somewhat more expansive enterprise than branding,

The Idea Garden

Branding guru Simon Anholt and I agree on many things, but we do not concur entirely on my characterization of branding. To quote Anholt at length:

> I dispute . . . your contention that branding is fundamentally a monologue. The best brand theory—and the best brand practice—today sees brand as [a] common purpose or shared vision that unites businesses with their staff, suppliers, and customers, and so is in every sense parallel to the mutuality of public and cultural diplomacy. A brand is also . . . as much an invitation to complaint as it is a promise of quality, so even in that rather literal sense it must always be about two-way communication. . . . Brand is very much more than "image" and the communication, management, or promotion of image. Brand strategy is almost synonymous with corporate strategy, and, at least in theory, there is a parallel notion in nation branding. Most firms these days would describe their brand as their relationship with their market and their other stakeholders.[46]

To that I reply, let one hundred flowers bloom. But when it comes time to pick the bouquet, it seems worth remembering that if branding is about selling the fragrance, public diplomacy is about discussing horticulture.

since, whereas almost all branding, in one way or another, constitutes PD, not all PD requires or even necessarily supports branding. But at the end of the day the point is not which is subsumed by the other; suffice it to say that the two concepts are intimately related but distinct. More important is the observation that their practitioners share the conviction that a country's international image requires active, ongoing management if international (and, by extension, domestic) policy is to be developed successfully.

Even with the best efforts, though, the results of branding in support of public diplomacy have been mixed. The Cool Britannia campaign launched by the UK in the late 1990s received much attention at the outset, but the novelty melted away as quickly as the ice cream it was named after in the heat of media scorn and ridicule.[47] Several attempts by the agents of Canada's public diplomacy to burnish the national brand received much less attention; the Upper North Side campaign in New York in 1998 and 1999 and the Think Canada Festival in Japan in 2001 appear to have achieved little of lasting value.[48]

In short, attempts to apply private-sector solutions to public-sector challenges do not always produce the results desired. Selling foreign policy, after all, is not like selling soda pop. In the wake of 9/11, marketing executive Charlotte Beers, onetime board chair of the advertising giant J. Walter Thompson, was asked by then Secretary of State Colin Powell to sell so-called Brand America in the Middle East. Beers's Madison Avenue tactics, evident in slogans like "Shared Values" and "Muslim Life in America," dissolved in fiasco. Although there were many complicating factors, she resigned less than a year into her appointment and the ads were pulled. This underscores the point that it is not enough to know how to connect from a technical standpoint; you must understand the culture and values of those you are trying to influence.[49]

Protocol to Persuasion, Démarche to Dialogue

I have emphasized that PD is most effective when meaningful exchange is wed to policy development and state behavior. As both instruments and elements of international relations, public diplomacy and branding are also techniques of statecraft. But they are something more even than that—namely, parts of a larger international policy process that works at various levels, in various time frames and dimensions.

What does this mean in practice? In the short term, the focus of PD and branding will be on event management and media relations, the latter being by nature principally reactive and crisis oriented. Dialogue, advocacy, and strategic communications are the hallmarks of the medium term; they involve initiating discussions with a view to being persuasive, obtaining inputs, and achieving outcomes. Over the long term, by sustaining the aforementioned activities while nurturing and promoting dense, robust cultural, educational, and scientific relations, practitioners will benefit from durable relationships and effective networks based on trust and respect.[50]

Speaking of cultural relations, we should consider that culture is indeed a key ingredient of public diplomacy, which helps to explain the substantial investments governments have made in institutions such as the British Council, the Alliance Française, and China's Confucius Institutes, which number more than 300 in 78 countries and counting. However, it is also—especially in the cases of the United States and Canada—among the most vulnerable components.[51] For example, in 1995, a foreign policy review titled *Canada in the World* proposed a major push in this area under the rubric of the Third Pillar. But the resources and internal support never materialized, and what was likely the single most promising initiative, the Canadian International Information Strategy—which would have placed Canada at the forefront of public diplomacy—lost the bid for funding to the landmine ban (itself a major exercise in public diplomacy) in 1997, a time of diminishing resources.[52]

To manage public diplomacy in such a manner as to convey forcefully the requisite brand characteristics of positive attitude and soul, the foreign ministry must carefully shape longer-term cultural relationships with international artistic and academic support programs.[53] That alone, however, will by no means be sufficient to secure improved performance. Much more will be required:

process and structural reengineering, the reallocation of resources and investment in public diplomacy tools, work planning and priority setting. That said, a coherent and well-executed public diplomacy and branding strategy, connected through the foreign ministry to a supportive domestic constituency, can make a real difference in advancing international policy objectives.

Although practitioners have tended to think of public diplomacy as a program and branding as a campaign, together they in fact constitute a paradigm—a new way of doing diplomatic business, of telling a country's story in an open and inclusive way. They represent the critical means to important ends, and accordingly must be engaged with care and forethought. Indeed, however tempting, it would be unwise to slip entirely into promotional mode when imagining the potential of public diplomacy and branding. These are innovative, evolutionary additions to the diplomatic toolbox, but they are not miraculous devices suitable for all circumstances. While very useful, there are real limits to what can be achieved with either.[54]

Good public diplomacy can't compensate for bad policy, and the most sophisticated branding campaign will fail if unsupported by facts. A central characteristic of brands is that they carry a promise to fulfill expectations: from whiter whites and superior handling to due process and the rule of law. However, to use marketing terms, if the brand experience does not tally with the brand message, credibility will be lost and the position of the source country weakened. Practitioners of public diplomacy sometimes refer to this as the "say-do gap," and the results can be devastating. To avoid them, the public diplomat must be prepared to stand up not only *for* one's country abroad but, when necessary, to one's country at home, say, when resources are insufficient or policy is incongruent with the inputs supplied by public diplomacy.[55] Only when the message and the experience, the saying and the doing, are in accord can legitimacy be demonstrated, relationships built, and networks reinforced. Walk the talk or risk exposure as a naked emperor.

To recapitulate: public diplomacy is enjoying a renaissance, and branding is a growth industry. These facts may be explained by three factors. First is the *tanking* of traditional diplomacy, which occupies an ever smaller niche in the diplomatic ecosystem and just doesn't work very well anymore; its actors, institutions, ethics, conventions, and legal framework require reform. Second is the *transnationalization* of diplomatic issues: globalization, the blurring of the lines between the international and domestic spheres, and the indivisibility of security—a threat to any state can easily become generalized—are forcing foreign ministries to rethink their roles and refocus their activities. And third is the *triangulation* of issue management, whereby diplomatic agents connect with host governments by engaging with populations rather than (or in addition to) making bilateral or multilateral overtures; this is becoming the new norm.

All this is not just fad or fashion. Diplomacy is evolving in the face of consequences that range from increasing irrelevance to outright oblivion. Public diplomacy and branding hold forth the promise of reconciling continuity with change not just for the representatives of the A-world but also for the advocates of the C-, T-, and E-worlds, whose access to and influence in Western capitals could increase with their mastery of the art of public diplomacy. All told, as the centerpiece of diplomatic practice, public diplomacy could help realize economic and political goals and make the world a safer place by contributing to both security and development.

The Human Dimension

The effective public diplomat will need all of the qualities of the traditional diplomat—judgment, tact, intellect, discretion—and a good many more that may be situation specific. What kind of institution might best develop such qualities? Let me turn now to a subject that has not received nearly the attention it deserves: the foreign service.[56]

The foreign service is the primary expression of the human factor in diplomacy. It consists of a distinct cadre of career employees who alternate between service at home and abroad and who specialize in negotiation, analysis, and cross-cultural representation as well as in particular issue clusters such as area knowledge, international law, and multilateral institutions. The public pays little attention to the foreign service either in the context of public diplomacy and branding or, for that matter, in any other respect. At more than a few dinner parties I have seen the eyes of some guests glaze over when members of the foreign service hold forth on the foibles of the institution in which they work. Often the subject is quickly dropped. That, I think, is a mistake, because it is very often the members of the foreign service who are the beating heart of diplomacy and the foreign ministry.

The capacity to produce the kind of value-added analysis that can only be born of intimate familiarity with a country or region has been a defining feature of the foreign service, but today—due to resource reductions, overstretch, and a debilitating mix of internal difficulties—that capacity is diminishing. Any competent public servant can assemble a briefing book or organize the program for a high-level visit. Far fewer can talk intelligently about, for example, the differences among British, French, Dutch, Spanish, and Portuguese colonialism, the economic impact of Taoism, or the comparative political influence of Islam. And while there is almost endless talk about knowledge workers, continuous learning, and professional development, the reality often subverts the rhetoric.

All of this matters because it is essential that the abilities of the foreign service complement the requirements of public diplomacy and branding, the success of each of which is dependent upon making interpersonal contacts, nurturing networks, and sustaining relationships. These cannot be accomplished by haughty snobs or sullen sociophobes. Nor can they be subcontracted entirely to local staff. Judgment, experience, and instinct are used to shape and calibrate PD and branding-related activity, thus reinforcing existing links or, when and where necessary, creating new ones. To date, the foreign service's ability to meet those imperatives has not been as evident as it should be, which might help to explain why public diplomacy and branding, in the overall mix of diplomatic practices, have themselves not always received as much recognition as they merit.

In an ideal world it might be possible to convince most people of the intrinsic value of the foreign service. Unfortunately, we don't live there, and in the real world many believe that anyone can do the job. That assumption is not only misguided but damaging (and too often complicated by feelings of resentment or envy in any case). To be sure, some political appointees and domestic public servants appointed to the foreign service have performed with distinction. Yet while there will always be a place for talented amateurs, in the foreseeable future most national governments will need the services of a highly dedicated group of rotational employees, both generalists and specialists, who are ready and willing to go almost anywhere and do almost anything, at almost any time. The talent pool must be deep, its dedication and commitment unwavering, and its positioning strategic. There is no equivalent to or substitute for the unique role that the foreign service plays in integrating the actions of national governments abroad. No other group of government employees understands the world better or has a broader view of the interconnectivity of issues than the members of the foreign service.

Spiraling Downward . . .

So much, then, for the defense of the realm. All of this begs a more fundamental question: are the foreign services that countries *have* the foreign services that they *need?* While my observations are based primarily on the Canadian example, my research and experience with colleagues from other foreign services have led me to the conclusion that Canada's case is in many respects representative.

Foreign services in the A-world, which are the focus of my comments here, are no longer the bastions of aristocracy or privilege they once were, but they still have a long way to go if they are to reflect the diversity and pluralism of domestic populations in the globalization age.[57] In a paper prepared for the Spanish foreign ministry, former British diplomat Shaun Riordan wrote, "Foreign services . . . were designed for a world that no longer exists. [They] . . . are no longer up to the challenges of defending and promoting national interests . . . [and] need radical reform in their structures, culture, recruitment, and training."[58]

Though it is severe, I tend to agree with this assertion. Foreign services everywhere appear to be in trouble—under siege on the domestic front, underresourced financially, and overstretched operationally. British diplomatic studies scholar Brian Hocking has suggested that diplomats will have to move from being "gatekeepers" to "boundary spanners."[59] There may well be something to that. But the image I have right now is rather more that of "margin minders." The foreign service, like its home department(s), has been displaced from the core of the international policy apparatus.

Not long ago considered the elite of the public service, in an increasing number of countries the foreign service has become something of an orphan—isolated, unloved, even ostracized. It may mostly be a function of demographics and generational change, but it is my experience that today's foreign service has become brittle and sclerotic rather than sleek and sinewy. It constitutes an awkward minority in departments increasingly dominated by others.[60] In Canada's case, for instance, the foreign service became a sort of boutique bargaining unit, unable to negotiate competitive terms and conditions of employment for its members—especially after the top three of its five tiers were lopped off and transferred to the government-wide executive group in the early 1980s. Although many qualified, high-end candidates still consider a foreign service career and thousands line up each year to take the entrance exams, unless some fundamental changes are made, the foreign service will continue to lose its standing in the public sector. It lacks the critical mass of other occupational groups and faces profound structural and demographic challenges, not the least of which is the pending retirement of the baby boomers and the ascent of the two-career, two-income family.

The sad tale of this once-proud institution, then, is a compendium of neglect, mismanagement, and missed opportunity. On the inside, much has been lost. A severe lowering of standards related to policy, regional, and linguistic expertise has ensured the widely held prophecy of the foreign service's impending irrelevance will be all but realized. The pressures from almost every direction have mounted unremittingly, while energy, imagination, and commitment on the part of decisionmakers have proven scarce. Denial and indecision have compounded the problems. Public diplomacy and branding are demanding activities and require creativity and perseverance. These attributes are hard to find among the worn down, wrung out, and beaten up.[61]

For the foreign service to survive—and certainly if it is to prosper—some fundamental innovation will be required. Governments must find ways to transform their nearly moribund foreign services into diverse and dynamic international groups of globalization managers with clearly articulated skill sets, recruited from across government and beyond.

. . . And Pulling Up

How to start? By employing the skills and instruments honed in service abroad to bring the outside in and turn the inside out. The good news is that despite everything, most foreign services, especially those in the A-world, still have some decent bench strength. Professionalism remains high, motivation is strong, and dedication to both the work and the institutions persists. Put another way, there remain considerable reserves of the very qualities that have traditionally characterized the foreign service brand. Acting in concert with allies and stakeholders—including, where appropriate, NGOs and business partners—the foreign service we have can be transformed, with determination and commitment, into the international service we need: a vital agent of whole-of-government international policy integration. This might usefully begin with the rehabilitation of professionalism. Many other recognized occupational groups within government—engineers, architects, doctors, lawyers—are offered real choices mid-career and can opt to pursue either a senior management or a senior professional position. Seasoned diplomats, analysts, negotiators, area specialists, and others with demonstrated expertise should be afforded no lesser opportunity. If diplomacy is to be defined as a profession, then it will have to correlate more closely with recognized achievement and experience.[62] It will also have to be elaborated in reference to an explicit skill set, such as demonstrated excellence in networking and building partnerships, advocacy and negotiation, policy development and analysis, and intelligence gathering and assessment. In this context, diplomats start to look less like decorous messengers and more like sage, cross-culturally attuned advocates and lobbyists.

At the other end of the spectrum, entry-level recruitment into the foreign service, long the main source of new talent, will in most cases have to be dramatically expanded. In the meantime, however, demographic changes in the labor force are creating many vacancies at all levels. To fill these gaps, in addition to relying on accelerated promotions, talent will have to be drawn from other occupational groups within host departments, from across the government, and from across the country. This could involve, among other things, the orchestration of a large-scale lateral entry process that would encompass everyone in government who is now doing international policy and international program work and whose experience, skills, and, especially, personal suitability and representational capacity would fit the bill. Such a campaign would also focus on employing specialists—perhaps especially those from science-based departments such as energy, health, and natural resources—to manage knowledgably the growing number of science-based files.

I am referring here to the construction of a bigger, better tent with larger, and more diverse, crowds inside. Secondments and exchanges would be encouraged whereby foreign service officers would be installed in strategic positions across government as well as in civil society and the private sector even as infusions of new blood increase energy levels in the foreign ministry. The new body would be elite but not elitist, selective yet inclusive—indeed expanded, but in a manner that maintains professional standards and not only does not disadvantage foreign service incumbents at any level but creates new opportunities for them.

To Recover the High Ground

Especially lacking has been a forward-looking strategy for rehabilitating the foreign service as an institution. I see here a real opportunity to address, among other things, some crucial issues related to the foreign service demographic—such as the need to bring in new candidates between the ages of thirty and forty-five, among them more women and visible minorities. Doing so will ensure that the institution is more reflective of the national population.

There are many ways to articulate the essential elements of an international service, but for starters they should be as follows:

- *Dynamism.* The mark of a vital and inclusive institution with a history and a future
- *Indispensability.* A critical component of the machinery of government, promoting security, prosperity, and identity among its constituents
- *Professionalism.* A function of skill sets, recognized standards, and rotationality rather than occupational fraternity
- *Adaptability.* Rapid responsiveness to change, capacity to work effectively within and across issues and departments both at home and cross-culturally abroad
- *Commitment.* Investment in the global pursuit of nationally defined values, policies, and interests
- *Expertise.* Thorough experience with advocacy and negotiation, partnerships and networking, strategic analysis and intelligence gathering

To summarize: in the future, analytical skill, personal suitability, and global or specialized knowledge rather than educational credentials or affiliations with either the host department or certain occupational groups should come to define membership in the international service. Only by restoring the health of their critical institutions will governments be able to bring the outside in and turn the inside out, thus improving performance and moving toward the whole-of-government and whole-of-country orientations that foreign ministries so desperately require. For public diplomacy and branding to achieve their considerable potential, nothing less will do.

If the assessment presented in this chapter is correct, then it should be absolutely clear that public diplomacy, branding, and the foreign service will all need rethinking. In particular, it must be recognized that members of the foreign service will not be in a position to communicate effectively abroad if they are preoccupied with bread-and-butter issues or face constraints on spontaneous interaction.

In 1965, in his song "Like a Rolling Stone," Bob Dylan referred memorably to a diplomat as someone who "wasn't really where it's at." More than forty years later, the line still rings true. How, then, might we might get from where we are to where we want to be?

To begin to crack that king-sized nut, it will be necessary both to review several of the issues covered in this chapter through a slightly different lens and to push the analysis further and in some entirely new directions.

Notes

1. Canada's approach to PD was elaborated further in the 2005 *International Policy Statement,* although changes in government and substantial cuts to public diplomacy programs have rendered that document of more historic than practical interest. For an excellent comparative look at public diplomacy in Canada and Norway, see Bàtora (2005). See also Potter (2009).

2. *Jyllands-Posten* (2005).

3. See P. Taylor (1997).

4. See Zaharna (2007). Her draft article, "Mapping out a Spectrum of Public Diplomacy Initiatives: Information and Relational Communication Frameworks," was made available to the author in a personal communication dated June 11, 2007.

5. It is its direct bearing on policy, governance, and broad political objectives rather than (necessarily) on the foreign ministry or state budget that qualifies an activity as public diplomacy. Absent those connections, the activity is more likely to constitute international public relations.

6. There are, however, certain monologic, unidirectional forms of political communication intended to influence governments directly that do qualify as PD. These would include communiqués or major speeches made by foreign ministers or heads of state during crises or in instances where bilateral diplomatic relations are nonexistent (as with the United States and Cuba during the missile crisis) or have broken down (for instance, the 1972 negotiations to end the Vietnam War).

7. See Australia Department of Foreign Affairs and Trade (2005), New Zealand Ministry of Foreign Affairs and Trade (2006). Many of these submissions are worth viewing at the Australian Senate's website, http://www.aph.gov.au/Senate/committee/fadt_ctte/completed_inquiries/2004-07/public_diplomacy/index.htm.

8. See US General Accounting Office (2003; 2007). See US Office of Management and Budget (2006). See, for example, US Senate (2008).

9. See Lord Carter of Coles (2005).

10. This document contained many elements of the DFAIT's FAC 21 plan cited earlier.

11. Why the renewed interest and activity? The spread of democracy means that public opinion—and relations with civil society generally—are more important to governments everywhere. A major assault on Western values has been launched by jihadists; it cannot go unanswered. Complex interdependence and the exigent, transnational nature of global issues—the environment, crime, terrorism—have combined to heighten the efficacy and appeal of public diplomacy generally. See Centre for Strategic and International Studies (1998) for an initial assessment.

12. The literature on PD has become extensive in recent years. For a general introduction, visit the website of the University of Southern California's Center on Public

Diplomacy at www.usc.publicdiplomacy.com; Public Diplomacy Institute at George Washington University (http://pdi.gwu.edu). See also Waller (2007b), Melissen (2007), and Anholt (2009). Phil Taylor has archived a vast and exceptionally good selection of articles on PD and many other communications issues. See http://129.11.188.64/papers/index.cfm?outfit=pmt). Broad surveys are available in three recent volumes dedicated to PD: *The Hague Journal of Diplomacy,* edited by Melissen and Sharp (2007); *The Annals of the American Academy of Political and Social Science* (2008), edited by Cowan and Cull; and Foreign and Commonwealth Office (2008). An extensive bibliography has been compiled by the Netherlands Institute of International Relations (2008). Bruce Gregory at GWU and John Brown at USC also track and usefully review additions to the literature.

13. The extent to which public diplomacy is actually new is a matter of some controversy. Clearly there has always been a public dimension to diplomacy, manifest mainly through propaganda activities and favored especially during wartime, hot or cold. But the emphasis on dialogue with populations and on integrating the results into the policy development process differs in kind from intergovernmental exchange and sets publc diplomacy apart from conventional diplomacy.

14. See Nye (2002; 2004b). On the relationship between soft power and PD, see Fisher and Brockerhoff (2008: 21–23). The phrase *soft power* was very much in vogue in Canada during the Axworthy years but now, like *human security,* has largely disappeared from the official discourse. At a panel presentation at the March 2007 meeting of the International Studies Association, Nye was criticized for predicating his analysis on an overconfidence in the endless reserves of US soft power as well as for situating his model in the context of power per se, because power is fundamentally instrumental—something used on others to assert your will. The association with power was seen to undercut the centrality of mutuality and synthesis to public diplomacy that some see.

15. See Zaharna (2007).

16. Sean Moore, for example, elaborates the process of *strategic inquiry,* whereby an issue and the environment in which it is situated are researched and analyzed and a plan established well in advance of any action being taken. This involves attention to aspects such as framing and positioning the "ask," the identification of obstacles and local allies, the consideration of fallbacks, and related practices of so-called issue scoping. Personal communication with author, January 14, 2008. See http://www.seanmoore.ca.

17. See Nye (2005), Kurlantzick (2006). A more comprehensive treatment is provided in Ramo (2007). See also Hutton (2007), Nye (2004c; 2006).

18. On the techniques and challenges of peace building, see Paris (2004).

19. See Melissen (2007).

20. It is worth emphasizing that soft power, however defined, remains, like any kind of power, instrumental. It is a means for getting what you want in the world. To quote my colleague Ali Fisher, "Given that soft power is about getting others to adopt *your* goals, it cannot be used in genuine exchange, which presents the possibility of both sides moving position." Personal communication with the author, March 4, 2009.

21. In the private sector, by way of contrast, the term *public affairs* is often used as code for "government relations" and lobbying.

22. See Nancy Snow, http://www.nancysnow.com. See also Cull (2006).

23. See Armistead (2004).

24. The Iraq War provides several examples of information warfare: disseminating disinformation, intercepting signals, jamming broadcasts, blocking websites, even amplifying music. In the second assault on Fallujah, for example, US marines in Iraq blared AC/DC's hard rock anthems "Highway to Hell" and "Back in Black" to pump themselves up and disorient those they were attacking. This tactic resembled that used

by the air cavalry that blasted Wagner's "Ride of the Valkyries" from helicopters during an airborne assault in the Coppola film *Apocalypse Now*.

25. Sean Moore, http://www.seanmoore.ca.

26. One of Canada's ambassadors to the United States in the 1980s, Allan Gotlieb, drew upon his own experience to capture the essence of this approach long before most. See Gotlieb (1991).

27. A full account of this sordid incident is offered by the Center for Media and Democracy at its website, PR Watch, at http://www.prwatch.org/books/tsigfy10.html. See also MacArthur (1993).

28. The term *diaspora communities* here refers to members of an exiled population who retain significant links to their country of origin. Beyond that, the term becomes notoriously difficult to define, raising questions about citizenship, generation, language, and so forth. For a wide-ranging treatment of diasporas, see Berns-McGown (2008).

29. If this contact were undertaken for purposes other than gathering general information, generating foreign intelligence, or influencing a particular situation abroad, however, it would in my view still qualify as outreach rather than public diplomacy.

30. DFAIT has no such practices in place now.

31. Ali Fisher has done interesting work in adapting the approach used in developing "open source" software to the practice of PD. See Fisher (2008).

32. Personal communication, February 19, 2007.

33. This point has been illustrated aptly by my former colleague Jeremy Kinsman, who, in the context of an ongoing project at Princeton on democracy promotion, lists the contents of the public diplomacy toolbox: initiating, participating, facilitating, demonstrating, sharing, convening, connecting, engaging, advising, and informing. Personal communication with the author, May 16, 2008.

34. See www.rachellelamb.com.

35. See Lamb (2005), Rosenberg (2003).

36. See Alinsky (1971).

37. Fitzpatrick (2007).

38. See Zaharna (2007).

39. Or, if not learned, at least recorded. See, for example, Cull (2007). On the use of strategic communications to combat violent extremism, see Corman, Trethewey, and Goodall (2008). For the views of the Bush administration's last undersecretary of state for PD, see Glassman (2008).

40. See Kelly (2007).

41. It is very difficult to be credible in promoting democracy, liberty, and freedom, for example, when you are supporting authoritarian governments, reducing civil liberties, and running a secret network based on extraordinary rendition, black prisons, and the use of methods of interrogation so harsh as to be classified as torture.

42. There have been, however, some exceptional cases of the use of monological PD to communicate directly with governments—for instance, President Woodrow Wilson's Fourteen Points address. Sometimes PD can also be used to foster direct contact between political figures, as at cultural events.

43. See Van Ham (2001) for what has proven a seminal work in this field.

44. In this respect, diplomats on assignment abroad can be seen to serve as local brand managers, foreign ministers as international branding coordinators, and the foreign ministry as world headquarters.

45. With its reliance upon market testing, client feedback, and customer satisfaction, branding is hardly unresponsive to changes in the public environment. However, compared to that in public diplomacy, the connection is episodic rather than continuous.

46. Personal communication, October 13, 2006. Anholt has developed a hexagonal model that sets out the principal elements of a nation's brand, including tourism, exports, policies, investment and immigration, culture and heritage, and people. On branding and development, see Anholt (2005); on the mother of all (nation) brands, see Anholt (2004); on branding nations, cities, and regions, see Anholt (2007).

47. Mark Leonard, architect of that UK rebranding initiative, offers his own take. See http://markleonard.net/journalism/coolbritannia.

48. Evan Potter, one of only a handful of Canadians with expertise in this field, assesses these campaigns closely in *Branding Canada* (2009).

49. Tiedeman's excellent MA thesis, "Branding America: An Examination of US Public Diplomacy Efforts After September 11, 2001," was submitted to the Fletcher School at Tufts University in April 2005.

50. John Ralston Saul is a powerful advocate of the role of culture in international policy; see, for instance, his 2004 John W. Holmes Memorial Lecture, "Projecting a Middle Power into an Imperial World." It opens with a quotation from William Fulbright: "In the long course of history, having people understand your thought is much greater security than another submarine." Similar arguments are found in Kirsten et al. (2007).

51. For a history of US cultural diplomacy in the twentieth century, see Arendt (2007). For a focus on the Cold War years, during which government-sponsored international cultural activities peaked, see Yale (2008). See also Rugh (2009), http://www.arabmediasociety.com/?article=709; Lugar (2009), http://lugar.senate.gov/sfrc/pdf/PublicDiplomacy.pdf; University of Southern California (2009), available at www.publicdiplomacymagazine.org.

52. The stillborn CIIS proposed major new resources, the creation of a worldwide satellite television broadcast service (the Canada Channel), the expansion of DFAIT's Internet presence, support for enlarged shortwave radio programming, and many other initiatives. The opportunity costs associated with the failure to pursue the CIIS are unrecoverable.

53. Adequate support for international broadcasting and the international activities of various granting councils is an essential element of both PD and branding, but as it falls largely outside of the realm of the foreign ministry and foreign service, it will not be treated here.

54. The literature critical of PD theory and practice is thin, but thickening. See Lucas and Ali (2009), Snow and Taylor (2008).

55. This in turn requires both guts and a fairly thick skin, neither of which is universally associated with diplomats.

56. Whereas foreign ministries and diplomacy are merely understudied, apart from publications designed mainly for members, the foreign service is barely studied at all. See the background and research papers available on the website of the Professional Association of Foreign Service Officers (www.pafso-apase.com), as well as its quarterly, *Bout de Papier.* By way of comparison, see the site of the American Foreign Service Association (www.afsa.org) and its superb *Foreign Service Journal.*

57. To the extent that this trait endures, it is found mainly, and somewhat ironically, in the diplomatic corps of the C- and T-worlds.

58. Titled "Reforming Foreign Services for the Twenty-First Century," this document was made available to the author in a personal communication dated March 26, 2007.

59. See Hocking and Spence (2002: introduction). For a multilateral context, see Cooper, English, and Thakur (2001).

60. I should know. In the 1980s and 1990s, I was elected five times to the Executive Committee of Canada's Professional Association of Foreign Service Officers, where I began my education in labor management relations—and passion for shaking up foreign ministries from within. My contribution was the PEG, or PAFSO Evaluation Guide, which was a systematic, comprehensive, membership-driven program used to rate the performance of DFAIT's managers from the unique perspective of those they supervised. The results were available to all participants. The goal was to identify and eventually isolate the worst managers, who tended to be those subscribing to the kiss-up, kick-down model of corporate behavior. We called this "managing managers." For details, contact the Professional Association of Foreign Service Officers at http://www.pafso-apase.com.

61. The human resource management function of DFAIT was comprehensively evaluated in 2007. While the auditor general's report contained few surprises for the initiated—the personnel branch is referred to by some in the department as its "heart of darkness—the local media described the findings as "devastating." Among their observations: "Serious problems need urgent attention . . . the department does not have a strategic plan [and] is struggling . . . unless it acts now the situation will get worse." See www.oag-bvg.gc.ca.

62. In Canada's case, working-level diplomats as an occupational group have been lumped into the "administrative and foreign service" category for collective bargaining purposes.

PART 4

The Way Ahead

International Policy Instruments: Relevant, Effective, Transformed 11

There is a conviction still popular in some circles that diplomacy is a special calling or vocation. Forget that. In the era of globalization, there is nothing sanctified about either diplomatic work or the instruments of international policy. All are underperforming. What to do?

To connect with populations and sustain an active, ongoing dialogue, members of the foreign service must analyze the issues, craft appropriate strategic messages, choose the appropriate communications tools and media, cultivate relations with journalists and opinion leaders, and seek partners among the like-minded in civil society and the business community. These rules apply equally to domestic and international situations and they involve raising the foreign ministry's competitive profile at home by using public diplomacy to enhance its nation's image and build the national brand worldwide.

This is the future of diplomacy, and it is daunting in scope. Its reach does not exceed the grasp of those most directly implicated, but again, if foreign service officers are to become globalization managers and foreign ministries globalization entrepôts, then there is work to be done. Practitioners will not least have to avoid falling into the trap described so vividly by Charles Taylor in his characterization of Canadian involvement in the Vietnam War: "They fooled themselves through a tragic misunderstanding of the issues . . . and a misguided faith in the prowess of their own diplomacy."[1]

Demonstrating Domestic Relevance

I stressed in Chapter 10 that in the context of diplomacy, any analysis of the big ideas and grand strategies underpinning global relations would not amount to much without sufficient attention devoted to diplomacy's domestic frontline, where the distinctions between public diplomacy and outreach, the importance of connecting with citizens in the policy development process, the need for an integrated approach to domestic constituency building, and so on are most visible. For far too long, members of the foreign service have doggedly slogged through major capitals and to the ends of the earth, laboring under the mistaken assumption that their work's value was evident to all, including opinion leaders and decisionmakers on the home front. Foreign ministries desperately need to recruit allies who can both support funding proposals submitted to the treasury and do more effective bidding during the annual government resource auction that is the budgetary allocation process. To gain the recognition that fosters cooperation, diplomats must (but rarely do) focus on developing a domestic political and communications strategy, dramatically cranking up outreach programs (especially for students and youth), establishing a national presence in cities across the country, and systematically infiltrating universities, NGOs, and think tanks.[2]

Clearly, members of the foreign service have lots to do. What they should *not* be doing is burning up scarce time and effort by playing catch-up and fighting to defend turf that should be happily surrendered insofar as domestic diplomatic engagement is moving to a higher plane. On the latter point, other government departments have long been leading in a vast array of functional areas; it is time for the foreign service to end its costly and counterproductive skirmishes over the custody of specific files (such as environmental law, resource regulation, international financial institutions, culture and the arts, the negotiation of various specialized treaties, and many more) and to begin a carefully planned and phased withdrawal from day-to-day work on particularistic issues. Only then can it begin to redouble its existing resources at a higher level of analysis, focusing on geographic priorities and those extant functional nodes to which it brings a unique, catalytic perspective.

In practice, this would involve a dedication and commitment to policy leadership and entrepreneurship. It would entail a much greater emphasis on planning and on the analysis of broad, crosscutting policy clusters such as governance, security, sustainable development, and the promotion of rights and democracy. These issues would then be coordinated and integrated across government. At the same time, country and regional expertise—a seriously undervalued and indeed depreciating asset—could be rebuilt. This geographically specific form of knowledge is of major benefit to foreign ministries; their network of missions abroad constitutes the basis of their comparative advantage over other government departments. They had better work it.

The Foreign Ministry as Broker, Guide, and Storyteller

Nowhere else in government do we find the foreign ministry's capacity to manage the number and kinds of trade-offs that characterize international policy and multistakeholder diplomacy. Foreign ministries are well placed to develop strategic overviews of their country's place in the world; to help integrate policies based on their firsthand examinations of the many facets of globalization; and to assess what their results might mean for citizens, governments, and future international policy objectives. But to achieve their potential, they will have to overcome the many obstacles set out in Chapters 9 and 10. At the highest level of analysis, international policy is an expression of the constantly shifting balance between the values and interests of the states involved in its formulation—that is, between what is seen as important (such as human rights, social justice, and democratic development) and what is pursued as desirable (such as prosperity through trade and investment; security through development, peacekeeping, or counterterrorism). Values and interests are often closely related in that the way the latter are pursued often reflects the former—manifest, for instance, in a preference for negotiations over confrontation or conflict. Similarly, the extent to which values are considered in decisionmaking often reflects underlying interests; take the example of complex trade-offs between achieving international environmental stewardship and developing resources or between the promotion of commercial relations and the protection of human rights. Occasionally, values and interests are for all practical purposes indistinguishable, as in support for rule of law, through the promotion of good governance and international treaties.

Because of the dynamic balance between values and interests in a constantly changing world, international policy is notoriously difficult to codify, and complete coherence is rare if not unattainable. That said, it is the responsibility of foreign ministries to manage the trade-offs and to communicate and implement the results. And if governments can create foreign ministries and international services dedicated to harmonizing policies and interests, serving as brokers in global issues and world affairs, and managing networks of missions abroad, will their achievement be sufficient? Probably not, but it would certainly help take diplomats a long way from that unenviable place in which they find themselves now. Rather than a quaint, quiet backwater or lowly source of logistical and support service to others, the foreign ministry and international service I envision would be fabulous places to work, providing a stimulating professional environment and retaining the loyalty and commitment of the best employees.

By pulling out of any area that is not a focal point of their core mission or a locus of decisionmaking activity, redeploying in support of demonstrable results, and reaching out to citizens, foreign ministries can increase both their relevance and their efficiency. That, I submit, is a pretty good formula for both job satisfaction and administrative effectiveness.

Delivering Measurable Results

I have suggested that the challenges and consequences of globalization have rendered public diplomacy key among the activities that foreign ministries and foreign service officers should be engaging in abroad. The practitioners of public diplomacy must routinely put their shoulders to the great wheel of public opinion, whether to nudge it forward, backward, or even sideways. From the perspective of national governments, however, what really counts is that these efforts pay off, producing outcomes in service of defined interests. To again quote former Canadian diplomat François Taschereau, now a senior public relations executive, "Diplomacy should be about results; it would force governments to concentrate resources where a difference can be made."[3] In these days of tightened budgets, heightened scrutiny, and fierce competition, nothing less will do.

If some basic refocusing is necessary, how might it be achieved? Government has been showing renewed interest in measuring performance and evaluating results. In the case of DFAIT, this is due in part to significant budget cuts to PD programs made in September 2006. Prior to those reductions, the department, regrettably, was unable to show that its PD activities were aligned with or helping to advance the government's international priorities. If a case for reinvestment in PD is to be made, its value must be demonstrable.

By measuring results, foreign ministries can show that they are responding to the challenges of globalization. Qualitative description will have a place here, but the narrative documentation of outcomes will have to be accompanied by the identification of performance indicators and the quantification of measured achievement.

Meaningfully measuring the results of public diplomacy, however, is notoriously difficult, and the success of efforts to date has been mixed even according to analysts and practitioners from countries with major investments therein, such as the UK and the United States.[4] Nor has the cause of measurement been much advanced in the growing literature on public diplomacy, where the focus has been on analyzing practice rather than on evaluating performance.

Nicholas Cull at the University of Southern California has likened the current fixation with quantification to the mania of auditors rushing out into a forest each morning to determine whether the trees grew overnight.[5] It is nevertheless clear that the imperatives of achieving results and demonstrating value in the field of public policy expenditure will require the generation of baseline data, both numeric and narrative, that can show that PD produces real returns. Only then will it be possible to construct a convincing argument for increased budgetary support.

Models for the measurement of results are under development and being tested by several foreign ministries, including those of the UK, the United States, Australia, and Canada. Definitive findings are still scarce, but it is nonetheless possible to begin to identify best practices and draw some preliminary conclusions. These include the need to identify in advance strategic objectives and specific performance indicators, to track and evaluate short-term versus long-term impacts, and to be in a position to analyze inputs (resources, time, expenses) against outputs (audience reach, partnerships, media coverage) and outcomes (changes in perception, policy, and behavior) in order to assess value for money. There are, however, six essential caveats:

1. The most effective PD practices and compelling metrics cannot compensate for and may instead reveal fundamental flaws in policy.[6]
2. Public opinion research (POR) is both expensive (particularly focus group testing and one-on-one interviews with opinion leaders) and highly prone to manipulation (as with the loading of questions and selection of multiple-choice answers or the treatment and weighting of the data).
3. In international policy there is a demonstrable dialectic between results and resources; the measurement and assessment of PD's efficacy will require financial and personnel support, either new or deployed from elsewhere.
4. The resulting expenditures on monitoring and analyzing foreign media, tracking changes in policy and opinion, and many other activities should be planned for and not imposed upon already overburdened employees in an underresourced field.
5. An increasingly significant component of PD is Internet based, yet this fact has not figured centrally in discussions of results measurement; it must.
6. It will rarely be possible to measure one very important category of outcomes: those that public diplomacy may have prevented, such as terrorist attacks.

Because the effectiveness of PD relies on successfully engaging with public opinion, POR might be expected to feature centrally in measurement exercises. Curiously, although it is perhaps the most obvious gauge of shifts in perception and attitude, little practical use has been made of it by officials.[7] Input from polling, focus groups, and interviews offer the promise of insight into the changing public environment but is nevertheless rarely used to guide the development of international policy. And although it could foster greater transparency and accountability, it is not routinely used to track the success or failure of efforts intended to "move the needle."

Such seeming underappreciation for a valuable tool may be attributed in part to limited budgets, but there are other constraints associated with POR. Polling makes for great headlines and often provides an accurate snapshot of opinion on a particular issue at a given moment in time, but it is less useful in mapping the broad landscape of attitudes and preoccupations as they evolve, particularly in the absence of long-term baseline data. Moreover, though polling is the dominant expression of POR, it is expensive, the findings are easily massaged, and it does not always produce actionable results. The other main forms of POR, focus groups and interviews, are more likely to yield useful insights, but governments are not generally enthusiastic about commissioning such studies, not least because the outcomes are less predictable. And at the political level, there will always be debate about whether to try to lead or follow public opinion.

How much use do foreign ministries make of POR on international issues? Much less than they should, in my view, notwithstanding the caveats mentioned above. Although used occasionally to obtain snapshots or, in the context of risk management, to gauge attitudes on controversial issues, it is otherwise underutilized. Most foreign ministries do a fairly good job of media monitoring and analysis, preparing daily surveys of coverage in the domestic and international press and producing thematic summaries as required. Focus group testing is sometimes used, but on a demand-driven more than a strategic and systematic basis. The same applies to polling: the results of major subscription-based research and data mining projects are distributed throughout government regularly, but custom polling, apart from annual exercises undertaken to track major international policy trends and foreign ministry performance, is initiated much less often and usually as a stand-alone project.

POR conducted abroad is even less rigorous and coordinated and is usually driven by immediate priorities, ranging from developments in Iraq and Afghanistan to the need for public support for intensifying relations with China and India or promoting commercial and investment ties with emerging economic centers elsewhere.[8] On balance, and perhaps not surprisingly, the best tracking research tends to concern issues of international trade, defense, and security, while the weakest concerns foreign policy, development assistance, diplomacy, and attitudes toward global issues.

Partly for the reasons just outlined, I remain somewhat skeptical about using the fruits of conventional survey research as bases for policy formulation and decisionmaking. What people say or expect that they will do is often quite different from what they actually do, especially with respect to international policy issues that may seem ephemeral. It is all too easy for polling firms to arrange to receive certain types of responses or to interpret the returns in such a way as to please their clients. For these reasons I believe that focus groups, especially of the more in-depth, deliberative type, and structured interviews can provide more useful information.

Where, then, does this leave the foreign ministry? In a somewhat uncomfortable place, I think. POR can help public diplomats determine whether or not they are connecting with populations; indeed, they have few alternatives for establishing performance metrics. With few exceptions, however, POR is not well integrated into international policy development. If feedback loops were working properly, policy planners and PD practitioners would be using POR systematically, especially as a means to understand emerging currents in the opinion of the internationally attentive public, but resource constraints, coupled perhaps with a certain culturally rooted disinclination toward consultation, ensure that they are not.

Why Brand Now?

With some sense in mind of the preconditions for delivering effective public diplomacy, creating a relevant foreign ministry, and producing a transformed foreign service, the questions must be put: Is this urgent? And can it make a difference? The answer in each case is an unequivocal yes, *but.* Negotiating globalization has been tough for most governments, especially those that have not benefited from its advent. Many countries today—including the UK, France, and Russia—occupy a significantly smaller place in the world than they did fifty years ago. The United States now finds itself at the top (if that) of the same slide. This gradual erosion of national power and influence on the part of status quo powers has had an element of inevitability in the post–World War II era, as Europe integrated, Japan rebuilt, and China, India, Mexico, and Brazil emerged. Nation branding is one way to halt or even reverse this trend.

As they do with the practice of e-diplomacy on the Internet, foreign ministries show some skepticism regarding the importance or even the existence of national brands. I do not share it. As a comparative example, consider the promotion of investment, commerce, and tourism in Europe; Switzerland undoubtedly benefits from its reputation for precision, France from its association with high culture and epicureanism, Italy from its premium on style and design, and Germany from its prowess in industrial engineering. At the other end of the spectrum, we can see the difficulties faced by Romania in shaking its association with vampires, gypsies, and Ceaucescu and by Serbia in living down the massacre at Srebrenica, the siege of Sarajevo, and the refuge it provided to war criminals. Somewhere in the middle of that pack, countries like Slovenia and any of the formerly Soviet Baltic states just don't make much of an impression of any kind.

To come at the issue from a different direction, anyone who has read the pronouncements that have routinely accompanied the terrorist attacks over the past decade will have realized that in the age of globalization, image problems and foreign policy are intimately intertwined. The strategists of jihad, for instance, have shown some sensitivity toward nation brands in the production of propaganda, and they spend more than a little time managing their own images and reputations.

Canada's experience may again afford some useful insights. The country has for years been coasting on an international reputation as a committed internationalist, preeminent peacekeeper, environmental activist, and generous aid donor—inferred in large part from the message of its brand. Recent developments in international policy and resources reduction have rendered that

Triple Jeopardy

Canada faces some real branding challenges. Its existing global brand—a scenic and resource-rich but frigid and almost empty land inhabited by Eskimos, trappers, and lumberjacks—is weak, amorphous, and, more important, obsolete. Contemporary virtues—dynamism, innovation, technology, tolerance, competitiveness, and multiculturalism—are conspicuously absent. Rather than an asset, Canada's brand image is a growing liability to its economic interests, political influence, and, ultimately, sovereignty and independence.

These problems were well illustrated a few years ago when Canada's US consuls general gathered in the New York offices of a leading public relations firm for a presentation on Canada's branding challenges.[9] It went something like this: participants were invited to view three slides that were supposed to summarize Canada's brand in the United States. The first was a blank screen, implying that most US citizens simply don't think much about their neighbor to the north. The viewers nodded grimly in agreement. The second was a collage of stock postcard images—the Royal Canadian Mounted Police, pristine lakes amid vast tracts of forest, happy fishermen, glowing igloos on the frozen tundra, Niagara Falls. This induced knowing smiles all around—a bit cute, but it worked to draw tourists. The third slide was a single image of shimmering, golden wheat fields framed by majestic, snow-peaked mountains. It didn't capture the vitality of Canadian cities, thought the consuls, but it seemed an improvement over its predecessor.

"Does anyone know what is wrong with this picture?" asked the presenter. The answer: it was taken in . . . Wyoming! If nature is placed at the center of your brand, he went on to explain, with few exceptions the lasting impression is more generic than distinctive. You can never own it. That makes firm association with your image, and hence any benefit from your brand, very difficult to sustain.

message inaccurate. Moreover, Canada's continued reliance on an outdated brand has left its interests exposed and its policies and positions vulnerable to attack.

With the end of the Cold War came severe budgetary cuts to the military, development assistance, and the foreign ministries throughout most of what had been the first and second worlds. This in turn forced a fundamental rethinking about the kinds of international policy results that might realistically be achieved. In many countries, and certainly in Canada, the long-standing emphasis on global-scale objectives such as poverty eradication, conflict resolution, nonproliferation, and environmental advocacy gave way to a more short-term, team-centered, and project-based approach. This new orientation inhered in brief bursts of concentrated energy and provided a tangible focus for such resources as were available.[10]

This was niche diplomacy; as observed in Chapter 9, it was extremely cost-effective and made a huge contribution to the development of public diplomacy. Priorities were identified on the basis of their susceptibility to or potential for Canadian leadership, their potential for rapid and successful delivery, and the likelihood of producing tangible outcomes. The main criterion was the possibility of making a difference. The probable results of successful niche diplomacy, rather than requiring measurement in small increments over decades, were palpable and highly media-friendly. Each project, from banning landmines to ending the conscription of child soldiers, had a clearly defined start and finish, and made the political leadership look good; when maximum gains had been extracted, the minister could simply declare victory and move on. It was a brilliant strategy, reinforcing Canada's reputation for international activism while simultaneously accommodating major expenditure reductions.

Under the watchful gaze of the Canadian foreign minister during this period, Lloyd Axworthy, DFAIT officials pushed the formula one step further by constructing thematic links between projects, thereby seemingly enlarging the scope of their enterprise. Making a virtue of necessity, Minister Axworthy and his team of human security activists had, by the end of his tenure, completed this stunning international policy retrofit to give the appearance of near-perfect policy coherence under the rubric of the human security agenda.[11]

When the national brand becomes dated, the immediate challenge for governments with limited hard power and constrained independence is to identify and bridge the gap between past and present before it becomes a credibility chasm. How? By using public diplomacy to rebrand, connecting the old to the new by projecting a vision that is contemporary, positive, and, above all, accurate. By promoting core values through visible action and in so doing creating a demonstration effect. By renovating a national image without compromising its integrity or losing accumulated brand equity. Ireland's metamorphosis from famine-ridden and civil-warring yet somehow quaintly charming emerald basketcase to Celtic tiger is an excellent example.[12] Its transformation is evident even in the catalog of totemic anthems by the Irish rock band U2, which went from "Sunday Bloody Sunday" in the 1980s to "It's a Beautiful Day" in the 1990s. South Africa, Poland, Spain, and Cuba have, to varying degrees, been similarly successful.

Raising the Bar

Have foreign ministries and foreign service officers kept pace with the challenges of globalization? The record is mixed. To be sure, in an ever-changing world there will always be work to be done. As we have discussed, an increasing number of major issues are rooted in science and technology—from global warming and climate change to weapons of mass destruction, to pandemic disease, to energy and the environment—yet many foreign ministries are still without a high-level international science adviser or an internship program designed to bring scientific perspectives to bear on the full range of international policy issues. With few exceptions, the looming significance of S&T concerns has not been adequately reflected in the structure or operations of diplomatic services.

Bringing science to the forefront of international policy and relations will require deliberate action. Courses on S&T issues need to be added to the curricula of diplomatic academies and training institutions and made mandatory for political and economic officers. Habits of close cooperation with science-based departments and specialized agencies, as well as with relevant universities, businesses, NGOs, and think tanks have yet to be developed. A systematic program of exchanges could make a real contribution here, as could the creation of an S&T specialty stream within foreign services.

If the new diplomacy is to emphasize the relationship between underdevelopment and insecurity, major changes in the distribution of resources throughout headquarters and, even more important, abroad must be made. Most countries' representational profiles, or *diplomatic footprints,* also require a makeover: they are not as supple or adaptable as they might be. Foreign ministries, however, are often hamstrung by the existence of standardized overseas mission molds; choice is usually restricted to micro, mini, medium, and large. These standards in turn govern such variables as the level and type of services offered, the amount of administrative support provided, the range of benefits (linen, china, crystal, domestic staff) that come with installment in the official residence, and so forth. In some places the diplomatic footprint needs to be large and visible—for example, in global network nodes such as New York, Paris, and Tokyo. In other places, small and light is just about right.

What kind of embassy does the future require?[13] Even today, foreign ministries still tend to privilege codification and formulas; what they need is unlimited representational flexibility to suit changing circumstances. Take, for example, the challenge of optimizing a state's diplomatic presence in London. A country like Canada should be thinking in terms of operating an embassy to the so-called world city of London rather than, or at minimum in addition to, a high commission to the UK.[14] The importance of bilateral ties has been diminishing gradually for over a century; so, then, have the resources needed to maintain them, especially over the past fifty years. Yet Canada's interest in enjoying greater visibility and capacity in a number of London's key sectors—merchant banking, shipping, cultural industries, venture capital, insurance—has, in the age of globalization, never been more acute. In other words, the economic, cultural, and international importance of London as a world city is rising, and this is occurring at a far faster rate than the importance of the bilateral political relationship is slipping. None of this has yet been reflected on the ground, and the result is a serious misalignment of capabilities and needs.

In all cases, more could be achievcd by emphasizing the role of the ambassador as the personal representative of the head of government. The same could be done for locally hired staff working at missions abroad who represent a tremendous resource—providing continuity and retaining institutional memory—that is not managed or used nearly as well as it should be. While members of this group cannot be substituted universally for members of the foreign service, with their innate advantage of cultural and linguistic fluency, they are better suited than anyone from the sending state to know what kind of public diplomacy will work best on the ground.

Why not experiment, where appropriate, with posting foreign service officers in-country—with full diplomatic status but without support staff, or a chancellery, or an official residence? Or furnishing them with ambassadorial titles and a modest discretionary budget but—apart from stipulating the results sought—leaving the administrative details (housing, office, support) entirely to their judgment? Why are foreign ministries so hung up on states? Some Fortune 500 companies are larger and more important than individual countries—why not post trade commissioners to corporations rather than to capitals?

Gateway missions, hub-and-spoke arrangements, shared services, colocation with the like-minded, additional honorary consuls—all constitute the types of alternative arrangements for representation abroad that foreign ministries should start to consider.[15] Sometimes Internet conferencing or a brass plaque on a hotel room door for a few days will be enough; in other cases a *virtual mission*—custom built, but of bytes rather than bricks—may suffice.[16] In conflict zones, a completely portable setup with a secure satellite uplink for communications but without any permanent physical presence may be most suitable. The point here is flexibility, and that can better be exercised if control over the management of missions abroad and the provision of support services to appointees from elsewhere in government are used to sharpen the influence of the foreign ministry generally. In practical terms, this will mean pushing back by senior foreign ministry managers.

Creativity and imagination do not flourish in a bureaucratic setting. Career interests and institutional biases frequently intervene. I have spoken of the importance of domestic outreach to constituency building; it can also play a vital role in idea generation and intellectual ventilation, especially by connecting with universities and think tanks. Why not bring the principles of *wikinomics* to diplomacy, leveraging knowledge by posting selected international policy issues and problems online for comment and proposed solution?[17] The creation of an e-marketplace—a virtual agora for ideas, if you will—might be undertaken in conjunction with that of an in-house source of intellectual stimulus, say, the appointment of a chief innovation officer.[18] This senior adviser could report directly to the deputy minister and would be responsible for identifying and analyzing leading-edge thinking on international policy, diplomacy, and public administration. Ideally, the appointee would be supported by a free-form, completely unstructured skunk-works type of operation that would operate outside of the usual bureaucratic constraints, preferably off-site.

The best decisions are made with a full view of all options and choices. To find the optimal way forward, decisionmakers should entertain the widest range of opinions and analyses. Apropos the promotion of alternative thinking, consideration might also be given to the establishment of a dissent channel open to all employees, who could offer critical assessments to senior decisionmakers without risk of filtration by those with conflicting views or interests.[19] For some, blessing the received wisdom may be preferable to embracing heresy, but the road between the two is growing shorter. In that spirit, I would suggest that the level of those with the authority to sign off on recommendations to cabinet secretaries and ministers could usefully be lowered from that of the deputy head to, say, the director general with line responsibility for the file.[20] Relocating authority downward would reduce convolution and speed flow.

Many countries could quite easily establish a diplomatic reserve drawn from a comprehensive database comprising not just retired heads of mission but all those from the foreign service and beyond with relevant experience and ability who might be willing to serve. The same goes for the creation of diplomatic SWAT teams—early responders whose skills can be identified in advance and who are available for deployment at short notice—and the appointment of roving ambassadorial problem solvers. All of this could be managed in tandem with the creation of an internal diplomatic float, consisting of those on training, long-term leave, or secondment who could be reassigned on short notice to deal with emergencies.

Perhaps more than any other single issue, though, diplomats and foreign ministries must find their way from the margins to the mainstream of popular and political culture and demonstrate that what they do really does matter. As the repository of institutional memory in the apparatus of international policy and the source of advice and expertise thereon, the foreign ministry and foreign service are irreplaceable. Greater attention must be devoted to ensuring that they are seen to be so. As it is, public opinion on diplomacy and its agents remains, in my experience, decidedly negative. Although this image problem must primarily be addressed through demonstrated improvements in performance, more also needs to be done by way of communications and outreach. To educate the domestic constituency on international policy, foreign ministries must increase their networking activities at home (for instance, by engaging with various diaspora and religious communities).[21]

Redoubled efforts to connect through the new media by, among other things, designing more user-friendly and interactive websites are an obvious starting point here; the ever-widening possibilities associated with ICT represent one powerful tonic for many of diplomacy's ailments.[22] Blogging is now over a decade old; responsive foreign ministers and some senior officials are doing it, and so too should more ambassadors, especially those posted to trouble spots. It is time to ventilate fully the structure and content of diplomacy, to democratize the inputs into decisionmaking, and to push accountability upward while delegating responsibility for decisionmaking downward. Hierarchical, authoritarian structures, like the Cold War–era thinking that produced them, are obsolete.

The agenda for change is clearly incomplete; some key reforms remain undone.[23] PD, as has been shown, is changing the way all other forms of diplomacy are practiced, but this fact is not yet reflected in a greater diversion of human and financial resources to the field. In Canada since 2005, PD spending has been drastically reduced from an already inadequate base; in the United States, despite some increases post-9/11, PD expenditures and levels of activity remain well below those of the Cold War period.[24]

How much, then, has been accomplished overall in recent years? Here I draw again on Canada's experience, which may be broadly indicative. Foreign service officers are now more fairly remunerated, with compensation and recognition better aligned with skills and experience; now senior diplomatic professionals—area experts, senior negotiators, subject-matter specialists—may not necessarily need to seek entrance to the executive group in order to have career fulfillment. Eligibility for entry to the foreign service has been broadened, and its composition now better reflects the diversity of the population.[25] A values and ethics division has been established and there is generally more openness, transparency, and accountability. Training at all levels has improved immeasurably, as learning by doing has been replaced by a full program of formal diplomatic instruction at the Canadian Foreign Service Institute.

A more systematic and objective approach has been taken to assignment practices and performance evaluations; promotions and bonuses no longer resemble the grand prizes of popularity contests. A diplomatic rapid reaction group was set up in 2005 to deal immediately—indeed, where possible, preventively—with crises: called START, or the Stabilization and Reconstruction Task Force, it is an interdepartmental coordinating and executive body with a secretariat housed in DFAIT and an annual budget of US$100 million.[26] The department is even considering a proposal to pre-position consular response teams in the field to deal with natural disasters and man-made emergencies, as its counterpart in the UK has already done. Finally, the department consults with clients and interested parties more widely and more often—for example, on issues of human rights, human security, and regional relations—and is using the Internet to test hypotheses and to ventilate in hopes of democratizing the policy development process; through the Canadian Foreign Service Institute, it is also putting the new media in service of distance learning.

And yet, and yet. Generally speaking, foreign ministries and foreign services are neither sufficiently valued as international policy institutions nor managed as capably or resourced as adequately as they should be. More attention needs to be paid to the development of skills relevant to present and future requirements—especially in the areas of public diplomacy and S&T, which comprise the strategic links between development and security. The establishment of Web-based social networking sites within foreign ministries could be particularly useful in providing a venue for the sharing of experiences and best practices, thereby fostering more vibrant communities of contemporary diplomatic practice.

Foreign ministries must move more decisively to put their own houses in order. Only then will they be able to show taxpayers and governments that investing in a well-staffed, well-resourced organization is highly cost-effective, for it ensures a quality work environment for diplomacy's most valuable asset: its people. Developing that asset is much less expensive than beefing up the military establishment, and it can produce more sophisticated results than buying influence through aid. The case for more substantial reinvestment remains to be made, but, if foreign ministries realign resources with priorities and reinvent the way they work, they will have a convincing case.

Seeking a Friendly Future

In today's unstable and dangerous world, diplomacy and diplomats form a spool that helps keep the skein of civilization from completely unraveling. By keeping channels of communication open across various divides, they can avert outright catastrophe. But bridging the gaps to connect resources to results will not be easy. It will require, at minimum, rebuilding a relevant foreign ministry with a structure and mandate that reflect the challenges of the twenty-first century, embracing public diplomacy as a core business model to ensure effectiveness, and transforming the foreign service into an international service—an agent of whole-of-government international policy integration that would once more be the envy of the public sector.

Relevance, effectiveness, transformation. Important details are missing, and much remains to be done. Yet these three words offer a mantra for foreign ministries organizing frontline responses to the challenge of globalization. The reform enterprise will need the support of colleagues in other government departments and other bargaining units, politicians, and even legislatures. But foreign ministries must start somewhere if they are to become the flexible, directed, and innovative international policy institutions that citizens want and governments require.

What, then, is the precise formula for improved diplomatic performance? One by which the vertical gives way to the lateral, the rigid to the fluid, and strategic direction displaces listless drift. The foreign ministry of the twenty-first century will be more organic and interlinked, less stretched and mechanistic. Authoritarian hierarchies—subverted by the leveling effects of the new technology and the norms of the nexus generation—will dissolve into limpid pools of teamwork and innovation. Those more comfortable making calls at the foreign ministry than plying the back channels will be displaced by street-smart advocates and cross-cultural communicators who combine rich area knowledge with an encyclopedic grasp of public relations and branding.

A Cautionary Tale

In diplomacy, as in international policy, there is always room for reform. But there is also a point at which even the most skillful use of soft power bumps up against hard fact. For example, Robert Greenhill provides a sobering assessment of Canada's international image and reputation in "Making a Difference? External Views on Canada's International Impact," a summary of the views of forty global opinion leaders interviewed during 2004.[27] I have come across no more powerful testament to the need to actively manage national image and reputation, and to bring international policy rhetoric in line with the facts on the ground.

The fiscal capacity exists, particularly in A-world countries and even in the midst of economic downturn, to do more, faster and better—to overcome the severe resource constraints that have plagued foreign ministries since at least the late 1990s. In many instances, with the infusion of a modest amount of capital—a few hundred million dollars in Canada's case, barely enough to register on the national accounts and a pittance by the standards of other government departments—great strides could be made toward delivering on the promise inherent in the aforementioned mantra of relevance, effectiveness, and transformation. Working smarter can only get you so far. If demands (for new missions, more visits, better consular service) keep increasing while supply (of human and financial resources) remains static or diminishes, performance will inevitably suffer. To do more, diplomats and foreign ministries need more. Resources, creatively managed, can produce results. But reinvestment is essential.

Here I find an interpretation of the sad tale of General Charles Gordon—the fabled Gordon of Khartoum—most instructive as a parable. Although one of Queen Victoria's most talented (and supposedly favorite) generals, despite his best efforts, Gordon was in the end unable to save Khartoum—or himself. But it was not for lack of trying. Sent, lacking in troops, to defend this remote corner of the empire, Gordon worked smarter, evacuating as many women and children as he could before the siege laid by the Chosen One, El Mahdi, and his desert tribe. He aligned directly his limited resources (soldiers, food, and munitions) with his priorities (survival). Manning sections of the ramparts with imitation soldiers (British uniforms stuffed with straw), he was relentless in his determination to innovate. He missed no chance to maximize the advantages conferred by superior technology—cannons, carbines, and gunboats. When reinforcements, delayed by political infighting and dithering in London, finally did arrive, it was two days too late. Gordon was in the end a victim of conflicting priorities at home and treachery within his own ranks. His defenses were eventually overwhelmed, and his head was paraded around Khartoum on the end of a pole.

What to make of that? If you want to know what is important in the public realm, watch what governments do, not what they say. And follow the money—or lack thereof. When all is said and done, there are very real limits to what can be achieved by cleverness. At a certain point, there is just no substitute for resources. The resources accorded diplomacy are clearly insufficient and incommensurate with the importance of the function.[28] In Canada, as in many other countries, the foreign ministry has been shrinking—as has its budget, especially when measured as a percentage of overall government spending. The defense budget, in contrast, has grown.[29] That is a false economy, and ill advised. All of which speaks in favor of devoting much more time, attention, and support to the foreign ministry, diplomacy, and the foreign service. Yet too often, senior managers and their political masters have failed to make the case aggressively—or at all. Instead, that task has fallen to others or been forgotten in the shuffle to find fiscal economies and secure resources in times of economic downturn.

As was General Gordon and his garrison to the British Empire, these institutions are on the front lines of globalization. Make them, or break them.

Notes

1. Taylor (1974).

2. There are, however, limits on what might realistically be achieved. The absence of a natural domestic constituency like that enjoyed by the departments of defense, transportation, or environment means, at the end of the day, that political leadership will be required when it comes to securing resources.

3. Personal communication with the author, February 19, 2007.

4. See, for example, Lord Carter of Coles (2005), British Council (2005–2006: 65–70). See, for instance, Edelstein and Krebs (2005: 91), Djerejian (2003: 65), J. Johnson (2006: 50). On the disconnect between the acknowledgment of the need to measure public diplomacy results and the near-complete lack of movement to that end as evidenced by detailed references to congressional reports, see Izadi (2007).

5. Personal communication to the author, March 9, 2006.

6. Consider US Undersecretary of State Karen Hughes's ill-starred "listening tour" of the Middle East in 2005. Other examples are legion. See Englehardt (2007).

7. I was responsible for DFAIT's POR activities from 2003 to 2006. I am nonetheless indebted to Bruce Gregory for pointing out that other neglected measurement tools include social networking assessment, ethnography, and automated sentiment analysis.

8. In many countries, and especially in parts of the T- and E-worlds, POR is virtually unknown and often alien to popular culture. I am accordingly highly suspect of polling done in places such as Afghanistan and Iraq, where POR activity will inevitably be affected by continuing conflicts.

9. This event was related by Terry O'Reilly in a feature on nation branding that was part of the series *The Age of Persuasion*; it aired on April 19, 2007, on CBC Radio One.

10. After a decade of cuts to DFAIT resources, the February 2005 federal budget contained new money—not a windfall, perhaps, but a significant investment of US$641 million over five years—for additional positions abroad as well as for public diplomacy, personnel safety, and international peace and security support. A substantial portion of that funding was clawed back following a change in government; in the budgets of 2006 and 2007, DFAIT came up short.

11. See Copeland (2001: 52–72). Michael Small, Don Hubert, Rob McRae, and Eric Hoskins are among the officials whose work on the human security agenda deserves more credit than it has received.

12. By 2009, Ireland's prospects had darkened dramatically, and it was being compared with (near-bankrupt) Iceland more frequently than with any of the Asian economic miracles of yore.

13. Some think tanks have begun to rethink the nature of diplomatic representation abroad. See, for example, Argyos, Grossman, and Rohaytn (2007).

14. Under globalization, a new order of world cities is emerging in which certain urban places, for various reasons, stand out from the rest. Within the top tier of these cities, London usually leads the pack by virtue of hosting critical activities in the greatest number of key sectors, edging out New York and Tokyo. Among the places in the next tier, Paris, Shanghai, Rome, Los Angeles, Bombay, Berlin, Rio de Janeiro, and many others may lead in one or two areas, but not across the board. Needless to say, this urban order is both subjective and subject to very rapid change.

15. The United States is experimenting with the establishment of what the State Department calls "American Presence Posts," which are neither full diplomatic missions nor even, necessarily, full-time. See, for example, http://busan.usconsulate.gov/102_2007.html.

16. In the context of the transformational diplomacy initiative we have described, the United States, through the establishment of so-called virtual presence posts, is the leader in this field. See, for example, http://tonga.usvpp.gov/. See also Niblock (2006).

17. Under the Office of eDiplomacy (http://www.state.gov/m/irm/c23839.htm), the State Department has, for purposes of knowledge management, also established an intranet wiki-style diplomatic encyclopedia called *Diplopedia*.

18. InnoCentive is a commercial example of this kind of site. See http://www.innocentive.com.

19. The State Department has long maintained such a facility, although I am told by my US colleagues that it is little used.

20. I would again emphasize, however, that neither the introduction of collaborative, online technology nor any amount of structural tinkering will produce results in the absence of an enabling organizational culture. Fear and loathing do not make for a healthy or supportive work environment.

21. Several foreign ministries have made progress here; in Canada, the Muslim Communities Working Group was established after 9/11 and has demonstrated a strong track record. See Treasury Board Canada (2004–2005) for a description.

22. A promising Canadian effort to draw civil society into a continuing collaborative conversation on international policy was launched in early 2008. See http://www.canadasworld.ca.

23. I have barely scratched the surface in terms of reform possibilities. How many foreign ministries have offices for network coordination, stakeholder relations, partnership management, and so on? The possibilities are vast. On the current crisis of US diplomatic readiness, see American Academy of Diplomacy and the Stimson Center (2008).

24. See Critchlow (2004). The depletion of PD assets in the 1990s is highlighted in Mark Leonard's impressive *Public Diplomacy* (2002).

25. Just as not everyone is suited to be a doctor or a social worker, not everyone would make a good diplomat. The foreign service's 2006 lateral entry exercise was conducted without interviewing candidates. Surely firsthand assessment of personal suitability is required for the sake of maintaining professional standards.

26. See Department of Foreign Affairs and International Trade Canada (2008) for a description of START. Former secretary of state Rice strongly supported the establishment of a US civilian response corps, a partnership of eight federal agencies with a roster of rapidly deployable experts with active, standby, and reserve components. See http://www.crs.state.gov/index.cfm?fuseaction=public.display&shortcut=4QRB.

27. See Greenhill (2004).

28. By way of illustration, over the course of my research two factoids, perhaps apocryphal, cropped up repeatedly: (1) that there are more musicians in the various branches of the US military than there are diplomats in the State Department and (2) that in recent years the annual increase in the defense budget has exceeded the total budget of the State Department—which includes official development assistance.

29. On the potential savings available within the current US defense establishment, see Turse (2008).

Guerrilla Diplomacy: Sharper, Faster, Lighter 12

Lord Acton is said to have once remarked, "There is no worse heresy than that the office sanctifies the holder of it." I have argued that old-style diplomacy, with its venerated conventions and its structural rigidities, will have a role in international relations for as long as states have formal business to conduct among themselves. But the domain associated with that kind of activity has narrowed and its importance has diminished as the operating environment has changed and the center of gravity in the global political economy has shifted. Much of what was once fixed and predictable has become diffuse and dynamic. Notwithstanding the persistence in the popular imagination of caricatures of men in top hats swanning about banquet halls, diplomacy's frontiers now extend far from quiet clubs, closed meeting rooms, grand hotels, and formal embassies. Today's diplomatic encounters are just as likely to take place in a barrio or a souk, in an Internet chat room or on a blog, on Main Street or in a Quonset hut set astride the wire.[1]

In all kinds of ways, some obvious, some subtle, diplomacy is under siege. The conventional diplomat, teetering on the brink of irrelevance, is an endangered species in an ecosystem under stress. Just as private security companies and mercenaries are doing jobs once reserved for soldiers, nongovernmental diplomatic service providers are now plying their trade pro bono, if not for hire.[2] This trend will almost certainly continue.

Letting Go

This chapter elaborates the concept of guerrilla diplomacy (GD), which, as both a diplomatic method and a doctrine of statecraft, carries the potential not only to improve the performance of foreign ministries and the efficacy of diplomatic practice but to make the world a more secure and prosperous place for a greater proportion of its inhabitants.[3] It can do this in the short term by contributing to the resolution of insurgency and, over the longer term, by contributing to development as a critical component of the new security.[4] The concept of guerrilla diplomacy, situated at the far end of a spectrum that features traditional diplomacy at the opposite pole and public diplomacy somewhere near the center, moves the general discourse in directions quite different from those that still characterize mainstream international relations. GD responds to the marginalization of dialogue, negotiation, and compromise that has come with the militarization of international policy. GD has been designed in response to the advent of the S&T-driven globalization age and, by placing maximum value on innovation, is at home in that transformed operating environment.

I am convinced that A-world states should adopt the practices of guerrilla diplomacy, but similar benefits would accrue elsewhere. Developing countries and their representatives could, for instance, do a much better job of advancing their issues in metropolitan centers.[5] In certain circumstances, GD will have particular resonance for smaller and medium-sized countries whose lack of colonial baggage and nonthreatening demeanor may at times be convertible into suitability or credibility as interlocutors. Intelligence garnered through GD might then be leveraged, perhaps to secure an influential place at an otherwise exclusive table. In these instances, image and reputation—or rather lack thereof—may be a country's strongest international asset. In all cases, from dignified chancelleries to storefront offices and from hotel rooms adorned with portable brass plaques and equipped with secure wireless networks to virtual missions, both the game and its players are changing. The diplomatic footprint—whether made by feet enclosed by oxfords, Reeboks, or sandals—is being customized and shaped to fit the client rather than the manufacturer. As to the latter, at least in the case of the guerrilla diplomat, we can discern from the mark he or she has left the emergence of a new age polymath equipped with energy, understanding, and a clear agenda.

Portrait of the Diplomat as Guerrilla

The appreciation of ambiguity and paradox is one of the mature pleasures of adulthood. In the previous chapters, we saw that the line between traditional and public diplomacy can be rather blurry. So, too, can the line between public and guerrilla diplomacy, where hard and fast distinctions are hard to come by. GD may best be understood as a subset of, or a specialty compartment of, the former; with a different ethic and more unconventional tactics, it is situated at the innovative end of the spectrum.

Popular and accessible rather than remote and hierarchical, guerrilla diplomacy is built on the foundations of public diplomacy and goes well beyond the so-called information operations conducted by militaries. It embraces improvisation, changing its orientation and approach as quickly as events move on the ground. Its agents are attuned to uncertain, even unstable situations in which developments are fast-breaking and the premium is on mobility, intelligence, and cultural adaptability—where garden-variety public diplomacy may for one reason or another be unsuitable or inadequate. Such circumstances, among them complex emergencies, are increasingly common—particularly in some of the tougher neighborhoods of the T- and E-worlds, where every embassy political officer should be a guerrilla diplomat.[6]

The guerrilla diplomat moves the yardstick—from looking to seeing, from hearing to listening, and from transmitting to receiving. But it is in the context of security and development that guerrilla diplomats set themselves apart from their more conventional cousins. GD is most clearly defined by the following:

- Autonomy, agility, acuity, and resilience
- The ability to generate and use intelligence
- Personal and situational sensitivity
- Local knowledge, cultural awareness, and linguistic and communications skills
- Irregular representational capabilities and characteristics
- An affinity for collaboration and teamwork
- Functionality in conflict situations
- Connectedness to the global political economy of knowledge
- The capacity, enhanced by S&T, to act with souplesse
- A catalytic and transformational orientation

Guerrilla diplomats use all of the tools of PD—but combine them with some of the classic qualities of guerrilla warfare: agility, adaptability, improvization, self-sufficiency, and popular support. Surprise may be a less common attribute, and ambush rarer still, but both do sometimes figure in GD. The aforementioned surprise appearance of Brian Tobin, then fisheries minister of Canada, on a barge in New York's East River in March 1995 during the fisheries dispute with Spain is a classic example of guerrilla diplomacy.

While the guerrilla diplomat's playbook will be informed more by an irregular and imaginative interpretation of the principles of public relations than by any reading of the doctrine of people's war, sensitivity to and knowledge of any immediate environment will be paramount. The guerrilla diplomat's ears will always be to the ground and his or her eyes on the horizon—but the success of any endeavor will turn especially on the collection of strategic intelligence, the development of alternative networks, and the production of demonstrable results. It may involve relying on technology and especially the new media as a force multiplier; on taking a less formal approach to representation; and, probably most importantly, on thinking outside the box and innovating relentlessly. Canada's General Romeo Dallaire played largely by the rules when he was UN force commander in Rwanda and did not receive the support he needed. General Peter Cosgrove of Australia, in contrast, used the media to engage both the global public and the UN bureaucracy when he was the commander of INTERFET in East Timor, and he got much of what he wanted.

To all of the critical advantages associated with PD—communication networks, relationship building, cultural ease, and creativity—GD adds an emphasis on the importance of abstract thinking, advanced problem-solving skills, and rapid-adaptive cognition. Ever inventive and prepared to improvise in order to achieve their objectives, guerrilla diplomats know what to do when things get sticky. Doing things by the book is not among the guerrilla diplomat's favored tactics; awaiting instructions, following orders, and referring to operating manuals rarely suffice in the sorts of fast-paced, high-risk environments best suited to GD.

The guerrilla diplomat will suffocate if confined to organizational silos and drown if submerged under waves of bureaucracy. Comfort with risk and an affinity for interaction—for taking a serious interest in what and how people think about the world—come with the GD territory. In political communications generally, and guerrilla diplomacy in particular, the question of *how* is at least as important as *what.* Neither cautious introverts, ambitious careerists, nor reckless and insensitive types need apply: guerrilla diplomats must have the street smarts to avoid offending their hosts or their home government colleagues.

All public diplomats must be networkers and knowledge workers, expert at dialogue, advocacy, and partnership building. Guerrilla diplomats, however, require far more specialized skills and a rather particular taste for the work involved. In order to hit the ground running, they must be able to use their intimate understanding of the local political, economic, and cultural terrain, thereby gaining access to critical information sources and navigating pathways of influence that others can't even detect. They will, where appropriate, operate unconventionally, outside of traditional metropolitan comfort zones. Guerrilla diplomats can bore deeply into the interstices of power or, like penetrating oil, soak into the operations of the opposition. They are also at ease with business culture, interacting variously with both local and multinational corporate representatives. Knowledge of S&T and mastery of ICT are GD prerequisites.

In ways that will only reveal themselves as circumstances require, guerrilla diplomats can connect directly with the key drivers of insecurity—anger, resentment, humiliation, alienation. They can also use their capacity for souplesse to tap into the global political economy of knowledge and thereby broach the difficult issues that underpin insecurity and perpetuate underdevelopment. In all cases this means getting out of the embassy and into the street—or slum, or desert, or jungle—to engage with friends and, where possible, with foes as well. It is their capacity for total but subtle penetration that allows guerrilla diplomats to earn confidence and trust, mobilize support, and gain insights unavailable to others.

In practical terms, the need to sustain an atmosphere of confidence, trust, and respect will result in guerrilla diplomats behaving in ways not always associated with their profession. Although the following list is indicative rather than comprehensive, by way of example, guerrilla diplomats will typically seek and consider diverse viewpoints, maintain contact with and pursue inputs from marginalized and underrepresented groups, give appropriate weight to background and context, eschew secondhand information in favor of first-hand accounts and validation, be accountable to both their superiors and their interlocutors, and admit their mistakes and acknowledge their faults.[7]

To summarize, cocktails are the same worldwide, but diplomats can't be. The guerrilla diplomat brings an informed, directed, special forces–style sensibility to bear on the broad objectives of diplomacy, maximizing self-reliance while minimizing the usual investment in plant, infrastructure, and logistical support. In a nutshell, vested with the triple-A attributes of agility, autonomy, and adaptability, the guerrilla diplomat will serve as the crucial link between and embodiment of thinking globally and acting locally. An emphasis on these attributes carries some important implications for conflict resolution.

Counterinsurgency: Guerrilla Warfare Meets Guerrilla Diplomacy

In the discussion of the relationship between development and security presented in Chapters 5 and 6, I touched on some emerging conceptual parallels between public diplomacy and counterinsurgency. COIN, or counterinsurgency, is coming rapidly back into fashion; along with so-called stabilization operations, it may even become the next major priority within the Pentagon.[8] COIN therefore merits closer investigation, and I would like to pick up that thread here in order to stitch together something that the guerrilla diplomat might usefully wear.

In 1929, T. E. Lawrence (of Arabia) wrote the entry for "guerrilla" in the fourteenth edition of the *Encyclopaedia Britannica.*[9] Referencing the Arab resistance to Turkish occupation of the Middle East, Lawrence asked, "Suppose [the insurgents] were an influence, a thing invulnerable, intangible, without front or back, drifting about like a gas? Armies were like plants, immobile as a whole, firm-rooted, nourished through long stems to the head." To control the land they occupied, the Turks "would have need of a fortified post every four square miles, and a post could not be less than twenty men. The Turks would need 600,000 men to meet the combined ill wills of all the local Arab people. They had 100,000 men available."

Is this sounding familiar? "The printing press is the greatest weapon in the armory of the modern [guerrilla] commander," Lawrence wrote further, accurately predicting Al-Qaida's modern-day use of the Internet. For insurgents, "rebellion must have an unassailable base. . . . It must have a friendly population—not actively friendly, but sympathetic to the point of not betraying rebel movements to the enemy. Rebellions can be made by 2 percent active in a striking force, and 98 percent passively sympathetic. . . . Granted mobility, security,

. . . time, and doctrine . . . victory will rest with the insurgents, for the algebraical factors are in the end decisive, and against them perfections of means and spirit struggle quite in vain." A century since their publication, these excerpts seem eerily if not chillingly prescient. Then as now, an encounter between guerrilla warfare and guerrilla diplomacy is overdue.[10]

The word *counterinsurgency* is generally used to describe the responses of regular armies to irregular resistance.[11] Those who theorize war and political-military relations have little choice these days but to ponder counterinsurgency, as it happens to be what most A-world armies are spending much of their time doing—not, it must be added, particularly well. "Why won't they just stand up and fight?" demand the exasperated generals. "Every time we meet on the battlefield, we prevail," they assert triumphantly. The problem is, the latter observation answers the former question, but not all of the generals in charge appear to have noticed.[12] Even if they did, there is not necessarily a directly proportional relationship between positive military outcomes and political progress. Indeed, if there is a relationship at all, it could well be inversely proportional, due at least in part to the inherent contradiction between the goal of control (military) and that of liberation (political).

Traditional diplomats, as we have seen, are running into difficulty because, in a world of proliferating nonstate actors, they are equipped primarily to deal with the representatives of other states. A-world militaries are similarly struggling with asymmetrical confrontations because they are organized—doctrinally, culturally, and materially—for larger-scale, more structured types of conflict.[13] In most instances of counterinsurgency, moreover, there is a disturbing pattern: A-world armies and generals are fighting their enemies in the T- and E-worlds with troops whose social status in their country of origin is linked often to the C- and T-worlds. This scenario appears to illustrate the power relations inherent in globalization, and may help explain why the results attributable to COIN operations have been mixed to poor.

Can insurgency in fact be successfully countered? Not easily. From the Roman Empire to the Third Reich, from the so-called Indian wars in the United States to the Boer War in southern Africa to the US campaign in the Philippines in the 1920s, some combination of disproportionate civilian casualties and extreme acts of brutality can usually be counted on to dampen the enthusiasm of the population for rebellion. Another tried-and-true technique is massive occupation—the deployment of, say, one soldier for something between every twenty and every 100 persons occupied, depending upon the ferocity of the resistance. If that means heavy casualties for the occupier, the disadvantage will still go to the occupied—for a while, anyway. Planning and resources are key. If the vacuum left after regime change is not filled quickly, then—as has been made painfully clear by the cases of Afghanistan and Iraq—someone not likely to be of the occupier's choosing will move in to fill it. If that occurs, recovery is difficult, even with money, manpower, and time.

In any event, in the age of globalization—marked as it is by widespread sensitivity and concern over human rights, mass media coverage, and limited public tolerance for casualties—neither of these two approaches is realistic. Domestic publics don't have the stomach or the patience. So what options remain to interested world leaders? They can quit. But that, for obvious reasons, is difficult. They can hand over control to a friendly local regime and let them deal with the aftermath of their failure. But finding credible, legitimate, and effective partners, particularly during an occupation, is a tall order, as has been shown in the cases of the Karzai and al-Maliki governments in the Afghanistan and Iraq governments, respectively.

In yet another illustration of the deterritorialization of political space, it is the population, not the place, that has become the locus in counterinsurgency. That reality puts a premium on political persuasion, on the ability to convince the public that your intentions are noble and constructive and that your efforts at protection deserve support—to the extent that force is avoided or used minimally and discriminately and that the emphasis is placed instead on political and economic instruments designed to distance the population from the insurgents. Yet this ability is rarely nurtured. Instead of reaching out to populations through dialogue and partnership, a variety of domination-oriented alternatives have been attempted, from establishing technological and weapons superiority and controlling territory (break, take, hold, repair the damage) to manipulating information flows and endlessly retooling command bureaucracies.[14]

Variations on the theme of shock and awe—a strategy that combines speed, advanced technology, and overwhelming force to establish "full-spectrum dominance"—might work in the act of regime change, but are highly counterproductive in the aftermath.[15] These deceptively outdated tactics are quite inappropriate in the face of a mobile, diffuse, and networked threat—especially one tied to a global insurgency movement that, like Al-Qaida, has become expert at the use of political communications and uses religion to motivate violent extremism.

In this type of conflict, as was the case in Vietnam, tactical victory is next to irrelevant. You can win every battle and still lose the war. If there is any chance of "winning"—a word that itself may in this context be inappropriate or outdated—the complexity of the challenge must be met by a response that is integrated, comprehensive, and long-term. Modern insurgency, in my view, is in large part a function of underdevelopment, and will best respond if treated accordingly. If all efforts are not directed ultimately toward locally sourced good governance, the rule of law, the provision of services, and political participation, then neither development nor security can be anticipated.

Distracted by terrorism and confounded by the political ideologies associated with Islam (or Islamism), we may finally have to acknowledge that the main currents of strategic thinking in Western countries do not fully reflect the sweeping realities of the globalization age. Specifically, the costs of the failure to come to terms with the political and developmental prerequisites of security are adding up, and now a fundamental change in direction is imperative. How might these shortcomings be addressed, especially at the pointy end of the diplomatic spectrum where armed conflict looms?

Here something quite unprecedented seems to be happening. Two strains of thought, though emanating (at least in some cases) from opposing ends of the intellectual continuum, are apparently converging. When it comes to dealing with asymmetric conflict, military and civilian analysts are arriving at more or less the same conclusion: engage populations. The clearest signs of this convergence are cropping up—if not always explicitly—in the literature on counterinsurgency, a good deal of which is written by active or retired service personnel.[16] Contemporary doctrine in this relatively neglected but now resurgent field of study is beginning to reflect conditions in the theater of operations.[17]

As did their predecessors regarding earlier conflicts in Vietnam, Malaya, and the like, contemporary strategists and practitioners of counterinsurgency are returning to the point made by Robert Thompson in the 1960s and repeated by David Kilcullen and others today: asymmetrical conflicts are prime candidates for the application of political methods of problem solving.[18] A recently declassified US military report, for instance, states that *information operations*—which they refer to as public affairs, public diplomacy, and psy-ops collectively—"are now critical to military success and will only become more so in the foreseeable future."[19]

Bottom line? Military strategists are acknowledging that while soldiers may have the watches, the guerrillas have the time. In that case, what to do? In my opinion, if COIN operations are 80 percent political, then one answer jumps immediately to mind—that soldiers are the wrong people to be accorded primary responsibility for completing them. Counterinsurgency is not primarily the job of armies. The entire issue needs to be reframed, viewed through a different prism. We might begin by considering how to adapt and apply public diplomacy in conflict zones. I say, leave the tanks at home and send in a busload of guerrilla diplomats for whom insurgent thinking will be second nature. And substitute ambassadors for generals at the top of the local food chain, so that critical decisions can be made in full view of all the relevant considerations. Let me set this out in context.

Public Diplomacy and Political War: Two Sides of the Same COIN?

I have tried to situate the issues treated so far within an analysis of grand strategy,[20] arguing that if development is the new security, then we need to adjust our approaches to diplomacy and international policy accordingly, in part by applying what we have learned from the Cold War to the era of globalization. In Chapter 5, I referred briefly to issues related to fourth generation war and other forms of unconventional warfare.[21] I observed that the conventional military, which exists mainly for the purpose of killing or capturing adversaries, is of limited use in counterinsurgency. In asymmetrical conflict, a reliance on the coercive power of armed force is more likely to create enemies than win friends.

Counterinsurgency offers great opportunity for adapting some of the central techniques of PD to the particular circumstances of war.[22] In fact, military theorists of counterinsurgency are again placing emphasis on connecting directly with the local population via such PD tactics as networked communications, cultural literacy, and relationship building—in other words, by talking rather than fighting.[23] This means that from a counterinsurgency perspective, the putative revolution in military affairs is irrelevant at best.

At the leading edge of this wedge is an apparent fusion in thinking about what might be described as military public diplomacy and political counterinsurgency. This convergence, although not usually identified as such, is reflected in some of the literature cited previously on topics such as the 3 Ds (that is, defense, diplomacy, and development), the three block war (combat, relief, and reconstruction or offense, defense, and stabilization) and contemporary counterinsurgency doctrine. Advocates (especially in US military circles) of a joined-up, foreign-domestic, civil-military approach to international counterinsurgency interventions sometimes treat this cluster of issues under the rubric of *foreign internal defense*.[24] Taken together, many of these considerations mirror my own thoughts on souplesse and guerrilla diplomacy. The following imperatives, for instance, are shared by GD and COIN:

- Establish new linkages between hard and soft power.
- Emphasize rapid-adaptive brainpower over firepower.
- Bridge cultural differences through networked communications.
- Focus on issues rather than targets.
- Favor agility, adaptability, and dialogue over force.
- Forge partnerships with and within civil society.
- Win hearts and minds through political communication.
- Demonstrate integrity through values-based action and ethical behavior.
- Use broadcast, interactive, and multimedia strategically.[25]
- Adopt new approaches to the collection and use of intelligence.

In short, political counterinsurgency and military public diplomacy are becoming two sides of the same coin. How would their fusion work, and what might it imply?

To *counter* insurgency, it is necessary to think like an insurgent, looking at the source of your opponent's strength in order to determine how it might best be turned into a weakness—a vulnerability that can be exploited. This is precisely what improvised explosive devices and suicide bombing have achieved against armor and fortified positions. Defeating such threats requires the kinds of detailed knowledge—intellectual, psychological, cultural—that can be provided by anthropologists and ethnologists as well as neighborhood residents and the local police force (which, if doing its job properly, should be close to the people).[26] Practical use of this type of human-centered expertise is a central feature of *human terrain systems,* a contemporary approach to counterinsurgency whose developers have tried to learn from the experience of the controversial Civil Operations and Rural Development Support Program—a variant of which was known also as Phoenix—implemented in Vietnam.[27]

The provincial reconstruction teams (PRTs) in Afghanistan and Iraq are intended to represent the contemporary incarnation of this approach; however, their performance, too, has been mixed.[28] As one veteran commented, "The main purpose of PRTs boils down to 'box-checking' . . . they are there so that governments can say that they are there. . . . [I]n numbers and influence, the military dominates and the diplomats and development staff rarely get out of their heavily fortified compounds . . . [but even] when they do, the procession is tightly scripted and heavily guarded."[29]

In this light, a reliance by counterinsurgency forces upon tanks, armored convoys, and Fort Apache–style strong points in insecure areas would seem mainly to multiply the number of targets; it sends all of the wrong messages. It is a sign of weakness rather than strength, which in turn suggests that defeat is closer than victory; think of the outposts of the French foreign legion in the Algerian Sahara or the disaster at Dien Bien Phu in Vietnam. (US attempts to create fortified hamlets in Vietnam did not fare much better.)

At present, the use of force is still privileged by COIN operatives, who typically turn to diplomacy and development only after an area has been "pacified" or made "secure." Those favoring a more politically driven approach would reverse this order, seeking to take the public terrain by consent and to secure the support of populations voluntarily. They would rely, in the first instance, not on the use of force but on diplomacy and development informed by extensive historical research, political knowledge, economic resources, and cross-cultural capacity. By tapping into the undercurrents of hostility and feeding the intelligence thereby gained back into the strategic planning and policy formulation process, diplomatic and development efforts that begin with short-term relief and evolve into longer-term cooperation could yield promising outcomes. Put another way, as means to earning the trust and confidence of the local population, inadvertently bombing schools and hospitals or driving tanks into living rooms will likely backfire. Action in accordance with an agreed political strategy, by contrast, just might work.

For many counterinsurgency ends, the military is simply the wrong means; overreliance on armed force is both costly and inefficient. Military public-affairs and civil-liaison officers and their colleagues—including those working out of the offices of provincial reconstruction teams in Afghanistan and regional coalition command centers in Iraq—can do some of what is necessary, but they are constrained by their organizational affiliations, and their approach tends to be acultural. Guerrilla diplomats, by contrast, with their dedication to continuous connectedness, can help provide the momentum required to avoid slipping into a reactive position, from which it can be very difficult to regain the initiative. In seeking to take the population by consent rather than by compulsion, guerrilla diplomats can secure the public terrain in a manner that renders firepower unnecessary.

That said, shooting messages rather than bullets will not in itself do the trick. No one likes being used for target practice, whatever the munitions. Addressing the challenges of COIN, one analyst has described the current approach of A-world governments as something akin to a "bizarro [evocation of] *Goldilocks*—not hot [hard power] enough, not cold [soft power] enough, but just right enough to alienate the population without pacifying them."[30] I think that is apt. Bringing people over to your side requires both talking the walk and walking the talk. Thus primary reliance on the military rather than the political is inappropriate. Those in uniform are seen to be responsible for imposing the will of outsiders and for inflicting tragedy upon innocents. Why ask soldiers to do something that for diplomats, and especially guerrilla diplomats, will come as second nature? It's like asking an arsonist to do the job of a fireman.

The main problem with COIN, in both theory and practice, is that it is frequently in the wrong box. That, in my view, goes much of the way toward explaining its troubled history.

Diplomatic and Humanitarian Alternatives

Imagine an irregular conflict situation wherein, amidst the bursts of violence, malaria was decimating the populace or water shortages were contributing to unsanitary conditions, crop failure, and hunger and mobilizing the insurgency. Enter the guerrilla diplomat. The mission? To connect with the population in an unthreatening manner. Undertake field research to identify the immediate causes of the misery and instability. Engage A-world capacity to tap into the global political economy of knowledge, drawing on the sources of specialized knowledge and expertise required to address the causal issues thus identified through technology, medicine, and/or humanitarian assistance. Work with other government and nongovernmental organizations to broach broader issues and to put more lasting solutions into place.

The diplomacy of deeds links aid to development and, in so doing, has a potent demonstration effect. That is souplesse in a nutshell, connecting COIN to grand strategy; in its absence, any gains on the ground either won't matter or won't last.

The overall goal would not be to put down insurgency by force but rather to provide an environment in which civil considerations would both trump and *be seen to trump* military options. In those circumstances, the opposition's inflammatory messages—usually litanies of grievances against the enemy—would be less likely to resonate, and the turbulence associated with anger and resentment would be more likely to subside. Instead of going after insurgents by brandishing weapons, crashing into compounds, and rounding up suspects, counterinsurgents would take immediate aim at the causes of fear and want. These would be identified through discussion and then pursued aggressively to prevent crisis from becoming chaos. To restate it, the overriding goal would be to create conditions in which security and development could flourish while suffering, anxiety, and discontent withered.

Of course, ideas emanating from academic conferences and specialized bodies of literature are one thing, actual events in conflict zones quite another. Current counterinsurgency practices still amount mainly to a reliance on violence as a means to compel submission and impose the will of outsiders. The heavy-handed use of force, backed by rigid positions, entrenched privilege, and the arrogance of power, continues only to backfire, leading the weak to turn to religious and political extremism of an ever more hazardous and irregular variety. The result is like putting out fires with gasoline: a conflagration of violence instead of a methodical smothering of the sparks.

In a tinderbox, gradually dousing the embers of discontent under a light spray is preferable to trying to disintegrate them with a water cannon, stamp them out with heavy machinery, or, worst of all, fan the flames. Better results could quite possibly be obtained by letting the bundles of cash saved by the termination of offensive operations rain down on insurgent populations. This is not a joke. Bombing restive communities with money rather than cluster bombs and bunker busters would stimulate consumption and generate employment rather than alienation and fury. The infusion of direct support would also circumvent the corruption and graft often associated with local government and foreign aid. In situations where conventional tactics are not working—and there is no shortage of those—the proposition is certainly worth considering, especially as the costs of staying the present course continue to mount.[31]

Many would argue that the existence of an organized and violent threat has been exaggerated to justify a response in kind—one that really serves to support the agenda of the military-industrial complex.[32] That may well be so; endless war, even if of dubious value as a macroeconomic instrument, is endlessly good for certain types of business, perhaps especially the defense and security contractors with guns for hire.[33] Patient police work and intelligence gathering just do not generate the same level of private-sector expansion.

As living conditions worsen in many parts of the world, greater numbers of the exploited and marginalized—and of those who empathize with their plight—will turn to desperate measures. These are chosen mainly out of anger, frustration, and a sense of injustice, but they are also encouraged and exploited by the very effective marketing campaign mounted by supporters of the global jihad to recruit and retain adherents. Note again the recurrent pattern of insurgent thinking: turn one of globalization's strengths, in this case the efficient international division of labor, into a weakness by recruiting the disaffected.

Active hostility and human-centered development are incompatible; the latter begins with resolving conflicts, the former with the more costly alternative of winning them. Sending in the marines may once have been the answer, but today that could well make matters worse. In cases of insurgency, it is diplomats rather than soldiers who are best equipped to initiate countermeasures. Because diplomacy is about talking things out—about understanding and negotiating differences rather than just fighting over them—it is what serves as the linchpin in conflict situations between present hostility and future cooperation. Guerrilla diplomats in particular employ intelligence, local knowledge, and cultural sensitivity in service of an alternative narrative to that of the insurgents—one that helps interpret events, inform strategy, direct policy, and guide action.

The apparent convergence of strategic thinking about COIN and PD is fascinating, and certainly deserves more intensive inquiry, especially with respect to the potential for further cross-fertilization. It may even be that elements of PD are finding a place near the heart of counterinsurgency doctrine, in which case they are likely to attract much attention. Such attention would be warranted, and the use of PD by counterinsurgents in war zones welcome.

Listening to Lawrence?

It is in many ways encouraging that the United States and Canada have recently issued counterinsurgency doctrines that feature some fresh thinking and emphasize (again) the importance of winning hearts and minds.[34] The content of these manuals, however implicitly, does support the contention that the thinking on political counterinsurgency PD and military information-operations PD is coalescing. Cross-cultural training—another essential component of effective communication with those of different national origins or ethnic backgrounds—has also become something of a growth industry, even in military academies.

A change in course may be at hand. Yet I would still hesitate to give either of these developments top billing. Apart from catchy terminology, there is not really much that is new in the resurgence of interest in counterinsurgency. The same old mistakes get made again and again, and important lessons are quickly forgotten. There is an apparent military pathology at work here that could do with further investigation. Even in a best-case scenario, recognizing the need of those in uniform to learn or relearn the politics of counterinsurgency is the easy part; establishing real two-way communications in situ with often hostile local populations and then taking meaningful action is quite another matter.

In any event, there is much else that can be done to counter insurgency, mainly through legal, police, and intelligence work. Innovative approaches can be pursued to rehabilitate convicted terrorists while in prison; for instance, employing counselors who are themselves former terrorists to conduct therapy sessions is a tactic that is finding some success in Indonesia and Saudi Arabia.[35] Intelligence officials can monitor jihadi websites and, when appropriate, close them down and prosecute the sponsors, much as is done with the websites of child pornographers and human traffickers (see Chapter 6).

It is also necessary to keep the relative importance of competing priorities in perspective. In my estimation, embarking on a process of serious engagement between the A- and the C-, T-, and E-worlds on broad issues of development—including the range of S&T concerns we have raised—remains the most promising way to defuse the kinds of tensions that, if ignored, may eventually find expression in violence. But this process would require focus, money, and decades of patient trial and error—and, for that matter, would be a nonstarter so long as defense departments dominate so much of the space allotted to international policy. War, in the final analysis, is still the antithesis of diplomacy. When the fighting starts, the talking tends to stop, and the scope for useful diplomatic enterprise, especially initially, becomes limited.

All of which brings us back to the here, the now, and the possible. The unique skills and tactics of the guerrilla fighter are ideally matched to the irregular conditions and uneven terrain characterizing so many of today's battlefields. In some situations the use of force may be unavoidable, especially if the provision of emergency relief would be otherwise impossible. In such cases, it would be for the military to do the fighting—and to provide security for assistance operations, but only if and as required. Aid workers—preferably many more of them than are typically available—would better be responsible for managing development cooperation. And those guerrilla diplomats that could be recruited, trained, and deployed would do what they could to keep it all together, ensuring that all activities were conducted in a manner suitable to conditions as they evolved on the ground.[36] Ultimately their goal could involve something as elemental as developing and promoting a better situational narrative than that being advanced by the adversaries.[37] In any case, to restore symmetry, we must reframe COIN by bringing the unconventional to bear on the unorthodox. It is time that the guerrilla warrior met the guerrilla diplomat.

Foreign Intelligence: Sensitive Ears, Sharp Eyes

There is a much greater potential role for certain types of public diplomacy in conflict situations than has generally been granted. NATO has provincial reconstruction teams all over Afghanistan, but their performance has not, to my knowledge, been rigorously evaluated or even much monitored. Ditto for coalition PRTs in Iraq. Some foreign ministries are experimenting with rapid deployment units specializing in preventive diplomacy and conflict resolution. In 2005, Canada's DFAIT, as we have noted, created START, or the Stabilization and Reconstruction Task Force, in order to deal with both conflict and emergency assistance.[38]

Though steps in the right direction, such initiatives tend to be inadequately resourced and removed from most other diplomatic business. Most diplomacy will continue to be conducted under less arduous circumstances. All diplomacy, however, will involve establishing and managing networks of contacts. Sometimes these activities will be tied to the realization of specific objectives—such as delivering a ministerial visit or high-profile cultural event—but on a day-to-day basis, networking is done for the purpose of collecting tactical and strategic information, which is to say intelligence, and cultivating beneficial relationships.[39] This will be increasingly true as foreign ministries move toward a PD model that features advocacy, partnerships, and, especially, dialogue—the font of what is referred to in the trade as *human intelligence* and the potential source of, among other things, valuable foreknowledge. In these respects—and in light of their extensive network of missions and representatives abroad and systems of secure communications—it seems foreign ministries are well positioned to increase their contribution to the collective intelligence-gathering effort.

Intelligence—an elusive and misunderstood commodity, especially within foreign ministries, for which there is great demand and very limited supply—is the calling card of the guerrilla diplomat. While I have not heard anyone suggest that the terms *diplomatic intelligence* and *foreign intelligence* are as oxymoronic as the military equivalent is often said to be, it remains true that diplomacy is not generally associated with intelligence gathering or assessment. In fact, just as people working in the field of development assistance often have an aversion to people in uniform, diplomats do not typically think highly of the intelligence function. It tends to be seen as a career backwater. Like so much else covered in this volume, that, too, must change.

Globalization has produced an explosion of available information and has enormously facilitated access thereto. This development has rendered intelligence—those grains of wheat hidden among bushels of chaff—invaluable. Intelligence is simply information whose value is based on its accuracy, timeliness, and relevance in relation to the objectives and priorities of the information consumer. In other words, intelligence represents a special type of information. It is set apart from chatter by its acuity and utility. While it may be generated through technical (eavesdropping and signal interception), covert (espionage, the use of running agents, impersonation), or other clandestine means, it has been my experience that the most worthwhile and accurate intelligence is usually the result of interpersonal communication—oral exchange, firsthand observation—and/or the careful reading of open, unclassified sources.

You don't need subterfuge to produce intelligence. For decades, *I. F. Stone's Weekly* published some of the most insightful criticism of the US government around, breaking confidential stories regularly without access to any classified material. My own experience as an intelligence analyst covering South, Central, and Southeast Asia during the world-changing shifts they underwent from 1989 to 1992 led me to similar conclusions. Open sources and expert analysis contained by far the most useful insights. I was struck especially by the evidence of ideological blinders that often obscured objective observation. Within the Western intelligence establishment, there was huge resistance to incontrovertible proof that the USSR was withdrawing its military forces from Afghanistan and Vietnam. So high was the comfort level with Cold War verities that many of those in the business of threat production and maintenance simply could not imagine events transpiring outside of that familiar framework.[40] Judgment, background knowledge, and discernment are the essential qualities for the intelligence analyst. Personal loyalty, the inclination to use positional power to suppress dissent, and ideological conviction are not.

Informed interpretation of diverse sources is the natural gift of the guerrilla diplomat, who will operate for extended periods semiautonomously and above the radar screen. Indeed, it is the self-reliance and visibility of guerrilla diplomats, in combination with their identified association with a state, that helps make them valuable both to their local contacts and to their employer.

One often hears of "good" or "bad" intelligence. I have always found this a dubious distinction. All bona fide intelligence is good—however difficult or inconvenient the policy or operational implications. If, by contrast, the information is wrong or has been manipulated to correspond to political imperatives or the wishful thinking of the boss, then it is not bad intelligence but something else—misinformation, disinformation, propaganda, anything but intelligence. One central, unresolved, and perhaps intractable problem, however, as we have just implied, is the frequent clash between intelligence and policy. Intelligence can support policy and be wrong. It can subvert policy and be right. Or there can be any number of permutations in between.

Policies tend to develop momentum, a life of their own based on fact, faith, career interests, or will. Sometimes intelligence will reinforce a given policy direction or be distorted to support a predetermined conclusion, as with the purported missile gap with the USSR in the 1960s and its descendant misrepresentations in the 1980s. One of the most notorious examples of this dishonest, disastrous practice was the so-called intelligence indicating the presence of weapons of mass destruction that justified the 2003 invasion of Iraq. In other cases, the supposed intelligence may simply prove wrong. For example, during the 1980s there were repeated allegations of the use of chemical or bacteriological agents such as yellow rain against Hmong tribespeople who had fought on contract for the CIA, particularly in Laos during the Indochina wars. With Canadian assistance, a UN mission was sent in 1984 into the refugee camps along the northeastern frontier of Thailand to examine the evidence being offered by the Hmong refugees (I was the team's escort). The team conducted extensive interviews, collected samples, and performed physical examinations. When the analysis was complete the experts concluded that the substance in question consisted mostly of a mixture of pollen and bee feces. The ideologues were infuriated.

On other occasions, bona fide intelligence is either missed or misinterpreted. The long list of colossal intelligence failures—to foresee the Iranian revolution in 1979 or the implosion of the USSR in 1989, to preempt the attacks on US embassies in Kenya and Tanzania in the late 1990s or on the World Trade Center and the Pentagon in 2001, and so on—provides a wealth

Policy and Intelligence: Strange Bedfellows?

Readers will doubtless be aware of other examples of ideologically or politically colored interpretations of intelligence, perhaps even some as zany as the yellow rain example. But the sparks really fly when intelligence subverts existing policy and argues in favor of a change in direction.

In November 1991, Indonesian troops broke up a peaceful proindependence demonstration in Dili, East Timor. Many hundreds were killed, wounded, or missing; it was a massacre. Interpretations varied widely. Area analysts tended toward the determination that events of this kind could be attributed to the nature of the Indonesian regime. While occurrences on such a scale were relatively rare, human rights violations in Indonesia were epidemic and systemic, the military was poorly trained and led, and more events of this kind could be expected. Other officials, particularly those whose job it was to promote political and economic relations with Indonesia, maintained that the massacre, however unfortunate, was in fact an aberration, a one-off episode unlikely to be repeated. They recommended against any drastic action, such as suspending aid—in their view an overreaction.

The Canadian foreign minister at that time, Barbara McDougall, received assessments of both varieties, albeit through different channels. In exasperation, she asked officials whom to believe. This evinced a high degree of discomfort and uneasiness among those in the room.[41]

The post-9/11 conflicts in Afghanistan and Iraq have generated similar kinds of tensions in and among Western capitals. The point here is that normative, prescriptive policy and objective, analytical intelligence do not always lead to the same conclusions. That speaks in favor of keeping the two functions at arm's length—something easier said than done, especially in the face of abiding pressures within large organizations to speak with one voice.

of examples.[42] These failures, however, usually have less to do with a lack of information than with a failure of analysis or the interference of policy or political biases, which skew the interpretation of such information as is available.

Major powers dominate the so-called intelligence community, the inner circle of which consists of the English-speaking allies of the twentieth century—the United States and the UK, principally, with Australia and Canada grateful to be cast in supporting roles. New Zealand was a member too, until the United States forced it out in the late 1980s on account of its decision to forbid visits to its ports by ships that might be armed with nuclear weapons. Most of the EU countries, especially France and Germany, are also active players in the Western intelligence field,[43] while Singapore, Malaysia, Morocco, and numerous others from the C- and T-worlds are also involved, although on a different level.[44] China, Russia, and India are players in their own right.

The close intelligence-sharing relationships among Western countries represent yet another Cold War carryover; whatever their virtues, the results can be less than ideal. Groupthink is rampant, and the tendency to interpret events and information from a Western perspective means that culturally significant clues—the type arising from the intimate local knowledge that would be a GD trademark—can easily be missed on the receiving end. Guerrilla diplomacy addresses these shortcomings by ensuring that its practitioners will know how to listen, how to be seen to be listening, and how to interpret what is heard, culturally and historically as well as linguistically.

Making Intelligence More Intelligent

Globalization has rendered the old alliance-based structures less relevant. But that's not all. Smaller states, notwithstanding their limited resources, have some built-in advantages over the heavyweights. They do not carry the latter's historical baggage. They are not detested or resented as imperialists (or formerly so). They do not have grand geopolitical or strategic ambitions. They are not threatening, in short. For these reasons, doors that may not be accessible to others can be opened. Sources are more likely to be prepared to talk candidly. For these reasons, these smaller countries are exceptionally well suited to the generation of valuable human-source intelligence, which in turn can be used to bolster the political positions of others—especially those in major capitals where bringing more to the table could produce tangible dividends.

Several recent publications on foreign policy have made reference to the record numbers of nationals traveling and working abroad and have encouraged governments to collectively consider such people, as well as foreign nationals with significant domestic ties, a potential diplomatic resource that might be harnessed to a much greater and more systematic extent than is done today.[45] In Canada, this idea was brusquely dismissed by some of the more hidebound old-schoolers as tantamount to a proposal to turn diplomatic missions abroad into drop-in centers for backpackers.

But pause on that for just a moment. In certain places—South and Southeast Asia come immediately to mind—I can think of no better or more cost-effective way to leverage information sources and expand networks. There are many places in the world where vacationers, entrepreneurs, businesspeople, retirees, and volunteers may hear and see things that would not come to the attention of officials. For example, backpackers have long been attracted to the unspoiled beaches of southern Thailand—some provinces of which, as noted previously, are also home to a sometimes nasty insurgency, which since the middle of the 2000s has intensified. Local rebels have allegedly developed ties to Al-Qaida, whose presence next door in Malaysia has been widely reported.[46] Diplomatic staff in Bangkok or Kuala Lumpur are unlikely to be in a position to produce much relevant intelligence on this kind of issue. They just are too far removed in every sense; they require the help of people who have spent time much closer to the ground—aid workers, teachers, NGO representatives. In such cases, why not open Internet cafes hosted by the friendly junior political officer (and aspiring guerrilla diplomat) who could serve coffee while sensitively chatting up a selection of guests in a directed way? Creating a social space at embassies that would serve the same function once provided by American Express mail drops makes good sense to me.

Netpolitik: ICT as a Force Multiplier

Diplomats, and in particular guerrilla diplomats, could be great generators of intelligence. But how else might useful information be effectively gathered and, in the context of international political communications, exchanged and disseminated? In answering these questions, issues surrounding use of the new media, especially the Internet, by foreign ministries in general and guerrilla diplomats in particular deserve extensive treatment in their own right. This is one area where the thinking has advanced considerably.[47] For example, John Arquilla and David Ronfeldt maintain that any analysis of the strategic role played by information in international relations cannot be confined to a narrow technical discussion about platforms and processes but must also take into account the values, identities, and practices reflected by the formation of global networks.[48] New technology has made possible both the creation of and access to a common life of the mind, a "web of living thought" that, as we have seen, was termed by Teilhard de Chardin as the noosphere.[49] While the great usefulness of the new media in efforts to directly engage populations at home and abroad and thus maximize scale economies, impact, and leverage is worth noting, we will be able only to touch on the subject here.[50] The point of departure is this: the explosive popularity of social networking possibilities associated with sites such as Facebook, MySpace, YouTube, LinkedIn, Twitter, Hi5, and Friendster may be enough to provoke communications theorist Manuel Castells to issue a revised edition of his landmark trilogy on the information age.[51] An increasingly large proportion of the world's population looks to the Internet as its primary source of information and communication; as higher transmission speeds and greater bandwidth expand audio- and video-streaming options, the Internet will only continue to edge out newspapers, television, radio, and conventional telephones as the primary communications medium. The most recent applications as of the time of this writing, summarized under the moniker Web 2.0 and featuring an emphasis on content sharing, social networking, interactivity, and downloadable audio and video podcasts in contrast to simple information presentation, promise to accelerate this trend.[52]

There is no doubt as to the power and pervasiveness of the medium. To offer just a sampling: campaigns on the Web were critical to the rise of the antiglobalization movement; they stopped the Multilateral Agreement on Investment in the late 1990s; they changed the outcome of a Korean presidential election; they have raised the profiles of consular cases in unprecedented ways. Citizen journalism is on the ascendancy, since anyone with a webcam and a digital uplink can become a reporter—think of the earliest footage of the 9/11 attacks in 2001, the Indian Ocean tsunami in 2004, the 2007 prodemocracy uprising in Burma, or the anti-Chinese rioting in Llasha, Tibet, in 2008. Almost none of those images were provided by professional media. And almost none of it could be suppressed by local authorities. Or think of blogs. In their immediacy and interactivity, blogs may not quite be the equivalent of face-to-face contact but certainly come closer than do documents posted on static websites, which makes them especially effective at breaking down cultural barriers. Blogs from Iraqi war zones and elsewhere in the Middle East have brought the human toll of those conflicts to desktops around the globe: executions have been streamed live on anti-occupation sites, and the Abu Ghraib prison pictures spread faster than Seymour Hersh's editorials in the *New Yorker* could ever be distributed.[53] Those images have effectively branded the US occupation. In the wake of developments such as these, it is not entirely surprising that Rand Corporation analysts have recommended that the US military try Internet marketing techniques to win hearts and minds in Iraq and Afghanistan.[54]

Diplomacy is also flirting with the new media and migrating toward the Web.[55] As is characteristic in the globalization age, it has not taken long to reach technological takeoff. The foreign ministers of Sweden and Britain have blogs, and certain US and UK diplomats do so as well.[56] Sri Lanka, Serbia, Colombia, Albania, Macedonia, the Republic of the Maldives, Estonia, and the Philippines have established virtual embassies in the 3-D virtual universe called Second Life.[57] The US State Department has established an Office of eDiplomacy, created a network of virtual presence posts, and is hosting a wiki-like intranet application called Diplopedia; Secretary Clinton has her own Web page, as did former assistant secretaries for public diplomacy Karen Hughes and James Glassman. Singapore and Hong Kong were way out in front in establishing Web-based identities for their city-states.

Public diplomats, then, can use the new media to connect directly with populations; finding better, more creative ways to do so will be one of GD's primary responsibilities, in part because the Internet can compensate for the increasingly severe constraints on personal contact imposed in an increasing number of locales by security considerations. For instance, guerrilla diplomats could work from virtual desks organized thematically or geographically, whereby they could create networks of expertise extending far beyond the foreign ministry. For example, the officer who covers Southeast Asia could share the Thai desk at headquarters with professors, NGO representatives, recently posted staff, businesspeople, Canadians working in Thailand, and anyone else with knowledge and expertise they were prepared to contribute. The virtual desk model, based on multiparty, horizontal issue management, would also be appropriate for dealing with the wide range of S&T challenges discussed earlier.

Not all guerrilla diplomats will be young, but many will have grown up with the new media. For members of this cohort, the full interactive potential of the medium and of its application to PD and branding will be obvious.[58] Such familiarity is advantageous because, just as the military needs rules of engagement, GDs need tools of engagement.[59] Guerrilla diplomats could thus become active in virtual worlds, using 3-D graphics, haptic technology (involving simulated sensory experience), and real-time voice communication to do things in cyberspace that could not easily be replicated on the ground. Examples using lifelike avatars with digital identities might include testing high-risk negotiating strategies, running alternative scenarios for conflict resolution, or talking to the Taliban. As the lines between the real and virtual worlds become less distinct and the Web 3.0 era dawns, the already evident appeal of various diplomatic cyberoptions is likely to increase, with a range of still-unclear consequences.

Still, using the Internet for public engagement, let alone guerrilla diplomacy, remains in many foreign ministries an untested, even suspect proposition. The blogosphere is exploding with content of interest to diplomats, but, like the rest of the Internet, it is not systematically tracked or monitored.[60] Because the norms of the new media favor the immediate and most traffic is unmediated, there can be a clash between IT management culture and that of conventional diplomacy. Some senior officials are suspicious because the pace is so fast and the public input so unpredictable. Others just don't get the revo-

e-Diplomacy 1.0

In the early days, Canada was at the forefront of e-diplomacy and thus again may serve as an instructive example. In December 1999, Ian Barnes visited Ottawa to relate the intriguing story of the British Council's Herculean efforts (which he led) to establish a global Internet brand. This was achieved, but only under threat by headquarters in London of taking down the first generation of sites that had been established independently by some of the council's more enterprising country program directors.

Intrigued, I organized a high-level interdepartmental seminar on branding at the Toronto offices of a global public relations firm. At that time enthusiasm for branding Canada internationally was widespread through the public service, but there was no defined center of responsibility or leadership; with limited financial support, those efforts went off in a variety of directions and ended inconclusively. A year later, in 2000, as part of the Government-On-Line initiative, I was charged with design and construction of Canada in the World, a multitiered, government-wide international policy facility that was accessible through the Canada International gateway.[61] That site lives on, though it has become something of an orphan.

In 2001, on behalf of DFAIT's Communications Bureau, I secured financing from the (now-defunct) Public Diplomacy Fund to enlarge the nascent Internet brand, "Canada. Cool. Connected," which we had developed over the course of the Government-On-Line exercise into a comprehensive international communications or branding framework. That effort bore fruit the following year with the Promoting Canada Abroad initiative, which was based on yet more adjectival themes that we felt captured the essence of contemporary Canada: competitive, civic, creative, caring, cosmopolitan, and captivating. To my knowledge, this formulation remains the closest thing to an international brand yet produced by Canada, but see if the material related to the initiative has been removed from the DFAIT website.

In any case, Canada was already ahead of most nations in its recognition of the Internet as a medium for exchange as well as broadcasting.[62] In 2003, then foreign minister Bill Graham initiated the Foreign Policy Dialogue, and began a series of interactive, online policy discussions that continued over the course of several months. Discussion papers authored by DFAIT officials were posted for consideration, comments solicited and received, and summaries prepared. At the end of the process, the government published its response.[63] At the time, this experiment represented an innovative, even radical use of the new media. It democratized decisionmaking and increased the accountability of the policy development process.

lutionary significance of the new media per se. Many governments, it should be added, are not yet ready to cede centralized control over communications and policy development.

The result is a paradox. For the very reasons that the Internet is so popular with youth and the NGO community—and thus the obvious locus of the diplomatic future—its place in the foreign ministry remains unclear: Is it a policy instrument? Communications vehicle? Technical service? PD and branding tool? All of the above? The full potential of the Internet has yet to be realized by diplomacy.[64] But in the foreign ministry's quest for greater relevance, it is up to guerrilla diplomats to find their way to the frontier of netpolitik, even if there are a few dead ends and detours along the way.[65]

Making It Happen

As the eyes and ears of their nation abroad, especially in difficult environments, guerrilla diplomats could use their IT and new media savvy to great advantage, becoming major producers of intelligence and firmly establishing the reputation of guerrilla diplomacy within international relations circles along the way. And they can use their souplesse to help bridge the digital divide, plugging into the global political economy of knowledge to match problems to solutions. That said, there are common capacity gaps in foreign ministries that first require attention. Possibly the most glaring is the overall lack of cultural literacy and foreign language facility, which is little short of shocking in this era of globalization, when so many talented first-generation immigrants are so readily at hand. This is one area in which buying or hiring the talent required may make more sense than training foreign service officers—a costly, slow, and uncertain process.

In developing this capacity, countries will need to align their human resources objectives directly with their geographic priorities. Most foreign ministries in the A-world, for example, need more staff fluent in Chinese (for communication with a quarter of the world's population); Spanish (to engage much of Latin America); German (for the rise in the so-called new Europe); Japanese (whose speakers control what is still the second largest economy in the world); Portuguese (the language of rising Brazil); Russian (the tongue of a resurgent population); and, not least, Arabic. Aside from facilitating dialogues on oil, Arabic would of course be particularly useful for those reaching out to moderate Islamic democracies with a view to developing cooperative security and intelligence-sharing arrangements. Foreign ministries in the C-, T-, and E-worlds, meanwhile, might have to add English to the list—still the lingua franca of diplomacy, business, and S&T, at least for now.

Prospective guerrilla diplomats would make a habit of using their cultural and linguistic skills to connect with diaspora and immigrant communities in their home countries. In places like the United States, the UK, Canada, and Australia, these groups represent a huge, largely untapped source of advice and intelligence on many countries of great international policy interest. China and India, two major immigrant source countries with growing economic and political significance, are obvious examples. Pakistan, Sri Lanka, Sudan, Mexico, Haiti, and the countries of Southeast Asia, Central America, and the Horn of Africa, to name a few, also come readily to mind.

In order to better connect with such communities, as well as to conduct more conventional outreach and constituency building, foreign ministries need to establish a presence—likely in the form of seconded political officers—on the ground in all of the major cities of the home countries in question. In many cases, costs could be kept down by installing these officers in regional offices that are already functioning in other capacities, such as trade promotion.

University campuses are another neglected source of intelligence; establishing lasting contacts among professors and students—perhaps especially foreign students—could produce huge returns down the road. Again, this would involve taking a much more rigorous and systematic approach to connecting with citizens and even former citizens abroad, and similar efforts would be required to maintain contact with those who have developed substantial ties to the sending state through education, emigration, and business. When posted as head of the political section at the Canadian High Commission in Kuala Lumpur, for example, I was surprised to discover that although an estimated 50,000 Malaysians had attended postsecondary schools in Canada, mostly under the auspices of the Colombo Plan, the High Commission had no list of graduates. Many of these former students had undoubtedly found their way into positions of power and influence, yet they were unknown to those whose job it was to build and maintain networks of contacts.

It should by now be clear why intelligence, speed, flexibility, adaptability, and mobility are all ideals of GD. A retuned workforce and a new model for representation abroad—one based more on the imperatives of PD and GD than on traditional diplomatic considerations—would give the foreign ministry the advantage over other government departments and, for that matter, the competition internationally. Temporary missions, colocation, hub-and-spoke arrangements, expanded honorary consular designations, and other innovative approaches to representation offer much promise, but real progress will require a sea change with regard to the still-dominant culture of risk aversion that prevails at the headquarters of most foreign ministries. A concerted effort to obtain buy-in on the part of ministers, policy planners, and senior officials will also be mandatory. Meanwhile, specialists in human resource management and public administration will have to get busy too; there is much yet to be done with respect to fleshing out the details of new organizational structures, lines of decisionmaking authority, financial accountabilities, and reporting relationships and responsibilities. Indeed, they may have to work some magic in order to reconcile the imperative of accountability with that of minimizing the bureaucratic overburden.

All of which leads naturally to the question: what kinds of people, which skills, will be needed? Pitching the rationale for GD is one thing; turning it into a proposal that can be used by human resource departments for staffing, promotion, and assignment purposes is quite another.

Building a Better Diplomat Is Job One

Beyond whatever formal or informal educational qualifications may be required (and building on the portrait presented at the beginning of the chapter), the recruiters of guerrilla diplomats should be looking, if I may borrow from analyst Jennifer Welsh, for those who are "at home in the world."[66] By this I mean they possess qualities that together amount to personal suitability: versatility, energy, critical consciousness, curiosity, an appreciation of diversity, an entrepreneurial spirit, physical stamina, spiritual resilience, and a dash of guile—combined, of course, with the courage of their convictions. Furthermore, as they address some of the more perplexing issues that confront the planet, guerrilla diplomats will need to exhibit a high degree of situational awareness, relying on their acutely developed judgment at those times when going along to get along just won't do. In short, guerrilla diplomats must be problem solvers who can think on their feet, improvise as required, and, when appropriate, push the envelope to achieve the necessary results.

Such people will be as effective in storefront operations as in boardrooms and as comfortable in teeming markets and conflict zones as they are in leafy suburbs and downtown office towers. Comfortable with risk and sensitive to the needs of others, they will choose hands-on teamwork over pencil pushing in bureaucratic isolation. Too many serving ambassadors are more adept at schmoozing with other diplomats inside the embassy walls than they are at mixing it up with the locals on the street. Exchanging anecdotes with diplomatic colleagues about what might be going on outside is a poor substitute for finding out personally. By contrast, guerrilla diplomats are as likely to have spent years exploring the world at ground level as acquiring the most impressive academic credentials.[67]

Of course foreign ministries that intend to establish guerrilla diplomacy as a modus operandi must develop training and research programs to that end. Courses in intelligence gathering and analysis, effective networking, cross-cultural communication, and complex problem solving would be central. That said, a more systematic approach to passing along the benefits of unique personal experience—the tricks of the diplomatic trade learned over years of service on the front lines of representation—would be at least as important. In both organized and informal settings, mentors could make a real contribution to enriching and enabling a foreign ministry's cadre of guerrilla diplomats.

Guerrilla Diplomat as Political Officer?

Globalization is placing growing pressure on foreign ministries to field a new type of diplomat—a political officer who is effective in counterinsurgency, who can play a defined and useful role in conflict zones, and, more generally, who is capable of delivering results, especially in underdeveloped and insecure parts of the world. This guerrilla diplomat would serve as a catalyst for unifying the objectives and activities of all the other players, including those in the military, aid agencies, and civil society. This catalytic function would flow directly from recognition of the position of the ambassador as the senior representative of the sending state's government in-country, yet the guerrilla diplomat is unlike either the political officer in a conventional embassy or the military officer in the battlefield.[68] If anything, the guerrilla diplomat most closely resembles the district officers serving in the most remote corners of the British empire. Unlike their counterparts in New Delhi or Hong Kong, these members of the colonial service were not "in the bubble." Instead they were left mainly to their own devices.

The case of some PRTs in conflict zones offers additional insights. In Canada's PRT in Kandahar, for example, a handful of diplomatic and development assistance staff are vastly outnumbered by military personnel. When the political officer wants to leave the heavily guarded compound—a kind of mini–green zone—to make a visit somewhere in the city or its environs, the military has had to be given forty-eight hours' advance notice in order to prepare a security and logistics plan for the outing—which, when and if it happens, will require a convoy of armored vehicles and dozens of soldiers. Talk about seeing you coming a mile away. This practice is the antithesis of guerrilla diplomacy. The guerrilla diplomat prefers to travel light.[69]

That, then, is my sketch. It is more, I hope, than a shadow, but it is still a faint outline, a work in progress. Is it possible to illustrate further guerrilla diplomacy through case studies and examples? I have mentioned Brian Tobin; former Canadian ambassador Ken Taylor's much-celebrated efforts to protect American diplomats in Tehran after the Islamic revolution in Iran from 1979 to 1980 would also qualify in terms of stealth and innovativeness.[70] Swedish diplomat Raoul Wallenberg's assistance in the removal to safety of thousands of Hungarian Jews during World War II illustrates the importance of risk tolerance, a commitment to humanitarian values, and the personal traits of heroism and courage. And the UN Special Representative for Iraq, Sergio Vieira de Mello, killed in a suicide bombing in Baghdad in 2003, demonstrated the role of interpersonal skills, adaptability, and pragmatism.[71] Still, the pool of obvious examples is not deep.[72] If there were many more examples, diplomacy might not be in such distress.

The Wrap: Can I Get Some Panacea with That?

Guerrilla diplomacy—a kind of supersensitized, rapid-adaptive PD with a permanent broadband satellite connection—is aligned with the emerging patterns and changing pace of international politics. Even under the most propitious circumstances of good intentions and ample resources, GD won't work in the absence of either a strategy that situates all activity within the context of larger goals and objectives or the intelligence that informs any necessary changes thereto. With those caveats in mind, I would assert that GD responds to the three greatest (and related) international policy challenges facing most countries:

1. Globalization, which, in tandem with international economic integration and social polarization, is fostering underdevelopment, breeding instability, increasing state failure, and undercutting the authority and capacity of governments everywhere
2. A transformed international environment, which, in combination with the preponderance of unilateral US military power, is disaggregating traditional, ideology-based alliances, replacing them with various regional groups—for example the EU, Mercosur, and Shanghai Cooperation Organization—and contributing to the proliferation of new, asymmetrical threats[73]
3. The emergence of a new constellation of unconventional security challenges, including global warming, pandemic disease, diminishing biodiversity environmental degradation, the proliferation of weapons of mass destruction, bio- and nanotechnologies, energy and resource scarcity, and genomics

If its benefits to humanity are to be maximized, globalization must coincide with equitable integration in the form of public-private partnerships, joint ventures between government and civil society, as well as (and relatedly) a willingness to experiment. Properly resourced and executed, GD can help with that, resolving conflicts and supporting development by improving access to S&T, connecting to the global political economy of knowledge, and acting with souplesse. By generating and using intelligence to provide distant early-warning systems, GD will inform preventative action at a fraction of the cost of acting, often militarily, after conflict has begun—or, worse, ended in ruins. In short, GD helps increase resilience and decrease vulnerability and thus contributes to a more secure world.

As the scope for applying GD has broadened, the implications for public administration and governance have multiplied. There will, for instance, be a major role for guerrilla diplomats inside the machinery of government in addition to that of representing it abroad, speaking truth to power, and resisting the arbitrary or self-serving application of power to truth. At minimum, to deliver results in the contemporary setting, foreign ministries will need more guerrilla diplomats in more places, performing vital functions not being done by anyone else. These will include not only networking, advocacy, and the analysis of critical events through the unique prism of national interests, policies, and values but also solving problems through the provision, for example, of consular services in difficult or dangerous environments.

The creation of a relevant foreign ministry, an effective business model for diplomacy, and a transformed foreign service is a prerequisite both for the incubation of a cadre of guerrilla diplomats and for the success of guerrilla diplomacy itself.[74] Because diplomats represent governments (or international organizations) and because these kinds of institutions are diminishing in the era of globalization, even the most astute guerrilla diplomats will not be able to address, let alone resolve, all of the world's problems. But even so, to the extent that governments remain even remotely important, performance could certainly be bettered. Guerrilla diplomacy, as one element in a grand strategy for the globalization age, can help to make a difference.

Notes

1. It is in these ways and more that foreign ministries clearly differ from other departments of government, especially more domestically focused ones like Public Works, Social Development, and the Treasury.

2. See, for example, http://www.independentdiplomat.com. The founder of this website, former British foreign officer Carne Ross, has written a book by the same title—see Ross (2007). For reviews, see Urquhart (2007) and his subsequent exchange with Ross, http://www.independentdiplomat.com/documents/pdf/NYROB%20letters.pdf. See also Copeland (2007).

3. I took a preliminary stab at defining the term a few years ago; see Copeland (2004). It may still seem to some readers too romantic or, conversely, confrontational. I, too, was somewhat torn, but in the end I was convinced by the appraisal of one of my younger reviewers, Laura Sunderland: "I like it. It grabbed my attention and speaks to me. It's not clunky. It's cool." That was enough for me.

4. In examining hard power applications of soft power, I am reminded of Sun Tsu's observation that speed and agility can in some circumstances more than compensate for differences in size and weight.

5. For this observation I am much indebted to my UK colleague Philip Fiske de Gouveia.

6. I have stated elsewhere that guerrilla diplomacy may also be thought of as *transformational public diplomacy.* See Copeland (2008c).

7. My focus has been on *how* guerrilla diplomats will work rather than on exactly what, in addition to addressing the drivers of insecurity and underdevelopment, they will be doing. The short answer to the *what* question is whatever the sending state wishes of them. This might involve working with and supporting civil society in the host country by promoting accountability, the rule of law, and respect for human rights; encouraging democratic development; or reinforcing good governance practices, to name a few of the possibilities.

8. See US Army Field Manual 3-07, *Stability Operations,* and US Army Field Manual 3-24, *Counterinsurgency.* The guide to stability operations, or nation building,

in particular, doctrinally elevates that activity to the level of conventional offensive, defensive, and COIN operations; emphasizes the importance of providing safety, security, and well-being for civilians; and asserts that the challenges of governance, economic development, and civil conflict are best addressed through soft power. If this advice sticks—and there are huge obstacles—it will represent a radical strategic departure.

9. See Lawrence (1929).

10. For a Western analysis of the thinking on guerrilla warfare pioneered by Mao Tse-tung and Vo Nguyen Giap, see Taber (2002).

11. See Nagl (2005) for an example of especially influential contemporary thinking. See also Thompson (1966), Trinquier (2006), Guala (2006). For a historical survey, see Marston and Malkasian (2008).

12. US CENTCOM commander David Petraeus is one obvious exception here.

13. See Record (2005), Sullivan (2007).

14. Because the numbers of those involved in COIN have been so small relative to the total populations in Afghanistan and Iraq, the formula has been more like "break, take, forsake." Yet the application of overwhelming force, especially if not followed by relief and reconstruction, almost always fails in these circumstances.

15. See Tomes (2005: 37–56).

16. See, for instance, Kilcullen (2006), Packer (2006, which highlights Kilcullen's contributions), Croke (2006), Milton-Edwards and Crooke (2004).

17. Given this convergence, it is not surprising that there are a growing number of calls for an integrated counterinsurgency strategy involving all of the key players. See, for example, US Department of State (2006).

18. See Thompson (1966), Kilcullen (2006).

19. US Department of Defense (2003: 3).

20. On the transformation of strategic affairs, see Freedman (2006).

21. A very good treatment of fourth generation war is offered in Hammes (2004).

22. I explore the theme of using PD as an invaluable tool in war communications in an article I prepared for the Foreign and Commonwealth Office; see Copeland (2008b).

23. See, for example, Ford (2005: 51–66). In Iraq, initially harsh US counterinsurgency methods turned much of the population against their supposed liberators, whom they came to regard instead as occupiers. See Hashim (2003). On the cross-cultural, organizational, and doctrinal difficulties faced by the US military in Iraq, see Aylwin-Foster (2005: 2–15).

24. See, for example, D. Jones (2006).

25. See Helmus et al. (2007), who advocates the use of modern marketing principles in COIN.

26. On the special role of the police and the sort of granular, tactical information they can provide, see Clutterbuck (1966). Der Derian has made a documentary film, *Cultural Warriors* (2009), that explores these issues from the perspective of moral hazard and personal risk.

27. See Kipp et al. (2006). For a comprehensive survey of the US experience, see Long (2006).

28. On counterinsurgent diplomacy from a US perspective, see Amend (2008), Green (2007).

29. From an interview conducted April 3, 2008, with a senior political officer who has served in Afghanistan and requested anonymity. Among countless sources advocating a fundamental shift in NATO's Afghanistan strategy, see Johnson and Mason (2008b).

30. Remark by Colin Kahl in response to a question by the author at a panel discussion on COIN at the International Studies Association's annual conference in San Francisco, March 29, 2008.

31. The Multi-National Force–Iraq's manual *Commander's Counterinsurgency Guidance,* for example, was issued in June 2008 and enjoins US and coalition troops to "employ money as a weapons system." Among other recommended actions are "secure and serve the population," "live our values," and "promote reconciliation." Cited in Kaldor (2008).

32. This line was finely articulated by Samantha Power in response to a question I asked following a presentation at DFAIT on October 31, 2006.

33. See C. Johnson (2008) on military Keynesianism.

34. The new Canadian COIN guidance is reviewed by Elmer and Fenton (2007). See "The Paradoxes of Counterinsurgency," *New York Times,* October 5, 2006, http://www.nytimes.com/imagepages/2006/10/05/world/20061005_doctrine_graphic.html.

35. See Kurlantzick (2007).

36. For a superb treatment of the overwhelming importance of highly contextualized cultural and historical knowledge in COIN, see Johnson and Mason (2008a).

37. Jihad, for example, has been spun into a powerful narrative of holy war. Not least in oral cultures such as Afghanistan's, the elaboration and deployment of a compelling alternative narrative—development as security, perhaps—could, if supported by actions and resources delivered in an integrated and consistent manner, achieve much in COIN.

38. See also Foreign Affairs and International Trade (2008).

39. On the intelligence function generally, see Shulsky and Schmitt (2005).

40. See MacPherson (2006).

41. I was the author of one of the dueling assessments, and had several occasions to discuss the incident with the former minister while working at the Canadian Institute of International Affairs, of which McDougall was the president and CEO.

42. For an overview, see Betts (2007).

43. Such countries have the resources and experience to assess information, including that gathered by technical means, and to carry out offensive intelligence operations—for instance, running agents, paying informers, and so forth.

44. See Porch (1995) and Brodeur, Gill, and Tollborg (2002). The war on terror has brought a range of new intelligence partners—among them Syria, Egypt, Jordan, and some central and eastern European states. Their relative importance may decline as new priorities emerge.

45. See Cohen, (2003), Welsh (2004), Canada25 (2004).

46. On this and many other points relevant to this part of the analysis, see National Commission on Terrorist Attacks upon the United States (2004).

47. An excellent survey is offered by Bollier (2003). See also Potter (2002).

48. On the use of networks by terrorists, see the seminal work by Arquilla and Ronfeldt (2002); on the implications for diplomacy, also see Arquilla and Ronfeldt (2007).

49. Arquilla and Ronfeldt (1999) do an excellent job of bringing Teilhard de Chardin's thoughts into the twenty-first century.

50. The US Institute of Peace has published a useful series of papers under the heading Virtual Diplomacy.

51. See Castells (1996; 1997; 1998).

52. The peer-reviewed Internet journal *First Monday,* produced a special issue on March 3, 2008, featuring critiques of Web 2.0.

53. See, for instance, Dahr Jamail, http://www.dahrjamailiraq.com.

54. See Helmus et al. (2007).

55. Some excellent PD websites include those hosted by the University of Southern California (http://uscpublicdiplomacy.com/index.php), George Washington University (http://pdi.gwu.edu), the Netherlands Institute of International Relations Clingendael (http://www.clingendael.nl), and the DiploFoundation (http://www.diplomacy.edu) based in Geneva and Malta. St. Thomas University School of Law tracks internet diplomacy; see www.diplomacymonitor.com/stu/dm.nsf/infoinetdiplo?OpenForm.

56. See, for instance, Foreign and Commonwealth Office, http://blogs.fco.gov.uk. The content provided by some of the heads of mission, for example Frances Guy in Lebanon, is exceptional.

57. See Second Life, http://www.secondlife.com.

58. In government as elsewhere, an e-generation gap is becoming apparent. On how the Internet is changing international relations, see Bollier (2003).

59. I am indebted to Barry Nesbitt for the formulation of this observation. Personal communication, February 9, 2008.

60. Technorati (2008) is unsurpassed on the growing importance of the blogosphere.

61. See http://www.canadainternational.gc.ca.

62. This contrast was made clear to me at a conference I attended in November 2003, "Diplomacy and the Web," organized at Lancaster House in London by the Oxford Internet Institute.

63. A similar facility lives on today in the form of DFAIT's online discussion forum. Recent topics have included failed states, nonproliferation, multilateralism, democracy promotion, and Canada in North America. Novel when it was introduced, the site today attracts rather less attention. See Foreign Affairs and International Trade Canada, http://geo.international.gc.ca/cip-pic/participate/menu-en.aspx.

64. For some further thinking on possible uses of the new media, see Maybury (2008).

65. Early versions of DFAIT's website were especially unimpressive; the version in use in the late 1990s was an off-the-shelf product that featured a boomerang-shaped arc with blue blobs along the axes. It bore a striking resemblance to the site in use by Canadian Airlines, which at the time was facing bankruptcy. In the spring of 2001, those of us working on the Canada in the World cluster commissioned what was effectively a branding audit. We arranged for local staff working at the international offices of a large public relations firm to visit our site and evaluate it against what we were trying to achieve in terms of content and user experience. Much as we had anticipated, they pronounced the baby ugly.

66. See Welsh (2004).

67. As I mentioned in Chapter 8, however, knowledge of S&T issues, being now so urgently required by most foreign ministries, is likely an important exception here.

68. Like most distinctions, this one, too, requires some nuance. With their intensive language and area knowledge, some foreign area officers from the military and "warrior diplomats" (to use journalist Tom Brokaw's term) from special forces may, apart from having different objectives, rather resemble guerrilla diplomats. If actual guerrilla diplomats were working in close cooperation with the military, the division of labor would have to be clear.

69. Exactly how much security guerrilla diplomats will require and whether it should be provided by public or private means will depend on particular circumstances. But if it is difficult to generalize, it is clear that excessive constraints render effective GD impossible.

70. See Woodrow Wilson International Center for Scholars (2005).

71. See Power (2008).

72. I would be grateful for reader suggestions regarding additional examples or case studies.

73. Riordan (2004) is especially good on the potential use of PD as a bridge to moderate Islam and a means to promote civil society.

74. If nurturing these qualities proves as arduous a task as it has to date, it may be necessary ultimately to remove PD and GD from the existing framework and establish new, stand-alone institutions. Something along these lines has been suggested in the United States in the form of the Center for Global Engagement. See Defense Science Board (2008).

Conclusions: None Foregone 13

Hope is a waking dream.
—Aristotle

It seems highly unlikely that Bruce Mau has ever thought about guerrilla diplomacy. But in 2004 to 2005, while touring to promote the release of his book *Massive Change,* he used as a point of departure a superbly relevant pair of epithets.[1] One was "It's not about the world of design. It's about the design of the world." The other: "Now that we can do anything, what do we want to do?"

These two elegant, double-hooked phrases epitomize what to look for in high-level strategic communications. They resonate at an elemental level. Indeed, they echo some of the fundamental questions that I have tried to address in this volume: What kind of a world do we live in? How should we interact with it? And to what end?

Design is by nature a positive, life-affirming activity that is premised on the assumption that by thinking and then acting differently, various aspects of our lives can be improved.[2] In this sense, hope, which buoys the spirit and nourishes the soul, is not faith based but rational. Design, rationality, and hope all have a place in international relations. Their role could usefully be accorded more scope.

The same holds true for innovation. Eager student to great creative thinker: "Please tell us, wise teacher, how do you always manage to think outside of the box?" Great creative thinker to eager student: "What box?"

Imagination, however, is a rare and precious thing. Sometimes the most obvious solutions to even the most everyday problems—let alone the more complex varieties—remain undiscovered for years and years. After all, it took several centuries after the invention of the suitcase to figure out that it would be a good idea to fit them with wheels and long handles.

Still Grappling with Globalization

This book is going to press in the midst of a brutal worldwide recession, which is showing signs of careening into a protracted depression. Whether or not the end of the globalization age is upon us, of some things we may be certain: you can't garrison against pandemic disease; you can't extraordinarily render climate change; and you can't surge militarily into democracy, good governance, or the rule of law. There are more reasons than ever to conclude that we must act now to prevent an accretion of fragile and failing states from snowballing into something much worse: a failed world. I have argued that in the age of globalization, not least because development is becoming the new security, much of diplomacy is moving into the public realm. Diplomacy matters. In the continuing quest for sustainable security, international policy planners must come eventually to grand strategy. During the Cold War, the grand strategy was deterrence backed by containment. In the globalization age, as articulated in the Pentagon's *Quadrennial Defense Review* of 2006 with its fixation on the so-called Long War, it is the global war on terror, even if no longer acknowledged as such.[3] The core of the crisis today is that this militarization of international policy and strategy, whereby war becomes the preferred option, has persisted. Policy, as Hew Strachan aptly observes, has become the instrument of war, rather than the other way around.[4]

This surely is the gravest of errors. Were diplomacy and development to displace defense as the centerpiece of grand strategy, humankind would benefit substantially. Underdevelopment, along with the insecurity that it engenders, is the central problem of globalization. That is why the management of globalization through the institutions of diplomacy and the medium of international policy must become the preoccupation of decisionmakers and, indeed, the ultimate political goal of grand strategy.

As a means of formulating and implementing international policy, diplomacy connects security to development. But development has been marginalized and diplomacy has failed to adapt, overcome by neglect and the aforementioned continuation of a Cold War–style militarization of international relations. Diplomacy of any type, if practiced principally in support of military objectives such as occupation, will be critically compromised from the outset. Whatever the implications for the role of PD and GD in counterinsurgency—and here I would stress that the application of soft power to the end of hard power will always present something of a conundrum—diplomacy works best before the fighting starts.

The result is systemic crisis: a diplomatic deficit, a performance gap. This dysfunction is evident in both the prevalence of conflict—a signature of diplomacy's failure—and the scope and scale of festering threats (political violence, economic polarization, cultural aggression, religious antagonism) as well as of unaddressed challenges, most rooted in science and driven by technology (pandemic disease, climate change, environmental collapse, and so forth).[5]

Morgenthau on the Deficit and War

In several, often overlooked chapters in his seminal work *Politics Among Nations,* realist scholar Hans Morgenthau offers some illuminating comments about diplomacy, which he situated at the forefront of his normative vision of international relations. Among his observations, the following bear special consideration for our purposes:

- Diplomacy must be divested of the crusading spirit.
- Never put yourself in a position from which you cannot retreat without losing face and from which you cannot advance without grave risks.
- Diplomacy must look at the political scene from the point of view of other nations.
- Never allow a weak ally to make decisions for you.
- The armed forces are the instruments of foreign policy, not its master.[6]

Citing examples such as these in an interpretive essay on Morgenthau's contribution to international relations, Robert Jervis observes:

> Much of international politics consists of a mutual adjustment of interests, and this involves not only exerting one's will over others but understanding what others want and why they want it. The protracted and patient interaction with others, the exploration of alternative solutions, [and] the accommodation of what others need constitute the essence of day-to-day diplomacy, which, if successful, does not produce those dramatic clashes [that] have so preoccupied scholars and given them a distorted view of how international politics does and should function.[7]

In a remarkable open letter to the *New York Times* published on April 18, 1965, Morgenthau set out his arguments against the Johnson administration's pursuit of the Vietnam War. They are worth quoting at length:

> We [Americans] like to think of . . . war as a . . . self-sufficient, technical enterprise, to be won as quickly, as cheaply, as thoroughly as possible and divorced from the foreign policy that preceded and is to follow it. Thus our military theoreticians and practitioners conceive of counterinsurgency as though it were just another branch of warfare, to be taught in special schools and applied with technical proficiency wherever the occasion arises.
>
> This view derives, of course, from a complete misconception of the nature of civil war. People fight and die in civil wars because they have a faith [that] appears to them to be worth fighting and dying for, and they can be opposed with a chance of success only by people who have at least as strong a faith.
>
> While normally foreign and military policy is based upon intelligence—that is, the objective assessment of the facts—the process here is reversed: a new policy has been decided upon, and intelligence must provide the facts to justify it. . . . To conduct foreign and military policy not on their own merits, but as exercises in public relations . . . the government fashions a world that

> pleases it, and then comes to believe in the reality of that world and acts as though it were real. . . . [T]hey are all misconceptions that conjure up terrible dangers for those who base their policies on them. . . . [T]hey lead us from the blind alley in which we find ourselves today to the rim of the abyss.[8]

In the age of globalization, few policymakers, and certainly not the neoconservatives, seem to have taken any of this into account. Forty-five years after Morgenthau's epistle, author Robert Fisk wrote a piece for *The Independent* titled "The Only Lesson We Ever Learn Is That We Never Learn." It too is worth a long look:

> And if there are, as I now calculate, twenty-two times as many Western troops in the Muslim world as there were at the time of the eleventh- and twelfth-century Crusades, we must ask what we are doing. Are we there for oil? For democracy? For Israel? For fear of weapons of mass destruction? Or for fear of Islam? . . . And I will hazard a terrible guess: that we have lost Afghanistan as surely as we have lost Iraq and as surely as we are going to "lose" Pakistan. It is our presence, our power, our arrogance, our refusal to learn from history and our terror—yes, our terror—of Islam that is leading us into the abyss.[9]

Different Century, Same Abyss . . .

Apropos our discussions of Cold War carryovers, the problems intelligence inherently poses, and the need to relearn counterinsurgency, I might add that the persistence of such tragic "misconceptions" goes much of the way toward explaining why, by most accounts, the world has in the intervening decades since the end of the Vietnam War become neither more peaceful nor more secure.[10] Even those maintaining a more optimistic view of global trends are careful to attach caveats to their findings. In the update to its generally positive 2005 report, for instance, the Human Security Centre notes that "four of the world's six regions have experienced increased numbers of conflicts since 2002, the past five years have seen a huge spike in the estimated death toll from terrorism, while negotiated settlements . . . have worryingly high failure rates."[11] In short, the essential qualities of globalization, exacerbated by some very serious strategic errors on the part of major players, are blowing back big-time.[12] The Bush Doctrine lies in tatters, with its costs on all fronts still mounting.[13]

To address these issues, I have taken readers on something of an analytical road trip across the terrain of grand strategy, starting by the side of the tranquil Chao Prya River in Thailand and ending on the jagged edge of the twenty-first century. Along the way, we traveled from the Cold War to the era of globalization and the transnational world order model I call ACTE, from defense to development as the new security, through terrorism and S&T, and through the foreign ministry and the foreign service to arrive, finally, at public and guerrilla diplomacy.

Moving through these times, spaces, and places, we have not paused for more than a moment. We have mapped, we have modeled, and we have reconsidered broad tracts of international relations. We could have stopped more often or stayed longer, but we didn't. Why? Because if the distances—intellectual and analytical—have been great, the risks of getting bogged down, sidetracked, or lost were greater still.[14] To get from there to here, it has been necessary to proceed somewhat unconventionally, moving outside of the usual scholarly confines of particular data sets and exclusive theoretical frameworks. Above all, while maintaining the high-altitude perspective necessary to apprehend the big picture and assess the various observations and findings generated by a range of different disciplines, I have tried not to lose sight of the overarching objective: the identification of practical ways to construct a world in which peace and prosperity might one day displace conflict and poverty.

To achieve that objective, I have argued that diplomacy as we know it has reached the limits of its usefulness and is thus at a critical juncture. To restore performance, diplomats need a more integrated conceptual map, a more comprehensive global analysis, a world order model that works, and reconstructed institutions: a relevant foreign ministry, an effective approach to diplomacy, and a transformed foreign service. These three elements, framed by government, governance, and the public environment, are the prerequisites to the restoration of the diplomatic ecosystem.

By nothing less than a holistic analysis of the complex international policy web can we hope to get at the fundamental issues. Like so many others, however, the diplomatic ecosystem is under duress from multiple sources; the habitat has changed, but diplomacy has failed to adapt—or even to demonstrate much resilience. Yet there is an important distinction. While other ecosystems are facing collapse as a result of overuse or overloading, contemporary diplomacy is operating at nowhere near its carrying capacity. Notwithstanding its potential as a catalyst for reconciling national interests, conventional diplomacy suffers from neglect and underutilization. Might guerrilla diplomacy, as a critical link between security and development, then be inserted to revive the ecosystem and hence burnish the prospects for peace? I believe so.

. . . And a World on Fire

There is much about life on this small planet, and indeed about the human condition, that remains inscrutable. This does not apply, however, to the subjects of these pages. The problems that I have considered and the responses they warrant are complex, but, like the five uneasy pieces I described in the introduction, they can be understood. And once understood, they can be managed. This is the domain of geodiplomatics as set out in Chapter 1 and defined as a nonviolent, dialogue-based approach to the effective management of the world's strategic nexuses.

As always, though, there are management challenges. Notwithstanding the more or less steady march of history, it remains true that single events can change the course of history—or stay it. Think of the assassination of Archduke Ferdinand in Sarajevo. Pearl Harbor. Hiroshima. Sputnik. The Gulf of Tonkin incident. 9/11.

In providing the pretext for launching the global war on terror, 9/11 and its aftermath have kept the world on a war footing. It must be asked: what has been achieved? Wars have been launched in Iraq and Afghanistan, resulting in tens of thousands of military casualties and the deaths of hundreds of thousands of innocent civilians. Civil, human, and legal rights have been seriously degraded and a climate of fear fomented. There have been mass incarcerations, secret renditions, and the legitimized (if not quite legalized) acts of torture. The world is both less humane and less secure than was the case on September 10, 2001.

The highest calling of the state is to find ways to provide for the security of its citizens. In the globalization age, that end cannot be achieved by the sole means of defense and the military, paramilitaries and profiteering. We can do better. Diplomacy, at least as linked to development, can help us to get back on our feet and regain the bearings we have lost.[15]

Treating the underlying threats to human survival—whether embedded in S&T or arising from increasing poverty and injustice—will involve more than tossing a few diplomats onto the razor's edge. It will require new ways of looking, seeing, and coming to terms with the world around us. Getting from bullets to bytes, from bricks to clicks, will require a commitment to solving problems through meaningful exchange and enlarged understanding. And it will require mobilizing the global political economy of knowledge, applying that knowledge with precision and in a strategic context (which is to say exhibiting souplesse), analyzing relentlessly, and reconstructing the institutions of international policy.

In the face of the new constellation of unconventional and asymmetrical threats spawned by globalization, it is for public institutions to respond swiftly and innovate rigorously. Governments desperately need to get moving if the fragile diplomatic ecosystem is not only to recover but to double as a bulwark against the militarization of international policy. After all, to reiterate, military power does not translate into political influence. Huge investments in defense establishments have not produced security.[16] Nor can they, for that matter; power grids, communications, fuel supplies, and transportation networks are sufficiently centralized that massive disruption is relatively simple. Above all, arms cannot suppress ideas.

Given a reasonable chance, most people would rather work to get ahead than fight. Sectarian ethnic, tribal, and ideological differences tend to recede in the face of real opportunity. While politicians must establish the agenda, diplomats can help set the scene and foster the conditions in which human-centered development can take hold and flourish.

It may be that the world is not quite ready yet to vault, in David Korten's words, from "empire to earth community."[17] Paradise has been lost, and today the imperative of mastery dwarfs that of harmony. Plunder characterizes our relationship with nature; so-called civilized man has learned little from the experience of so many of the world's aboriginal peoples. The will to dominate colors our interactions not just with the earth but with most of its inhabitants. Documentary filmmaker Edward Burtinsky summarized this well when he remarked that because we are all part of nature, we are destroying ourselves when we ransack the natural world.[18]

John Mearsheimer has observed that, these days, the core international policy prescriptions of the neoconservatives and those of the "liberal imperialists" are close to indistinguishable: defeat terror, spread democracy, promote markets.[19] That approach, in my view, is not working. Surely a better job can be done of shaping our common future.

The case has been made for a much greater reliance on diplomacy as a systematic alternative to the threat or use of force in response to global challenges. But given the state of diplomacy, that would be a tall order even if we had plenty of time to fill it. And given the substantial policy and resource implications, it is also one that is highly political. Still, if we fail to recognize this emerging imperative—or deny the amount of sober decisionmaking and resource reallocation its fulfillment would entail—the continued erosion of image and reputation, values and interests, power and influence, most of all the A-world's, appears inevitable. The persistence of these multiple huge, tragic disconnects—between theory and practice, strategy and tactics, ends and means—is in some respects discouraging. With security by Blackwater and sanitation by Halliburton, even the smattering of global green zones we might be left with will eventually become uninhabitable, surrounded by a seething sea of wretched red.[20]

But a significant dimension of our humanity is anchored in hopefulness. And, without descending into mysticism or irrationality, hope we must.[21] Hope nourishes the soul and buoys the spirit while sensory experience and empirical evidence move the mind. And in that observable, measurable, empirical world, there are an increasing number of signs that the balance is shifting. Public tolerance of the obvious anomalies and contradictions in post-9/11 international policy is wearing thin and perceptions of the status quo are becoming increasingly critical.[22]

Tipping Point at Hand?

When I began this book in mid-2006, there was very little talk of diplomacy in either the scholarly or the popular media, among either the political elites or the policymakers. Today, in all of those circles, there is some evidence of diplomacy's rehabilitation.[23] As globalization shakes down the world financial system, it is becoming increasingly difficult to conflate defense with security or to explain the absence of S&T from mainstream political discourse. War may be a legitimate last resort if vital national interests are at stake—as was the case in World War II—but as an instrument of discretionary regime change it is deeply flawed; as we have seen, its costs can be unbearable and its potential for generating instability enormous. At a certain juncture, the accumulation of evidence that subverts existing policy and the received wisdom on which it is based will result in what physicist Thomas Kuhn coined a paradigm shift. This term, however overused, is nonetheless useful for describing the sudden acceptance of a new way of thinking that not a moment before had been considered heresy.[24]

Kuhn did a superb job of illustrating this concept using the evolution of scientific theory, but the underlying dynamic is ultimately illustrative of the Hegelian dialectic—thesis, antithesis, synthesis—and of Karl Marx's application thereof to the broad movement of history.[25] Tad Homer-Dixon acknowledges the universality of the model and uses a similar construction to help explain what he describes as the *ingenuity gap*.[26] What these and many other variations boil down to is simply that, over time, the intellectual center of gravity—and with it the prevailing line of thought on essential issues—can shift, sometimes radically. As anomalies accumulate, rebuttals recede, dismissals become more difficult to sustain, and the scales of orthodoxy tilt quickly. Such wholesale transformations do not happen often—but when they do, it's out with the old, in with the new. The result is a new way of seeing.

Kuhn showed how the Copernican revolution overwhelmed all of the old assumptions associated with the Ptolemaic universe. Something similar could happen if diplomacy and development were moved into the center of our thinking about international relations. With globalization in crisis and public support ebbing for the war on terror, defense as security, and the militarization of international policy, I am beginning to detect signs of such a movement.

The convergence of these trends just might lead thinking people to reflect carefully upon the complex dynamics of globalization and the role of S&T therein—and then to look to diplomacy and development as promising alternatives to war and want.

Take Nothing for Granted

As I prepared this book, the airwaves were again being saturated with chilling tales and horrifying images, evoking fear and dread. Between the Pentagon's penchant for "surging" years after its initial display of so-called shock and awe on the one hand and ever more deadly truck bombs and improvised explosives on the other, it is clear the CNN effect—whereby the very fact of constant press coverage in and of itself influences foreign policy decisions—has been elevated to an art form.[27] At the economic end of the spectrum, the globalization of financial markets continues to result in investor stampedes, such as that which precipitated the global market meltdowns of 2008–2009. Various reassurances from the red suspender set notwithstanding, I see little to prevent the recurrence of 1990s-style runs on entire nations or regions. Together, these fragments add up to more than a distraction, but they are much less than the whole picture. They obscure a larger and in many respects even darker reality that daily afflicts broad tracts of humanity: the banal, structural violence that is well-known to a significant percentage of the earth's population. Unlike the more familiar forms of conflict—a state collapse here, a terrorist incident there, an armed intervention somewhere else—this kind of violence is systemic rather than episodic. And for most inhabitants of advanced, postindustrial countries, except when they're tripping over the homeless, it is also largely invisible. The ever restless lens of the mass media, the unrelenting pressures of the news cycle, and market preferences for infotainment see to that.

The need to pursue an alternative path seems clear. But there is an informal consensus in favor of the status quo among powerful corporate and political interests expert at conjuring threats and manufacturing fear and loathing. These interests resist dialogue, supporting instead an agenda characterized by huge investments in framing and spin, litigation and special pleading. The result? Legislated spending on new weapons programs, enormous contracts for private security and reconstruction, good jobs for the faithful in key electoral districts, and the advantages for some that flow from a war economy without end.

Perhaps the best-known matrix of institutions, businesses, and people benefiting from the perpetuation of conflict is the near-legendary US military-industrial complex. This household phrase dates from President Eisenhower's oft-quoted farewell address of January 17, 1961. Its prescience continues to inspire: "In the councils of government, we must guard against the acquisition of unwarranted influence, whether sought or unsought, by the military industrial complex. The potential for the disastrous rise of misplaced power exists and will persist."[28] This warning, issued back in the early days of the Cold War, has only gained currency with its frequent repetition since. As one analyst has concluded, "Informal relationships between and among the 'iron triangle' of defense contractors, military establishments, and governments can undermine the ability to think clearly . . . [and thus can] corrupt their judgement."[29]

Many believe that as a result of the continuing dominance of the military-industrial complex, public resources are squandered on unnecessary weapons systems and programs while arms races are sought and provocations actively solicited by an interconnected network of military personnel, congressional representatives, and weapons merchants. Think tanks—including the American Enterprise Institute, the Heritage Foundation, and others—play an increasingly important part in sustaining this nexus of influence. It is not a conspiracy but rather a consensus among the beneficiaries—managers, stockholders, employees, and politicians with military bases or defense production facilities in their districts. Their collective perception of self-interest in the status quo has proven an ongoing obstacle to reform. That grip must be broken.

The Public Environment Is Tough

In Chapter 3, I discussed in general terms the impact of globalization on domestic politics, governance, and civil society. In Chapter 10, when considering the outreach function of diplomacy, I touched on the need for diplomats to connect with citizens and stakeholders to ensure that international policy goals and messages were resonating nationally. It is inevitable at this point that I return again to these issues: outreach is essential for building a public constituency, addressing the negative public narrative that characterizes diplomats as a pampered and privileged elite, and demonstrating the domestic relevance of diplomacy, the foreign ministry, and the foreign service. Indeed, engaging on the home front through the delivery of a political strategy supportive of democracy represents the missing link for all three institutions in the international policy triad: such a strategy will be critical in efforts to secure improved performance in the annual resource auction.

But this won't be easy. The preoccupations of the domestic audience are for the most part elsewhere, which will make them difficult to reach.[30] Moreover, both diplomats and their employers suffer from a bad reputation—they're seen as coddled, ineffective, outdated. And if only this was the whole of the problem.

Throughout the A-world, much has been made of the irony that even as we become ever more cosmopolitan and buy ever more completely into the culture and ethos of globalization, the coverage of international affairs in the mainstream media continues to flag. Whether the issue is the sideswiping of the national economy or a run on the national currency as a result of financial decisions made in other countries; the migration of jobs due to free trade or the impact of foreign takeovers on export performance; shifting patterns of land use and settlement due to climate change; or the impact of SARS, BSE, or avian flu on tourism and investment decisions, there is no doubt that all countries have become painfully exposed to events originating beyond their borders. Yet this reality is rarely reflected in the overall news mix, and even less so in the content behind the headlines. Why? Media multiplication and segmentation; budget and personnel cuts; a loss of institutional memory; the closure or consolidation of foreign bureaus; less frequent and shorter stories; an absence of analysis; a fixation on the sensational—earthquakes, tidal waves, train wrecks. Fewer journalists, their resources increasingly stretched, are covering the international relations beat, and there appears to be a widespread conviction among media managers that readers and viewers just aren't interested in world affairs. Those who are have little choice but to rely upon specialized sources and the Web for anything but the most basic information.

But there always is an "other hand" when the topic is globalization. Globalization also provides access to new voices through technology—the proliferation of satellite TV stations is an excellent example. On a visit to Moscow in early 2008, I was able to view by commercial cable hundreds of channels in scores of different languages. CNN's monopoly on all-news broadcasting was broken long ago by the established US networks, then by the likes of BBC World, Sky News, and CBC Newsworld. Today, many more sources as diverse as Al Jazeera and Russia Today are transmitting 24/7, worldwide, and in English. They offer a different perspective on world events, and even though distribution has been blocked in some places, I have little doubt that over time the impact of this profusion of new sources will be felt, surpassing, in some instances, the influence of some states.

Such changes in the structure of media coverage have both prefigured and reflected major shifts in the public environment, which has itself been subject to the same powerful influence of globalization. This process of historical conditioning is producing a new division of labor at all levels, fracturing some communities while creating others, and simultaneously generating wealth for some and misery for others. If few A-world citizens are sufficiently aware of the increase in their links to the C-, T-, and E-worlds, they are nonetheless buffeted by the consequences, which have produced tectonic shifts in all dimensions of life and extend well beyond the visible impact of immigration. Hot air gratings, food banks, and shelters have become more crowded as public spending on health, education, and social programs has declined. Economic and social aspects of the T- and E-worlds have arrived in A-world cities, while A-world wealth and comfort are now widely dispersed in pockets of gated prosperity elsewhere.

In the swirl of ambiguity and uncertainty that these developments have unleashed—only intensified by the ascendancy of single- and special-interest lobbies—international affairs has become a hard sell. The public's preoccupation with infotainment, lack of a strong sense of domestic constituency, and the negative stereotype of diplomats have combined to make the latter's job all the more difficult.

Perception Is Reality

The reasons for the inhospitality of the domestic environment go well beyond the blurring of the lines between the national and the global, the rising prominence of government departments outside the purview of the foreign ministry, or the activism of other levels of government, including that of cities. Trends in the domestic polity are now deeply influenced by the rise of issue-driven advocacy, job insecurity, generational change, and other matters closer to home that have served to increase disquiet but have also induced fatigue, apathy, and, in some quarters, cynicism.

Not that long ago, there existed a broad, comfortable, nonpartisan consensus on most matters of international policy. But that entente has been shattered, a development hastened not only by the unpopular wars in Afghanistan and Iraq, but by the growing popularity of highly particularistic, single-interest lobbies—be their cause the rain forest or the coral reefs, East Timor or Tibet, human rights or hunger, bans on small arms or child soldiers. It is often difficult to reach, let alone draw together, such a fragmented constituency.

Perhaps feeling adrift in this turbulent and confusing world, many appear to have redrawn the lines of their individual moral engagement closer to their front doors. Beset by lingering doubts about governance at home and facing a range of vexing if not intractable challenges abroad, people seem to be looking inward just when they should be looking out. That has certainly been my personal and professional observation over the past decade, and it is backed up by compelling survey research. Citizens now see their government's priorities as overwhelmingly domestic—health care, education, the environment, and the economy dominate, with all aspects of international affairs, from defense to foreign aid, barely registering in comparison.[31] Though there are occasional spikes in the attention they pay to the world around them—9/11, the war in Iraq, events in Iran or North Korea—these are at best minor peaks in a valley of indifference. Even the hardy perennials of global peace, development, and human rights are rarely at the front of most respondents' minds. International policy, like the S&T issues within it, exists in a kind of floating world.

In short, the importance of aligning both international and domestic populations with PD and GD objectives could not be clearer, but engaging the latter has become very difficult—at least, that is, in the A-world. But compare that audience to those in Palestine or Israel, Cuba or Kosovo. For these and many other publics, whether they are on the receiving or initiating end, international policy has a palpable reality quotient, with equally tangible and wide-ranging implications for both thought and action.

I made the case in Chapters 9 through 11 that organizing diplomacy to perform effectively abroad will be difficult, but not impossible. While diplomacy may appear to many ineffective today, once you have the right people doing the right things in the right places, performance—and perceptions thereof—will improve. It will then be easier to construct arguments for placing more representatives in the field, where they can add maximum value to the diplomatic enterprise. Some of the budgetary resources required to cover those incremental costs will come from the savings born of technological advances and the move to a flatter, more policy-focused structure at headquarters.[32] Granted, even at that, additional resources will have to be found, and, in an economic downturn and the inevitable attendant scramble to find new fiscal economies, particular vigilance will be necessary. All of which makes the need to engineer success on the home front all the more crucial.

Once Were Diplomats

Speaking of home, for most of the book I have tried to resist the temptation to rely exclusively upon Canadian examples, which I believe might be too particular and in some cases too parochial for what is intended as a generic assessment. Nonetheless, in the final chapters I have drawn on some of my own observations and experience to illustrate points I consider to be germane to the larger argument.

At that level of analysis, I see five broad points derived from events north of the forty-ninth parallel that might be abstracted for wider consideration:

1. To produce results in international policy, efforts to perfect organizational structure and bureaucratic process are not enough. Personal commitment and capable, even driven, leadership, mainly political but also in the public service, is essential. Recourse to armed force is usually not.
2. The active and strategic management of a country's international reputation and image can yield high dividends; anything less can incur serious costs.
3. Dialogue-based PD works—but not without commitment, resources, and a clear sense of the nature, possibilities, and limitations of PD and branding.
4. Intelligence collection and analysis are a central but undervalued diplomatic function. There is a large but largely unrealized potential for doing more.
5. Creating a relevant foreign ministry, adopting an effective diplomatic business model, and transforming the foreign service are prerequisites to sustaining success in all of the above.

Delivering outcomes in international relations entails the right policies, programs, personnel, and instruments. Even that, however, will not necessarily suffice. Because so much turns on the personal and the situational, on luck and timing, the stars must also align. And if they do, then it just might be possible to make things happen. But getting the physics, the chemistry, and even the mantra right won't work if other preconditions, often impossible to identify or predict in advance, are not met.

Five Paradoxes for Policymakers

Stepping back slightly further, we can see that our quest for a strategic perspective on this sprawling tableau contains a number of paradoxes. Each is intimately associated with international policy and relations, and each goes beyond the underperformance of diplomacy as a function of the diminishing importance of the state in the age of globalization.

First, when it comes to public diplomacy, the actor can vitiate the product and the messenger the message.[33] Diplomats work mainly for governments, and the foreign ministry is an integral part of the apparatus of the state. Governments exist, inter alia, to defend interests, pursue policies, and project values. When members of civil society encounter diplomats, therefore, chances are the diplomat—especially if he or she has initiated the exchange—will almost certainly be after something: an expression of support, a shift in position, a useful insight, a gem of intelligence. There is nothing at all the matter with that. But it is not a neutral point of departure and may give rise to suspicion or mistrust. No amount of active listening can overcome the handicap of reading from a script or seeking preordained conclusions, whereby the integrity of the exchange could be undermined and the chances of arriving at a mutually beneficial outcome lessened, especially if the foreign ministry lacks influence over decisionmaking at home.

Second, these are not the same old, same old times, but most states, saddled with antiquated institutions, are behaving as if they were. As has been shown, diplomats are faced with an agenda dominated by issues far removed from the sorts of political, ideological, and territorial differences that have traditionally given rise to interstate conflict. Today, their path is being determined by the dynamic of globalization, which, by exacerbating distributive injustice, has engendered a host of new connections among diplomacy, security, and international policy. The instruments of international policy, however, remain brittle and sclerotic, trapping the value that could be added by diplomacy within dysfunctional administrative machinery. Reform as well as resources are urgently required.

Third, to the extent that remedies have been embraced, they have tended to be the wrong ones. The Cold War ended almost twenty years ago, yet the principal thrust of international policy in most Western countries is toward containing terrorism, just as it used to be toward containing communism. A secondary objective, promoting democracy, is equally ill-suited to violent imposition. Democracy is best assisted rather than imposed, and even then the primary impetus must be local, and the support homegrown. As long as thought and action in the A-world remain militarized and the armed forces continue to attract the lion's share of public resources vis-à-vis development agencies and diplomatic services, conditions in the rest of the world are unlikely to improve. This translates into a prescription for unending underdevelopment and insecurity.[34]

Fourth, diplomats, notwithstanding their crucial role at the intersection of development and security, for the most part don't *do* aid. Yet as a response to globalization, development is in large part the answer to insecurity. Defusing the anger and resentment that find expression in violence means committing to a more equitable and sustainable division of the world's wealth and resources, which will in turn mean placing a much greater emphasis on and more resources into development. The full measure of horsepower inherent in the diversity of the diplomatic ecosystem has not been harnessed to this wagon, and summoning the will, finding the political direction, targeting the recruits, and providing the appropriate training will not be easy.

Last, S&T has become an increasingly prominent feature of the international policy landscape, but the priorities and practice of diplomacy do not reflect as much. Profound threats to the survival of the species—among them the science-based, technologically driven challenges already cited—have not received the attention they deserve in either theory or practice, especially within foreign ministries. As a driver of insecurity, S&T has not been adequately recognized; as a central part of any remedy, it has not been sufficiently engaged. Besides, even when diplomats do fully acknowledge that S&T is part of both the problem and the solution, they'll lack the knowledge, the institutional structure, and the policy expertise to take action. Diplomats do not know what they need to know, where or how to get the knowledge, or what to do with it if they do get it.[35] This, too, must be remedied. So the times have changed, but key policies and institutions have not.

The result is a disconnect, the impact of which has been calamitous. The West is fighting a global war on terror with no end in sight using an inappropriate set of tools and concepts carried over from the Cold War. The mindset? Confrontational and angry. The threat? Universal and generalized. The response? Armed and dangerous.

The substitution of the war on terror for the Cold War as the central organizing principle in international relations has brought the world to the brink. As both the diagnosis and the prescription are wrong, it is hardly surprising that intelligence estimates have concluded that the present course is exacerbating rather than reducing insecurity. A majority of experts now agree that this war is not only being lost, but is making matters worse.[36] Until a way is found to jettison the baggage of Cold War ideology, performance is unlikely to improve.

A Marshall Plan for the Middle East? It would surely be preferable to military occupation. The hard-line policies pursued to date have wrought unpredictable and undesirable results, not least of which are an increase in the chronic instability associated with economic and political polarization, an associated rise in identity politics, frequent collateral damage, and the serious erosion of rights, liberties, and freedoms. That is not a tenable combination.

In short, the arrival of the globalization age has engendered a host of both new connections and new contradictions among diplomacy, security, and international policy. Thinking these through leads inexorably to a simple conclusion: the old approaches won't do.

The Design of Diplomacy

In my estimation, the implications of the arguments for changing how we think about international relations as well as how we design and deliver public administration are immense. They are also largely ignored.[37] But they can't be dismissed for much longer. States are responsible for security. Diplomats represent states. If globalization has made security indivisible and if development is the prerequisite to security, then diplomats must play a larger role in the pursuit of development, not least by broaching issues related to international cooperation in S&T.

Looking ahead, we see a world very different from that encapsulated by the title of Chapter 2, "Cold War Comfort." Now more than ever, the importance for diplomacy of staying tuned to developments in the margins remains constant. The nature of globalization as assessed in Chapter 3 is polarized and unpredictable, hence our need for the kind of world order model set out in Chapter 4. In Chapter 5, I have tried to parse the ramifications of these arguments for our thinking about security and to underscore the reasons that terrorism is flourishing. But terrorism is more accurately seen as a symptom than a cause of insecurity. That cause, I argue in Chapter 6, may more than any other single factor be attributable to underdevelopment, which must accordingly become the preoccupation of diplomatic activity.

In this deterritorialized milieu of global insurgency and increasing state failure, military power, though not irrelevant, has demonstrated its limits, particularly in the face of unconventional and asymmetrical threats. However menacing some of these long-bottled, newly freed tribal, ethnic, and religious genies may appear, initiating an exchange with them is, I argue, in the end more likely to produce favorable results than shooting at them. This is particularly true in light of the new array of global challenges rooted in science and driven by technology that we examined in Chapters 7 and 8.

This point deserves special emphasis. Science creates knowledge about the world around us. Through R&D that leads to technological innovations, we can test that knowledge and apply it to specific problems or challenges, from the need for alternative energy sources and pollution control to the development of disease-resistant grains. And those technologies can be disseminated and implemented—not just by market forces and specialized international organizations but as a matter of science diplomacy.

It is my sense that the kinds of issues and shifting power relations discussed in Chapter 8 may provide the moral impetus and the force majeure necessary both to restore the public's faith in the relevance of diplomacy and to sharpen the effectiveness of its practice. Take just one file, climate change. It has now been almost twenty years since international agreement on the Framework Convention at the Rio Conference (UNCED) in 1992. There is a real opportunity here for coordinated, cooperative international action motivated by common interest. Considering the inaction to date and depending on the severity and consequences of the likely disruption, it is not unreasonable to anticipate the need for drastic measures.[38] Access to clean air and water may one day in the not-so-distant future be enshrined in international law as a basic human right, for instance in the UN *Universal Declaration.* With that, mandatory emission reductions could be imposed. New coal-fired electrical power generation plants could be banned and existing plants be made subject to controls. A moratorium could be placed on logging in boreal and tropical rain forests. A UN force to police the Amazon? International satellite surveillance of northern forests in Russia and Canada? Protected networks of air monitoring stations in China and India? Restrictions on motor vehicle use in the United States? None can be ruled out. How will it happen? There is only one option. Diplomacy.

In researching the drivers of insecurity both present and future, I found that the attraction of ideas, often disseminated over the airwaves and in cyberspace, is edging out compulsion on the ground in the calculus of power and influence. In analyzing both causes and remedies, I also found myself arriving repeatedly at the same conclusion: the interconnected triad of the foreign ministry, diplomacy, and the foreign service, which are covered in Chapters 9, 10, and 11. They merit far more support and attention than they have received. As the repositories of institutional memory, resident policy expertise, and unique area knowledge, these institutions represent vital national resources when it comes to the peaceful management of divergent values and interests. They should be treated as such.

Globalization, with its concomitant shift from the international to the transnational, is contributing to the accumulation of capital, expediting innovation, and maximizing all kinds of efficiencies. But, by socializing costs while privatizing benefits, globalization is also a primary source of economic instability, political insecurity, and state failure. The diplomatic skills necessary to cope are to some extent universal, but in the rough-and-tumble world of globalization the *context* of diplomacy has changed radically, and this carries significant practical implications. As the world has moved beyond the state-centric Westphalian model of international relations, diplomats need to connect directly with populations, which in turn requires new skills, namely cross-cultural capacity and a high degree of confidence and comfort—what the French call *aisance.* These qualities are usually neither apparent nor required in dealings with other diplomats or the representatives of local elites, who tend to be Westernized in nature and orientation.

This lack of skills and capacity, in combination with the transformed environment, has created a diplomatic performance gap, or deficit, whereby threats go unchecked, conflict unabated, and major challenges unaddressed. This is why, as I advocated in Chapter 12, the moment has arrived to embrace guerrilla diplomacy. Were the required resources put into place and a full court press delivered on reform, the transformation of diplomatic practice could be effected in relatively short order.

If this book's main message could be encapsulated in a phrase, it might be this: the purpose of diplomacy in a world of insecurity is to address the root causes of underdevelopment. In other words, the place in the globalization age for the agents of diplomacy and the foreign ministry, as those best able to cohere the national interest and manage it strategically, is at the nexus between security and development. If development is the new security and security is best achieved through talking rather than fighting, then I see no alternative: diplomats must get over their Cold War habits and become more integrally involved in the business of development, especially the management of S&T files.

If we increase the level and intensity of personal and professional contact by including diplomats and aid workers in the same occupational group (the foreign/international service), we can expedite this repositioning. In the end, however, more integration will also be required at the political decisionmaking level. This integration could be achieved below the level of head of government via the delegation of authority to a senior minister who could chair a high-level cabinet committee on international policy, operations, and strategic direction. That would mean bringing each of the interdepartmental players together under the overall guidance of a single minister, possibly the foreign minister, who would then answer to the head of government regarding policy coordination and cohesion.[39] The foreign and trade ministries, defense, immigration, the aid and foreign intelligence agencies, and all departments involved in major international scientific and technological enterprise would be subject to this oversight. Were this to eventuate, policy coherence, while never complete, would certainly be improved. Indeed, I would estimate that the full package of management and public administrative reforms could be accomplished within about five years.

Remember the Past

Many of these arguments have been gestating for years. Consider, for example, the memorable and remarkably prescient words of University of Toronto historian James Eayrs. Penned at the height of the Cold War, they are no less apt today:

> The . . . fact of modern international life accounting for the impotence of force and the weakness of great powers is . . . the heightened constraint of opinion and the nature of the only kind of war the great powers are free to fight. This is not big war, thermonuclear war. It is little war, guerrilla war. And for great powers no experience is more frustrating. It frustrates not least because the

> targets are so few, and so fleeting . . . the enemy always knows more about what's going on. After all, it's his country . . . There's always an intelligence gap in these conflicts . . . the great power is invariably disadvantaged. . . .
>
> Twentieth-century war is increasingly an instrument of doctrinal conviction. Doctrinal war, more than war fought for gain or preemptive attack, is likely to be . . . brutal war. Crusades are notorious for their cruelty. . . .
>
> Those who serve the state as warriors are largely spared these stresses and strains. They are protected by their training and their ethic which, more than in any other profession, cultivate the ideal of unquestioning obedience to higher command. The diplomatist may well experience malaise when required to execute policies [that] seem to him likely to result in war; for the onset of war is to him a signification of his failure.[40]

War, as Eayrs observed, represents the failure of diplomacy, which is the antithesis of recourse to violence. And in a world of multiplying information sources and pathways, of proliferating actors and media, the importance of direct personal contact and connection is increasing. Distilled to its essence and at its best, diplomacy embodies and gives voice to three of the most elemental human qualities: reason, understanding, and the capacity to communicate. Diplomacy may be, in the words of retired US ambassador Charles Freeman, "the most difficult of the political arts."[41] Yet it alone holds the key to approaching a fraught future by design rather than by default.

They Created Devastation, and Called It Peace

So spoke Tacitus of the Roman Empire almost two millennia ago. Performance can be improved. In my efforts to set out the crisis facing contemporary diplomacy, enlarge our sense of the causal links, and indicate how the failings might be corrected, I have doubtless missed some important points. Still, I believe the world set out in the preceding pages, as modeled by ACTE, to be a reasonable facsimile of our own. If it is, then at the highest level of analysis, the implications for policymakers of the main arguments I have advanced should be straightforward, perhaps even obvious. But they are nonetheless far-reaching:

1. During the Cold War, when security was predicated on armies and weapons, development was seen by some as morally imperative, but by most as optional. In the globalization age, development, rather than defense, has become essential to security, and hence is best seen as a strategic rather than an ethical necessity. International policy and relations should therefore be demilitarized, international policy resources redeployed, priorities reordered, and instruments recast. This means that baggage carried over from the Cold War—including all tendencies to inaccurately characterize the threat, emphasize armed force, and take a binary, reductionist worldview—will have to be set

aside. It should be exchanged, at least in part, for a renewed commitment to human-centered, sustainable, and equitable development as the basis for global security going forward.

2. Government departments and diplomatic services should be retooled to take full account of S&T as both a primary driver of the future threats and challenges associated with globalization and a source of remedial opportunities.[42] They must engage more meaningfully with the global political economy of knowledge; invest in both basic and advanced education to provide an enabling environment for progress; and, through their commitment to extensive interchange, training, and professional development, nurture the capacity to bridge the digital divide and act with souplesse.
3. International institutions—including but not limited to diplomatic services in A-world countries—should undertake the measures necessary to mainstream public diplomacy and develop a capacity for guerrilla diplomacy. By connecting with nontraditional partners at home and abroad at all levels of government and in civil society, they can cultivate key constituencies that will help offset the diminishing importance of the state. This will mean they must forge new relationships with the media, the private sector, NGOs, diaspora and religious groups, and the academic community. In all of this, the rehabilitation of the intelligence function, and, in some cases, the adaptation of public diplomacy for application to the conditions of counterinsurgency, will be crucial.

More broadly, immediate action is required to address the most egregious effects of underdevelopment and insecurity through the purposeful redeployment of resources from defense to development and diplomacy, and through the pursuit of directed pro-poor policies in the T- and E-worlds.

Eventually, we might have cause to make the case that policy planners in the A-world should focus in the short to medium term on one level of the model that has escaped much discussion here: the C-world.[43] This is the contingency zone, which can be considered the strategic crossroads of globalization. It is here that the movement of people, countries, and regions into the A-world may be most quickly and easily expedited—above all by concentrating A-world cooperation and assistance efforts on the C-world's critical S&T sector. Those in the T- and E-worlds might also thus experience new opportunities for upward mobility, as the integration of the global political economy created demand-driven vacancies in the C-world.[44]

Of course, we cannot be certain either that all of this would occur or that it would be sustainable if it did. But given that quick hits and easy wins can only facilitate the change process, an early focus on certain elements of the C-world may be a policy objective worth considering. At minimum, it would allow for deliberate action intended to push or pull participants up the development ladder. That seems much preferable to a model that offers, at best, the possibility that development benefits might incidentally trickle down.

Anticipating the Times to Come

I planned this book as an analytical survey and reconnaissance mission, and accordingly have passed lightly over large tracts of intellectual terrain. There remains much to be explored, and the possible directions for research are almost endless. I will mention only a few of the more obvious candidates.

The ramifications of the case presented here could usefully be applied to the unique circumstances obtaining in various parts of each of the A-, C-, T-, and E-worlds, be they nations, regions, cities, or groups. A full assessment of these implications for trade and immigration policies, international organizations, and multilateral financial institutions could be most illuminating. Much more also needs to be said about the interface between the public and private sectors and civil society.

We must also develop a better understanding of why S&T remains ensconced in institutions and corporations, away from the public mind and largely disconnected from the diplomatic agenda. How to better align S&T investments with common interests? The roles of foreign direct investment, basic research, and technology transfer require much fuller illumination.

Considerable work could be done to enlarge understanding of the global political economy of knowledge; bringing the existing scholarship on the noosphere and netpolitik to bear on these issues could yield important insights. Dan Tapscott and, from a different perspective, David Bollier offer some compelling grounds for optimism on these issues. Tapscott, for example, argues convincingly that the active sharing of intellectual property can stimulate mass collaboration in a way that produces the desired results more effectively and efficiently than could ever be achieved through conventional corporate secrecy and competition.[45]

The concept of souplesse could certainly be further developed, bench-tested, and fleshed out with illustrations. The same goes for the notion of the diplomatic ecosystem. And of course guerrilla diplomacy itself requires much fuller elaboration and critical evaluation. Diplomats will have to find better ways to interact with business and to connect with business intelligence and commercial risk assessment networks—as well as with the growing world of private philanthropy.

As the lines between the real and virtual worlds become increasingly indistinct, the scope for diplomatic experimentation with the new media will continue to grow. The technological hardware and software available for transnational exchange and advocacy have already become so powerful that skepticism over the potential for meaningful crossover between the real and virtual domains has diminished in recent years.[46] Much more analysis, however, will be required on the issue of how diplomacy can better realize the possibilities inherent in the digital universe. Even now, there is room to accomplish objectives in cyberspace that would be difficult or impossible to achieve on this side of the screen.[47]

Finally, attention could usefully be directed toward assessing the likely nature of the diplomatic agenda over the medium term of the next five to ten years. For instance, we will need to prepare to deal with the raft of S&T issues raised in these pages as well as to embark on such diplomatic megaprojects as readying populations for the emergence of the noncarbon economy in the years beyond the peak of oil production. A host of related global resource management issues require similar attention. There is at this moment also an urgent need to organize for the global power shift already under way in the forms both of Asia's economic and political reemergence and the rapid comeback of multi-, or heteropolarity. The failures of the twentieth century in accommodating change of this magnitude must not be repeated. Finally, gearing up for the outreach required to keep publics in favor of this rebalancing of power will take some doing.

It will be for the scholars of public administration to determine how all of this might be achieved—especially the interlinking of diplomacy and development in ways that will allow foreign ministries to broach the overarching issues of S&T. Experts in governance will also be called upon to advise guerrilla diplomats in treating the many unconventional and asymmetrical afflictions we have covered.

Last Post

Of this we may be sure: as globalization erupts in a series of financial and economic shocks that are shaking its very foundations, a new world order is emerging. Though the outline remains indistinct, it appears likely that there will be a substantial number of new players wanting a place at the table—while Asia, the rapidly rising powerhouse of the integrated global economy, takes its seat at the head. One hopes that this transformation can be accommodated more peacefully and managed more adroitly than was the case in the twentieth century, when conflagrations surrounding the emergence of Germany, Japan, the United States, and the Soviet Union resulted in catastrophic losses. Add to this a changing climate, a growing population, a deteriorating environment, diminishing resources, and a demand for energy that outstrips the supply, and all of the elements are in place for a highly conflicted future.

For these reasons and more, serious attention needs to be paid, above all, to diplomacy per se. Here the message may be basic, but it is nonetheless worth repeating. History illustrates that diplomacy can be crucial to the prevention and the resolution of conflict. The end of unipolarity means an inevitable restructuring and some degree of rebalancing. Balancing requires compromise, and much of whatever happens will have to be negotiated. This will place the diplomats on the leading edge.

Less widely appreciated is the durable contribution that diplomacy can make toward achieving international security writ large. It can do this by addressing—through dialogue, engagement, and the orchestration of concerted action—not only the immediate causes of organized violence, but also the more complex underlying issues related to underdevelopment, insecurity, and the role of S&T. Diplomacy must therefore be placed at the center of grand strategy in the twenty-first century.

To span the digital divide by addressing the R&D deficits that separate the beneficiaries of globalization from its casualties, diplomats require specialized skills and experience. Yet most diplomatic practitioners—and the establishments they populate—lack the subtle, supple capacity to act effectively in the contemporary milieu. They are equipped neither to prevail over the myriad challenges of the twenty-first century nor to deliver the kinds of remedial policies and effective responses that this era requires. To bridge the performance gap, not only diplomacy but the diplomat him- or herself must be reimagined and re-created completely.

In the quest to maximize the benefits and minimize the costs associated with the globalization age, the foreign ministry, diplomacy, and the foreign service *do* matter. It is long past time—that most scarce and nonrenewable of resources—that they were treated accordingly. As the human face of international relations, it is the talker, not the fighter—the diplomat, not the soldier—who is best suited to address the complex requirements of development and peace. Especially when that face is attached to the body of a high-functioning, street-smart, renaissance humanist with well-developed instincts, a BlackBerry, and, when necessary, a Kevlar vest.

Guerrilla diplomacy, as a contribution to the management of global relations in an insecure world, may offer one way ahead. It's time, then, to bring our portrait of a guerrilla diplomat to life. Lonely sentinels on guard duty? No thanks. Exit new world orderlies, enter network nodes.

Notes

1. Mau, *Massive Change,* http://www.massivechange.com/about.

2. I am grateful to Canadian designer Anne Carlisle for this observation. Personal communication, February 12, 2008. I would venture to add the arrival of the Obama team provides reasonable justification for being at least cautiously hopeful. As we go to press, for example, there are renewed plans for convening a regional meeting to find ways to encourage security and development in Afghanistan. Iran is to be invited, which would have been inconceivable prior to January 2009. And there have been a flurry of other overtures—to Russia, Syria, Indonesia, and Turkey. Secretary of State Clinton and Vice President Biden can't seem to stop talking about smart power, soft

power, and diplomacy. Harvard professor Joseph Nye is becoming almost a household name. Special envoys have been appointed, thorny issues broached, executive orders signed, and new directions indicated. But combining hard and soft into smart power is difficult alchemy, and the mix potentially explosive. Trying to turn anthropologists into human terrain systems interpreters, soldiers into diplomats, and diplomats into counterinsurgents can be hazardous morally and dangerous personally. In my view, ways must be found to make dialogue work, and to make it work without the skewing effects that attend the threat or use of violence.

3. At the time of this writing, the evidence suggests that all terrorism, and especially the variety motivated by political Islam, may now be declining. Human Security Report Project (2008), "Human Security Brief 2007." May 21, http://www.humansecuritybrief.info.

4. See Strachan (2008: 44).

5. An increasing number of authors are reaching similar conclusions. Abbott, Rogers, and Sloboda (2007), for instance, cite climate change, competition over resources, the marginalization of the majority, and militarization as the main drivers of insecurity.

6. Paraphrased; all responsibility for misinterpretation is mine.

7. See Jervis (1994).

8. See Morgenthau (1965).

9. See Fisk (2008). On the West's calamitous misreading and mismanagement of its relations with Pakistan, Afghanistan, and Central Asia, see Rashid (2008).

10. *Foreign Policy* and the Fund for Peace identify sixty vulnerable states. See *Foreign Policy* (2007). The International Crisis Group (2008) estimates that in 2007, the world was afflicted by seventy-five major conflicts, of which seven were worsening (namely those in Algeria, Spain's Basque region, Chad, Kenya, Kyrgyzstan, Lebanon, and Pakistan); one, in Nepal, was improving; and sixty-seven were unchanged from 2006.

11. Human Security Centre (2007).

12. It will be difficult to match Chalmers Johnson's now complete trilogy on the unintended consequences of empire. See C. Johnson (2000; 2004; 2007).

13. See Englehardt (2008). On the link between imperial overstretch and the financial crisis, see Huq (2008).

14. Consider, for instance, the amount of time and effort that was devoted to constructing deterrence theory during the Cold War. Beyond historical or intellectual interest, what good is all of that material now?

15. A more coordinated and balanced approach and a greater reliance on diplomacy and development as the centerpieces of Canada's engagement in Afghanistan were among the main recommendations contained in the January 2008 report from the Independent Panel on Canada's Future Role in Afghanistan, chaired by former deputy prime minister John Manley.

16. Nor, some would argue, is war good for business after all; certainly not over the economic long term. See Johnson (2008b).

17. See Korten (2006).

18. Burtinsky's *Manufactured Landscapes* (2007) is a must-see for all with an interest in the impact of industrialization.

19. Comment recorded by the author at an ISA panel discussion in San Francisco, March 27, 2008.

20. Blackwater and Halliburton are large US corporate contractors whose activities in Iraq and elsewhere have been harshly critiqued. On Blackwater, see Scahill (2007). See also Halliburton Watch, http://www.halliburtonwatch.org/home.html.

21. There are all kinds of reasons to be hopeful. To cite just one, Tapscott and Williams (2006) argue that the new media have made problem solving through mass collaboration so attractive that collaboration may be edging out competition as the primary motivator of business behavior. Browse their blog at http://www.wikinomics.com.

22. At the 2009 ISA conference in New York, there was much discussion about the direction and orientation of US foreign policy under the Obama administration. Some expressed reservation over the early enthusiasm for "smart power," a potentially volatile mix of hard and soft power more easily said than effectively used. Although views were mixed, a slim majority, by my reckoning and not least because the war on terror was seen as deeply "sedimented" in the Washington bureaucracy, were forecasting a continuation of familiar policy directions, even if the packaging evolves. On smart power and the new government, see Nye (2009), http://www.latimes.com/news/opinion/commentary/la-oe-nye21-2009jan21,0,3381521.story. On continuity in foreign policy, see Brose (2009). For broader prescriptions, see Sanger (2009), Slaughter (2009), Graubard (2009), and Engelhardt (2009). On fixing the foreign service, see Holmes (2009).

23. I refer here to various statements by candidates in the 2008 US presidential primaries and since, Canadian parliamentarians in all parties, and the British foreign minister, who spoke of the need for a "diplomatic surge." See Miliband (2008).

24. See Kuhn (1996).

25. I am indebted to Scott Bury for reminding me of the link to Hegel.

26. "Yes, you're right; it's all the same," said Thomas Homer-Dixon in response to a comment I made to this effect at an event hosted by DFAIT on February 18, 2006.

27. Since the advent of television, world affairs have been coming into the living rooms of the nation, thus heightening reality content and contributing to the compression of space. For a useful survey of the various aspects of the CNN effect, see Livingston (1997).

28. The televised version of the critical two-and-a-half-minute passage is well worth viewing. Available at http://www.youtube.com/watch?v=8y06NSBBRtY.

29. See McMaster (2008).

30. Some of the material in this section was presented, in a slightly different context, in Copeland (2006: 20–30).

31. See, for example, Bricker (2006), Davis (2008).

32. The rule of thumb is that when the overhead costs are fully figured into the calculation, it is approximately three to four times more expensive to keep a foreign service officer in the field than at headquarters.

33. For this formulation I am indebted to my colleague Martin Rose, director of the British Council in Canada.

34. When governments favor military over diplomatic options, most diplomats swallow hard and get on with it. There are exceptions, however. Veteran US foreign service officers J. Brady Kiesling, John Brown, and Ann Wright resigned in March 2003 over the decision to invade Iraq. Kiesling noted in an interview with the *New York Times* that "no one of my colleagues is comfortable with our policy . . . [but] the State Department is loaded with people who want to play the team game. . . . We have a very strong premium on loyalty." That has cost everyone. See Felicity Barringer (2003), "U.S. Diplomat Resigns, Protesting 'Our Fervent Pursuit of War,'" *New York Times,* February 27.

35. If diplomats are to use the full potential associated with S&T advancements, they will need all the help they can get. The Munk Centre for International Studies at the University of Toronto, for example, has established the Citizen Lab, which has a mandate to conduct "advanced research and development at the intersection of digital

media and world civic politics." See Munk Centre for International Studies, http://www.citizenlab.org.

36. The recommendations of those surveyed are striking from the perspective of this analysis. They advocate more attention to branding, addressing issues of economic and social development, and relearning what works in ideological struggles. See Marks (2007). In mid-2009, less is being heard about the war on terror, but even if gone from the political rhetoric, the enormous inertia generated by the pursuit of this priority since 2001 will ensure that it remains with us for some time. Vast organizations exist to fight it, troops are deployed worldwide in support of it, careers and promotions depend on it.

37. For a general overview of these issues, see Copeland (1997–1998) and Copeland (1997). See also C. Johnson (2000). For a forceful counterargument, see Saul (2005).

38. In the absence of comprehensive and immediate international action—and perhaps even with such measures—climate change may engender conflict on many levels. See Dyer (2008). See also Friedman (2008), McKibben (2009). Alternatively, climate change may represent a universally compelling catalyst for global cooperation.

39. The same sort of delegated authority would apply to the role of the ambassador at missions abroad.

40. Eayrs (1971).

41. See Freeman (2007). His essay "Diplomacy in the Age of Terror," adapted from a speech to the Pacific Council on International Policy in 2007, concisely critiques the present course of US foreign policy, and provides eloquent testimonial to many of the arguments offered here. The piece anticipates with some prescience a number of the key international policy themes that have emerged from Washington since the departure of the Bush administration. For an especially stinging indictment of the former president, see Pitt (2009), available at http://www.truthout.org/010709J; Warde (2009).

42. The private sector has already awakened to this new reality and is moving to harness the full potential of collaborative technology, not least in order to solve scientific problems with commercial potential. See InnoCentive, http://www.innocentive.com.

43. A broadly similar analytical conclusion—presented largely in an anecdotal travelogue format—may be found in Khanna (2008).

44. Because the ACTE model encompasses but is not anchored in territorial or spatial relationships, it would be a mistake to frame any discussion solely in geographic or regional terms. That said, to the extent that there is scope for that type of consideration, Southeast Asia (a once wildly popular region of so-called baby tigers that, since the economic crisis of the late 1990s, has largely disappeared from view) and African, Middle Eastern, and the Mediterranean rim countries come immediately to mind.

45. See Tapscott and Williams (2006), Bollier (2007), at http://www.re-public.gr/en/?p=136. See also Bollier's (2009) history of the digital commons, at http://creativecommons.org/weblog/entry/12448; Tapscott (2009); Sanderson, Gordon, and Ben-Ari (2008).

46. How blurred have the lines become and how powerful is the technology? See the category entitled "those rated most jaw dropping" at http://www.ted.com/index.php/talks/list; see also the amazing work of Johnny Chung Lee at http://www.cs.cmu.edu/~johnny.

47. Such experiments are occurring. See Second Life, http://secondlife.com. In early 2009, reports surfaced to the effect that Second Life may be in trouble. See Owen Thomas (2009), "The End of Second Life," February 22, at http://gawker.com/5158190/the-end-of-second-life. For a scholarly treatment of virtuality, see Boellstoroff (2008).

Bibliography

Abbott, Chris (2008). "An Uncertain Future: Law Enforcement, National Security and Climate Change." *Oxford Research Group,* January. http://www.oxfordresearchgroup.org.uk/publications/briefing_papers/pdf/uncertainfuture.pdf.

Abbott, Chris, Paul Rogers, and John Sloboda (2007). *Beyond Terror: The Truth About the Real Threats to Our World.* London: Rider.

Alam, M. Shalid (2000). *Poverty from the Wealth of Nations: Integration and Polarization in the Global Economy Since 1760.* Basingstoke: Palgrave Macmillan.

——— (2003). "Scholarship or Sophistry? Bernard Lewis and the New Orientalism." *Counterpunch,* June 28. http://www.counterpunch.org/alam06282003.html.

Alinsky, Saul (1971). *Rules for Radicals: A Pragmatic Primer for Realistic Radicals.* New York: Random House.

Allison, Graham (2006). "The Ongoing Failure of Imagination." *Bulletin of the Atomic Scientists* (September–October).

Amadae, S. M. (2003). *Rationalizing Capitalist Democracy: The Cold War Origins of Rational Choice Liberalism.* Chicago: University of Chicago Press.

Amend, Kurt (2008). "Counterinsurgency Principles for the Diplomat." *Small Wars Journal,* July 19. http://smallwarsjournal.com/mag/docs-temp/75-amend.pdf.

American Academy of Diplomacy and the Stimson Center (2008). "A Foreign Affairs Bid for the Future: Fixing the Crisis of Diplomatic Readiness." *Stimson,* October. http://www.stimson.org/budgeting/Publications/Long_Final_11_08.pdf.

American Foreign Service Association. *American Foreign Service Association.* http://www.afsa.org.

———. *Foreign Service Journal.* http://www.afsa.org/fsj.

Amin, Samir (1977). *Imperialism and Unequal Development.* New York: Monthly Review Press.

Anderson, M. S. (1993). *The Rise of Modern Diplomacy, 1450–1919.* London: Longman.

Anderson, Sarah, and James Cavanagh (2000). *A Field Guide to the Global Economy.* New York: New Press.

Anholt, Simon (2004). *Brand America.* London: Cyan.

——— (2005). *Brand New Justice.* Amsterdam: Elsevier.

——— (2007). *Competitive Identity.* Basingstoke: Palgrave Macmillan.

———, ed. (2008). *Journal of Place Branding and Public Diplomacy.* Basingstoke: Palgrave Macmillan.

Arendt, Richard (2007). *The First Resort of Kings: American Cultural Diplomacy in the Twentieth Century*. Dulles, VA: Potomac Books.

Argyos, George, Marc Grossman, and Felix Rohatyn (2007). *The Embassy of the Future.* Washington, DC: Center for Strategic and International Studies. http://www.csis.org/media/csis/pubs/embassy_of_the_future.pdf.

Armistead, Leigh (2004). *Information Operations: Warfare and the Hard Reality of Soft Power*. Dulles, VA: Brassey's.

Armitage, Richard, and Joseph Nye (2007). *CSIS Commission on Smart Power: A Smarter, More Secure America.* http://www.csis.org/media/csis/pubs/071106_csissmartpowerreport.pdf.

Arquilla, John, and David Ronfeldt (1999). *The Emergence of Noopolitik: Toward an American Information Strategy.* Santa Monica: Rand Corporation. www.rand.org/pubs/monograph_reports/MR1033/index.html.

——— (2002). *Networks and Netwars.* Santa Monica: Rand Corporation.

——— (2007). "The Promise of Noopolitik." *First Monday* 12(8). http://firstmonday.org/htbin/cgiwrap/bin/ojs/index.php/fm/article/view/1971/1846.

Atkinson, George (2006). "Science and Technology: A Bridge Between Cultures and Nations." *eJournalUSA* 11(3): 4. http://www.america.gov/media/pdf/ejs/1006ej.pdf#poupup.

——— (2007). "The Globalization of Science and Technology: U.S. and International Strategies." Presentation given at the Global Forum: Building Science, Technology, and Innovation Capacity for Sustainable Growth and Poverty Reduction, February 14. http://web.worldbank.org/wbsite/external/topics/extstiglofor/0,,contentMDK:21183804~menuPK:3156763~pagePK:64168445~piPK:64168309~theSitePK:3156699,00.html.

Australia Department of Foreign Affairs and Trade (2005). *Public Diplomacy Handbook.* Canberra: DFAT.

Australia Senate (2007). *Inquiry into the Nature and Conduct of Australia's Public Diplomacy.* http://www.aph.gov.au/Senate/committee/fadt_ctte/public_diplomacy/submissions/sublist.htm.

Avant, Deborah (2005). *The Market for Force: The Consequences of Privatizing Security.* Cambridge: Cambridge University Press.

Axworthy, Lloyd (2003). *Navigating a New World: Canada's Global Future*. Toronto: Knopf.

Aylwin-Foster, Nigel (2005). "Changing the Army for Counterinsurgency Operations." *Military Review* (November–December): 2–15.

Azzam, Maha (2006). "Islamism Revisited." *International Affairs* 82(6): 1119–1132.

Bacevich, Andrew (2004). *American Empire: The Realities and Consequences of U.S. Diplomacy.* Cambridge, MA: Harvard University Press.

——— (2008). *Limits of Power: The End of American Exceptionalism.* New York: Metropolitan Books.

Bailey, Ronald (2005). "Under the Spell of Malthus." *Reasononline,* August–September. http://www.reason.com/news/show/33122.html.

Bank for International Settlements (2005). "Central Bank Survey of Foreign Exchange and Derivatives Market Activity in 2004." *Bank for International Settlements,* March 17. http://wsww.bis.org/press/p050316.htm.

Bar, François, and Hernan Galperin (2006). "Wireless Communication and Development: Micro and Macro Linkages." *Information Technologies and International Development* 3(2): 1–2.

Baran, Paul A. (1957). *The Political Economy of Growth.* New York: Monthly Review Press.

Barber, Benjamin (2002). "Democracy and Terror in the Era of Jihad vs. McWorld." *Worlds in Collision: Terror and the Future of World Order,* eds. Ken Boothe and Tim Dunne, 245–262. New York: Palgrave Macmillan.

——— (2003). *Fear's Empire: War, Terror, and Democracy.* New York: W. W. Norton.

Barkawi, Tarak (2006). *Globalization and War.* Oxford: Rowman and Littlefield.

Barlow, Maude (2005). *Too Close for Comfort: Canada's Future Within Fortress North America.* Toronto: McClelland and Stewart.

Barnaby, Frank (1992). *The Role and Control of Weapons in the 1990s.* London: Routledge.

Barnett, Roger (2003). *Asymmetrical Warfare: Today's Challenge to US Military Power.* Dulles, VA: Potomac Books.

Barnett, Thomas P. M. (2004). *The Pentagon's New Map: War and Peace in the Twenty-First Century.* New York: G. P. Putnam's Sons.

——— (2009). *Great Powers: America and the World After Bush.* New York: Putnam.

Barston, Ronald Peter (2006). *Modern Diplomacy,* 3rd ed. London: Longman.

Bàtora, Jozef (2005). "Public Diplomacy in Small and Medium-Sized States." *Discussion Papers in Diplomacy* no. 97. The Hague: Clingendael.

——— (2008). *Foreign Ministries and the Information Revolution.* Leiden, the Netherlands: Martinus Nijhoff Publishers.

Bergen, Peter, and Paul Cruikshank (2008). "The Unraveling: The Jihadist Revolt Against Bin Laden." *New Republic,* June 11. http://www.tnr.com/politics/story.html?id=702bf6d5-a37a-4e3e-a491-fd72bf6a9da1.

Berger, Peter L. (1997). "Four Faces of Global Culture." *National Interest* 49(Fall): 23–30.

Berns-McGown, Rima, ed. (2007–2008). "International Journal: Special Edition on Diasporas." *International Journal* 63(1).

Berridge, Geoff (2005). *Diplomacy: Theory and Practice.* New York: Palgrave Macmillan.

Best, Jacqueline (2003). "From the Top-Down: The New Financial Architecture and the Re-embedding of Global Finance." *New Political Economy* 8(3): 363–384.

Betts, Richard K. (2007). *Enemies of Intelligence: Knowledge and Power in American National Security.* New York: Columbia University Press.

Bezanson, K., et al. (1999). *Vietnam at the Crossroads: The Role of Science and Technology.* Ottawa: International Development Research Centre.

Bezanson, Keith, and Francisco Sagasti (2005). *Prospects for Development Thinking and Practice.* New York: Rockefeller Foundation. http://www.rockfound.org/about_us/news/2006/111006dev_think_practice.pdf.

Bhutto, Benazir (2008). *Reconciliation: Islam, Democracy, and the West.* New York: HarperCollins.

bin Laden, Osama (1998). "Fatwah." *PBS.* http://www.pbs.org/newshour/terrorism/international/fatwa_1998.html.

Bobbitt, Philip (2002). *The Shield of Achilles: War, Peace, and the Course of History.* New York: Knopf.

——— (2008). *Terror and Consent: Wars for the Twenty-First Century.* New York: Knopf.

Boellstoroff, Tom (2008). *Coming of Age in Second Life: An Anthropologist Explores the Virtually Human.* Princeton, NJ: Princeton University Press.

Bollier, David (2003)."The Rise of Netpolitik: How the Internet Is Changing International Politics and Diplomacy." *Aspen Institute.* http://www.aspeninstitute.org.

——— (2009). *Viral Spiral: How the Commoners Built a Digital Republic of Their Own.* New York: New Press.

Bond, David (2001). "U.S.-French Aviation Deal Clears Path for Delta Alliance." *Aviation Week and Space Technology,* October 29.

Boot, Max (2002). *The Savage Wars of Peace: Small Wars and the Rise of American Power.* New York: Basic Books.

Bottome, Edgar M. (1986). *The Balance of Terror: Nuclear Weapons and the Illusion of Security, 1945–1985.* Boston: Beacon Press.

Bound, Kirsten, Rachel Briggs, John Holden, and Samuel Jones (2007). "Cultural Diplomacy." *Demos.* http://www.demos.co.uk/files/Cultural%20diplomacy%20-%20web.pdf.

Brenner, Neil, and Roger Keil, eds. (2006). *The Global Cities Reader.* New York: Routledge.

Bricker, Darrell (2006). "Of Government's List of Five Priorities, Canadians Rate 'Patient Wait Times Guarantee' at the Top." *Ipsos News Center,* March 27. http://www.ipsos-na.com/news/pressrelease.cfm?id=3028.

British Council (2005–2006). *Annual Report 2005–06: Measuring Success.* http://www.britishcouncil.org/bc-annual-report-2005-2006.pdf?mtklink=bc-annual-report-2005-2006.

Brodeur, J., P. Gill, and D. Tollborg, eds. (2002). *Democracy, Law, and Security: Internal Security Services in Contemporary Europe.* Burlington, VT: Ashgate.

Brose, Christian (2009). "The Making of George W. Obama." *Foreign Policy* (January–February): 52–55.

Brown, John (2007). "Karen Hughes and Her 'Diplomacy of Deeds.'" *Common Dreams,* April 9. http://www.commondreams.org/archive/2007/04/09/411.

Bruce Mau Design and the Institute without Boundaries. *Massive Change.* http://www.massivechange.com.

Brunnee, Jutta, and Stephen Toope (2006). "Norms, Institutions, and UN Reform: The Responsibility to Protect." *Behind the Headlines* 63: 3.

Brzezinski, Zbigniew, et al. (1992). *New Dimensions in International Security.* London: Brassey's.

Bull, Hedley (1977). *The Anarchical Society: A Study of Order in World Society.* New York: Columbia University Press.

Burnham, G., et al. (2006). "Mortality After the 2003 Invasion of Iraq: A Cross-Sectional Cluster Sample Survey." *The Lancet* 368(9545): 1421–1428.

Campbell, Robert, Leslie A. Pal, and Michael Howlett (2004). *The Real Worlds of Canadian Politics: Cases in Process and Policy.* Peterborough, Ontario: Broadview Press.

Canada International Portal. Government of Canada. http://www.canadainternational.gc.ca/ci-ci/index.aspx.

Canada's World. "Global Inequality." *Canada's World.* http://www.canadasworld.ca/learnmor/ninenewr/globalin.

Canadian International Development Agency (2005). "Canada's International Policy Statement—A Role of Pride and Influence in the World." *Canadian International Development Agency.* http://www.acdi-cida.gc.ca/CIDAWEB/acdicida.nsf/En/JUD-2107401-GV3.

Cardoso, Fernando Henrique, and Enzo Faletto (1979). *Dependency and Development in Latin America.* Trans. Marjory Mattingly Urquidi. Berkeley: University of California Press.

Carothers, Thomas, and Marina Ottaway, eds. (2005). *Uncharted Journey: Promoting Democracy in the Middle East.* Washington, DC: Brookings Institution Press.

Carvalho, Soniya (2006). *Engaging with Fragile States: An IEG Review of World Bank Support to Low-Income Countries Under Stress.* Washington, DC: World Bank.

Castells, Manuel (1996). *The Rise of the Network Society: The Information Age—Economy, Society, and Culture,* 2nd ed., Vol. I. Oxford: Blackwell.

——— (1997). *The Power of Identity: The Information Age—Economy, Society, and Culture,* 2nd ed., Vol. II. Oxford: Blackwell.

——— (1998). *End of Millennium: The Information Age—Economy, Society and Culture,* Vol. III. Cambridge, MA: Blackwell.

——— (2000). *The End of the Millennium: The Information Age—Economy, Society, and Culture,* 2nd ed., Vol. III. Oxford: Blackwell.

——— (2003). "The Rise of the Fourth World." *The Global Transformations Reader: An Introduction to the Globalization Debate,* 2nd ed., eds. David Held and Anthony McGrew, 430–439. Malden, MA: Polity Press.

CBC News (2006a). "Aboriginal Children Are Poorest in Country: Report," November 24. http://www.cbc.ca/canada/story/2006/11/24/child-poverty.html.

CBC News (2006b). "Kashechewan: Water Crisis in Northern Ontario," November 9. http://www.cbc.ca/news/background/aboriginals/kashechewan.html.

CBC-TV (2008). *The Al Qaeda Code.* Documentary broadcast, April 3.

Center for Arms Control and Non-Proliferation. *The Center for Arms Control and Non-Proliferation.* http://www.armscontrolcenter.org.

Center for Media and Democracy. *PR Watch.* http://www.prwatch.org.

———. *Source Watch.* http://www.sourcewatch.org/index.php?title=BP.

Center for Systemic Peace (2007). *Global Conflict Trends.* http://www.systemicpeace.org/conflict.htm.

Central Intelligence Agency. "Rank Order—Military Expenditures." *The World Factbook.* https://www.cia.gov/library/publications/the-world-factbook/rankorder/2034rank.html.

Centre for Strategic and International Studies (1998). "Reinventing Diplomacy in the Information Age." *Institute of Communications Studies,* October 9. http://ics.leeds.ac.uk/papers/pmt/exhibits/799/reinventingdip.pdf.

"The Charge of the Think-Tanks" (2003). *The Economist,* February 15: 33.

Chatham House (2006). "Islamism Revisited." *Chatham House Briefing Paper,* September.

Chernus, Ira (2006). "The Day That Changed Everything Wasn't 9/11." *TomDispatch,* September 11. http://www.tomdispatch.com/post/119758/chernus_cornered_empire_the_legacy_of_9_11.

Chesterman, Simon, and Chia Lehnardt, eds. (2007). *From Mercenaries to Market: The Rise and Regulation of Private Military Companies.* New York: Oxford University Press.

Chesterman, Simon, et al., eds. (2005). *Making States Work.* Tokyo: United Nations University Press.

Chomsky, Noam (1988). *Manufacturing Consent: The Political Economy of Mass Media.* New York: Pantheon Books.

——— (2006). *Failed States: The Abuse of Power and the Assault on Democracy.* New York: Metropolitan Books.

Chua, Amy (2004). *World on Fire: How Exporting Free Market Democracy Breeds Ethnic Hatred and Global Instability.* New York: Anchor Books.

Chung Lee, Johnny. *Carnegie Mellon University.* http://www.cs.cmu.edu/~johnny.

Clarke, Richard (2004). *Against All Enemies: Inside America's War on Terror.* New York: Free Press.

Cleveland, Cutler J., Ida Kubiszewski, and Merrill Miller (2007). "United Nations Conference on Environment and Development (UNCED), Rio de Janeiro, Brazil." *The Encyclopedia of the Earth,* November 9. http://www.eoearth.org/article/United_Nations_Conference_on_Environment_and_Development_(UNCED),_Rio_de_Janeiro,_Brazil.

Clutterbuck, Richard (1966). *The Long, Long War: Counterinsurgency in Malaya and Vietnam.* New York: Praeger.

Cohen, Andrew (2003). *While Canada Slept: How We Lost Our Place in the World.* Toronto: McClelland and Stewart.

Collier, Paul (2007). *The Bottom Billion: Why the Poorest Countries Are Failing and What Can Be Done About It.* Oxford: Oxford University Press.

Consortium for Science, Policy, and Outcomes. "Highlights of the 2007 Forum on S&T Policy." *Consortium for Science, Policy, and Outcomes.* http://www.cspo.org/outreach/stforum2007/program.htm.

"Convention on Biological Diversity." June 5, 1992. *United Nations Treaty Series* 1760, no. 30619: 79.

"Convention on the Prohibition of the Development, Production, and Stockpiling of Bacteriological (Biological) and Toxin Weapons and on Their Destruction (April 10, 1972)." September 3, 1992. *United Nations Treaty Series* 1974, no. 33757: 45.

"Convention on the Prohibition of the Development, Production, Stockpiling and Use of Chemical Weapons and on Their Destruction." September 3, 1992. *United Nations Treaty Series* 1974, no. 33757: 45.

"Convention on the Prohibition of the Use, Stockpiling, Production, and Transfer of Anti-Personnel Mines and on Their Destruction." September 18, 1997. *United Nations Treaty Series* 2056, no. 35597: 211.

Cooper, Andrew F. (2007). *Celebrity Diplomacy.* Boulder: Paradigm Publishers.

Cooper, Andrew F., John English, and Ramesh Thakur, eds. (2001). *Enhancing Global Governance: Towards a New Diplomacy.* Tokyo: United Nations University Press.

Cooper, Andrew F., Brian Hocking, and William Maley (2008). *Global Governance and Diplomacy: Worlds Apart?* Basingstoke: Palgrave Macmillan.

Cooper, Robert (2000). *The Postmodern State and the World Order.* London: Demos.

——— (2003). *The Breaking of Nations: Order and Chaos in the Twenty-First Century.* New York: Atlantic Monthly Press.

Copeland, Daryl (1988). "Withered Recovery in Africa." *International Perspectives* (May–June): 17–19.

——— (1989a). "Rethinking Adjustment." *International Perspectives* (January–February): 4–7.

——— (1989b). "Foreign Service in the Nineties." *PAFSO Papers* 1: 1. Ottawa: Professional Association of Foreign Service Officers.

——— (1992). "Bureaucratoxis." *PASFSO Papers* 1: 2. Ottawa: Professional Association of Foreign Service Officers.

——— (1997). "Foreign Policy, Foreign Service and the 21st Century: The Challenge of Globalization." *Canadian Foreign Policy* 4(3): 105–112.

——— (1997–1998). "Globalization, Enterprise, and Governance." *International Journal* 53(1): 17–37.

——— (2001). "The Axworthy Years: Canadian Foreign Policy in the Era of Diminished Capability." *Canada Among Nations,* eds. Fen Hampson, Norman Hillmer, and Maureen Molot, 152–172. Toronto: Oxford University Press.

——— (2004). "Guerilla Diplomacy: Delivering International Policy in a Digital World." *Canadian Foreign Policy* 11(2): 165–175.

——— (2005). "New Rabbits, Old Hats: International Policy and Canada's Foreign Service in an Era of Reduced Diplomatic Resources." *International Journal* 60(3): 743–762.

——— (2006). "Three Ps in Search of a Pod: A Personal Perspective on Public Diplomacy, Public Opinion Research and the Public Environment." *Public Diplomacy: Practitioners, Policymakers and Public Opinion,* ed. J. Fouts, 20–30. Santa Monica: Figueroa Press.

——— (2007). "James Eayrs on Diplomacy, Foreign Policy, and International Relations: A Retrospective." *International Journal* 62(2): 241–262.

——— (2008a). "Independent Diplomat." *International Journal* 61(4): 988–991.

——— (2008b). "No Dangling Conversation: Portrait of the Public Diplomat." *Engagement: Public Diplomacy in a Globalised World*, eds. Jolyon Welsh and Daniel Fearn, 134–145. London: FCO.

——— (2008c). "Transformational Public Diplomacy: Rethinking Advocacy for the Globalization Age." *Place Branding and Public Diplomacy*, forthcoming.

Corman, Steve, Angela Trethewey, and Bud Goodall, eds. (2008). *Weapons of Mass Persuasion: Strategic Communication to Combat Violent Extremism.* New York: Peter Lang Publishing.

Corn, Tony (2006). "World War IV as Fourth Generation War." *Policy Review*, January. http://www.hoover.org/publications/policyreview/4868381.html.

Council on Foreign Relations (2002). "Public Diplomacy: A Strategy for Reform—A Report of an Independent Task Force on Public Diplomacy." *Council on Foreign Relations.* http://www.cfr.org/publication/4697/public_diplomacy.html.

——— (2003). "Finding America's Voice: A Strategy for Reinvigorating U.S. Public Diplomacy." *Council on Foreign Relations.* http://www.cfr.org/content/publications/attachments/public_diplomacy.pdf.

Cowan, Geoffrey, and Nicholas Cull (2008). "Public Diplomacy in a Changing World." *The Annals of the American Academy of Political and Social Science* 616(1): 6–8.

Critchlow, James (2004). "Public Diplomacy During the Cold War." *Journal of Cold War Studies* 6(1): 75–89.

Croke, Kevin (2006). "Rethinking the War on Terrorism." *Policy Report.* Progressive Policy Institute, November 30.

Cull, Nicholas (2007). "Seven Lessons from Past US Public Diplomacy." Paper presented at the annual meeting of the International Studies Association, Chicago, March 3.

——— (2008). *The Cold War and the United States Information Agency: American Propaganda and Public Diplomacy, 1945–89.* Cambridge: Cambridge University Press.

Curtis, Andrew (2004). *The Power of Nightmares.* BBC documentary. http://news.bbc.co.uk/2/hi/programmes/3755686.stm.

Davis, Jeff (2008). "Where Did the Mission in Afghanistan Go?" *Embassy Newspaper Online*, October 16. http://www.embassymag.ca/page/view/afghanistan_mission-10-16-2008.

Defense Science Board (2004). "Report of the Defense Science Board Task Force on Strategic Communication." *Office of the Under Secretary of Defense for Acquisition, Technology and Logistics.* http://www.acq.osd.mil/dsb/reports/2004-09-Strategic_Communication.pdf.

Deffeyes, Kenneth (2002). *Hubbert's Peak: The Impending World Oil Shortage.* Princeton, NJ: Princeton University Press.

Demos. *The Atlas of Ideas.* http://www.demos.co.uk/projects/atlasofideas/overview.

Der Derian, James (2001). *Virtuous War: Mapping the Military-Industrial-Media-Entertainment Network.* New York: Basic Books.

Diamond, Jared (2005). *Collapse: How Societies Choose to Fail or Succeed.* New York: Penguin.

Diebert, Ronald (1997). *Parchment, Printing and Hypermedia: Communication in World Order.* New York: Columbia University Press.

DiploFoundation. *DiploFoundation.* http://www.diplomacy.edu.

The Diplomatic Pouch. *The Diplomacy Ring.* http://c.webring.com/hub?ring=diplomacy.

The Diplomatic Pouch. *The Diplomatic Pouch.* http://www.diplom.org.

Dizard, Wilson (2004). *Inventing Public Diplomacy: The Story of the U.S. Information Agency.* Boulder, CO: Lynne Rienner Publishers.

Djerejian, Edward P. (2003). "Changing Minds, Winning Peace: A New Strategic Direction for U.S. Public Diplomacy in the Arab and Muslim World." *Report of the Advisory Group on Public Diplomacy for the Arab and Muslim World,* October 1. http://www.state.gov/documents/organization/24882.pdf.

Dollar, David, and Aart Kraay (2002). "Spreading the Wealth." *Foreign Policy* 81(1): 120–133.

Dowlah, C.A.F. (2004). *Backwaters of Global Prosperity: How Forces of Globalization and GATT/WTO Trade Regimes Contribute to the Marginalization of the World's Poorest Nations.* Westport, CT: Praeger.

Doz, Yves, et al. (2006). *Innovation: Is Global the Way Forward?* Fontainbleu, France: Booz Allen Hamilton/INSEAD.

Duffield, Mark (2001). *Global Governance and the New Wars: The Merging of Development and Security.* London: Zed Books.

Dufour, Paul (2007). "Development of Science and/or Science for Development?" Presentation given at AAAS Annual Forum on Science and Technology Policy, Washington, DC, May 3–4. http://www.aaas.org/spp/rd/forumdufour.pdf.

Dyer, Gwynne (1996). "Globalization and the Nation State." *Behind the Headlines* 53(4): 1.

——— (2008). *Climate Wars.* Toronto: Random House.

Eaves, David (2004). "From Middle Power to Model Power: Recharging Canada's Role in the World." *Canada25.* http://www.canada25.com/collateral/canada25_from_middle_to_model_power_en.pdf.

Eayrs, James (1971). *Diplomacy and Its Discontents.* Toronto: University of Toronto Press.

Eberwein, Wolf-Dieter, and Bertrand Badie (2006). "Prevention and Sovereignty: A Vision and a Strategy for a New World Order?" *Global Society* 20(1): 1–24.

Edelstein, David M., and Ronald R. Krebs (2005). "Washington's Troubling Obsession with Public Diplomacy." *Survival* 47(1): 89–114.

Eisenhower, President Dwight D. (1961). "Farewell Address," January 17. http://www.youtube.com/watch?v=8y06NSBBRtY.

el-Nawawy, Mohammed, and Shawn Powers (2008). *Mediating Conflict: Al-Jazeera English and the Possibility of a Conciliatory Media.* Los Angeles: Figueroa Press. Available at http://ajerp.com/wp-content/uploads/2008/11/ajerp-el-nawawy-powers.pdf.

Ellis, Karen (2008). "How to Achieve Growth: The Million Dollar Question." *Overseas Development Institute,* February. http://www.odi.org.uk/resources/odi-publications/opinions/95-karen-ellis-achieving-growth.pdf.

Elmer, John, and Anthony Fenton (2007). "Canada's Counterinsurgency Strategy." *ZNet,* March 27. http://www.zmag.org/znet/viewArticle/1737.

Emerson, Steven (2003). "Statement of Steven Emerson to the National Commission on Terrorist Attacks Upon the United States." *Third Public Hearing of the National Commission on Terrorist Attacks Upon the United States*, July 9. http://www.9-11commission.gov/hearings/hearing3/witness_emerson.htm.

Englehardt, Tom (2007). "Empire of Stupidity." *TomDispatch,* September 4. http://www.tomdispatch.com/post/174832.

——— (2008). "The Global War on Terror Report Card." *TomDispatch,* October 21. http://www.tomdispatch.com/post/174992/the_global_war_on_terror_report_car.

——— (2009). "Addicted to Force, Addicted to Failure." *TomDispatch,* March 10. http://www.tomdispatch.com/post/175044/addicted_to_force_addicted_to_failure.

Environmental Defense Fund (1996). "EDF Dismisses Ethyl's Claim of Trade Discrimination on MMT; Cites New Survey Showing Over 85% of US Oil Co.'s Reject Use of MMT Gas Additive." *Environmental Defense Fund,* September 10. http://www.environmentaldefense.org/pressrelease.cfm?contentID=1762.

Fanon, Frantz (1965). *The Wretched of the Earth.* New York: Grove Press.

Farson, Richard (2007). "Paradoxes in Making Friend of Enemies." *USC Center on Public Diplomacy,* January 4. http://uscpublicdiplomacy.com/index.php/newsroom/pdblog_detail/070104_paradoxes_in_making_friends_of_enemies.

"A Fast-Fading World of Good Intentions" (2008). *International Herald Tribune,* September 25: 8.

Fearon, James D. (2004). "Separatist Wars, Partition and World Order." *Security Studies* 13(4): 394–415.

Fedoroff, Nina (2009). "Science Diplomacy in the 21st Century." http://www.state.gov/g/stas/2009/116182.htm.

Ferguson, Niall (2004). *Colossus: The Price of America's Empire.* New York: Penguin.

Fergusson, Yale H., and Richard H. Mansbach (2004). *Remapping Global Politics: History's Revenge and Future Shock.* Cambridge: Cambridge University Press.

First Monday (2008). "Special Issue—Critical Perspectives on Web 2.0." *First Monday,* March 3. http://www.uic.edu/htbin/cgiwrap/bin/ojs/index.php/fm/issue/view/263/showToc.

Fisher, Ali (2008). "Music for a Jilted Generation: Open Source Public Diplomacy." http://wandrenpd.files.wordpress.com/2008/05/music-for-a-jilted-generation-open-source-public-diplomacy1.pdf.

Fisher, Ali, and Aurelie Brockerhoff (2008). *Options for Influence: Global Campaigns of Persuasion in the New Worlds of Public Diplomacy.* London: Counterpoint, British Council. http://www.counterpoint-online.org/download/587/Options_for_influence_PDF_download.pdf.

Fisk, Robert (2008). "The Only Lesson We Ever Learn Is That We Never Learn." *The Independent,* March 19. http://www.independent.co.uk/news/fisk/robert-fisk-the-only-lesson-we-ever-learn-is-that-we-never-learn-797816.html.

Fitzpatrick, Kathy (2007). "Advancing the New Public Diplomacy: A Public Relations Perspective." *The Hague Journal of Diplomacy* 2(3): 187–211.

Ford, Christopher (2005). "Speak No Evil: Targeting a Population's Neutrality to Defeat Insurgency." *Parameters* 35(2): 51–66.

Foreign Affairs and International Trade Canada (2003). "Beyond Peace: Canada in Afghanistan." *Canada World View* 20.

——— (2008). "START." *Foreign Affairs and International Trade Canada.* http://www.international.gc.ca/fac/start-gtsr/index.aspx.

——— "Policy eDiscussions." *Foreign Affairs and International Trade Canada.* http://www.international.gc.ca/cip-pic/discussions/index.aspx?menu_id=13.

Foreign and Commonwealth Office (2008). *Engagement: Public Diplomacy in a Globalised World.* London: FCO. http://www.fco.gov.uk/en/about-the-fco/publications/publications/pd-publication/.

Foreign and Commonwealth Office (UK). *FCO Bloggers: Global Conversations.* http://blogs.fco.gov.uk/roller/.

Foreign Policy (2007). "The Failed States Index." *Foreign Policy,* July–August. http://www.foreignpolicy.com/story/cms.php?story_id=3865.

Foreign Policy/Center for American Progress (2006). "The Terrorism Index." *Center for American Progress,* June 14. http://www.americanprogress.org/issues/2006/06/b1763813.html.

Fouts, J., ed. (2006). *Public Diplomacy: Practitioners, Policymakers and Public Opinion.* Santa Monica: Figueroa Press.

Fowler, Bob (2000). "Report of the Panel of Experts on Violations of Security Council Sanctions Against UNITA." *United Nations Security Council,* March 10. http://www.un.org/News/dh/latest/angolareport_eng.htm.

Frank, Andre Gunder (1969). *Capitalism and Underdevelopment in Latin America: Historical Studies of Chile and Brazil.* New York: Monthly Review Press.

Franko, Patrice (2003). *The Puzzle of Latin American Economic Development.* Lanham, MD: Rowman and Littlefield.

Freedman, Lawrence (2006). "The Transformation of Strategic Affairs." *International Institute of Strategic Studies Adelphi Paper* no. 379.

Freeland, Richard M. (1972). *The Truman Doctrine and the Origins of McCarthyism: Foreign Policy, Domestic Politics, and Internal Security, 1946–1948.* New York: Knopf.

Freeman, Chas W. (2007). "Diplomacy in the Age of Terror." Remarks to the Pacific Council on International Policy. *Middle East Policy Council,* October 4. http://www.mepc.org/whats/100407.asp.

Freire, Paulo (1970). *Pedagogy of the Oppressed.* New York: Herder and Herder.

Fried, Robert (1990). *Nightmare in Red: The McCarthy Era in Perspective.* New York: Oxford University Press.

Friedman, Thomas (1999). *The Lexus and the Olive Tree.* New York: Anchor Books.

——— (2005). *The World Is Flat: A Brief History of the Twenty-first Century.* New York: Farrar, Straus and Giroux.

——— (2008). *Hot, Flat, and Crowded: Why We Need a Green Revolution.* Toronto: Douglas and McIntyre.

Fukuyama, Francis (1992). *The End of History and the Last Man.* New York: Free Press.

——— (2004). *State Building: Governance and World Order in the 21st Century.* Ithaca, NY: Cornell University Press.

Gaddis, John Lewis (1991). "Toward the Post–Cold War World." *Foreign Affairs* 70(2): 102–122.

——— (1997). *We Now Know: Rethinking Cold War History.* New York: Oxford University Press.

Gardner, Dan (2008). *Risk: The Science and Politics of Fear.* London: Virgin Books.

Garrett, Geoffrey (2003). "Global Markets and National Politics." *The Global Transformations Reader: An Introduction to the Globalization Debate,* 2nd ed., eds. Anthony Held and David McGrew, 384–402. Malden, MA: Polity Press.

Gates, Robert (2007). "Landon Lecture." *US Department of Defense,* November 26. http://www.defenselink.mil/speeches/speech.aspx?speechid=1199.

——— (2008). Untitled text of remarks at the National Defense University. *US Department of Defense,* September 29. http://www.defenselink.mil/speeches/speech.aspx?speechid=1279.

George, Susan (1976). *How the Other Half Dies.* New York: Penguin.

George Washington University. *The George Washington University Institute for Public Diplomacy and Global Communication.* http://pdi.gwu.edu.

Ghani, Ashraf, and Clare Lockhart (2008). *Fixing Failed States: A Framework for Rebuilding a Fractured World.* New York: Oxford University Press.

Gilpin, Robert (2001). *Global Political Economy: Understanding the International Economic Order.* Princeton, NJ: Princeton University Press.

Glasser, Susan B. (2005). "U.S. Figures Show Sharp Global Rise in Terrorism." *Washington Post,* April 27.

Glassman, James (2008). "The New Age of PD." *Chatham House,* September 11. http://www.chathamhouse.org.uk/files/12130_110908glassman.pdf.

Glatzer, Miguel, and Dietrich Rueschemeyer, eds. (2005). *Globalization and the Future of the Welfare State.* Pittsburgh, PA: University of Pittsburgh Press.

Gordon, Philip (2007). *Winning the Right War: The Path to Security for America and the World.* New York: Henry Holt.

Gotlieb, Alan (1991). *I'll Be with You in a Minute, Mr. Ambassador: The Education of a Canadian Diplomat in Washington.* Toronto: University of Toronto Press.

Graham, Carol, and Sandip Sukhtankar (2004). "Does Economic Crisis Reduce Support for Markets and Democracy in Latin America? Some Evidence from Surveys of Public Opinion and Well-Being." *Journal of Latin American Studies* 36(6): 349–377.

Grant, George (1969). *Technology and Empire: Perspectives on North America.* Toronto: Anansi.

Grant, Richard (2004). "The Democratization of Diplomacy: Negotiating with the Internet." *Oxford Internet Institute, Research Report No. 5*, November. http://www.oii.ox.ac.uk/research/publications.cfm.

Graubard, Stephen (2009). "A Broader Agenda: Beyond Bush-Era Foreign Policy." *Foreign Policy* (January–February): 176–181.

Green, Dan (2007). "The Political Officer as Counterinsurgent." *Small Wars Journal,* September. http://smallwarsjournal.com/documents/swjvol9.pdf.

Greenhill, Robert (2004). "Making a Difference? External Views on Canada's International Impact." *Canadian Institute of International Affairs,* February. https://idl-bnc.idrc.ca/dspace/bitstream/123456789/33024/1/120694.pdf.

Gregory, Frank, and Paul Wilkinson (2005). "Riding Pillion for Tackling Terrorism Is a High-Risk Policy." *Chatham House Briefing Paper,* January. http://www.chathamhouse.org.uk/pdf/research/niis/BPsecurity.pdf.

Griffith-Jones, Stephany, and Osvaldo Sunkel (1985). *Debt and Development Crisis in Latin America: The End of an Illusion.* Oxford: Clarendon Press.

Grogin, Robert C. (2004). *Natural Enemies: The United States and the Soviet Union in the Cold War, 1917–1991.* Lanham, MD: Lexington Books.

Guala, David (2006). *Counterinsurgency Warfare: Theory and Practice.* New York: Praeger.

Gurtov, Mel (2006). *Superpower on Crusade: The Bush Doctrine in US Foreign Policy.* Boulder, CO: Lynne Rienner Publishers.

Halliday, Fred (2000). "Transnational Paranoia and International Relations: The Case of the 'West Versus Islam.'" *The New Agenda for International Relations,* ed. S. Lawson, 37–53. Cambridge: Polity Press.

Hamilton, Keith A., and Richard Langhorne (1995). *The Practice of Diplomacy: Its Evolution, Theory, and Administration.* New York: Routledge.

Hammes, Thomas (1994). "The Evolution of War: The Fourth Generation." *Marine Corps Gazette,* September.

——— (2004). *The Sling and the Stone: On War in the 21st Century.* St. Paul, MN: Zenith.

Hardt, Michael, and Antonio Negri (2000). *Empire.* Cambridge, MA: Harvard University Press.

Harris, Jerry (2005). "To Be or Not to Be: The Nation-Centric World Under Globalization." *Science and Society* 69(3): 329–340.

Harris, Richard L., and Melinda Seid, eds. (2000). *Critical Perspectives on Globalization and Neoliberalism in the Developing Countries.* Boston: Brill.

Harrison, Graham, ed. (2004). *Global Encounters: International Political Economy, Development and Globalization.* Basingstoke: Palgrave Macmillan.

Hashim, Ahmed S. (2003). "The Sunni Insurgency in Iraq." *Middle East Institute Policy Brief,* August 15.

Held, David, and Anthony McGrew, eds. (2003). "Introduction." *The Global Transformations Reader: An Introduction to the Globalization Debate,* 2nd ed. Cambridge: Polity Press.

Helmus, Todd, et al. (2007). "Enlisting Madison Avenue: The Marketing Approach to Earning Popular Support in Theaters of Operation." *Rand Corporation*. http://www.rand.org/pubs/monographs/2007/RAND_MG607.pdf.

Herr, Donald (2008). "Changing Course: Proposals to Reverse the Militarization of US Foreign Policy." International Policy Report. *Center for International Policy*, September. http://www.ciponline.org/nationalsecurity/publications/ipr/Mil_USFP_IPR0908.pdf.

Hirsh, Michael (2004). "Bernard Lewis Revisited." *Washington Monthly* 36(11): 13–19.

Hobbs, Heidi H., ed. (2000). *Pondering Postinternationalism: A Paradigm for the Twenty-First Century?* Albany: State University of New York Press.

Hocking, Brian, ed. (1999). *Foreign Ministries: Change and Adaptation*. Basingstoke: Palgrave Macmillan.

Hocking, Brian, and David Spence, eds. (2003). *Foreign Ministries in the European Union: Integrating Diplomats*. Basingstoke: Palgrave Macmillan.

Hoekman, Bernard, and Beata Javorcik, eds. (2006). *Global Integration and Technology Transfer*. Washington, DC: World Bank.

Hoffman, David (2002). "Beyond Public Diplomacy." *Foreign Affairs* 81(2): 83–95.

Hoge, James F., and Gideon Rose, eds. (2005). *Understanding the War on Terror*. New York: Council on Foreign Relations.

Holmes, J. Anthony (2009). "Where Are the Civilians?" *Foreign Policy* (January–February): 148–160.

Homer-Dixon, Thomas (1999). *Environment, Scarcity, and Violence*. Princeton, NJ: Princeton University Press.

——— (2006a). "Five Years After." *Globe and Mail*, September 11: A-15.

——— (2006b). *The Upside of Down: Catastrophe, Creativity and the Renewal of Civilization*. Toronto: Knopf.

Homer-Dixon, Thomas, and Jessica Blitt, eds. (1998). *Ecoviolence: Links Among Environment, Population and Security*. Lanham, MD: Rowman and Littlefield.

Hudson, Rex A. (1999). "The Sociology and Psychology of Terrorism: Who Becomes a Terrorist and Why?" *Library of Congress, Federal Research Division*, September. http://www.loc.gov/rr/frd/pdf-files/Soc_Psych_of_Terrorism.pdf.

Human Security Centre (2005). *The Human Security Report 2005: War and Peace in the 21st Century*. New York: Oxford University Press.

——— (2007). "The Human Security Brief 2006." *Human Security Report Project*. http://www.humansecuritybrief.info/2006/contents/finalversion.pdf.

Humphreys, Macartan (2003). "Economics and Violent Conflict." *HPCR International*. http://www.preventconflict.org/portal/economics/Essay.pdf.

Hunter, William C., George G. Kaufman, and Thomas H. Krueger, eds. (1999). *The Asian Financial Crisis: Origins, Implications, and Solutions*. Norwell, MA: Kluwer Academic Publishers.

Huntington, Samuel P. (1991). *The Third Wave: Democratization in the Late Twentieth Century*. Norman: University of Oklahoma Press.

——— (1997). *The Clash of Civilizations and the Remaking of World Order*. New York: Simon and Schuster.

Huq, Aziz (2008), "Use It or Lose It? How to Manage an Imperial Decline." *TomDispatch*, October 16. http://www.tomdispatch.com/post/print/174990/Tomgram.

Hurrell, Andrew (2003). "Order and Justice in International Relations: What Is at Stake?" *Order and Justice in International Relations*, eds. Rosemary Foot, John Lewis Gaddis, and Andrew Hurrell, 24–48. New York: Oxford University Press.

Hurrell, Andrew, and Ngaire Woods, eds. (1999). *Inequality, Globalization and World Politics*. New York: Oxford University Press.

Husband, Jon. *Wirearchy*. http://www.wirearchy.com.

Hutton, William (2007). *The Writing on the Wall*. London: Little, Brown.

iCasualities.org. *Iraq Coalition Casualty Count*. http://icasualties.org/Iraq/index.aspx.

Ignatieff, Michael (2005). *American Exceptionalism and Human Rights*. Princeton, NJ: Princeton University Press.

Ikenberry, John G., ed. (2002). *America Unrivaled: The Future of the Balance of Power*. Ithaca, NY: Cornell University Press.

Ikenberry, John G., and Anne-Marie Slaughter (2006). "Forging a World of Liberty Under Law: U.S. National Security in the 21st Century." *Princeton Project on National Security*, September 27. http://www.princeton.edu/~ppns/report/FinalReport.pdf.

Independent Panel on Canada's Future Role in Afghanistan (2008). "Independent Panel on Canada's Future Role in Afghanistan." *Government of Canada Depository Services Program*. http://dsp-psd.pwgsc.gc.ca/collection_2008/dfait-maeci/FR5-20-1-2008E.pdf.

Industry Canada (2007). *Mobilizing Science and Technology to Canada's Advantage*. http://www.ic.gc.ca/eic/site/ic1.nsf/vwapj/S&Tstrategy.pdf/$file/S&Tstrategy.pdf.

Innis, Harold (1950). *Empire and Communications*. Oxford: Clarendon Press.

InnoCentive. *InnoCentive*. http://www.innocentive.com.

InterAcademy Council (2004a). "Inventing a Better Future: A Strategy for Building Worldwide Capacities in Science and Technology." *InterAcademy Council*. http://www.interacademycouncil.net/Object.File/Master/6/720/0.pdf.

——— (2004b). "Realizing the Promise and Potential of African Agriculture: Science and Technology Strategies for Improving Agricultural Productivity and Food Security in Africa." *InterAcademy Council*. www.interacademycouncil.net/File.aspx?id=8972.

——— (2005). "Joint Statement from International Scientific, Engineering, and Medical Organizations on UN Millennium Development Goals." *InterAcademy Council*, September. http://www.interacademycouncil.net/Object.File/Master/9/585/UN%20Statement%20(4).pdf.

Intergovernmental Panel on Climate Change. *Fourth Assessment Report: Synthesis for Policymakers*. http://www.ipcc.ch/.

International Atomic Energy Agency. *International Atomic Energy Agency*. http://www.iaea.org/index.html.

International Commission on Intervention and State Sovereignty (2001). *The Responsibility to Protect*. Ottawa: International Development Research Centre.

International Council for Science (2002–2003). "ICSU Series on Science for Sustainable Development No. 1-11." *International Council for Science*. http://www.icsu.org/2_resourcecentre/Resource.php4?rub=8&id=29.

——— (2005). "Strengthening International Science for the Benefit of Society: Strategic Plan 2006–2011." *International Council for Science*. www.iupesm.org/ICSU%20Strategic%20Plan.pdf.

International Crisis Group (2008). "Crisis Watch No. 53." *International Crisis Group*. http://www.crisisgroup.org/home/index.cfm?id=5247.

International Development Research Centre (IDRC) (2001). *The Responsibility to Protect: Report of the International Commission on Intervention and State Sovereignty*. http://www.idrc.ca/en/ev-9436-201-1-DO_TOPIC.html.

International Studies Association. *ISA Conventions and Conferences*. http://www.isanet.org/conventions.

Iraq Body Count. *Iraq Body Count*. http://www.iraqbodycount.org.

Izadi, Foad (2007). "Culture of Measurement in US Public Diplomacy." Paper presented to the International Studies Association Annual Conference, Chicago, February 28–March 3.

Jamail, Dahr. *Dahr Jamail's Mideast Dispatches*. http://www.dahrjamailiraq.com.

Japan Ministry of Education, Culture, Sports, Science and Technology (2005). "Strategic Promotion of the International Activity of Science and Technology." *Ministry of Education, Sports, Science & Technology*. http://www.mext.go.jp/english/news/2005/04/05062301.htm.

Jensen, Nathan M. (2006). *Nation-States and the Multinational Corporation: A Political Economy of Foreign Direct Investment*. Princeton, NJ: Princeton University Press.

Jervis, Robert (1994). "Hans Morgentheau, Realism, and the Study of International Politics." *Social Research* 61(4): 853–876.

Johns Hopkins Bloomberg School of Public Health (2006). "Updated Iraq Survey Affirms Earlier Mortality Estimates." *Johns Hopkins Bloomberg School of Public Health,* October 11. http://www.jhsph.edu/publichealthnews/press_releases/2006/burnham_iraq_2006.html.

Johnson, Chalmers A. (2000). *Blowback: The Costs and Consequences of American Empire*. New York: Metropolitan Books.

——— (2004). *The Sorrows of Empire: Militarism, Secrecy, and the End of the Republic*. New York: Metropolitan Books.

——— (2007). *Nemesis: The Last Days of the American Republic*. New York: Metropolitan Books.

——— (2008). "How to Sink America." *TomDispatch,* January 22. http://ww.tomdispatch.com/post/174884.

Johnson, Joe (2006). "How Does Public Diplomacy Measure Up?" *Foreign Service Journal* 83(10): 44–52.

Johnson, Thomas, and Chris Mason (2008a). "No Sign Until the Burst of Fire: Understanding the Pakistan-Afghanistan Frontier." *International Security* 32(4): 41–77.

——— (2008b) "All Counterinsurgency Is Local." *The Atlantic,* October. http://www.theatlantic.com/doc/200810/afghan.

Jones, D. (2006). "Ending the Debate: Unconventional Warfare, Foreign Internal Defense, and Why Words Matter." *Defense Technical Information Center Online*. http://www.dtic.mil/cgi-bin/GetTRDoc?AD=ADA451259&Location=U2&doc=GetTRDoc.pdf.

Jones, Lucy (2005). "Karen Hughes' 'Listening Tour' and Its Aftermath: Selling America to the Muslim World." *Washington Report,* December. http://www.wrmea.com/archives/December_2005/0512024.html.

Jones, Seth, and Martin Libicki (2008). "How Terrorist Groups End: Lessons for Countering al Qa'ida." Santa Monica: Rand Corporation. http://www.rand.org/pubs/monographs/2008/RAND_MG741-1.pdf.

Jönsson, Christer, and Martin Hall (2005). *Essence of Diplomacy*. New York: Palgrave Macmillan.

Joseph, Sarah (2003). "Pharmaceutical Corporations and Access to Drugs: The 'Fourth Wave' of Corporate Human Rights Scrutiny." *Human Rights Quarterly* 25(2): 425–452.

Jyllands-Posten (2005). "Muhammeds ansigt" (editorial cartoons). September 30: 3.

Kahl, Colin (2008). "The Other Side of the COIN: The Evolution of Counterinsurgency in Iraq." Paper presented at the International Studies Association, San Francisco, March 29.

Kaldor, Mary (2008). "New Thinking Needs New Direction." *Open Democracy,* September 25. http://www.opendemocracy.net/article/yes/kaldor/new-thinking.

Kaplan, Robert (1994). "The Coming Anarchy." *Atlantic Monthly* 273(February): 44–76.

——— (2000). *The Coming Anarchy: Shattering the Dreams of the Post–Cold War.* New York: Vintage.

——— (2005). *Imperial Grunts.* New York: Random House.

Kapstein, Ethan B. (1999). *Sharing the Wealth: Workers and the World Economy.* New York: W. W. Norton.

Kearns, Ian, and Ken Gude (2008). "The New Front Line: Security in a Changing World." *Institute for Public Policy Research,* February. http://www.ippr.org/publicationsandreports/publication.asp?id=588.

Keck, Margaret, and Kathryn Sekkink (1998). *Activists Beyond Borders: Advocacy Networks in International Politics.* Ithaca, NY: Cornell University Press.

Keller, Wolfgang (2002). "Geographic Distribution of International Technology Distribution." *American Economic Review* 92(1): 120–142.

Kelly, John Robert (2007). "Constructing Relevant Public Diplomacy Strategy for the 21st Century." Paper presented at the International Studies Association, Chicago, February 28–March 3.

Kennan, George (1946). "861.00/2-2246: Telegram. The Charge in the Soviet Union (Kennan) to the Secretary of State." *George Washington University,* February 22. http://www.gwu.edu/~nsarchiv/coldwar/documents/episode-1/kennan.htm.

Khanna, Parag (2008). *The Second World.* New York: Random House.

Khouri, Rami G. (2004). "The US Public Diplomacy Hoax." *The Daily Star,* February 11. http://ics.leeds.ac.uk/papers/vp01.cfm?outfit=pmt&folder=7&paper=1359.

Kiesling, John (2003). "Letter of Resignation to Secretary of State Colin L. Powell." *New York Times,* February 23. http://www.nytimes.com/2003/02/27/international/27WEB-TNAT.html?ex=1235970000&en=d7252afe38adb528&ei=5070.

——— (2006). *Diplomacy Lessons: Realism for an Unloved Superpower.* Dulles, VA: Potomac Books.

Kilcullen, David J. (2006). "Three Pillars of Counterinsurgency." *Maxwell-Gunter Air Force Base.* http://www.au.af.mil/au/awc/awcgate/uscoin/3pillars_of_counterinsurgency.pdf.

——— (2009). *The Accidental Guerrilla: Fighting Small Wars in the Midst of a Big One.* New York: Oxford University Press.

Kimmage, Daniel (2008). "The Al-Qaeda Media Nexus." *RFE/RL Special Report.* http://docs.rferl.org/en-US/AQ_Media_Nexus.pdf.

Kinzer, Stephen (2006). *Overthrow: America's Century of Regime Change from Hawaii to Iraq.* New York: Times Books.

Kipp, Jacob, et al. (2006). "Human Terrain Systems: A CORDS for the 21st Century." *Military Review,* September–October. http://www.army.mil/professionalwriting/volumes/volume4/december_2006/12_06_2.html.

Klein, Joe (2006). *Politics Lost: How American Democracy Was Trivialized by People Who Think You're Stupid.* New York: Doubleday.

Klein, Naomi (2000). *No Logo: Taking Aim at the Brand Bullies.* Toronto: Knopf.

——— (2007). *Shock Doctrine: The Rise of Disaster Capitalism.* Toronto: Knopf.

Koeppel, Dan (2007). "China's iClone." *Popular Science,* August. http://www.popsci.com/popsci/technology/e7e48a137b144110vgnvcm1000004eecbccdrcrd.html.

Korten, David (2006). *From Empire to Earth Community.* San Francisco: Berrett Koehler.

Kremer, Michael (2002). "Pharmaceuticals and the Developing World." *The Journal of Economic Perspectives* 16(4): 67–90.

Kuhn, T. H. (1996). *The Structure of Scientific Revolutions.* Chicago: University of Chicago Press.

Kurlantzick, Josh (2006). "China's Charm: Implications of Chinese Soft Power." *Policy Brief* no. 47. New York: Carnegie Endowment for International Peace.

——— (2008a). "Fighting Terrorism with Terrorists." *Los Angeles Times,* January 6. http://www.carnegieendowment.org/publications/index.cfm?fa=view&id=19823&prog=zgp&proj=zusr.

——— (2008b). "Flight of the Diplomats." *Mother Jones,* September–October. http://www.carnegieendowment.org/publications/index.cfm?fa=view&id=22180&prog=zgp&proj=zme,zusr.

Lal, Deepak (2006). *Reviving the Invisible Hand: The Case for Classical Liberalism in the 21st Century.* Princeton, NJ: Princeton University Press.

Lamb, Rachelle (2005). *Communication Basics: An Overview of Non-Violent Communication.* Victoria, British Columbia: Centre for Non-Violent Communication.

———. *Mindful Communication.* http://www.rachellelamb.com.

Langley, Chris (2005). "Soldiers in the Laboratory: Military Involvement in Science and Technology—and Some Alternatives." *Scientists for Global Responsibility,* January. http://www.sgr.org.uk/ArmsControl/Soldiers_in_Lab_Report.pdf.

Larson, James F. (2004). "The Internet and Foreign Policy." *Headline Series* no. 325. New York: Foreign Policy Association.

Lawrence, T. E. (1929). "Guerrilla." *Encyclopedia Britannica.* http://www.bellum.nu/literature/lawrence001.html; site now discontinued.

Lens, Sidney (1971). *The Forging of the American Empire.* New York: Cromwell.

Leonard, Mark (1998). "It's Not Just Ice-Cream [Cool Britannia]." *New Statesman* 127(4392): 15–16.

——— (2002). *Public Diplomacy.* London: Foreign Policy Center.

Levi, Michael, and Michael d'Arcy (2005). "Untapped Potential: U.S. Science and Technology Relations with the Islamic World." *Analysis Paper* no. 8. Brookings Institution, March. http://www3.brookings.edu/fp/saban/analysis/darcy20050419.pdf.

Lewis, Bernard (1990). "The Roots of Muslim Rage." *The Atlantic* 266(3): 47–60.

——— (1992). "Rethinking the Middle East." *Foreign Affairs* 71(4): 99–119.

——— (1997). "The West and the Middle East." *Foreign Affairs* 76(1): 114–130.

——— (2001). *What Went Wrong.* Oxford: Oxford University Press.

——— (2005). "Freedom and Justice in the Modern Middle East." *Foreign Affairs* 84(3): 36–51.

Lind, William (2004). "Understanding Fourth Generation War." *Antiwar,* January 14. http://www.antiwar.com/lind/index.php?articleid=1702.

Lind, William, et al. (1989). "The Changing Face of War: Into the Fourth Generation." *Military Review* (October): 2–11.

Livingston, Steven (1997). "Clarifying the CNN Effect: An Examination of Media Effects According to Type of Military Intervention." *Research Paper R-18.* http://www.hks.harvard.edu/presspol/publications/papers/research_papers/r18_livingston.pdf.

Lockhart, Clare, and Simon Maxwell (2006). "Making States Work." *Overseas Development Institute.* http://www.odi.org.uk/annual_report/ar2006/making_states_work_spread_web.pdf.

Lomborg, Bjorn (2007). *Cool It: The Sceptical Environmentalist's Guide to Global Warming.* London: Cyan and Marshall Cavendish.

Long, Austin (2006). *On Other War: Lessons from Five Decades of Rand Counterinsurgency Research.* Santa Monica: Rand Corporation. http://www.rand.org/pubs/monographs/2006/RAND_MG482.pdf.

Lord, Carnes (2006). *Losing Hearts and Minds: Public Diplomacy and Strategic Influence in the Age of Terror.* New York: Praeger.
Lord, Kristin (2008). "Voices of America: U.S. Public Diplomacy for the 21st Century." Washington, DC: Brookings Institution Press. http://www.brookings.edu/reports/2008/11_public_diplomacy_lord.aspx.
Lord, Kristin, and Vaughan Turekian (2007). "Time for a New Era in Science Diplomacy." *Science* 315(9): 769–770.
Lord Carter of Coles (2005). "Public Diplomacy Review." *Foreign and Commonwealth Office,* December. http://www.fco.gov.uk/resources/en/pdf/public-diplomacy-review.
Lu, Catherine (2007). "Humanitarian Intervention: Moral Ambition and Political Constraint." *International Journal* 62(4): 942–952.
Lucas, Scott, and Ali Fisher (2009). *Projection and Power: The Trials of Public Diplomacy.* Leiden, the Netherlands: Brill.
Lugar, Richard (2009). "U.S. Public Diplomacy—Time to Get Back in the Game." Report from Senator Richard Lugar (R-IN), Ranking Member, to Members of the Committee on Foreign Relations, United States Senate, February 13. http://lugar.senate.gov/sfrc/pdf/PublicDiplomacy.pdf.
M. S. Swaminathan Research Foundation. *The M. S. Swaminathan Research Foundation.* http://www.mssrf.org.
MacArthur, John (1993). *Second Front: Censorship and Propaganda in the 1991 Gulf War.* Berkeley: University of California Press.
Macmillan, Margaret (2001). *Paris 1919.* New York: Random House.
MacPherson, Myra (2006). *All Governments Lie: The Life and Times of Rebel Journalist I. F. Stone.* New York: Scribner.
Mahbubani, Kishore (2008a). "The Case Against the West." *Foreign Affairs* (May–June).
——— (2008b). *The New Asian Hemisphere: The Irresistible Shift of Global Power to the East.* New York: Public Affairs.
Mansbach, Richard (2000). "Changing Understandings of Global Politics: Preinternationalism, Internationalism, and Postinternationalism." *Pondering Postinternationalism: A Paradigm for the Twenty-First Century?,* ed. Heidi H. Hobbs, 7–24. Albany: State University of New York Press.
Marburger, John (2005). "Science and Technology Policy Towards the Islamic World." Remarks delivered at the Brookings Institution, Washington DC, January 4. http://www.ostp.gov/pdf/jhmbrookingsstislamicworld.pdf.
Marden, Peter (2003). *The Decline of Politics: Governance, Globalization and the Public Sphere.* Burlington, VT: Ashgate.
Marks, Alexandra (2007). "A New Push for Change in the War on Terror." *Christian Science Monitor,* August 22: 3. http://www.csmonitor.com/2007/0822/p03s03-usmi.html.
Marshall, Peter (1999). *Positive Diplomacy.* Basingstoke: Palgrave Macmillan.
Marshall, Peter, and Nabil Ayad, eds. (1996). *Are Diplomats Really Necessary?* London: Marylebone.
——— (1997). *The Information Explosion: A Challenge for Diplomacy.* London: Marylebone.
Marston, Daniel, and Carter Malkasian, eds. (2008). *Counterinsurgency in Modern Warfare.* New York: Osprey Publishing.
Maswood, Javed (2000). *International Political Economy and Globalization.* Hackensack, NJ: World Scientific Publishing.
Mau, Bruce (2004). *Massive Change.* London: Phaidon Press.

Maybury, Mark (2008). "Trends in New Media." *Local Voices/Global Perspectives*, ed. Alan Heil. Washington, DC: Public Diplomacy Council.

Mayer, Jane (2008). *The Dark Side: The Inside Story of How the War on Terror Turned into a War on American Ideals.* New York: Doubleday.

McKibben, Bill (2009). "Climate Change." *Foreign Policy* (January–February): 32–38.

McLuhan, Marshall (1964). *Understanding Media: The Extensions of Man*. New York: McGraw-Hill.

McLuhan, Marshall, and Bruce R. Powers (1989). *The Global Village: Transformations in World Life and Media in the 21st Century.* New York: Oxford University Press.

McMaster, H. R. (2008). "On War: Lessons to Be Learned." *Survival* 50(1): 19–30.

Meadows, Donna H., Jorgen Randers, and Dennis Meadows (2004). *Limits to Growth: The 30 Year Update.* White River Junction, VT: Chelsea Green Publishers.

Melissen, Jan (2007). "Wielding Soft Power: The New Public Diplomacy." *Clingendael Diplomacy Papers* no. 2. The Hague: Netherlands Institute of International Relations/Clingendael.

———, ed. (2007). *The New Public Diplomacy.* Basingstoke: Palgrave Macmillan.

Melissen, Jan, and Paul Sharp (2007). "Special Issue on Public Diplomacy." *The Hague Journal of Diplomacy* 2(3).

Mendes, Errol, and Mehmet Ozay (2003). *Global Governance, Economy and Law: Waiting for Justice.* London: Routledge.

Metz, B., et al., eds. (2007). "Climate Change 2007: Mitigation." *Contribution of Working Group III to the Fourth Assessment Report of the Intergovernmental Panel on Climate Change.* Cambridge: Cambridge University Press.

Meyerson, Harold (2004). "Wal-Mart Loves Unions (in China)." *Washington Post,* December 1: A25. http://www.washingtonpost.com/wp-dyn/articles/A23725-2004Nov30.html.

Milanovic, Branko (2005). *Worlds Apart: Measuring International and Global Inequality*. Princeton, NJ: Princeton University Press.

Miliband, David (2007). "Europe 2030: Model Power Not Superpower." Address to the College of Europe, Bruges, November 15. www.Brugesgroup.com/miliband brugesspeech.pdf.

——— (2008). "Stand by for Our Diplomatic Surge." *Sunday Times,* January 6. http://www.timesonline.co.uk/tol/comment/columnists/guest_contributors/article3137534.ece.

Milton-Edwards, Beverley, and Alistair Crooke (2004). "Should We Talk to Political Islam?" *Re-imagining Security,* ed. Rosemary Bechler, 10–23. London: British Council.

Miniwatts Marketing Group. "Internet Usage Statistics for Africa." *Internet World Stats.* http://www.internetworldstats.com/stats1.htm.

Mirovitskaya, Natalia, and William Ascher, eds. (2002). *Guide to Sustainable Development*. Durham, NC: Duke University Press.

Mittelman, James H., and Norani Othman, eds. (2001). *Capturing Globalization.* New York: Routledge.

"Montreal Protocol on Substances That Deplete the Ozone Layer." September 16, 1987. *United Nations Treaty Series* 1522, no. 26369: 3.

Moore, Sean. *Sean Moore*. http://www.seanmoore.ca/.

Moore, Barrington, Jr. (1966). *Social Origins of Dictatorship and Democracy: Lord and Peasant in the Making of the Modern World.* Boston: Beacon.

Morgan, Jon (2001). "Fanatical, Yes, but Not Insane." *Baltimore Sun,* September 19: A2.

Morgenthau, Hans (1965). "We Are Deluding Ourselves in Vietnam." *New York Times Magazine,* April 18. http://www.mtholyoke.edu/acad/intrel/vietnam/hans'.htm.

——— ([1948] 2005). *Politics Among Nations: The Struggle for Power and Peace.* New York: McGraw-Hill.

Moses, Jonathon, and Torbjorn Knutson (2001). "Inside Out: Globalization and the Reorganization of Foreign Affairs Ministries." *Discussion Papers in Diplomacy.* London: Sage.

Mullen, James, et al. (1999). *Science, Technology, and Innovation in Chile.* Ottawa: International Development Research Centre. http://www.idrc.ca/openebooks/315-1.

Muller-Wille, Bjorn (2002). "EC Intelligence Cooperation: A Critical Analysis." *Contemporary Security Policy* 23(2): 61–86.

Multi-National Force–Iraq (2008). *Commander's Counterinsurgency Guidance,* June 21. http://www.mnf-iraq.com/images/CGs_Messages/080621_coin_%20guidance.pdf.

Munk Centre for International Studies at the University of Toronto. *CitizenLab.* http://www.citizenlab.org.

Nagl, John (2005). *Learning to Eat Soup with a Knife: Counterinsurgency Lessons from Malaya and Vietnam.* Chicago: University of Chicago Press.

Naidu, Ravi, et al., eds. (2006). *Managing Arsenic in the Environment: From Soil to Human Health.* Collingwood, Victoria: CSIRO Publishing.

National Commission on Terrorist Attacks Upon the United States (2004). *The 9/11 Commission Report.* http://www.9-11commission.gov/report/911Report.pdf.

National Defence Canada (2006). *A Soldier's Guide to Army Transformation.* http://www.army.forces.gc.ca/lf/English/5_4_1.asp.

National Research Council (1999). *The Pervasive Role of Science, Technology, and Health in Foreign Policy: Imperatives for the Department of State.* Washington, DC: Committee on Science, Technology, and Health Aspects of the Foreign Policy Agenda of the United States. http://www.nap.edu/catalog.php?record_id=9688#toc.

——— (2006). *The Fundamental Role of Science and Technology in International Development: An Imperative for the U.S. Agency for International Development.* Washington, DC: Committee on Science and Technology in Foreign Assistance.

National Security Council (1950). *NSC 68: United States Objectives and Programs for National Security,* April 14. http://www.fas.org/irp/offdocs/nsc-hst/nsc-68.htm.

Nef, Jorge (1999). *Human Security and Mutual Vulnerability: The Global Political Economy of Development and Underdevelopment.* Ottawa: International Development Research Centre. http://www.idrc.ca/openebooks/288-0/.

Negroponte, Nicolas. *One Laptop per Child.* http://laptop.org/en/.

Netherlands Institute of International Relations/Clingendael. *Clingendael.* http://www.clingendael.nl.

——— (2008). "Literature on Public Diplomacy." *Clingendael.* http://www.clingendael.nl/library/literature/public-diplomacy.pdf.

"The New Titans: A Survey of the World Economy" (2006). *The Economist* 380(8495): 3–8.

New Zealand Ministry of Foreign Affairs and Trade (2006). *Public Diplomacy Handbook.* Wellington: MFAT.

Niblock, Thomas (2006). "The Virtual Presence Post: Transforming Our Diplomatic Tool Kit." July 26. http://tonga.usvpp.gov/.

Nicolson, Sir Harold George (1980). *Diplomacy,* 3rd ed. London: Oxford University Press.

Nossal, Kim Richard (2007). "Right and Wrong in Foreign Policy 40 Years On: Realism and Idealism in Canadian Foreign Policy." *International Journal* 62(2): 263–278.

Nye, Joseph (1990). *Bound to Lead: The Changing Nature of American Power.* New York: Basic Books.

——— (2002). *The Paradox of American Power: Why the World's Only Superpower Can't Go It Alone.* Oxford: Oxford University Press.

——— (2004a). *Power in the Global Information Age: From Realism to Globalization.* New York: Routledge.

——— (2004b). *Soft Power: The Means to Success in World Politics.* New York: Public Affairs.

——— (2004c). "The Decline of American Soft Power." *Foreign Affairs* 83(3): 16–20.

——— (2005). "The Rise of China's Soft Power." *Wall Street Journal Asia,* December 29. http://belfercenter.ksg.harvard.edu/publication/1499/rise_of_chinas_soft_power.html.

——— (2006). "Global Opinion: The Spread of Anti-Americanism." *Trends 2005.* Washington, DC: Pew Research Center.

——— (2009) "The U.S. Can Reclaim Smart Power." *Los Angeles Times,* January 21. http://www.latimes.com/news/opinion/commentary/la-oe-nye21-2009jan21,0,3381521.story.

Office of the Auditor General (2007). "Human Resources Management—Foreign Affairs and International Trade Canada." *Office of the Auditor General,* May. http://www.oag-bvg.gc.ca/internet/English/mr_20070501_e_15413.html.

O'Reilly, Terry (2007). "The Age of Persuasion." *CBC Radio One,* April 19.

Organization for Economic Cooperation and Development (2004). "Science, Technology and Innovation for the 21st Century—Meeting of the OECD Committee for Scientific and Technological Policy at Ministerial Level." *Organization for Economic Cooperation and Development,* January 30. http://www.oecd.org/document/0,2340,en_2649_34487_25998799_1_1_1_1,00.html.

——— (2006). "China Will Become World's Second Highest Investor in R&D by End of 2006, Finds OECD." *Organization for Economic Cooperation and Development,* April 12. http://www.oecd.org/document/26/0,3343,en_2649_34451_37770522_1_1_1_1,00.html.

Osterholm, Michael (2007). "Unprepared for a Pandemic." *Foreign Affairs* 86(2): 47–58.

Overseas Development Institute (2008a). "Pro-Poor Growth and Development." *Briefing Paper 33,* January. http://www.odi.org.uk/resources/odi-publications/briefing-papers/33-pro-poor-growth-development.pdf.

——— (2008b). "Supporting Pro-Poor Growth Processes: Implications for Donors." *Briefing Paper 34,* January. http://www.odi.org.uk/resources/odi-publications/briefing-papers/34-pro-poor-growth-processes-donors.pdf.

——— (2008c). "The Political Economy of Pro-Poor Growth." *Briefing Paper 35,* January. http://www.odi.org.uk/resources/odi-publications/briefing-papers/34-pro-poor-growth-processes-donors.pdf.

Packer, George (2006). "Knowing the Enemy." *New Yorker,* December 18. http://www.newyorker.com/archive/2006/12/18/061218fa_fact2.

"The Paradoxes of Counterinsurgency" (2006). *New York Times,* October 5. http://www.nytimes.com/imagepages/2006/10/05/world/20061005_Doctrine_Graphic.html.

Paris, Roland (2004). *At War's End: Building Peace After Civil Conflict.* Cambridge: Cambridge University Press.

Patman, Robert, ed. (2006). *Globalization and Conflict: National Security in a New Strategic Era.* London: Routledge.

Patomaki, Heikki (2001). *Democratizing Globalization: The Leverage of the Tobin Tax*. London: Zed Books.

Paul, Christopher (2009). *Whither Strategic Communication: A Survey of Current Proposals and Recommendations*. Occasional Paper. Santa Monica: Rand Corporation. http://www.rand.org/pubs/occasional_papers/2009/RAND_OP250.pdf.

Pelton, Robert (2007). *Licensed to Kill: Hired Guns in the War on Terror*. New York: Three Rivers Press.

Pew Research Center (2003). "America's Image Further Erodes: Europeans Want Weaker Ties but Post-War Iraq Will Be Better Off, Most Say." *The Pew Research Center for the People and the Press*, March 18. http://people-press.org/reports/display.php3?ReportID=175.

——— (2004). "A Year After Iraq War: Mistrust of America in Europe Ever Higher, Muslim Anger Persists." *The Pew Research Center for the People and the Press*, March 16. http://people-press.org/reports/display.php3?ReportID=206.

——— (2006). *Conflicting Views in a Divided World*. http://pewglobal.org/reports/pdf/DividedWorld2006.pdf.

———. *Pew Global Attitudes Project*. http://pewglobal.org.

Pfeffermann, Guy (2002). "The Eight Losers of Globalization." *The Globalist*, April 19. http://www.theglobalist.com/StoryId.aspx?StoryId=2429.

Phares, Walid (2008). *The War of Ideas: Jihadism Against Democracy*. Basingstoke: Palgrave.

Pickering, Thomas R., and Chester A. Crocker (2008). *America's Role in the World: Foreign Policy Choices for the Next President*. Washington, DC: Georgetown University Institute for the Study of Diplomacy. http://isd.georgetown.edu/Americas_Role_in_the_World.pdf.

Pitt, William Rivers (2009). "The Greatest Greatness of George W. Bush." *Truthout*, January 7. http://www.truthout.org/010709J.

Pollin, Robert, and Heidi Garrett-Peltier (2008). "The Wages of Peace." *The Nation*, March 31. http://www.thenation.com/doc/20080331/pollin.

Porch, Douglas (1995). *The French Secret Services: From the Dreyfus Affair to the Gulf War*. New York: Farrar, Straus and Giroux.

Posen, Barry, and Andrew Ross (1996–1997). "Competing Visions for U.S. Grand Strategy." *International Security* 21(3): 5–53.

Postman, Neil (1986). *Amusing Ourselves to Death: Public Discourse in the Age of Show Business*. New York: Penguin.

Potter, Evan. (2009). *Branding Canada: Projecting Canada's Soft Power Through Public Diplomacy*. Montreal: McGill-Queen's University Press.

———, ed. (2002). *Cyber-Diplomacy*. Montreal: McGill-Queen's University Press.

Power, Samantha (2008). *Chasing the Flame: Sergio Vieira de Mello and the Fight to Save the World*. New York: Penguin.

Prebisch, Raul (1962). *The Economic Development of Latin America and Its Principal Problems*. New York: United Nations Press.

Preble, Christopher A. (2004). *John F. Kennedy and the Missile Gap*. DeKalb: Northern Illinois University Press.

The Professional Association of Foreign Service Officers. *The Professional Association of Foreign Service Officers*. http://pafso.com/index2.cfm.

The Project for the New American Century. *The Project for the New American Century*. http://www.newamericancentury.org.

Pugh, Michael (2007). "Normative Values and Economic Deficits in Postconflict Transformation." *International Journal* 62(3): 479–494.

Pugwash Conferences. *Pugwash Online: Conferences on Science and World Affairs.* http://www.pugwash.org.

Putnam, Robert D. (2000). *Bowling Alone: The Collapse and Revival of American Community.* New York: Simon and Schuster.

Radu, Michael (2002). "The Futile Search for the Root Causes of Terrorism." *Foreign Policy Research Institute,* April 23. http://www.fpri.org/enotes/americawar.20020423.radu.futilesearchforrootcauses.html.

Ramo, Joshua Cooper (2004). "The Beijing Consensus." *The Foreign Policy Centre,* May 11. http://fpc.org.uk/fsblob/244.pdf.

——— (2007). "Brand China." *The Foreign Policy Centre,* February. http://fpc.org.uk/fsblob/827.pdf.

Rana, K., and J. Kurbalija, eds. (2007). *Foreign Ministries: Managing Diplomatic Networks and Optimizing Value.* Geneva: Diplo Books.

RAND Corporation. "Worldwide Terrorism Incident Database." *RAND Corporation.* http://www.rand.org/ise/projects/terrorismdatabase/index.html.

Rashid, Ahmed (2008). *Descent into Chaos: The United States and the Failure of Nation-Building in Pakistan, Afghanistan and Central Asia.* New York: Viking.

Raven, Peter H., and Linda R. Berg (2006). *Environment.* Weinheim, Germany: Wiley-VCH.

Record, Jeffery (2005). "The Limits and Temptations of America's Conventional Military Primacy." *Survival* 47(1): 33–49.

Rice, Condoleezza (2006). "Transformational Diplomacy." Address delivered at Georgetown University, January 18.

Richmond, Yale (2003). *Cultural Exchange and the Cold War: Raising the Iron Curtain.* University Park: Pennsylvania State University Press.

Riordan, Shaun (2003). *The New Diplomacy.* London: Polity Press.

——— (2004). "Dialogue-Based Public Diplomacy: A New Foreign Policy Paradigm?" *Discussion Papers in Diplomacy* no. 95. The Hague: Netherlands Institute of International Relations/Clingendael.

——— (2007). "Reforming Foreign Services for the Twenty-First Century." *The Hague Journal of Diplomacy* 2(2): 161–173.

Robb, John C. (2007). *Brave New War: The Next Stage of Terrorism and the End of Globalization.* Hoboken, NJ: Wiley.

Robertson, Raymond (2004). "Relative Prices and Wage Inequality: Evidence from Mexico." *Journal of International Economics* 64(2): 387–409.

Rockefeller Foundation (2006). *New Conceptions, New Directions.* http://www.rockfound.org/about_us/news/2006/111006conceptions_directions.pdf.

Rodrik, Dani (2003). "Has Globalization Gone Too Far?" *The Global Transformations Reader: An Introduction to the Globalization Debate,* 2nd ed., eds. Anthony Held and David McGrew, 379–383. Malden, MA: Polity Press.

Rogers, Paul (2002). "Political Violence and Global Order." *Worlds in Collision: Terror and the Future of World Order,* eds. Ken Booth and Tim Dunne, 215–225. New York: Palgrave Macmillan.

——— (2007). *Why We're Losing the War on Terror.* Cambridge: Polity Press.

Rome Statute of the International Criminal Court (1998). U.N. Doc. A/CONF.183/9. July 17.

Rosenau, James (2003). *Distant Proximities: Dynamics Beyond Globalization.* Princeton, NJ: Princeton University Press.

Rosenberg, Marshall (2003). *Non-Violent Communication: A Language of Life.* Chicago: Puddledancer Press.

Ross, Carne (2007). *Independent Diplomat.* London: Hurst.

Rotberg, Robert I. (2003). *When States Fail: Causes and Consequences*. Princeton, NJ: Princeton University Press.

——— (2004). "Weak and Failing States: Critical New Security Issues." *Turkish Policy Quarterly* 3(2): 57–69.

Rudolph, Christopher (2003). "Security and the Political Economy of International Migration." *American Political Science Review* 97(4): 603–620.

Rugh, William A. (2009). "Repairing American Public Diplomacy." *Arab Media & Society* 7. http://www.arabmediasociety.com/?article=709.

Rumsfeld, Donald (2002). "Transforming the Military." *Foreign Affairs* 81(3): 20–32.

Rupert, Mark, and M. Scott Solomon (2005). *Globalization and International Political Economy: The Politics of Alternative Futures*. Lanham, MD: Rowman and Littlefield.

Sachs, Jeffrey (2004). "Welcome to the Asian Century: By 2050, China and Maybe India Will Overtake the U.S. Economy in Size." *Fortune,* January 12. http://money.cnn.com/magazines/fortune/fortune_archive/2004/01/12/357912/index.htm.

——— (2005). *The End of Poverty: Economic Possibilities for Our Time*. New York: Penguin.

——— (2008). *Common Wealth: Economics for a Crowded Planet*. New York: Penguin.

Sageman, Mark (2004). *Understanding Terror Networks*. Philadelphia: University of Pennsylvania Press.

——— (2008). *Leaderless Jihad: Terror Networks in the Twenty-First Century*. Philadelphia: University of Pennsylvania Press.

Said, Edward (1978). *Orientalism*. New York: Pantheon.

——— (2002). "Impossible Histories: Why the Many Islams Cannot Be Simplified." *Harper's Magazine* 305(1826): 69–75.

Sandbrook, Richard, ed. (2003). *Civilizing Globalization: A Survival Guide*. Albany: State University of New York Press.

Sanderson, Thomas, David Gordon, and Guy Ben-Ari (2008). *International Collaborative Online Networks: Lessons Identified from the Public, Private, and Nonprofit Sectors*. Washington, DC: Center for Strategic and International Studies.

Sands, Philippe (2005). *Lawless World: America and the Making and Breaking of Global Rules from FDR's Atlantic Charter to George W. Bush's Illegal War*. New York: Viking.

Sanger, David (2009). *The Inheritance: The World Obama Confronts and the Challenges to American Power*. New York: Harmony Books.

Satow, Sir Ernest (1979). *Guide to Diplomatic Practice*. London: Longmans.

Saul, John Ralston (2004). "Projecting a Middle Power into an Imperial World." John W. Holmes Memorial Lecture, Glendon College, Toronto, February 25. http://www.gg.ca/media/doc.asp?lang=e&DocID=4399.

——— (2005). *The Collapse of Globalism and the Reinvention of the World*. Toronto: Viking.

Scahill, Jeremy (2007). *Blackwater: The Rise of the World's Most Powerful Mercenary Army*. New York: Nation Books.

Scharpf, Fritz (2003). "Globalization and the Political Economy of Capitalist Democracies." *The Global Transformations Reader: An Introduction to the Globalization Debate,* 2nd ed., eds. Anthony Held and David McGrew, 370–378. Malden, MA: Polity Press.

Schell, Jonathan (1982). *The Fate of the Earth*. New York: Knopf.

Scholte, Jan Aart (2005). *Globalization: A Critical Introduction*, 2nd ed. New York: Palgrave Macmillan.

Schur, Michael (2004). *Imperial Hubris: Why the West Is Losing the Global War on Terror.* Dulles, VA: Potomac Books.

Schweitzer, Glenn E. (1989). *Techno-Diplomacy: U.S.-Soviet Confrontations in Science and Technology.* New York: Plenum Press.

Second Life. *Second Life.* http://secondlife.com.

Sen, Amartya (2006). *Identity and Violence: The Illusion of Destiny.* New York: W. W. Norton.

Sennholz, Hans (2002). "Deep in Debt, Deep in Danger." *Ludwig Von Mises Institute,* May 24. http://www.mises.org/story/967.

Shah, Anup (2008). "World Military Spending." *Global Issues,* March 1. http://www.globalissues.org/article/75/world-military-spending.

Sharp, Paul (1997). "Who Needs Diplomats? The Problem of Diplomatic Representation." *Diplomacy* 3: 58–78.

——— (1999). "For Diplomacy: Representation and the Study of International Relations." *International Studies Review* 1(1): 33–57.

Sharp, Paul, and Geoff Wiseman, eds. (2008). *The Diplomatic Corps as an Institution of International Society.* New York: Palgrave Macmillan.

Sheehan, Neil (1988). *Bright Shining Lie: John Paul Vann and America in Vietnam.* New York: Random House.

Shishani, Murad al- (2006). "Al-Zawahiri Addresses Reform in Muslim World." *Terrorism Focus* 3(3): 2–3.

Shulsky, Abram, and Gary Schmitt (2005). *Silent Warfare: Understanding the World of Intelligence.* Dulles, VA: Potomac Books.

Siddiqui, Haroon (2006). *Being Muslim.* Toronto: Groundwood Books.

Sindermann, Carl J. (2006). *Coastal Pollution: Effects on Living Resources and Humans.* Boca Raton, FL: CRC Press.

Singer, P. W. (2007). *Corporate Warriors: The Rise of the Privatized Military Industry,* updated ed. Ithaca, NY: Cornell University Press.

Singer, Peter (2007). "Put Science at the Centre of CIDA's Agenda." *National Post,* April 26: A-23.

Slaughter, Anne-Marie (2004). *A New World Order.* Princeton, NJ: Princeton University Press.

——— (2009). "America's Edge: Power in the Networked Century." *Foreign Affairs* (January–February): 94–113.

Slavin, Barbara (2005). "Hughes Embarks on 'Listening Tour' to Patch U.S. Image." *USA Today,* September 22. http://www.usatoday.com/news/world/2005-09-22-hughes-listening-tour_x.htm.

Smith, Rupert (2005). *The Utility of Force: The Art of War in the Modern World.* London: Allen Lane.

Smith, Steve (2002). "The End of the Unipolar Moment? September 11th and the Future of World Order." *International Relations* 16(2): 171–183.

Snow, Nancy. *Dr. Nancy Snow: American Persuasion, Influence, and Propaganda.* http://www.nancysnow.com.

Snow, Nancy, and Phil Taylor, eds. (2008). *The Routledge Handbook of Public Diplomacy.* New York: Routledge.

Soros, George (1998). *The Crisis of Global Capitalism: Open Society Endangered.* New York: Public Affairs.

——— (2006). *The Age of Fallibility: The Consequences of the War on Terror.* New York: Public Affairs.

Sosale, Sujartha (2003). "Envisioning a New World Order Through Journalism: Lessons from Recent History." *Journalism* 4(3): 377–392.

St. Thomas University School of Law. *Diplomacy Monitor.* http://www.diplomacymonitor.com/stu/dm.nsf/infoinetdiplo?OpenForm.

Stairs, Denis (2007). "Intellectual on Watch: James Eayrs and the Study of Foreign Policy and International Affairs." *International Journal* 62(2): 215–240.

Stålenheim, Petter, Damien Fruchart, Wuyi Omitoogun, and Catalina Perdomo (2006). "Military Expenditure." *Stockholm International Peace Research Institute Yearbooks*. http://yearbook2006.sipri.org/chap8.

Statistics Canada (2006). "Causes of Death 2003." *Statistics Canada.* http://www.statcan.ca/english/freepub/84-208-XIE/2005002/tables.htm.

Steans, Jill (2003). "Globalization and Gendered Inequality." *The Global Transformations Reader: An Introduction to the Globalization Debate,* 2nd ed., eds. Anthony Held and David McGrew, 455–462. Malden, MA: Polity Press.

Stein, Josephine Anne (2002). "Introduction: Globalisation, Science, Technology and Policy." *Science and Public Policy* 29(6): 402–408.

Steinbock, Dan (2007). "New Innovation Challengers: The Rise of China and India." *The National Interest* (January–February): 67–73.

Steingart, Gabor (2008). *The War for Wealth: The True Story of Globalization, or Why the Flat World Is Broken.* New York: McGraw-Hill.

Stewart, Rory (2006). *The Places in Between.* Fort Washington, PA: Harvest Books.

Stiglitz, Joseph (2002). *Globalization and Its Discontents.* New York: W. W. Norton.

——— (2006). *Making Globalization Work.* New York: W. W. Norton.

Stockholm International Peace Research Institute. *Stockholm International Peace Research Institute.* http://www.sipri.org.

Strachan, Hew (2008). "Strategy and the Limitation of War." *Survival* 50(1): 31–54.

Strange, Susan (1996). *The Retreat of the State: The Diffusion of Power in the World Economy.* Cambridge: Cambridge University Press.

Sullivan, Patricia L. (2007). "War Aims and War Outcomes: Why Powerful States Lose Limited Wars." *Journal of Conflict Resolution* 51(3): 496–524.

Swaminathan, M. S. (2001). "Now for the Evergreen Revolution." *For a Change,* August–September. http://www.forachange.co.uk/browse/1712.html.

Taber, Robert (2002). *War of the Flea: The Classic Study of Guerrilla Warfare.* Dulles, VA: Potomac Books.

Tapscott, Don (2009). *Grown Up Digital: How the Net Generation Is Changing Your World.* Toronto: McGraw-Hill.

Tapscott, Don, and Anthony Williams (2006). *Wikinomics.* Toronto: Portfolio. http://www.wikinomics.com.

Taylor, Charles (1974). *Snow Job: Canada, the United States and Vietnam (1954–1973).* Toronto: Anansi.

Taylor, Phil (1997). *Global Communications, International Affairs and Media Since 1945.* London: Routledge.

———. *Phil Taylor's Web Site.* http://129.11.188.64/papers/index.cfm?outfit=pmt.

Technorati. "State of the Blogosphere." *Technorati.* http://www.technorati.com/blogging/state-of-the-blogosphere.

TED. *TED.* http://www.ted.com/index.php/talks/list.

Teilhard de Chardin, Pierre (1965). *The Phenomenon of Man.* Trans. Bernard Wall. New York: Harper and Row.

Third World Academy of Sciences (2004). *Building Scientific Capacity: A TWAS Perspective.* www.ictp.trieste.it/~twas/pdf/CapBuildReport.pdf.

Thomas, Caroline (2001). "Developing Inequality: A Global Fault-Line." *The New Agenda for International Relations: From Polarization to Globalization in World Politics,* ed. S. Lawson, 71–90. Malden, MA: Polity Press.

Thompson, Sir Robert (1966). *Defeating Communist Insurgency: The Lessons of Malaya and Vietnam.* New York: Praeger.

Tiedeman, Anna (2005). "Branding America: An Examination of U.S. Public Diplomacy Efforts After September 11, 2001." *The Fletcher School at Tufts University.* http://fletcher.tufts.edu/research/2005/Tiedeman.pdf.

Todorov, Tzvetan (2005). *The New World Disorder: Reflections of a European.* Cambridge: Polity Press.

Tomes, Robert (2005). "Schlock and Blah: Counter-insurgency Realities in a Rapid Dominance Era." *Small Wars and Insurgencies* 16(1): 37–56.

Treasury Board Canada (2004–2005). "DPR 2004–2005: Department of Foreign Affairs and International Trade." *Treasury Board of Canada.* http://www.tbs-sct.gc.ca/rma/dpr1/04-05/FAC-AEC/FAC-AECd4501_e.asp.

"Treaty on the Non-Proliferation of Nuclear Weapons" (July 1, 1968). *United Nations Treaty Series* 729, no. 10485: 161.

Trinquier, Roger (2006). *Modern Warfare: A French View of Counterinsurgency.* New York: Praeger.

Tulchin, Joseph S., and Gary Bland (2005). *Getting Globalization Right: The Dilemmas of Inequality.* Boulder, CO: Lynne Rienner Publishers.

Turse, Nick (2008). "The Trillion Dollar Tag Sale: How the Pentagon Could Help Bail Out America." *TomDispatch,* October 26. http://www.tomdispatch.com/post/174994.

Uchitelle, Louis (2006). *The Disposable American: Layoffs and Their Consequences.* New York: Knopf.

UK House of Commons (2005). "Oral Evidence Taken Before the Home Affairs Committee." *Parliament Publications and Records,* October 11. http://www.publications.parliament.uk/pa/cm200506/cmselect/cmhaff/515/5101101.htm.

UN (1992). "Agenda 21: The Rio Declaration on Environment and Development, and the Statement of Principles for the Sustainable Management of Forests." *UN Department of Economic and Social Affairs: Division for Sustainable Development.* http://www.un.org/esa/sustdev/documents/agenda21/index.htm.

——— (2000). *United Nations Millennium Declaration.* http://www.un.org/millennium/declaration/ares552e.htm.

——— (2004). *A More Secure World: Our Shared Responsibility—Report of the High-level Panel on Threats, Challenges and Change.* New York: United Nations Press.

———. *Gateway to the UN System's Work on Climate Change.* http://www.un.org/climatechange.

UN Conference on Trade and Development (2003). "Science and Technology Diplomacy Initiative: Policy Dialogue on GMO Adoption and Trade—Policy Options for Developing Countries." Conference held July 18. Geneva, Switzerland.

——— (2007–2008). *Information Economy Report 2007–2008.* http://www.unctad.org/en/docs/sdteecb20071_en.pdf.

——— (2008). "Science and Technology for Development: The New Paradigm of ICT." *UNCTAD Information Economy Report 2007–2008.* http://r0.unctad.org/ecommerce/ecommerce_en/ier07_en.htm.

———. "Foreign Direct Investment." *UNCTAD.* http://www.unctad.org/Templates/StartPage.asp?intItemID=2527&lang=1.

———. *StDev.* http://stdev.unctad.org/themes/ict/docs.html.

UN Development Programme (1995). *Human Development Report 1994.* New York: Oxford University Press.

———. *Human Development Reports.* http://hdr.undp.org/en.

UN Economic and Social Council (2006). "Bridging the Technology Gap Between and Within Nations." *Commission on Science and Technology for Development.* Ninth Session, May 15–19.

UN General Assembly, Fiftieth Session (1996). *Comprehensive Nuclear-Test-Ban Treaty.* September 10. Doc. A/50/1027. http://www.ctbto.org/fileadmin/content/treaty/treaty_text.pdf.

UN Millennium Project (2005). *Innovation: Applying Knowledge in Development.* London: Earthscan. http://www.unmillenniumproject.org/documents/Science-complete.pdf.

University of East London. *Global Systems and Policy Design for the European Research Area (GLOSPERA).* http://www.uel.ac.uk/ssmcs/research/funded_projects/glospera.htm.

University of Southern California. *USC Center on Public Diplomacy.* http://uscpublicdiplomacy.com/index.php.

University of Southern California (2009). "New President. New Public Diplomacy?" *PD Magazine* (Winter). www.publicdiplomacymagazine.org.

"U.S., France Open Skies Paves Way for SkyTeam Immunity" (2001). *Aviation Daily* 346(15): 3.

US Army Field Manual 3-07 (2008). *Stability Operations,* October. http://www.fas.org/irp/doddir/army/fm3-07.pdf.

US Army Field Manual 3-24 (2006). *Counterinsurgency,* June. http://www.fas.org/irp/doddir/army/fm3-24fd.pdf.

US Department of Defense (2003). *Information Operations Roadmap,* October 30. https://scholarsbank.uoregon.edu/xmlui/bitstream/handle/1794/2169/27_01_06_psyops.pdf?sequence=1.

US Department of Energy. *Energy Information Administration.* http://www.eia.doe.gov.

US Department of State (2000). "Science and Foreign Policy: The Role of the Department of State." *Report of the Senior Task Force on Strengthening Science at State,* March 28. http://www.state.gov/www/global/oes/science/000328_dos_science_rpt.html.

——— (2002). *World Military Expenditures and Arms Transfers 1999–2000.* http://www.state.gov/t/vci/rls/rpt/wmeat/1999_2000.

——— (2006). "Counter-insurgency in the 21st Century—Creating a National Framework." *Bureau of Political-Military Affairs,* September 11. http://www.au.af.mil/au/awc/awcgate/state/72027.htm.

——— (2007). "American Presence Post, Busan, Korea." http://busan.usconsulate.gov/102_2007.html.

———. "Introduction to the Civilian Response Corps." *Office of the Coordinator for Reconstruction and Stabilization.* http://www.crs.state.gov/index.cfm?fuseaction=public.display&shortcut=4QRB.

———. *Office of eDiplomacy.* http://www.state.gov/m/irm/c23839.htm.

———. *Office of the Science and Technology Advisor.* http://www.state.gov/g/stas.

———. *Open Skies Agreements.* http://www.state.gov/e/eeb/tra/ata/.

———. *Open Skies Partners.* http://www.state.gov/e/eeb/rls/othr/ata/114805.htm.

US General Accounting Office (2003). "U.S. Public Diplomacy: State Department Expands Efforts but Faces Significant Challenges." *GAO Report GAO-03-951,* September 4. http://www.publicdiplomacy.org/21.htm.

——— (2007). *Actions Needed to Improve Strategic Use and Coordination of Research.* http://www.gao.gov/highlights/d07904high.pdf.

US Institute of Peace. "Virtual Diplomacy." *United States Institute of Peace.* http://www.usip.org/virtualdiplomacy/index.html.

US Office of the Director of National Intelligence (2006). "Trends in Global Terrorism: Implications for the United States." *Declassified Key Judgments of the National Intelligence Estimate,* April.

US Office of Management and the Budget (2006). "Program Assessment: Public Diplomacy." *Expect More.* http://www.whitehouse.gov/omb/expectmore/summary/10004600.2006.html.

US Senate (2008). "A Reliance on Smart Power: Reforming the Public Diplomacy Bureaucracy." *Committee on Homeland Security and Government Affairs, Sub-Committee on Oversight of Government Management,* September 23. http://hsgac.senate.gov/public/index.cfm?FuseAction=Hearings.Detail&HearingID=be7d1e94-9621-40bf-93ca-fa9910fafd78.

US White House (2002). *The National Security Strategy of the United States,* September. http://www.globalsecurity.org/military/library/policy/national/nss-020920.pdf.

——— (2005). *Analytical Perspectives, Budget of the United States Government, Fiscal Year 2005.* http://www.gpoaccess.gov/usbudget/fy05/pdf/spec.pdf.

——— (2006). *The National Security Strategy of the United States,* March. http://georgewbush-whitehouse.archives.gov/nsc/nss/2006/.

Urquhart, Brian (2007). "Are Diplomats Necessary?" *New York Review of Books,* October 11. http://www.nybooks.com/articles/20671.

Valentine, Douglas (1990). *The Phoenix Project.* New York: William Morrow.

Van Creveld, Martin (1991). *The Transformation of War.* New York: Free Press.

Van Ham, Peter (2001). "The Rise of the Brand State." *Foreign Affairs* 80(5): 2–6.

Velasco, Andrees (2002). "Dependency Theory." *Foreign Policy* (133): 44.

Verkuil, Paul (2007), *Outsourcing Sovereignty: Why Privatization of Government Functions Threatens Democracy and What We Can Do About It.* Cambridge: Cambridge University Press.

Vogel, David, and Robert Kagan, eds. (2004). *Dynamics of Regulatory Change: How Globalization Affects National Regulatory Policies.* Berkeley: University of California Press.

Wade, Robert, and Martin Wolf (2003). "Are Global Poverty and Inequality Getting Worse?" *The Global Transformations Reader: An Introduction to the Globalization Debate,* 2nd ed., eds. David Held and Anthony McGrew, 440–446. Malden, MA: Polity Press.

Wagner, Caroline (2008). *The New Invisible College: Science for Development.* Washington, DC: Brookings Institution Press. http://www.brookings.edu/press/Books/2007/newinvisiblecollege.aspx.

Waller, Michael J. (2007a). *Fighting the War of Ideas Like a Real War.* Washington, DC: Institute of World Politics Press.

——— (2007b). *The Public Diplomacy Reader.* www.lulu.com.

Wallerstein, Immanuel (1974). *The Modern World System.* New York: Academic Press.

——— (2008). "Commentary No. 226, Feb. 1, 2008: The Demise of Neoliberal Globalization." *Binghamton University.* http://www.binghamton.edu/fbc/eng2008.htm.

Warde, Ibrahim (2009). "Epitaph to George Bush." *Le Monde Diplomatique.* February 6, pp. 6–7.

Watkins, Alfred (2008). "Building STI Capacity for Sustainable Development and Poverty Reduction." Presentation to the AAAS Meetings, Boston, MA. February 17.

Weapons of Mass Destruction Commission (2006). "Weapons of Terror: Freeing the World of Nuclear, Biological, and Chemical Arms." *Final Report of the Weapons of Mass Destruction Commission to the UN Secretary-General*, June 1. http://www.wmdcommission.org/files/english.pdf.

Weart, Spencer R. (1998). *Never at War: Why Democracies Will Not Fight One Another.* New Haven, CT: Yale University Press.

Weiss, Thomas (2007). *Humanitarian Intervention: Ideas in Action.* Malden, MA: Polity Press.

Welsh, Jennifer (2004). *At Home in the World: Canada's Global Vision for the 21st Century.* Toronto: HarperCollins.

Wike, Richard, and Nilanthi Samaranayake (2006). "Where Terrorism Finds Support in the Muslim World: That May Depend on How You Define It—and Who Are the Targets." *Pew Research Center for the People and the Press,* May 23. http://pewresearch.org/pubs/26/where-terrorism-finds-support-in-the-muslim-world.

Williamson, John (1993). "Development and the 'Washington Consensus.'" *World Development* 21: 1239–1336.

Willis, Gary (2006). "A Country Ruled by Faith." *New York Review of Books,* November 16.

Wilson, Ernest J., III (2008). "Hard Power, Soft Power, Smart Power." *The Annals of the American Academy of Political and Social Science* 616(1): 110–124.

Wolf, Naomi (2007). *The End of America.* White River Junction, VT: Chelsea Green Publishing.

Woodrow Wilson International Center for Scholars (2005). "Revisiting Canada's Contribution to Resolving the Iranian Hostage Crisis." *Woodrow Wilson International Center for Scholars,* March 1. http://www.wilsoncenter.org/index.cfm?event_id=107570&fuseaction=events.event_summary.

Woods, Ngaire (2006). *The Globalizers: The IMF, the World Bank and Their Borrowers.* Ithaca, NY: Cornell University Press.

World Bank (2003). "Breaking the Conflict Trap: Civil War and Development Policy." *The World Bank,* June. http://econ.worldbank.org/wbsite/external/extdec/extresearch/extprrs/extbctcwdp/0,,menuPK:477815~pagePK:64168092~piPK:64168088~theSitePK:477803,00.html.

——— (2005a). *Dying Too Young: Addressing Premature Mortality and Ill Health Due to Non-Communicable Diseases and Injuries in the Russian Federation.* http://siteresources.worldbank.org/INTECA/Resources/DTY-Final.pdf.

——— (2005b). *World Development Report 2006: Equity and Development.* Washington, DC: World Bank.

——— (2006). *Global Economic Prospects 2007: Managing the Next Wave of Globalization.* Washington, DC: World Bank.

——— (2007). "Global Forum: Building Science, Technology, and Innovation Capacity for Sustainable Growth and Poverty Reduction." Washington, DC, February 13–15. http://web.worldbank.org/wbsite/external/topics/extstiglofor/0,,menuPK:3156763~pagePK:64168427~piPK:64168435~theSitePK:3156699,00.html.

———. *World Development Indicators Database.* http://publications.worldbank.org/WDI/.

———. *PovcalNet.* http://iresearch.worldbank.org/PovcalNet/jsp/index.jsp.

———. *World Development Reports.* Washington, DC: World Bank.

World Commission on Environment and Development (1987). *Our Common Future.* Oxford: Oxford University Press.

World Commission on the Social Dimension of Globalization (2004). "A Fair Globalization—Creating Opportunities for All." *International Labour Organization.* http://www.ilo.org/public/english/wcsdg/docs/report.pdf.

World Health Organization. "Avian Influenza." *World Health Organization.* http://www.who.int/csr/disease/avian_influenza/en/index.html.

———. "National Health Accounts." *World Health Organization.* http://www.who.int/nha/en.

World Intellectual Property Organization (2007). *WIPO Patent Report: Statistics on Worldwide Patent Activities.* http://www.wipo.int/export/sites/www/freepublications/en/patents/931/wipo_pub_931.pdf.

World Wildlife Fund (2006). "The Living Planet Report 2006." *World Wildlife Fund.* http://assets.panda.org/downloads/living_planet_report.pdf.

X (1947). "The Sources of Soviet Conduct." *Foreign Affairs* 25(July): 566–582. http://www.foreignaffairs.org/19470701faessay25403/x/the-sources-of-soviet-conduct.html.

Yale, Richmond (2008). *Practicing Public Diplomacy: A Cold War Odyssey.* New York: Berghahn Books.

Yergin, Daniel, and Joseph Stanislaw (2002). *The Commanding Heights: The Battle for the World Economy.* New York: Simon and Schuster.

Zaharna, Rhonda (2007). "The Network Communication Paradigm: Creating Soft Power in a Global Communication Era." Paper presented at the annual meeting of the International Studies Association, Chicago, March 3.

Zakaria, Fareed (2008). *The Post-American World.* New York: W. W. Norton.

Zartman, I. William (1995). *Collapsed States.* Boulder: Lynne Rienner Publishers.

Index

About the Book

Daryl Copeland charts the course for a new kind of diplomacy, one in tune with the demands of today's interconnected, technology-driven world.

Eschewing platitudes and broadly rethinking issues of security and development, Copeland provides the tools needed to frame and manage issues ranging from climate change to pandemic disease to asymmetrical conflict and weapons of mass destruction. The essential keystone of his approach is the modern diplomat, able to nimbly engage with a plethora of new international actors and happier mixing with the population than mingling with colleagues inside embassy walls.

Through the lens of *Guerrilla Diplomacy,* Copeland offers both a call to action and an alternative approach to understanding contemporary international relations.

Daryl Copeland is an analyst and educator who writes and speaks extensively on issues of diplomacy, international policy, and public management. From 1981 to 2009 he served as a Canadian diplomat, with postings in Thailand, Ethiopia, New Zealand, and Malaysia, and from 1996 to 1999 he was national program director with the Canadian Institute of International Affairs. He is currently research fellow at the University of Southern California's Center on Public Diplomacy and senior fellow at the University of Toronto's Munk Centre for International Studies. Visit www.guerrilladiplomacy.com to view his personal website, which contains more information about his work.